Y0-EHS-519

THE
PLOT TO KILL
THE
PRESIDENT

OTHER BOOKS BY G. ROBERT BLAKEY

Racket Bureaus:
Investigation and Prosecution of
Organized Crime
Perspectives on the Investigation
of Organized Crime (3 volumes)

OTHER BOOKS BY RICHARD N. BILLINGS

Power to the Public Worker

THE
PLOT TO KILL
THE
PRESIDENT

G. Robert Blakey
and
Richard N. Billings

NYT
Times
BOOKS

Published by TIMES BOOKS, a division of
Quadrangle/The New York Times Book Co., Inc.
Three Park Avenue, New York, N.Y. 10016

Published simultaneously in Canada by
Fitzhenry & Whiteside, Ltd., Toronto.

Library of Congress Cataloging in Publication Data

Blakey, George Robert, 1936-
The plot to kill the President.

Bibliography: p. 403
Includes index.
1. Kennedy, John Fitzgerald, Pres. U.S. 1917-1963 — Assassination.
I. Billings, Richard N., joint author. II. Title.
E842.9.B56   1980   364.1'524   80-5139
ISBN 0-8129-0929-1

We are indebted to a number of photographers whose work is reproduced in
the picture section appearing between pages 261 and 278.

Dallas Times Herald, ©1963 by Bob Jackson, picture number 4.
K. Jewell, picture number 8.
National Archives, picture number 6.
Lynn Pelham, Life Magazine, ©1967 Time Inc., picture number 40.
United Press International Photo, picture numbers 3, 7, 9, 10, 13, 17, 18, 21,
22, 25, 26, 29, 31, 34, 42, 44.
Hank Walker, Life Magazine, ©1960 Time Inc., picture number 1.
Wide World Photos, picture numbers 2, 5, 12, 14, 15, 16, 19, 20, 23, 24, 27,
28, 30, 32, 35, 36, 37, 39, 41, 43, 45, 46, 47.

To Elaine,
who not only critically read,
but typed the manuscript;
and to our seven children,
Michael, Matthew, Elizabeth, Anne, Jack, Katy, and Megan,
who not only put up with an absentee father
during the investigation,
but with a grouch while the book was being written.

And, likewise,
to my daughters Sarah and Deborah, and to Johanna.

Acknowledgments

The authors are deeply indebted, it goes without saying, to the publisher, Times Books, in particular Edward T. Chase, vice president and editorial director; and James W. Fitzgerald, managing editor. Further, the congressional investigation on which the book is based depended on the full support of the House Select Committee on Assassinations. The authors are especially grateful for the efforts of Louis Stokes of Ohio, chairman of the Committee; Richardson Preyer of North Carolina, chairman of the Kennedy assassination subcommittee; and Samuel L. Devine of Ohio, the ranking minority member. The staff of the Committee, by laboring long and hard in the investigation, contributed to the conclusions of the book, and there were some who helped directly: Gary T. Cornwell, the deputy chief counsel who was in charge of the Kennedy investigation; Michael Goldsmith and Donald A. Purdy, Jr., senior staff counsel; and Michael Ewing and Dan L. Hardway, staff researchers. Finally, there were the scientists and other experts whose work was essential, in particular James E. Barger of Bolt, Beranek and Newman Inc.; Mark Weiss and Ernest Aschkenasy of Queens College, City University of New York; and Ralph Salerno, a nationally recognized expert on organized crime.

The Committee's conclusions and a summary of its reasons and the evidence it relied upon appear in H. Rep. No. 95-1828 (pts. 1 and 2), Select Committee on Assassinations, House of Representatives, 95th Cong., 2d Sess. (Washington, D.C.: U.S. Government Printing Office 1979). The Committee's public hearings appear in Volumes I through V, *Hearings before the Select Committee on Assassinations,* House of Representatives, 95th Cong., 1st Sess. (Washington, D.C.: U.S. Government Printing Office 1979). Volumes VI through VIII contain scientific reports of the photographic evidence panel, the medical evidence panel, the firearms panel, the acoustics panel, and the handwriting and fingerprint evidence studies. Volumes IX through XII contain staff reports on organized crime; anti-Castro activities and organizations; Lee Harvey Oswald in New Orleans; the evolution and implication of CIA-sponsored assassination conspiracies against Fidel Castro; the Warren Commission; analysis of the support provided to the Warren Commission by the CIA; the Dallas motorcade; military investigation of the assassination; conspiracy witnesses in Dealey Plaza; Oswald-Tippit Associates; George de Mohrenshildt; depositions of Marina Oswald Porter; a study of defectors to the Soviet Union; and an investigation of Oswald in the Soviet Union and the defection to the United States of Yuri Nosenko.

The literature on the assassination of President Kennedy is abundant. Volume XII contains a bibliography with over 1,000 entries. While they were used extensively, they will not be reprinted here. The President's Commission on the Assassination of President Kennedy published its conclusions in 1964 in an 888-page *Report*. The Commission also published a major part of the evidence it collected in Volumes I through XXVI, *Hearings Before the President's Commission on the Assassination of President Kennedy* (Washington, D.C.: U.S. Government Printing Office 1964). There were also contemporaneous news accounts to draw upon: in *The New York Times, The New York Post, The Washington Post, The Washington Star, The Chicago Tribune, The Chicago Sun-Times, The Philadelphia Inquirer, The New Orleans Times-Picayune, The Tampa Times, The Tampa Tribune, The Miami Herald, The Dallas Morning News, The Dallas Times Herald, The Sunday Oklahoman, Life, Time, Newsweek, Colliers, Look,* and *New York Magazine*. There was also an ample amount of literature on organized crime (*Organized Crime: A Bibliography,* containing 1,600 entries, was published in 1977 by the Cornell Institute on Organized Crime), much of which need not be reprinted. The principal works in the public domain that were used as sources for the book are listed in the bibliography at the back of the book on page 403.

Contents

Preface

John F. Kennedy — few among us did not look on him with envy for his lot in life. He was young, idealistic, vigorous, handsome, intelligent, rich, well-married, and powerful. Yet our envy turned into pity on that November day in 1963. Reports of the assassination are no less dreadful when read in retrospect.

From Dallas, at 1:30 P.M. on November 22, the UPI teletyped: "Kennedy . . . wounded; perhaps seriously; perhaps fatally; by assassin's bullet." A *Washington Post* writer captured the reaction of a bereaved nation: ". . . disbelief; then, as the news sank in . . . shock."

Few among us who are old enough to remember that day have forgotten where we were or what we were doing when we learned of the President's assassination. My own memory of the tragedy is vivid. As a young prosecutor with the Department of Justice in Washington, I had spent the morning with Attorney General Robert F. Kennedy discussing investigations in Chicago, where I was about to be assigned to a field unit in the government's stepped-up drive on organized crime. One of the subjects to be taken up that afternoon was a contemplated effort to prosecute Sam Giancana, a Chicago organized-crime figure. During the lunch break, I learned the President had been shot. The meeting was not reconvened, and I never made it to Chicago. The organized-crime program faltered after the President's death, and I left the Justice Department to teach at the Notre Dame Law School, meeting my first class in September 1964, the month the Warren Commission issued its report, which found that Lee Harvey Oswald, acting alone, had assassinated the President.

As did most Americans, I accepted the verdict of the Commission. But unlike most Americans, I had a personal reason to have faith in *The Warren Report*. Key members of the staff that organized and directed the investigation were lawyers with whom I had worked at Justice, and I knew them as men of high integrity and unquestioned competence. When I read *The Warren Report*, I recognized the signs of their professional craftsmanship.

It follows that I was not troubled by the doubts that developed over the Commission's conclusions, anymore than I was perturbed by the controversy over the FBI investigation of the assassination of Dr. Martin Luther King, Jr., in April 1968. In fact, I was personally skeptical that there had been plots in either death. Consequently, when the House Select Committee on Assassinations was chartered in September 1976 to undertake a congressional inquiry into the Kennedy and King murders, I was merely an interested observer — but not all that interested. And I was quite surprised when I got a call from Congressman Christopher Dodd of Connecticut, who asked if I would accept the position of Chief Counsel and Staff Director of the Committee. I was then a professor at the Cornell Law School and, as I told Dodd, not inclined to leave teaching. But I said I would give it some thought, adding that my decision would ultimately depend on a frank discussion with him and the other members of the Committee. The Committee had been highly publicized in a none-too-flattering fashion, and I did not want to make up my mind on the strength of what I had read in the newspapers.

I went to Washington and my discussions with the Committee were comprehensive and wide-ranging. I put it as bluntly as I could: Were the members open-minded on the crucial questions of conspiracy, no matter who might be implicated, and possible bungling by agencies of our government, extending even to a cover-up? I was told the Committee was interested only in a professional product, based on the facts, that was crafted without fear or favor and based on an investigation that was consistent with the dignity of the House of Representatives. I, in turn, was asked if I might be influenced by having worked for Robert Kennedy when he was U.S. Attorney General. I said I owed nothing to anyone and expected nothing from anyone, but, I added, my respect for the memory of President Kennedy and Dr. King would prevent me from participating in any exploitation of their deaths, political or otherwise.

The give-and-take was, of course, a ritual that commonly occurs in the interview of any candidate for any position. It is a bit more ceremonial in Washington but no more consequential. Nevertheless, I found the Committee's questions to the point and appropriate, and their answers to my questions were refreshingly candid. While only one of my professional associates — and not one of those whom I knew in the Senate or the House — recommended that I take the job, as I thought it over, I came to the conclusion that the Committee was dedicated to the truth and had no intention of trying to exploit either tragedy. I consider truth a crucial value in a democratic society, for it is the foundation of the trust on which public institutions are based. If the Committee's work could help restore trust in public institutions — a trust that had declined due to the controversies over both assassinations — it would make an important contribution. So I had decided to accept the job, professionally open-minded but personally believing that the chief function of the investigation would probably be to lay ugly rumor to rest, when Committee Chairman Louis Stokes called on June 13, 1977.

I faced a formidable task when I arrived in Washington. Precious time had been lost, since a former chief counsel had apparently been more interested in personal publicity than serious investigation. We were following a cold trail to begin with, and as a congressional committee, we lacked the legal tools necessary to conduct a wide-ranging criminal investigation. It was not clear that we would be permitted to inspect the files of government agencies, such as the FBI and the CIA. I could not help thinking that if there had been a conspiracy in either case, witnesses to it were not going to cooperate voluntarily. In addition, the staff was in disarray — morale was low, and there was no sense of direction.

The first order of business was to hire some key deputies to help tackle the job ahead. They were lawyers, for the most part, like Gary Cornwell, who was named Deputy Chief Counsel for the Kennedy investigation. Cornwell, who had served with the Organized Crime Strike Force in Kansas City, was a tough, hard-driving investigative prosecutor. I also needed an editor with a number of qualities: someone who had investigative experience and breadth of vision, since the deep involvement of Kennedy and King in national affairs meant we would be looking into more than the facts of two homicides; someone who was an accomplished word craftsman, since one of the most durable products of the investigation would be our report, which I wanted to be technically sound and at the same time understandable to the American people; and someone I could trust. I therefore turned to Dick Billings, who is the coauthor of this book. I had known Billings since 1967. As an associate editor of *Life*, he was in charge of a hard-hitting series of articles on the Mafia, and he had called on me for legal advice at the time the series was published. We had remained good friends over the following years.

Billings had not been as detached from the subject of assassination as I had, though I considered his attitude to be open-minded and fair. He had actually covered the Kennedy assassination for *Life*, having flown to Dallas from the Miami Bureau, and he was responsible for the magazine's thoughtful reappraisal of *The Warren Report*. Billings's story, "A Matter of Reasonable Doubt," was one of the first by a national news organization to take a skeptical view of the single-assassin verdict of the Warren Commission, and it won the Sigma Delta Chi award for distinguished service in journalism in 1966. Billings also covered for *Life* the assassination investigation of New Orleans District Attorney Jim Garrison, though he soon determined that probe was a fraud.

This book is not, however, a joint memoir of a law professor and an investigative journalist who played key roles in a congressional investigation of the assassination of the President. Neither is it a book about two men named Blakey and Billings. Our role is simply that of narrators of the events the book *is* about, events that began with a fateful trip to

Texas. This book is the story of what happened in Dallas on November 22, 1963, and of how our national leadership responded to it. It is the tragic story of the murder of the 35th President of the United States by agents of a conspiracy whose complicity, until the two-year, $5.5 million House Select Committee investigation, was hidden from public view. It is, in short, an analysis of the evidence that established that organized crime was behind the plot to kill John F. Kennedy.

G. Robert Blakey
Notre Dame, Indiana
September 1980

THE
PLOT TO KILL
THE
PRESIDENT

Murder will out.
Geoffrey Chaucer
The Canterbury Tales

1

The Fateful Trip to Dallas

*Look upon that last day always. Count no mortal man happy till he
has passed the final limit of his life secure from pain.*

Sophocles,
Oedipus Rex

The Trip to Texas

It was politics that took John F. Kennedy to Texas in the fall of 1963,
"Presidential politics, pure and simple," as his Vice-President and successor, Lyndon B. Johnson, would one day write. The election was but a
year away, and while Kennedy was hardly trembling over the prospective candidacy of Barry Goldwater, the conservative Republican senator
from Arizona, he was anxious to shore up his sagging popularity. His
Gallup approval rating had plummeted from a remarkable 83 percent in
1961 to 59 percent, which while still quite respectable, was ample cause
for the President to worry about gaps in his support. In 1960, with na-
tive-son Johnson on the ticket, Kennedy had managed a mere 46,000-
vote plurality over Richard M. Nixon, and by 1963, according to a
Texas poll, he was favored by only 38 percent of the state's voters.

Both Johnson and Governor John B. Connally took issue with the
notion that Kennedy came to Texas to settle a dispute between liberal
and conservative factions in the state Democratic Party. They each
claimed — Johnson in his memoirs, Connally in testimony before us —
that the trouble had stemmed from a patronage agreement Johnson had

3

extracted from Kennedy as a condition for joining the ticket in 1960.
That Johnson would be empowered to pass on all federal appointments
in Texas was deeply resented by Ralph Yarborough, the senior U.S.
senator and leader of the liberals. As Connally told us in his public
testimony in September 1978:

> And indeed if the President was interested in resolving that difficulty, he
> had President Johnson right across the street in the old Executive Office
> Building, he had Senator Yarborough right here on the Hill, and he could
> have gotten them together in ten minutes. But that wasn't the purpose of
> his trip to Texas at all. It had nothing to do with it.

The 35th President of the United States, forty-six on the day he died,
Kennedy was the youngest elected Chief Executive in the nation's
history. During his brief term, he had wrestled with a steady succession
of difficult issues, the two most explosive of which came to a boiling
point simultaneously in October 1962. In confrontations with Southern
segregationists (over the admission of the first black student to the
University of Mississippi) and with the Soviet Union (over the em-
placement of intercontinental ballistic missiles in Cuba), he demonstrated his commitment to a domestic civil rights program and to U.S.
dominance in the Western Hemisphere.

It was over the issues of civil rights and Cuba that the President had
gotten into trouble with conservative constituencies in Texas and other
states of the South and West. In June 1963 he had sent a special
message to Congress in support of the most sweeping civil rights legislation since Reconstruction, a bill that would include guarantees of access
to public accommodations and the right to vote. It would also cost Kennedy the support of an estimated 3.5 million voters. As for Cuba, it was
learned in mid-1963 that while standing up to Khrushchev over the
missiles, Kennedy had made a no-invasion pledge, and his policy of re-
straining Cuban exile attacks on the forces of Cuban Premier Fidel
Castro had, by then, become evident.

In addition, thanks to his Keynesian economic policies (deficit spending in a time of sluggishness to overcome joblessness), his inclination
to favor costly welfare programs and his unyielding opposition to a steel
price increase in early 1962, Kennedy was considered a dangerous foe
of business interests. He was, in the eyes of political opponents, a rich
dilettante who had never had to work for a living and did not understand the free enterprise system; quite the opposite of Governor Connally, for example, who was born the same year as Kennedy, but to a
poor, working-class family. Connally had come to appreciate the cap-
italistic system by having struggled to succeed within it. When they first
discussed the Texas trip, he had explained to Kennedy that he should

concentrate on gaining favor with "moderate-to-conservative business leaders, political leaders of the state, who had not supported him, who were not enthusiastic about him . . ." Connally's reasoning that Kennedy had to win the admiration of the business community led him to insist that the President address a luncheon on November 22 at the Trade Mart in Dallas, a commercial center, where attendance would be limited to the city's business hierarchy, rather than at the Women's Building, which would have accommodated 4,000 guests. Connally even threatened to boycott the visit if he did not get his way on the luncheon site. In turn, the Trade Mart luncheon led the White House to proceed with plans for a motorcade through the center of Dallas, despite the objections of Connally, who contended it would overly fatigue the President, and Frank Erwin, executive secretary of the Texas Democratic Party, who was fearful of a confrontation with right-wing extremists. Erwin was not acting the role of unwarranted alarmist, for only weeks before the scheduled presidential trip, United Nations Ambassador Adlai E. Stevenson had been crudely assaulted by an unruly mob in Dallas. Byron Skelton, the Texas National Democratic Committeeman, wrote the President's brother, Attorney General Robert F. Kennedy, on November 4, urging that the trip to Dallas be canceled altogether. What concerned Skelton was the mood in Dallas, which he considered a good deal more ominous than what might be implied by a lukewarm enthusiasm of disgruntled businessmen. As evidence, he quoted the statement of a local luminary: "Kennedy is a liability to the free world," a remark to be expected of staunch Dallas conservatives whose passionate hatred Kennedy had earned, men like H. L. Hunt, the fanatically anti-communist oil billionaire, and Edwin A. Walker, the Army general whom Kennedy had removed from his European command for circulating right-wing literature to his troops. But Kennedy was adamant about the motorcade, which he believed was his only means of contact with working-class and minority citizens of Dallas.

The right-wing antagonism was brought home to Kennedy in a full-page advertisement placed by extremists in *The Dallas Morning News* on November 22, in which he was accused, among other sins: of responsibility for the imprisonment and persecution of thousands of Cubans; of selling food to the Communists in Vietnam; and of making a secret deal with the U.S. Communist Party. As disturbing as the ad itself was the realization that it had been accepted by an esteemed metropolitan daily newspaper, though the President might have been prepared for that by an earlier encounter he had had with the owner of *The Morning News*, E. M. "Ted" Dealey. Kennedy had been in office less than a year when Dealey came to a meeting of publishers at the White House, where he charged that the country had a "weak sister" for a President, when what was needed was "a man on horseback to lead this nation." If, on the morning of November 22, 1963, Kennedy missed the significance of the Dealey connection, he certainly would not have been aware that a statue of Ted Dealey's father, the founder of *The Morning News*, stood along the route of the motorcade, facing downtown Dallas with his back to the plaza that bore his name — G. B. Dealey (1859–1946).

President Kennedy never had an opportunity to do battle with the conservative extremists or to seek a truce with the moderates, as Governor Connally had urged. He died on the way to the confrontation, assassinated by forces that apparently were not directly related to the ideological differences of the new and the old frontier.

Kennedy and Death

As his family and close associates were aware, John F. Kennedy had a preoccupation with death. They explained this as a lasting effect of his close brush in the Pacific during World War II, when a Japanese destroyer sliced his PT boat in two, plunging him and his crew into a sea aflame with ignited fuel. Twice in his early political career, Kennedy was struck by near-fatal illness: in 1951, while traveling as a congressman in Japan, he was hospitalized with a fever of 106°; and in 1954, when he was in the Senate, a staphylococcus infection that resulted from unsuccessful back surgery was serious enough for a priest to administer last rites. It was not surprising to learn that he told his bride in 1953 that his favorite poem was "I Have a Rendezvous with Death" by Alan Seeger.

> It may be he shall take my hand
> And lead me into his dark land
> And close my eyes and quench my breath . . .

Arthur M. Schlesinger, Jr., the historian who served as a White House special assistant, coupled death with courage as the dominant theme of Kennedy's life. "Courage — and death. The two are related," Schlesinger wrote in *A Thousand Days*, "because courage, if it is more than reckless bravado, involves the exquisite understanding that death may be its price." Kennedy had good reason to ponder death, quite apart from his own narrow escapes: the death of a brother and a brother-in-law in the war in Europe, coming in quick succession a year after his own mishap on PT 109; and the loss of a sister in a plane crash in 1948. Small wonder that Kennedy's widow was said by Schlesinger to have remarked, "The poignancy of men dying young haunted him."

Kennedy was fatalistic about the risk of assault, an attitude no doubt nurtured by his wartime experiences: if the bullet has your name on it, death is inevitable. When it was brought to his attention as he was running for the presidency that, since 1840, no President elected in a year ending in a zero had left the White House alive, Kennedy wrote: "I feel that the future will have to necessarily answer this for itself — both as to my aspirations and my fate should I have the privilege of occupying the White House." Once in office, he could be grimly specific, as he was in a prophetic observation to his longtime and loyal aide, Kenneth O'Donnell, while they were traveling to Texas:

> . . . if anybody really wanted to shoot the President . . . it was not a very difficult job — all one had to do was get on a high building someday with a telescopic rifle, and there was nothing anybody could do to defend against such an attempt.

Kennedy's fatalism was a factor in his assassination to the extent that it permitted him to disregard the danger of a decision that was based on the political merits. He was restless by nature and an inveterate campaigner, who interspersed diplomatic missions abroad with vote-getting jaunts across the country. No less than eighty-three times in 1963, the Secret Service had to reckon with the menace of a marksman peering through a telescopic rifle sight from a tall building, or an assailant coming out of a crowd, firing a handgun at point-blank range. Since Kennedy believed there was little that could be done to stop a determined assassin, he recklessly resisted protective measures. He would not abide blaring sirens to trumpet the coming of a campaign caravan, and only once — earlier in November 1963, in Chicago, where a threat against him had been reported — did he permit his limousine to be flanked by motorcycle police. (On November 22, in the absence of such a threat in Dallas, escort motorcycles were kept to the rear of the limousine.) Kennedy was also opposed to posting bodyguards on the rear of his limousine, so the one precaution that might have saved his life, a human shield, was vetoed by the President himself.

After the assassination, O'Donnell told Gerald Behn, Special Agent-in-Charge of the Secret Service White House Detail, "Politics and protection don't mix." Aside from influencing the relatively incidental issues of police motorcycle positions and the posting of bodyguards, politics had a bearing on some larger pre-Dallas decisions by the White House, such as going along with Connally on the limited-invitation Trade Mart luncheon for business leaders, rather than a larger, more representative gathering at the Women's Building. The Secret Service preferred the Women's Building, for it could be entered via only two entrances, while the Trade Mart had about sixty doorways and a network of catwalks suspended over the dining area that also had to be covered. There was another security advantage in going to the

Women's Building that was only realized later. The route to the Women's Building would have been along Main Street eastward to the County Fairgrounds, southeast of downtown Dallas, and the motorcade would have approached Main Street by moving through Dealey Plaza from west to east at a relatively high speed (forty to fifty miles per hour). To get to the Trade Mart, west of downtown, the route was west on Main, north on Houston, and west again on Elm. It was this last turn, a 120-degree hairpin from Houston to Elm, that required the presidential limousine, an outsize open Lincoln, to slow down to an agonizing eleven miles an hour as it passed directly in front of the Texas School Book Depository.

While physical protection of the President was the responsibility of the White House detail (the advance agent from Washington who made an inspection tour on November 13 was more confident than the chief of the Dallas Field Office that the Trade Mart could be secured), intelligence fell within the province of the Protective Research Section, the eyes and ears of the Secret Service. It was up to the PRS to study threat information for signs of an assassination plot or the presence of deranged, potentially dangerous individuals. With regard to Dallas in November 1963, the PRS had nothing of consequence to report — no conspiracies and no mental cases, save several in which the subjects were confined to an institution.

There was no shortage of material to analyze, however, for between March and November 1963 the PRS had reviewed over 400 threats to President Kennedy. Three of the threats were deemed sufficiently serious to warrant further investigation or necessitate a last-minute modification of a trip plan. They were, if read that way, omens of a coming tragedy. One, a postcard warning that the President would be shot while riding in a motorcade, resulted in extra protection when he went to Chicago in March. The two others were related to trips by Kennedy to Chicago and Miami earlier in the very month he was murdered in Dallas. On October 30 the Secret Service learned that Thomas A. Vallee, a Chicago man who had been outspokenly critical of Kennedy foreign policy, had obtained arms and ammunition and had requested time off from work on November 2. The President was due to be in Chicago that day, but the trip was canceled, probably because of a crisis in South Vietnam following the overthrow and murder of President Ngo Dinh Diem. Vallee, who had been arrested by Chicago police with an M-1 rifle, a handgun, and 3,000 rounds of ammunition in his car, was released from custody on the evening of November 2. Then, on November 9 a Miami police informant secretly recorded a conversation with Joseph A. Milteer, a right-wing extremist, who told of a plan to assassinate Kennedy with a high-powered rifle from a tall building. There was no motorcade when Kennedy came to Miami on November 18. Instead, he traveled from the airport to a Miami Beach hotel by helicopter, although there was nothing to indicate this precaution was dictated by the Milteer threat, since it just as easily could have been prompted by the highly charged atmosphere generated by the Cuban exiles living in Miami.

In the twenty-day period between the canceled trip to Chicago and the assassination in Dallas, the Secret Service learned more about Vallee: he was a Marine Corps veteran with a history of mental illness while on active duty, a John Bircher, and a self-proclaimed expert marksman. This information was transmitted to the Protective Research Section in Washington, but it was not forwarded to agents of the White House detail or the Dallas field office. As for Milteer, the Secret Service learned before the assassination that he had been associated with radical right-wing organizations and that he was suspected of having participated in the September 1963 bombing of a church in Birmingham, Alabama, in which four young black girls were killed. His threat was relayed by the PRS to Secret Service agents conducting advance preparations for the President's trip to Miami, but no effort was made to pass it on to Winston G. Lawson, the advance agent in Dallas, or Forrest Sorrels, the Dallas special agent-in-charge. As Robert I. Bouck, the special agent-in-charge of the PRS, explained to us, the data on a threat by a right-wing extremist was not thought to be relevant to security in Dallas.

There were, in addition, threats the Secret Service or other government agency did not look into prior to the President's murder, presumably because they did not know about them. They were uttered, not only by right-wing radicals, but by anti-Castro exiles, embittered by the tragedy of the Bay of Pigs early in Kennedy's term and by governmental restraints on their guerrilla raids; and by racketeers who were reacting strongly to an unprecedented effort by the federal government to investigate and prosecute them. American gangsters were also upset over the failure to overthrow Castro, since he had taken away their lucrative gambling interests in Havana.

The Last Campaign

President Kennedy was in high spirits when he was awakened by his valet in Suite 850 of the Hotel Texas in Fort Worth at 7:30 on the morning of November 22. If he was more than a little bit miffed by the refusal of some trustees of Texas Christian University to go along with the idea of awarding him an honorary degree, he did not show it. Instead, he exuded confidence over the prospect of a successful reelection campaign, and he was particularly pleased with the way the Texas trip had been going so far, especially the dinner the night before for Congressman Albert Thomas in Houston. Governor Connally remembered:

I was looking and watching all through the crowd during the entire speech.
He was indeed reaching these people; he was communicating with them.
It just could not have been a better day in both San Antonio and Houston.

It was drizzling when Kennedy walked across the street from the hotel to address a gathering — workingmen, for the most part — in a parking lot, but he shook his head when Bill Greer, the Secret Service driver of his limousine, offered him his raincoat. "There are no faint hearts in Fort Worth!" the President shouted, and the crowd cheered. "We're going forward," Kennedy promised, winding up his remarks and heading back to the hotel for his second political appearance of the day, a Chamber of Commerce breakfast in the ballroom, where he was joined by his wife. "Yes, and there were 2,500 people at the breakfast that morning," said Connally. "So, the idea that he was meeting with a few exclusive, handpicked people is hardly true."

Back in Suite 850 at about 10 A.M., Kennedy placed two phone calls — one to former Vice-President John Nance Garner, who was celebrating his ninety-fifth birthday at his home in Uvalde, Texas, and one to thank a Fort Worth matron, Mrs. J. Lee Johnson, III, who had borrowed several original French Impressionists' paintings from private collections to hang in the presidential suite. Then Vice-President Johnson came by to introduce his sister and her husband, and Kennedy told them: "We're going to carry two states next year if we don't carry any others — Massachusetts and Texas."

Kennedy the realist knew full well that the political picture in Texas was not that rosy. He had just read in *The Dallas Morning News* about the feud in the Democratic Party, which had caused Senator Yarborough to refuse to ride in the Vice-President's car the day before. (Kennedy, on the morning of November 22, issued an order to O'Donnell that Yarborough would either ride with Johnson or walk.) In addition, there was an account in *The Morning News* of Richard Nixon's address the day before at a soft-drink bottlers convention in Dallas, in which the former Vice-President predicted that Kennedy would drop Johnson from the ticket in 1964. And on page 14, there was the full-page condemnation, the ad that had been purchased by the Birchers. "You know who's responsible for the ad," Kennedy said to O'Donnell. "Dealey. Remember him?"

O'Donnell was in the process of making a decision that some have thought crucial — whether or not to mount the bubbletop on the limousine for the drive through Dallas. (In fact, the bubbletop was not bullet-proof.) As a campaign signal caller, he was hoping for a break in the weather that would mean bigger crowds and enable the presidential party to ride in the open. So when Roy Kellerman, who was standing in for Gerald Behn as chief of the Secret Service detail, got word from Forrest Sorrels and Winston Lawson at Love Field that it appeared to be clearing, O'Donnell was relieved.

It was 11:38 Dallas time when Air Force One touched down at Love Field, the weather having turned "absolutely marvelous." Connally recalled in his public testimony:

> The crowd at the airport was several thousand people. It was, again, an extremely receptive group of people who were out there, enthusiastic group of people. I recall that after President and Mrs. Kennedy shook hands with those in the receiving line, they went over and Vice-President and Mrs. Johnson accompanied them, and they went over for five minutes or so, walked up and down the fence where there were thousands of people gathered . . .

On the presidential wavelength of the Secret Service radio net, it was not President and Mrs. Kennedy, it was Lancer and Lace. O'Donnell must not have been pleased with Kennedy's code name, for its phallic symbolism could only do damage in the Bible Belt. But Lancer did fit Kennedy, whose nocturnal adventures had occasionally caused consternation for a White House detail accustomed to calling it a day when Dwight Eisenhower had played his last hand of bridge. There actually had been times in 1960 when Kennedy just disappeared for brief periods, and little was more disturbing to a Secret Service agent than to lose track of the candidate or President-elect he had been assigned to protect. On this trip, however, the detail did not have to worry about Lancer's vanishing acts, for Lace had come along, difficult as it was for her to bear up under the strain of an arduous campaign trip. Connally was observing her closely:

> In San Antonio, she was rather stiff, I thought, rather unused to this. She had not been traveling much and campaigning much with the President and she was not noticeably ill at ease at all, but nevertheless, reserved, quiet and perhaps a little bit — frightened is too strong a word — but apprehensive about this whole thing. Not apprehensive in the sense of being fearful of violence, but just not being used to it.

Clouds had given way to warm sunshine as the motorcade left Love Field at 11:50, led by an unmarked white Ford sedan with Dallas Police Chief Jesse E. Curry at the wheel and Sheriff J. E. (Bill) Decker and Secret Service Agents Lawson and Sorrels as passengers. Curry was in contact with units of his command over Dallas Police Radio Station KKB-364, which operated on two channels, One and Two. Curry was tuned to Channel Two:

> Chief Curry: *Just made the turn out of Love Field onto Cedar Springs now.*
> Dispatcher: *. . . they are just leaving the field now on Cedar Springs at 15 mph.*

The President kept reminding his wife to take off her dark glasses so the people could get a look at her fine face. Kennedy was an old-fashioned politician, to whom his wife's beauty was a campaign asset. That was his style, as was the risky practice of working the crowds. He knew the history of presidential assassinations in America — Lincoln, Garfield, McKinley, all gunned down at close range in a public setting — but he seemed to pay it no mind. Back at Love Field, where he had lingered momentarily, touching hands with well-wishers through a steel-mesh fence, Ronnie Dugger of *The Texas Observer* jotted a note: "Kennedy is showing he is not afraid."

> Chief Curry: *At Lemmon, approaching Inwood at approximately 12 mph. (12:01 P.M.) . . . to motorcycle leading — drop back closer, hold up about 50 feet ahead of us . . . we are approaching underpass — Cotton Belt — near Loma Alta.*
> Dispatcher: *. . . now on Lemmon near Loma Alta (12:05).*
> Chief Curry: *. . . to motorcycle escort — three or four miles faster . . . pull those cars off the street . . . cut traffic at Oak Lawn.*

Connally was not exactly afraid, as he explained it, but he was nervous. He had opposed the motorcade, not only because it was crammed into the middle of a fifteen-hour marathon of public appearances. He told us:

> There was one other reason, and that was simply that I thought we ran the risk of having some embarrassing placards or signs or a few pickets along the way. I frankly never had any fear of physical harm or violence. That never entered my mind, but the idea that we probably would encounter a sign or two did enter my mind. . . .

> Chief Curry: *Just turning off Turtle Creek.*
> Dispatcher: *Just turning off onto Turtle Creek off Lemmon.*
> Chief Curry: *12 mph . . . at the MK&T Underpass at Turtle Creek.*
> Dispatcher: *10-4, 12:14 P.M.*
> Chief Curry: *. . . to motorcycle escort — three or four miles faster, let's try it.*

Connally's concern was justified, for up on the balcony of an old run-down house, a man held a sign that read, "Kennedy go home." Connally testified:

> But it was on the left side of the car . . . and the President was on the right side in the back seat, and I hoped he didn't see it, but he finally turned and said, "Did you all see that sign?" I said, "Yes, Mr. President, but we were hoping you didn't." He said, "Well, I saw it. Don't you imagine he's a nice fellow?"

Dispatcher: *. . . are you approaching Ross?*
Chief Curry: *Just approaching at this time.*
Dispatcher: *10-4, 12:20 P.M.*

As the motorcade reached the heart of the city, the crowds began to swell — a hearty welcome to which Kennedy responded by having his car stop two or three times, as Connally remembered:

> . . . there was this little girl — I guess she was eight years old — who had a placard that said, "President Kennedy," something like, "will you shake hands with me? . . ." Well, he immediately stopped the car and shook hands with this little girl, and, of course, the car was mobbed . . . .
>
> The other stop, we were halfway downtown, I suppose, when there was a nun, a sister, with a bunch of schoolchildren . . . right by the car. And he stopped and spoke to them . . .

Chief Curry: *Good shape, we are just about to cross Live Oak.*
Dispatcher: *12:22 P.M.*
Chief Curry: *. . . to escort — drop back. We will have to go at a real slow speed here on now . . . to motorcycle — hold up escort. O.K., move along. Check to see if we have everything in sight. Check with the rear car.*

The motorcade route had been well publicized, it was lunch hour, the weather was perfect; so a big turnout could be expected in the center of town. That is what Connally recalled most vividly:

> . . . and when we got down on Main Street, the crowds were extremely thick. They were pushed off of curbs; they were out in the street; and they were backed all the way up against the walls of buildings. They were just as thick as could be . . . there were at least a quarter of a million people on the parade route that day . . .

Chief Curry: *Crossing Lamar Street.*
Dispatcher: *10-4. Pretty good crowd there, 12:28 P.M.*
Chief Curry: *Big crowd, yes.*

* * *

Dispatcher: *. . . now on Main, probably just past Lamar.*
Chief Curry: *Just crossing Market Street.*

There had been the option for the procession to take Main Street directly through Dealey Plaza and reach the Trade Mart via Industrial Boulevard. That route was rejected, according to a Dallas police official, George L. Lumpkin, who had been consulted by the Secret Service, for it would have meant driving through a run-down neighborhood. Instead, the big Lincoln turned right and went one block north on Houston Street, then lumbered around the turn onto Elm Street, gradually picking up speed as it rolled westward down a slight grade. The scene now was the parklike plaza, with open green space on either side of the street. On the right, a pin oak tree, then a sign directing traffic to a ramp leading to the Stemmons Freeway, the way to the Trade Mart. Up a hill beyond the sign, there was a concrete wall and a concrete structure called a pergola, for lack of a more accurate description, and behind the pergola, a picket-fenced parking lot with a clump of thick-foliaged trees behind it; just ahead, the railroad, crossing at a point where Elm, Main, and Commerce streets converge, forming a triple underpass; directly to the rear, at the corner of Houston and Elm, a seven-story, red-brick building that served as a storage facility for the Texas School Book Depository. The crowd had thinned out noticeably by now — just a single line of onlookers along the curb.

Chief Curry: *Approaching triple underpass.*
Dispatcher: *12:30 P.M. KKB 364.*

At the turn from Houston onto Elm, Connally's wife, Nellie, spoke to the President for the first time since leaving Love Field, as she told us:

> . . . we were having such a wonderful reception, and we were all so excited . . . I had restrained myself up to that point . . . but I could no longer stand it, so I turned around to the President and I said, "Mr. President, you can't say Dallas doesn't love you."

"Obviously," the President answered, and then shots rang out.

Chief Curry: *Go to the hospital — Parkland Hospital. Have them stand by. Get a man on top of that triple underpass and see what happened up there. Have Parkland stand by.*

* * *

Dispatcher:	*. . . any information whatsoever?*
Chief Curry:	*Looks like the President has been hit. Have Parkland stand by.*
Dispatcher:	*10-4. They [Parkland] have been notified.*

*　　　　* * *

Chief Curry:	*Headed to Parkland. Something's wrong with Channel One.*

*　　　　* * *

Dispatcher:	*Unknown motorcycle — up on Stemmons with his mike stuck open on Channel One . . . [12:34 P.M.].*

The Channel One log, in fact, confirmed that there was a stuck microphone switch that prevented transmissions during the crucial moments of the assassination. At 12:26, the dispatcher announced, ". . . transmitter stuck, can't read anything for some time . . ."

While Curry barked commands to his units, his lead car, in the dark of the underpass, was nearly rammed by the fast-accelerating limousine that was negotiating the ramp to Stemmons Freeway. It was speeding to Parkland Memorial Hospital four miles away, the two fallen leaders cradled in the arms of their wives. "John said nothing," Nellie Connally recalled. "I said only to him from the time I saw one little movement, . . . 'Be still, it is going to be all right; be still, it is going to be all right.' I have read stories where I screamed and he screamed and all these things. There was no screaming in that horrible car. It was just a silent, terrible drive."

At Parkland, Jacqueline Kennedy declined to permit her fatally wounded husband to be taken from her until a Secret Service agent — Clint Hill, the man who had mounted the rear of the limousine at the sound of shots to shield the First Lady — offered his suit jacket for her to wrap around the President's shattered head.

As to what happened — the origin of the shots and the number — the eyewitness and earwitness accounts varied so greatly that they would have to be considered of less significance than other evidence. Undoubtedly, some of the most reliable testimony came from the motorcycle escorts, trained police officers riding just to the rear of the limousine, but even they were not in total accord. Bobby W. Hargis, who had been positioned to the left rear of the limousine (close enough to be sprayed by blood and brain fragments when the President was shot in the head), was able to recall just two shots, and he was so convinced of shooting from the right front that he parked his machine and ran up on the railroad overpass to investigate. On the other hand, D. L. Jackson, riding abreast of Hargis on the right side, heard three shots and was certain the fatal bullet had come from behind:

. . . and I thought, "Someone is shooting at them" . . . I looked then back to my right and behind me, then looked back toward Mr. Kennedy and saw him hit in the head . . . just above the right ear. The top of his head flew off away from me. . . . I knew that the shooting was coming from the right rear and I looked back that way but I never did look up.

Officer Jackson followed the limousine to Parkland, arriving in time to help lift the wounded men from the car, first the governor, since he was sprawled on a jump seat nearest the door, and then the President.

Clyde Haygood, two cycles behind Jackson, was so startled that he rammed a curb and overturned, then got up and followed Hargis on foot up the overpass embankment, his pistol drawn. M. L. Baker, riding behind Haygood, was so sure of where a sniper had been lurking that he dismounted and ran into the Texas School Book Depository, up to the second floor, where he encountered a man he judged to be about thirty, five feet nine, 165 pounds. Baker approached the man, but he lost interest in him when the manager of the Book Depository said he was an employee by the name of Lee Harvey Oswald. Fifteen minutes later, however, when Oswald disappeared from the building, the police radio broadcast a description.

Dispatcher: *Attention all squads, the suspect in the shooting at Elm and Houston is supposed to be an unknown white male, approximately 30, 165 lbs . . .*

H. B. McLain was riding on the left side, two cycles behind Hargis. He had just made the right turn from Main to Houston when he heard what he believed to be two shots, and saw pigeons fly from the roof of the Texas School Book Depository. When he heard Curry's order to go to Parkland, he followed Vice-President Johnson's car to the hospital, where he helped Mrs. Kennedy get out of the back of the presidential limousine.

Connally and Kennedy were wheeled to adjacent trauma rooms: the governor was taken to surgery that would lead to his recovery; but feverish efforts by physicians to resuscitate the President were futile. He was pronounced dead by Dr. William Kemp Clark at 1 P.M. Central Standard Time.

2

The Aftermath—Confusion, Grief, and an Inquiry

The full story of the assassination and its stunning sequel must be placed before the American people and the world in a responsible way by a responsible source of the U.S. Government.

The New York Times
November 25, 1963

The Immediate Aftermath

John F. Kennedy had been officially dead for fifteen minutes when a White House press aide, Malcolm Kilduff, asked Lyndon B. Johnson if he might issue a public statement. Johnson, who was huddled in a ward of Parkland Hospital with a reinforced squad of Secret Service agents, said, "No, wait. We don't know whether it's a Communist conspiracy or not. . . . Are they prepared to get me out of here?" They were. In fact, Rufus Youngblood, the chief of Johnson's Secret Service detail, was edgy, and anxious to get moving. "We don't know what type of conspiracy this is, or who else is marked," he told Johnson. They left Parkland in two cars, unmarked police cruisers: Johnson in the first, crammed in the back seat between Youngblood and Congressman Homer Thornberry, with Chief Curry at the wheel and Congressman Albert Thomas next to him; Lady Bird Johnson, among others, in the second. It was Youngblood's theory, as he ordered Johnson to duck his head below the level of the rear window, that if would-be assassins recognized the new First Lady, they would attack the wrong car. Arriving at Love Field, which was surrounded by Dallas police, the new Pres-

17

ident's ragtag entourage scurried up the steps to Air Force One in time to hear Kilduff's announcement reported on television. It was 1:40 P.M. Central Standard Time.

The shocking word from Dallas was flashed to the world within minutes by United Press International, whose White House correspondent, Merriman Smith, was on the phone from a press car in the motorcade. At 1:45 Washington time, an hour later than it was in Dallas, FBI Director J. Edgar Hoover telephoned Attorney General Robert F. Kennedy, who was having lunch at his home in Virginia with Robert M. Morgenthau, the U.S. Attorney for the Southern District of New York (Manhattan). "I have news for you," said Hoover. "The President has been shot. I think it's serious. I am endeavoring to get details. I'll call you back when I find out more." Edward M. Kennedy, the youngest of the brothers, was presiding over the U.S. Senate when he was told. Senior officials of the government were spread far and wide: a delegation of Cabinet members, headed by Secretary of State Dean Rusk, was high over the Pacific en route to Tokyo; Secretary of Defense Robert S. McNamara was at the Pentagon, working on his budget with McGeorge Bundy, the White House Assistant for National Security; General Maxwell Taylor, Chairman of the Joint Chiefs of Staff, was taking a break from a round of meetings with visiting generals from Germany; and Chief Justice Earl Warren was in conference with his associates on the Supreme Court when he was passed a note from his secretary. Robert Kennedy, when he first heard from Hoover, had called the Director of Central Intelligence, John A. McCone, at his office in Langley, Virginia, asking him to come over. It was just a mile or so from CIA Headquarters to Hickory Hill, Robert Kennedy's estate, so McCone was with the attorney general and his wife, Ethel, when Hoover called back. "The President is dead," the FBI chief reported. Kennedy had already heard the grim news from the White House.

Lyndon Baines Johnson was sworn in as the 36th President of the United States aboard Air Force One by U.S. District Judge Sarah T. Hughes, an old friend, at 2:38 P.M. Dallas time. He had waited for nearly an hour for Mrs. Kennedy, who had refused to leave Parkland Hospital without the body of the late President. A confrontation had resulted over the refusal of the Dallas County medical examiner, Dr. Earl Rose, to release the body before an autopsy had been performed, as required by Texas law. During a prolonged standoff, a local official was understood to remark that the assassination was "just another homicide," whereupon the beleaguered Kennedy band, O'Donnell in the lead, defiantly wheeled the casket to an awaiting hearse and ordered it driven to Love Field, where it was loaded aboard Air Force One. Mrs. Kennedy attended the two-minute swearing-in ceremony, accepting Johnson's condolences in stunned silence, then retired to her bedchamber for takeoff. Once the plane was airborne — at 2:47 — she walked to a rear lounge and took a chair beside the casket for the flight to Washington. O'Donnell and the other loyalists stayed with her. At "altitude," which was exceptionally high for security reasons (the pilot was also directed to fly a zigzag course, and the Air Force was on the lookout for unfriendly aircraft), Major General Chester V. Clifton, Kennedy's military aide, went forward to the communications shack to put in a call to Bundy at the White House. Clifton wanted to know if there were indications of an international conspiracy. It was not the sort of question to ask over an open network, so Bundy was guarded: the Pentagon was taking steps, he replied. The mood in Washington was actually one of apprehension: there would be time for grieving later; more pertinent now was national defense. The immediate reaction of McNamara and Taylor had been to alert U.S. forces around the world and to order additional Strategic Air Command bombers into the air. Undersecretary of State George Ball and CIA Director McCone had conferred by phone and agreed it would be appropriate to order the Watch Committee to study foreign intelligence with extra care for hints of an international plot. Secretary of State Rusk cabled from Hawaii to suggest that international soundings be taken, and he wondered who was in control of the nuclear button. To the Cabinet delegation en route to Tokyo, which had turned around and was flying back to Washington, the possibility of a coup d'etat was remote, but there were related fears. Secretary of the Treasury C. Douglas Dillon was concerned that the American people might blame the Soviet Union or Cuba or both and demand retaliation.

Air Force One set down at Andrews Air Force Base outside Washington at 5:59 P.M. Eastern Standard Time. As President Kennedy's body was being driven to the naval hospital in Bethesda, Maryland, President Johnson, accompanied by McNamara and Ball, who briefed Johnson on defense readiness and the reaction abroad to the assassination, flew by helicopter to the White House.

Dallas police arrested a man in the Texas Theatre about 1:55 P.M. He was Lee Harvey Oswald, twenty-four, of 1026 North Beckley Avenue in the Oak Cliff section of the city. Although Oswald had originally been apprehended in the shooting of a police officer, he was charged as well with the assassination of the President. "This man shot and killed President John F. Kennedy and Police Officer J. D. Tippit and wounded Governor John Connally," the rap sheet read. The immediate reason for identifying Oswald as the possible assassin was that he was an employee of the Texas School Book Depository and had departed from the

building right after the shooting, leaving a rifle, subsequently determined to be his, and three empty shell cases behind. At 2:50 P.M., Gordon Shanklin reported the arrest to Washington FBI Headquarters and
advised that a check of the files had shown that Oswald, who had
defected to the Soviet Union in 1959, was the subject of an internal security file, which read in part:

> In Moscow he went to the American Embassy and tried to renounce his
> American citizenship. He returned to the U.S. . . . 6/13/62, and brought
> with him a Russian bride. . . .

The FBI quickly developed more information on Oswald from the
files of the State Department and the Office of Naval Intelligence. When
he went to Russia in 1959, he tried to renounce his U.S. citizenship,
declaring, "I am a Marxist," and offered to give away military secrets
that he had learned from serving as a radar technician in the Marine
Corps. Back in the United States in 1962, he was interviewed in Fort
Worth by FBI agents, who characterized him as "very curt and short in
answering many questions . . . cold and arrogant." On August 13,
1963, he was sentenced to a $10 fine or ten days in jail for disturbing the
peace in New Orleans after he precipitated an incident by passing out
"Fair Play for Cuba" leaflets. On a subsequent radio debate on the
Cuban issue, Oswald reaffirmed his dedication to Marxism.

Late the same afternoon in Washington, Deputy Attorney General
Nicholas de B. Katzenbach was on the phone with the FBI speculating
that Oswald's pro-Cuban and pro-Soviet activities "would come into
mounting prominence," if, in fact he was the assassin. That very reality
and the consequent danger of its leading to World War III was Topic A
at the State Department. Two former ambassadors to the Soviet Union,
Averell Harriman and Llewellyn Thompson, insisted that the Kremlin
would not have an American Head of State murdered, but U. Alexis
Johnson, number three in the department under Rusk and Ball, worried what effect just a suspicion of Soviet complicity would have on detente.

At Dallas Police Headquarters, formal charges against Oswald were
brought separately before a Justice of the Peace: at 7:10 P.M. on November 22, for the murder of Officer J. D. Tippit; and at 1:30 A.M. on
November 23, for the assassination of President Kennedy. While he
had persistently protested his innocence, claiming to have been a "patsy," the FBI was busy assembling an overwhelming case against him.
Within twenty-four hours of the shooting, the bureau was so sure it had
the right man that it was rejecting leads that were not compatible with

the evidence against Oswald. An FBI report to President Johnson on November 23 summarized that evidence:

Oswald had been employed at the Texas School Book Depository, determined to have been the building from which the shots had been fired.

A fellow employee had observed him to carry to work, on the morning of November 22, a package of sufficient length to contain a rifle.

He had been observed on the fifth floor of the Book Depository at 11:50 A.M. [It later turned out he was seen on the sixth floor at about 11:45.]

He had been observed inside the Book Depository shortly after the shooting, but he had then disappeared.

A witness stated he had seen the shots being fired from a sixth-floor window of the Book Depository by a man resembling Oswald, though he could not make a positive identification after viewing the suspect in a police lineup.

A housekeeper at a rooming house at 1026 North Beckley Avenue said that Oswald, who had lived there since October 14 as "O. H. Lee," had come by about 1 P.M. on November 22 to pick up a jacket and had departed hurriedly.

A 6.5 caliber Italian rifle, found on the sixth floor of the Book Depository, had been sent from Chicago to one "A. Hidell," the name on a Selective Service card in Oswald's possession at the time of his arrest.

A bullet found on a stretcher at Parkland Hospital and fragments from the presidential car had been identified as having been fired from the rifle found in the Book Depository.

A latent fingerprint on a brown paper bag found near the window from which the shots had been fired — possibly the bag that had been used to conceal the rifle as it was being brought into the Book Depository — had been identified as the left index finger impression of Lee Harvey Oswald.

The President's Commission

On November 24 the main concern of FBI Director Hoover was the need to convince the public that Oswald was the actual assassin. Katzenbach was thinking along the lines of a presidential commission; Hoover countered with a proposal that the FBI submit, via the Justice Department, an investigative report that President Johnson could make public, if he wished. Acceptance of Hoover's plan depended on the sort of serenity that comes when it is determined that the calamity was a bizarre occurrence with no rhyme or reason to it. This isolated-event idea was pretty well destroyed, however, when at 11:21 that Sunday morning in Dallas, a local nightclub operator named Jack Ruby stepped out from a crowd of newsmen and police officers, gathered in the basement of Police Headquarters to watch Oswald being transferred to the county jail, and shot the suspected assassin in the stomach. Oswald, whose murder had been carried live on national television, was pronounced dead at Parkland Hospital at 1:07 P.M. Less than two hours later, Shanklin reported by phone to FBI Headquarters on the questioning of Ruby by Dallas police. ". . . Ruby claims no one else is involved, that no one knew he . . . was going to do it. . . ." Ruby refused to say why he had killed Oswald, except that it was not premeditated, although Shanklin had picked up a rumor that he had been prompted by an emotional reaction to the prospect of Mrs. Kennedy having to come to Dallas to testify in an assassination trial. As to the character insights or associations that might have shed light on a motive, Shanklin could only offer a bit of conjecture: the Chicago-born strip-joint owner, who had never been married, "may have homosexual tendencies," since an item in the file of the Dallas FBI office indicated his "association with a pervert."

The idea of two unrelated lone assassins striking within forty-eight hours was more than most people could accept. When Shanklin's Secret Service counterpart, Forrest Sorrels, discussed the shooting of Oswald by phone with Gerald Behn, chief of the White House detail, he agreed there was a plot. The Chairman of the Joint Chiefs, General Taylor, would later confide to William Manchester, the author of *The Death of a President*, that he had expected there to be a suspicion that Oswald had been killed "to suppress something." And President Johnson, as he struggled to decide how best to explain Dallas to a nervous nation, would one day write in his memoirs:

> With that single shot the outrage of a nation turned to skepticism and doubt. The atmosphere was poisonous and had to be cleared. I was aware of some of the implications that grew out of the skepticism and doubt. Russia was not immune to them. Neither was Cuba. Neither was the State of Texas. Neither was the new President of the United States.

It was also on Sunday, November 24, that the late President lay in state in the Rotunda of the Capitol, as mourners paid their last respects before his burial at Arlington National Cemetery. The eulogies were devoted for the most part to his qualities of greatness, "deep faith, complete confidence, human sympathy, and broad vision," as Speaker of the House John W. McCormack enumerated them. But there were also pointed references to evil forces suspected of a responsibility for his loss, described by Senate Majority Leader Mike Mansfield as ". . . the hatred, prejudice, and the arrogance which converged at that moment of horror to strike him down." Or, in the words of Chief Justice Earl Warren:

> What moved some misguided wretch to do this horrible deed may never be known to us, but we do know that such acts are commonly stimulated by forces of hatred and malevolence, such as today are eating their way into the bloodstream of American life. What a price we pay for this fanaticism.

By Monday, November 25, two senior FBI officials had been dispatched to Dallas to supervise the marshaling of evidence for the report to Johnson that Hoover hoped would stay the mounting clamor for a high tribunal. Hoover reiterated his views in a memorandum that morning, explaining how he had prevailed upon the editors of *The Washington Post* to kill an editorial calling for a presidential commission: ". . . we told the *Post* that a . . . full report will be made . . . by either the President or some distinguished jurist. . . ." The man in charge at the Department of Justice, Deputy Attorney General Katzenbach, was straddling the fence, trying to accommodate Hoover but, at the same time, heeding the pressure of public opinion that seemed to indicate a majority of the American people believed there were assassins still at large. Katzenbach urged, in a note to White House aide Bill Moyers on November 25, the prompt release of the FBI's report, maintaining that the reputation of the bureau would offset any inconsistency between the report and statements of Dallas police officials implying a Communist conspiracy. The alternative, Katzenbach went on, would be a presidential commission to review the evidence, which had "both advantages and disadvantages" and could ". . . await publication of the FBI report and public reaction to it here and abroad." Johnson did direct that the FBI report be submitted, but when influential members of the House and Senate started calling for a congressional investigation, and Texas Attorney General Waggoner Carr established a Court of Inquiry, the President told Hoover the only way to stop the "rash of investigations" was to appoint a blue-ribbon panel to evaluate the report. Hoover, of course, relented, although on the more substantive issue of Oswald's single-handed guilt he was virtually in a position to direct the verdict. He had, for example, sent the two supervisors to Dallas, whose assignment, in the words of Assistant to the Director Alan H. Belmont was ". . . to set out the evidence showing that Oswald is responsible for the shooting that killed the President. We will show that Oswald was an avowed Marxist, a former defector to the Soviet Union and an active member of the FPCC (Fair Play for Cuba Committee), which has been financed by Castro." In his note to Moyers, Katzenbach was merely echoing Hoover when he listed certain "facts" of the assassination that he believed ought to be made public: ". . . Oswald was the assassin . . . ; he did not have confederates . . . ; and the evidence was such that he would have been convicted at trial." Katzenbach suggested further that speculation about Oswald's motive should be checked. ". . . we should have some basis for rebutting thought that this was a Communist conspiracy or (as the Iron Curtain press is saying) a right-wing conspiracy to blame it on the Communists."

On the afternoon of November 29 President Johnson summoned Earl Warren to the White House, realizing that the Chief Justice had already refused a request that he serve as chairman of the presidential commission, which had been transmitted to him that morning by Katzenbach and Solicitor General Archibald Cox. A renowned persuader and manipulator, Johnson was at his best. He appealed to the patriotism of the old World War I soldier, implying that rumors buzzing around the world could lead to war, probably nuclear war. He then drew for Warren a frightening picture of how several congressional committees and the Texas Court of Inquiry ". . . would compete with each other for public attention, and in the end leave the people more bewildered and emotional. . . . " He named six distinguished men who would be appointed to the panel: Senator Richard B. Russell, Democrat of Georgia; Senator John Sherman Cooper, Republican of Kentucky; Representative Hale Boggs, Democrat of Louisiana; Representative Gerald R. Ford, Republican of Michigan; Allen W. Dulles, former director of the CIA; and John J. McCloy, who had served as U.S. High Commissioner for Germany and as president of the World Bank. Finally, the clincher, as Johnson would describe it in retrospect:

> I said I didn't care who brought me a message about how opposed he was to this assignment. When the country is confronted with threatening division and suspicions, I said, and its foundation is being racked, and the President of the United States says you are the only man who can handle the matter, you won't say, "no," will you?
>
> [Warren] . . . swallowed hard and said, "No, sir."

On the evening of November 29, 1963, Johnson signed the executive order that created the President's Commission on the Assassination of President Kennedy, the Warren Commission, as it soon came to be known. It was charged with ". . . the responsibility for finding the full facts of the case and reporting them, along with appropriate recommendations, to the American people.''

The FBI was upset enough to decline to send a representative to the initial meeting of the Commission on December 5, but it did prepare its report with dispatch. On December 9, the day it was forwarded to the Commission, Katzenbach was still urging — futilely, since even the bureau was opposed by this time — immediate release of the key points: that the evidence had established beyond a reasonable doubt that Oswald shot the President; and that an exhaustive conspiracy investigation (hundreds of persons questioned, numerous leads run out) had proven negative. It was that evening, December 9, that Robert Kennedy was visited by Arthur Schlesinger, Jr., the historian who was a White House aide. As Schlesinger wrote in *Robert Kennedy and His Times*, the Attorney General for obvious reasons was not taking an active part in the investigation, but he had been kept posted on its progress. "What about Oswald?" Schlesinger asked. "There could be no serious doubt that Oswald was guilty," Kennedy replied, "but there was still argument if he had done it by himself or as part of a larger plot, whether organized by Castro or gangsters." Kennedy said that Hoover thought Oswald had done it by himself, but CIA Director McCone thought two people had been involved.

At the outset at least, it was Warren's view that the Commission's role should be more judicial than investigative or prosecutorial, that it should evaluate the case that had been developed by law enforcement agencies, the FBI in particular, rather than assemble new evidence. ". . . I believe that . . . we can start with the premise that we can rely upon the reports of the various agencies that have been engaged in the investigation . . . ," he said at the Commission meeting on December 5. There would, therefore, in the view of the Chief Justice, be no need for an independent investigative staff, that the Commission could make do with fourteen attorneys to be recruited by J. Lee Rankin, the former Solicitor General, who was sworn in as Commission General Counsel on December 16. Nor would it be necessary to seek subpoena power. (Warren was overruled on this point, however, and it was granted by a congressional resolution.) When the Commission met for a second time on December 16, Warren's faith in the reliability of the FBI had been severely undermined by the quality of the report the bureau had submitted a week earlier. According to Commission members, the FBI report was difficult to decipher, much of its content had been leaked to the press, and it left, as Congressman Boggs put it, "millions of questions" unanswered. Rankin, who would be instrumental in the ultimate decision to rely entirely upon the resources of the federal agencies, remarked that it just did not seem as though the FBI was "looking for things that this Commission has to look for in order to get the answers that it wants and it's entitled to." Beyond the defects of the voluminous FBI report, the Commission was faced with the antagonism of Hoover, who was defensive to the point of paranoia over a concern that the Bureau would be charged with dereliction and his reputation would be ruined. William C. Sullivan, Assistant FBI Director in 1963, told a Senate Committee on Intelligence Activities in 1976 that Hoover adamantly opposed a thorough inquiry, ". . . for fear that it would discover important and relevant facts that we in the FBI had not discovered. . . ." According to Sullivan, Hoover's favorite tactic was media manipulation, ". . . to leak to the press the FBI investigation, believing that this would tend to satisfy everybody and perhaps the authorities would conclude that an investigation of great depth would not be necessary." Fifteen years later, Katzenbach explained the dilemma to us. The FBI would have been deeply troubled, he said in testimony to us, by evidence that contradicted its conclusions that Lee Harvey Oswald was the lone assassin. For its part, the CIA was not as reluctant to cooperate, though it took the position, as we were told by Richard M. Helms, who in 1963 was the Deputy Director for Plans, that the Commission would only receive responses to specific inquiries. That is, no information would be volunteered, a policy that eventually would prove more damaging to the Commission's credibility than Hoover's outright opposition.

The most vexing problem for the Commission, one it would never fully resolve, was referred to by Rankin as "tender spots," potential embarrassments to the FBI and CIA that would inhibit a free flow of information between the agencies and the Warren Commission. The CIA's "tender spot" would not be aired in public until a Senate investigation of intelligence activities in the mid-1970s, but the FBI's was dropped in the lap of the Commission in January 1964 by Texas Attorney General Waggoner Carr, who reported a rumor that Oswald had been a bureau informant. It led Rankin, for one, to call into question the FBI's quick determination that there had not been an assassination conspiracy. ". . . they have not run out all kinds of leads," he noted at a January 22 Commission meeting, "in Mexico or in Russia, . . . but they are concluding that there can't be a conspiracy. . . ." Rankin went on to say it would, of course, be in the FBI's best interest to get the Commission to close the case, if there was any truth to the Oswald-as-informant rumor. This in fact was what the bureau had been trying to do with its assurances that it had found the one and only assassin. Rankin suggested that he put the question directly to Hoover, explaining that he merely wanted to put the rumor to rest, but Warren disliked the idea of going to the FBI without a prior effort to learn the facts behind the charge. Russell argued that to elicit a response from Hoover, and then to proceed with an investigation, would appear to impeach the FBI. Rankin could not see how the country would accept the conclusions of the investigation, if it could not be satisfied on this issue, but Dulles, talking from the experience of a long career in the CIA, said the charge would be "a terribly hard thing to disprove."

Boggs:	*You could disprove it, couldn't you?*
Dulles:	*No.*
Boggs:	*Let's take a specific case; that fellow Powers [U-2 pilot Gary Francis Powers] was one of your men.*
Dulles:	*. . . not an agent. He was an employee.*
Boggs:	*Let's say Powers did not have a signed contract but was recruited by someone in the CIA. The man who recruited him would know, wouldn't he?*
Dulles:	*Yes, but he wouldn't tell.*
Warren:	*Wouldn't tell it under oath?*
Dulles:	*I wouldn't think he would tell it under oath, no. . . . He ought not to tell it under oath.*
McCloy:	*. . . suppose the President of the United States comes to you and says, "Will you tell me, Mr. Dulles?"*
Dulles:	*I would tell the President of the United States anything, yes; I am under his control. He is my boss. I wouldn't necessarily tell anybody else, unless the President authorized me to do it.*

Boggs was aghast, telling Dulles, "What you do is make our problem utterly impossible because you say this rumor can't be dispelled under any circumstances." Dulles replied, "I don't think you can unless you believe Mr. Hoover, . . . which probably most people do." Warren announced he favored a two-sided approach — the rumor had to be checked out both with Hoover and independently, but that was not what was to happen. Rankin discussed the rumor with Hoover on January 28 and was told flatly, "Oswald had never been an informant of the FBI." Then, on February 6, Hoover submitted an affidavit to the Commission, stating a search of FBI records had shown that Oswald had never been an informant, and on February 13 affidavits were filed by each of the ten FBI agents who had been in contact with Oswald, all of whom denied he had been an informant. These denials were supported by the testimony on May 6 of Assistant to the Director Belmont and on May 14 by the word of Hoover himself. That the Commission never was able to check out the rumor on its own was not important as an indication to the Commission that an Oswald connection with the bureau might be concealed by the FBI, for our investigation would show there was no such connection. What was significant, however, was the ability of the FBI to intimidate the Commission, in light of the bureau's predisposition on the questions of Oswald's guilt and whether there had been a conspiracy. At a January 27 Commission meeting, there was another dialogue:

McCloy:	*. . . the time is almost overdue for us to have a better perspective of the FBI investigation than we now have . . . We are so dependent on them for our facts. . . .*
Rankin:	*Part of our difficulty in regard to it is that they have no problem. They have decided that it is Oswald who committed the assassination, they have decided that no one else is involved, . . .*
Russell:	*They have tried the case and reached a verdict on every aspect.*
Boggs:	*You have put your finger on it.*

Conclusion: Oswald a Lone Assassin

Hoover need not have been so worried — the Commission did not discover any important evidence that the FBI overlooked, which is not to say it failed to try. The testimony of 552 witnesses and the thousands of exhibits of analyzed evidence attest to an enormous effort to sift truth from a monumental accumulation of information. The performance of the Commission's staff was all the more exceptional in view of the pressure: an impossible June 30 deadline for the final report. The White House wanted the job done in advance of the presidential nominating conventions in the summer of 1964, for fear the assassination would become a political issue. When the 888-page report did appear — on September 24, nearly three months behind schedule — it was a remarkably well-crafted and comprehensive document. More important, it was, for the time being at least, generally accepted as the truth: "No material question now remains unresolved," wrote the Pulitzer Prize-winning journalist Anthony Lewis, in an introduction to *The New York Times* edition of *The Warren Report*. The case against Oswald was overwhelming, so much so that Chief Justice Warren would, in his *Memoirs*, reflect on it from the perspective of his former position of prosecutor in a large metropolitan California county as open and shut: ". . . I have no hesitation in saying that had it not been for the prominence of the victim, the case against Oswald would have been tried in two or three days with little likelihood of any but one result."

The Commission concluded that the shots had been fired from a sixth-floor southeast corner window of the Texas School Book Depository; they were at least two, probably three, in number — one a probable miss, one that wounded Kennedy in the neck and Connally in the chest, right wrist, and left thigh, and one that hit Kennedy in the head, killing him; and they had all been fired by Oswald. The origin of the shots was based on the testimony of witnesses, who said they had seen a rifle being fired from the sixth-floor window; from ballistics tests on a nearly whole bullet found on Connally's stretcher at Parkland Hospital and on bullet fragments found in the front seat of the limousine, indicating they had been fired from a 6.5 millimeter Mannlicher-Carcano rifle found on the sixth floor of the Book Depository; from tests on three cartridge cases, also found on the sixth floor of the Book Depository, indicating they had been fired in the Mannlicher-Carcano; and from inspection of the windshield of the limousine, which had been struck by a bullet fragment on its inside surface. Further, the nature of the wounds suffered by Kennedy and Connally, determined by medical testimony, and the location of the limousine at the time of the shots, determined by a movie film taken by a spectator, Abraham Zapruder, established that the shots had come from above and behind. Kennedy was first hit by a bullet that entered the back of his neck and exited at his throat; while he might have survived this wound, he then suffered a fatal wound to the head. As for Connally's wounds, although the Commission said its essential findings did not depend on just which shot had hit the governor, the determination it did make would later ignite a heated controversy: ". . . there is very persuasive evidence . . . to indicate that the same bullet which pierced the President's throat also caused Governor Connally's wounds." Oswald's guilt was based on the following evidence: he had owned the 6.5 millimeter Mannlicher-Carcano from which the shots were fired; he had carried the rifle into the Book Depository on the morning of November 22; he had been at the window at the time the shots were fired; the rifle had been found, shortly after the assassination, partially hidden on the sixth floor along with a paper bag in which he had brought the weapon into the building. By way of other evidence, the Commission established that a rifleman of Oswald's capabilities could have fired the shots from the Mannlicher-Carcano in the elapsed time of the assassination; that he had lied to the Dallas police after his arrest; and that he had attempted to assassinate Major General Edwin A. Walker on April 10, 1963, "demonstrating his disposition to take human life."

The Commission also concluded that Oswald had murdered a Dallas police officer, J. D. Tippit, which it considered corroboration of his guilt in the assassination: nine eyewitnesses had identified Oswald as Tippit's killer; cartridge cases found at the scene had been fired from a revolver in Oswald's possession at the time of his arrest, a revolver he in fact had purchased; and Oswald's jacket had been found along the path of flight from the scene. Within thirty-five minutes of the Tippit murder — eighty minutes after the assassination of the President — Oswald had resisted arrest at the Texas Theatre, attempting to shoot another police officer.

Conspiracy Theories Rejected

The Warren Commission told the American public that it found no evidence of a conspiracy, and while the wording of its conclusion left room for a reversal based on contradictory facts not available in 1964, the Commission went to great length (131 pages in its *Report*) to dismiss the idea of a plot. It said that no "limitations [had] . . . been placed on the Commission's inquiry . . . [and that] all government agencies [had] . . . fully discharged their responsibility to cooperate with the Commission in its investigation." The Commission added, ". . . if there is any . . . evidence [of a plot], it has been beyond the reach of all the investigative agencies and resources of the United States. . . ." In addition, it invoked some powerful names, those of top-level leaders, who, it said, had reached the same conclusion independently: Secretary of State Rusk, Secretary of Defense McNamara, Secretary of the Treasury Dillon, Attorney General Kennedy, FBI Director Hoover, and CIA Director McCone. Having decided that Oswald had acted without confederates, the Commission sought to decipher a reason for the assassination from the character of the assassin, but since he was dead, it could only study his background, about which it was able to compile a considerable volume of detail. From it, the Commission proposed a number of possible motives: Oswald's deep-rooted resentment of authority, his inability to enter into meaningful relationships, his urge to find a place in history, his capacity for violence, and his commitment to Marxism. While finding none of these satisfactory, if judged by the "standards of reasonable men," the Commission theorized they may well have been the "moving force of a man whose view of the world had been twisted." The Commission believed it was closest to discovering the motive when it drew a psychological portrait of a totally alienated man:

His life was characterized by isolation, frustration and failure. He had very few, if any, close relationships with other people and he appeared to have great difficulty in finding a meaningful place in the world. He was never satisfied with anything. When he was in the United States he resented the capitalist system. . . . He seemed to prefer the Soviet Union and he spoke highly of Cuba. When he was in the Soviet Union, he apparently resented the Communist Party members, who were accorded special privileges and who he thought were betraying communism, and he spoke well of the United States. He accused his wife of preferring others to himself and told her to return to the Soviet Union without him but without a divorce. At the same time he professed his love for her and said that he could not get along without her. Marina Oswald thought that he would not be happy anywhere, "Only on the moon, perhaps."

The Commission's conclusion that there was no conspiracy was the product of a systematic examination of the issue that, on its face, was thorough and foolproof. It was premised on the same meticulous approach that was used to establish Oswald's guilt: first, a step-by-step analysis of his modus operandi in the assassination, to determine if there were any indications that Oswald had been assisted; then, careful scrutiny of Oswald's life from the time he was discharged from the Marine Corps in September 1959, to learn if the seeds of conspiracy might have been sown during his defection to the Soviet Union, or in his period of political activism on return to the United States in June 1962. Further, the Commission probed the possibility that Jack Ruby had been a participant in a plot, and, finally, it sought to lay to rest a proliferation of rumors (126 items of speculation were rebutted in an appendix of the report).

Specifically, the Commission found nothing sinister in the choice of the motorcade route (it had been appropriately based on destination, Kennedy's desire for a heavy turnout and traffic patterns), or in Oswald's employment at the Texas School Book Depository (it had apparently been secured through a chance conversation between Marina's friend, Ruth Paine, and a neighbor, the sister of a Book Depository employee, Buell Wesley Frazier, on October 14, which, as far as the Commission could determine, was over a month before it was known publicly that the Depository building would be on the presidential route). While it was Frazier who asserted that Oswald had carried an object the size and shape of a rifle into the Book Depository on the morning of November 22, the Commission was satisfied that his assistance had been limited to giving Oswald a ride to work and that Frazier was in no way involved. The arrangement of cartons at the window from which the shots were fired and fingerprints other than Oswald's on the cartons gave no indication of an accomplice; and the testimony of a witness who had been sitting on a wall on the southwest corner of Houston and Elm streets, identifying Oswald as the single individual in the window, was more credible to the Commission than that of a witness who had been standing on the east side of Houston, asserting the presence of a second man in the window.

Oswald's decision to defect to Russia had been made, the Commission concluded, a good two years beforehand, giving rise to speculation that he had been recruited by Soviet agents while stationed with the Marines in the Far East. The Commission, however, found reason to doubt that he had been: if the Soviet agents had made contact with such a likely turncoat, he would have been of far more value to them as a Marine radar operator than as a defector. Further, the Commission could find nothing that had occurred in the course of Oswald's defection

— in the processing of his visa application, for example — to indicate that he had become a Soviet agent prior to entering the U.S.S.R. in October 1959. There remained the possibility that he had been recruited after he defected, though the Commission found that just as unlikely, once it considered the circumstances surrounding some major events of his stay in Russia. When Oswald appeared at the U.S. Embassy in Moscow on October 31, 1959, to announce his desire to become a Russian citizen and was stalled by a consular official, he vowed that he would reveal to the Soviet government military secrets that he had learned as a Marine radar specialist, an indiscretion that served to persuade the Commission that he had not been under the tutelage of the KGB, the Soviet intelligence agency. "Certainly a statement of this type would prejudice any possibility of his being an effective pro-Communist agent," the Commission remarked in its *Report*. The Commission also reasoned that the preferred treatment Oswald had received in Minsk — a well-paying job in a radio and television factory, a monthly subsidy from the Russian Red Cross and an apartment for the ruble equivalent of $6 a month — did not imply a clandestine arrangement, but was intended as an inducement to Oswald to remain in Russia. As for Oswald's marriage to Marina Prusakova on April 30, 1961, the Commission commented: "It seems unlikely that the Soviet authorities would have permitted Oswald to marry and to take his wife with him to the United States if they were contemplating using him as an agent." And the Commission considered Marina, with her inability to speak English and her ignorance of the United States, to have been an unlikely member of an "agent team." Finally, the Commission sifted the details of the Oswalds' emigration to the United States for hints of the KGB's handiwork, but to no avail. The State Department and the Immigration and Naturalization Service advised they could find no indication that Oswald had been coached by Soviet authorities when he wrote to the U.S Embassy in Moscow for permission to return to the States; his letters displayed the "arrogant attitude which was characteristic of him" and showed "about the same low level of sophistication, fluency, and spelling" as other letters he had composed. Other evidence indicated to the Commission that, "rather than facilitate the departure of the Oswalds," the Soviet government "first tried to dissuade Marina Oswald from going to the United States and then, when she failed to respond to the pressure, permitted her to leave without undue delay."

The Commission found no conspiratorial implications in Oswald's associations, once he had returned to the United States. It examined his personal contacts: with the Russian-speaking community of Dallas-Fort Worth, whose members had befriended Marina, although their relationship with Oswald was "short-lived and generally quite strained";

with George de Mohrenschildt, specifically, a "highly individualistic" man who "frankly admits his provocative personality," and his China-born White Russian wife, Jeanne, who, like her husband, had never displayed "subversive or disloyal conduct"; and with Ruth and Michael Paine, she a Quaker, whose interest in U.S.-Russian relations had induced her to cultivate a friendship with Marina; he the son of a Trotskyite, but whose security clearance as an engineer with Bell Helicopter put him above suspicion (even though he and Oswald attended a political meeting together in the fall of 1963). The Commission also pursued Oswald's left-wing affiliations, compiling a wealth of detail on his dealings in 1962–63 with the Communist Party, the Socialist Workers Party, the Socialist Labor Party, and the Fair Play for Cuba Committee. Most of Oswald's activities consisted of harmless correspondence — between the national FPCC headquarters and his one-man chapters in Dallas and New Orleans, for example — but there was one incident with violent overtones. While passing out "Hands Off Cuba!" leaflets in New Orleans in August 1963, Oswald was arrested in a street fight with anti-Castro Cubans. The Commission concluded that the incident did not imply an incipient conspiracy, even though he was in the company of two confederates, one of whom was never identified. The Commission terminated its inquiry into a possible political conspiracy by turning its attention to right-wing extremist groups that had circulated a "Wanted for Treason" handbill in Dallas on November 20 and 21 and had placed an equally disparaging "Welcome, Mr. Kennedy" advertisement in *The Dallas Morning News* on November 22, concluding it could find no connection between the conservative forces in question and Lee Harvey Oswald or the assassination.

The Commission found nothing sinister in Oswald's journey to Mexico even though it occurred just eight weeks before the assassination under circumstances mysterious enough for Oswald to have cautioned Marina that it was to be kept strictly secret. She honored his admonition to the extent of lying to the FBI when asked if she had known about the trip beforehand, a denial she admitted was false when she testified before the Warren Commission on February 3, 1964. Even then, Marina knew very little about the trip itself, but the Commission was able to piece together a chronology from travel records and statements of persons who had come in contact with Oswald: in particular, Silvia Tirado de Duran, a Mexican national employed at the Cuban Embassy in Mexico City, who was questioned by Mexican authorities.

Oswald arrived in Mexico City on the morning of September 27, 1963, having traveled by bus from New Orleans. He spent two days trying to obtain a visa to go to Cuba. It was for the purpose of continuing on to the Soviet Union, he said, although he had told Marina that he intended to remain in Cuba, a version the Commission found to be credible. Oswald was informed at the Cuban Embassy he would not be granted a visa for travel to Cuba unless he first got one to enter the U.S.S.R.; and he subsequently learned at the Soviet Embassy that his application would take about four months to process. Senora Duran said that Oswald had become so angered over the impasse that she had summoned Cuban Consul Eusebio Azcue, who had engaged in a heated exchange with Oswald. Oswald spent the balance of his stay in Mexico City sightseeing and checking back with the Soviet Embassy on his visa application. He left for the United States by bus on October 2, arriving in Dallas disappointed and discouraged, according to Marina.

The Commission felt assured it had acquired better-than-adequate corroboration of its account of the trip from a variety of sources: the Mexican government and U.S. officials who had worked with Mexican authorities; the Cuban government, which had been asked to confirm Senora Duran's testimony; CIA handwriting experts, who had verified that the visa application had in fact been signed by Oswald; and "confidential sources of extremely high reliability." In addition, the Commission was confident that Oswald had not been in contact with individuals who had not been identified, so all-inclusive had the coverage been of persons he had encountered, ". . . including passengers on the buses he rode, and the employees and guests of the hotels where he stayed, . . ." The Commission learned, for instance, that on the bus to Mexico, Oswald sat next to an itinerant preacher named Albert Osborne, whose denial that he had shared a seat with Oswald was judged to be unreliable by the Commission, although it found no reason to suspect that Osborne had participated in the assassination. The Commission checked "literally dozens" of allegations in connection with Oswald's trip to Mexico (he had been hired, for example, by Castro agents), each of which it determined to be "without any factual basis." In short, the Commission determined that Oswald's trip to Mexico was in no way connected with the assassination, and it uncovered no evidence of a sinister role that it could attribute to the Cuban government.

The Commission methodically deflated several other conspiracy allegations that it judged to have been either incorrectly interpreted or grounded on erroneous information. It pointedly attached no significance to Oswald's rental of three post office boxes in Dallas and New Orleans in 1962–63, since he had not done it secretively, and it could not be established that he had ever used them for receiving surreptitious messages. As for Oswald's regular use of aliases, the Commission found them to be compatible with "his antisocial and criminal inclinations" and used to conceal his purchase of the murder weapons (Oswald had signed "A. J. Hidell" when he ordered by mail the Mannlicher-Carcano rifle and the Smith & Wesson revolver), but it did not see them as indicative of a "conspiracy with others." Other conspiracy leads were dismissed because they were based on claims of Dallas citizens whose stories the Commission plainly did not believe. One was the report of an employee of a sporting goods store in Irving, the Dallas suburb where the Paines lived, that shortly before the assassination a telescopic sight had been mounted and boresighted on a rifle for Oswald, implying that Oswald had owned a weapon that had not been accounted for, since his Mannlicher-Carcano had come with a telescopic sight attached. Another came from several witnesses, placing Oswald — at times alone, at times with associates — practicing with his rifle at ranges around Dallas, implying a complex conspiracy. There was also the testimony of a Lincoln-Mercury salesman that identified Oswald as the prospective purchaser of an automobile in November 1963, indicating he was a proficient driver (he was hardly able to drive at all, according to the testimony of Ruth Paine, who had been giving him lessons) and suggesting that Oswald, considered destitute by all accounts, had expected to come into enough money to afford a car. (The Commission did an extensive analysis of Oswald's finances, which indicated that from the time he returned from the Soviet Union on June 13, 1962, to November 22, 1963, his living pattern "was consistent with his limited income," which for the seventeen-month period was $3,665.89, against cash disbursements of $3,501.79.) Finally, the Commission dismissed claims that Oswald was in the company of men who appeared to be Cubans, or at least Latins, in the late summer and early fall of 1963. It simply noted with skepticism the separate assertions of a lawyer and a bartender in New Orleans, each of whom said he had seen Oswald in the summer of 1963 with Latin-looking individuals; and it decided not to credit the story of a Cuban exile in Dallas, Silvia Odio, who told of a visit to her home one evening in September 1963 by Oswald and two Latins who identified themselves as anti-Castro activists. Oswald confederates in an unlikely cause, the Commission reasoned, which was a reference to Oswald's loudly professed allegiance to the Castro regime.

Insinuations that Oswald had been a U.S. government agent were among the most troublesome the Commission had to tackle, for it is always difficult to prove a negative, and the circumstantial evidence that Oswald had been some sort of intelligence agent was strong. The strategy employed to refute the rumors was to dispense with lengthy analysis (they were treated in only three pages in the *Report*), issue an unequivocal denial, and hope the matter would be settled once and for all. The Commission declared: ". . . close scrutiny of the records of the Federal agencies involved and the testimony of the responsible officials of the U.S. Government establish that there was *absolutely* no type of informant or undercover relationship between an agency of the U.S. Government and Lee Harvey Oswald *at any time* [emphasis added]." As it would turn out, the Commission, no doubt pressed by the thin-skinned leadership of the FBI, need not have protested so vigorously, for the innocence of the government's relationship with Oswald withstood the test of our investigation, which went considerably beyond taking affidavits of denial. But as it stood in 1964, the skeptical reader was entitled to question the flat assertions of the Warren Commission. For a man of his limited education and ability, Oswald, in his peculiar way, had come in contact with more than one federal agency, including the FBI.

The Commission's investigation of the charges entailed a review of Oswald's repeated dealings with federal agencies, beginning with his application for a passport prior to defecting to the Soviet Union in 1959: the one he turned in at the U.S. Embassy in Moscow when he tried, in October, to renounce his citizenship. "Thereafter . . . Oswald had numerous contacts with the American Embassy, both in person and through correspondence." In 1961 he applied for a renewed passport, which was granted, and his application for admittance to the United States, with his Russian wife, was approved by the Immigration and Naturalization Service and the Department of State. Just before sailing for the States, he secured a State Department loan to help cover transportation costs. The FBI subsequently interviewed Oswald on three occasions, while he was residing in Dallas-Fort Worth and New Orleans in 1962–63, and he was under government surveillance when he campaigned for the Fair Play for Cuba Committee in New Orleans. The government also learned that he visited the Soviet Embassy in Mexico City. The Commission took note of the allegations that Oswald had been something more to the intelligence agencies than the subject of their surveillance, and its approach was to interrogate the sources of the charges (including Marguerite Oswald, who had claimed her son had been a U.S. spy in Russia), to review the federal files on Oswald and to take testimony from officials of the FBI and the CIA. Finally, the Commission sought to discover why the name of Dallas Special Agent James P. Hosty appeared in Oswald's address book, and it was satisfied with the explanation of both Hosty and Ruth Paine, who proposed it was the result of Hosty's visit to the Paine home on November 1, 1963, in search of Oswald.

Oswald and Ruby Not Connected

The Commission apparently made a careful inspection of Jack Ruby's every known move from the evening of Thursday, November 21, to the moment he murdered Oswald in the basement of Dallas Police Headquarters, 11:21 A.M., Sunday, November 24, on the theory that his activities and associations would have indicated a conspiracy had there been one. The study revealed, according to the Commission, that Ruby had been a restless gadabout and a night owl. On Thursday evening he ate dinner with an old friend, Ralph Paul, the proprietor of the Bull Pen, a drive-in in Arlington, Texas, and at midnight he joined Lawrence Meyers, a Chicago businessman, in the Bon Vivant Room of the Dallas Cabana Motel. The study showed that, on hearing the news of the assassination, Ruby had become visibly upset and had decided to shut down his clubs, the Carousel and the Vegas, for three nights and had even considered selling his business interests and returning to his native Chicago. It emphasized Ruby's preoccupation with the "Welcome, Mr. Kennedy" advertisement in *The Dallas Morning News*, which, he had become convinced, was the work of either "Commies or Birchers," designed to discredit Jews. The study developed evidence of the ease with which Ruby had been able to move about police headquarters for no official purpose, citing as an example his attendance at a midnight Friday news conference at which reporters were permitted to observe the suspected assassin. It indicated that Ruby was, within hours of the assassination, aware of Oswald's background, at least to the extent of knowing that he had belonged to the Fair Play for Cuba Committee, not the "Free Cuba Committee," as he so informed District Attorney Henry M. Wade, who had got it wrong at the midnight Friday news conference. The Commission found nothing suspect in the extent of Ruby's knowledge of the assassin's background (he could have learned it from the newspapers, the Commission reasoned), or his willingness to assert it in public. Finally, the Commission, from its study of Ruby, was able to give an account of the events of Sunday morning, telling how he said he had left home about 11, gone to Western Union to wire $25 to Karen Carlin, a Carousel striptease dancer, who had phoned him at 10:19, and had then proceeded across Main Street and into the basement of police headquarters.

In its evaluation of Ruby's activities, the Commission said it could not discover any "sign of any conduct which suggests that he was involved in the assassination" and that "his response to the assassination had been one of genuine shock and grief." Saturday night phone calls by Ruby to Ralph Paul and Breck Wall were ultimately found not "to indicate that [Ruby] . . . had conspiratorial" contacts. It determined that Paul had been a close friend, business associate, and adviser to Ruby and that Wall, a onetime business associate, was a former official of the American Guild of Variety Artists, who had commiserated with Ruby over the failure of his competitors to close their clubs after the assassination, as he had done. Further, checks by the FBI and CIA disclosed no evidence that either Paul or Wall had "ever engaged in any form of subversive activity." The Commission checked another potentially suspicious telephone call, the one from Karen Carlin at 10:19 on Sunday morning asking for $25, ". . . to determine whether that call was prearranged for the purpose of conveying information about the transfer of Oswald or to provide Ruby an excuse for being near the police department." The Commission found no evidence of a link between Karen Carlin or her husband, Bruce Ray Carlin, and the shooting of Oswald. But the key piece of evidence in the Commission's case that Ruby had not participated in an assassination plot was its finding that Ruby and Oswald had never been acquainted, though here again, the Commission was in the position of having to prove a negative. It was able to do it, at least to its own satisfaction, by demonstrating that all of the reported links between the two men had been cut from whole cloth. Oswald was said to have visited Ruby at the Carousel by at least one witness, an entertainer who did a memory act, but the Commission was convinced that Oswald had never set foot in the nightclub. The Commission was equally certain that Ruby and Oswald had not met at the Dallas YMCA, although Ruby had been a member at a time when Oswald had lived there briefly, and it found no validity at all in rumors of a homosexual relationship. The Commission went beyond the reported links and looked for mutual associations that might have provided indirect links. Another boarder at Oswald's rooming house had been acquainted with a woman who had known and worked for Ruby; the housekeeper at the rooming house, Earlene Roberts, was the sister of a woman who had discussed a business venture with Ruby four days before the assassination. But these and other clues to a possible Ruby-Oswald connection — including the fact that they had lived about a mile from one another in Oak Cliff — did not impress the Commission as meaningful. Finally, the Commission considered an allegation by Marguerite Oswald that an FBI agent had shown her a picture of Ruby the day before he murdered her son, but the Commission was satisfied that the man in the photograph, which had been taken, according to the Cuban government, by a CIA surveillance camera in Mexico City, bore no resemblance to Jack Ruby.

The Commission acknowledged that Ruby was feared by his employees for his violent tirades. It also acknowledged that Ruby had been arrested by Dallas police eight times prior to being charged with the murder of Oswald, but the Commission considered the arrests to have been minor. While the Commission recognized that Ruby had known numerous underworld figures, men like Paul Roland Jones who had criminal records, and that one of his closest friends was Lewis McWillie, a professional gambler in Havana who was visited by Ruby in

1959, it took the position that the evidence did not establish a link between Ruby and organized crime, citing testimony of both federal and state officials who believed no such connection existed.

The Commission's portrait of Ruby is easily summarized. He grew up in Chicago, the son of Jewish immigrants; he lived in a home disrupted by domestic strife; he was troubled psychologically as a youth and not well educated; his temperament had been described as ranging from "mild mannered" to "violent." In 1963 Ruby was fifty-two and unmarried; he ran a cheap Dallas nightclub not very successfully. His acquaintances included a number of Dallas police officers who frequented his club, as well as business associates and customers, many of whom lived on the shady side of legitimacy. Ruby had a violent temper; he had broken the law several times in a minor way, but he was not connected to organized crime, and there was no credible evidence that linked him to the assassination of the President.

3

The Decline of Credibility: 1964-1976

[T]he monumental record of the President's Commission will stand like a Gibraltar of factual literature throughout the ages to come.

Gerald R. Ford
Portrait of the Assassin

Critical Analysis

Early reviews of *The Warren Report* by legal scholars and journalists were duly respectful of the diligent investigation on which it was based, and they generally accepted its interpretation of the Kennedy assassination as accurate and its conclusions as final. "Each fact is to be found in its proper place to sustain each conclusion," wrote the distinguished British jurist, Lord Devlin, in *The Atlantic.* "The minor conclusions support the major, and on the major, the verdict rests." There was, however, among the American populace a body of dissent that was reflected in a Louis Harris poll published on October 19, 1964: 31 percent of the people doubted Oswald had acted alone. That figure would double in just a few years, as the credibility of the Warren Commission would begin to crumble under the assault of a growing host of critical authors.

Many of these critics, however, had special axes to grind. As a result of our investigation, the Committee found that "criticisms leveled at the Commission . . . [were] often biased, unfair and inaccurate . . .

40

[and] . . . the prevailing opinion of the Commission's performance was undeserved." The best example of a critic who fit the Committee's "unfair and inaccurate" description was Mark Lane, a New York attorney long identified with left-wing causes and author of *Rush to Judgment*, which was published in 1966. It was a widely read book in which Lane catalogued actions and statements by the Commission that he perceived to be errors, misjudgments, or distortions. (Lane also was an active critic of the FBI investigation of the assassination of Dr. Martin Luther King, Jr., and he represented James Earl Ray, the convicted assassin of Dr. King, before the Committee, which had this to say of Lane's role in that case: "Lane was willing to advocate conspiracy theories . . . [without checking] them, [and his] . . . conduct resulted in public [misperception . . .].") Next to Lane in prominence among the first wave of critics was Harold Weisberg, a former U.S. Senate investigator whose series of privately published harangues (*Whitewash, Whitewash II, Photographic Whitewash*, etc.) were centered on the theme of government complicity and cover-up, but because his rhetoric was so obscure, his arguments so dependent on accusation rather than logic, the effect of Weisberg's work was to make complex issues confusing.

In the late 1960s a number of more thoughtful critics emerged, writers whose analyses, though not without a point of view, were more objective and less strident. Josiah Thompson, an authority on the Danish philosopher Kierkegaard, took leave from Haverford College in Pennsylvania, where he was a philosophy professor, to produce *Six Seconds in Dallas*, in which he attempted to go beyond a denunciation of the Warren Commission and reconstruct what actually had happened in Dealey Plaza from his analysis of eyewitness testimony and the medical and ballistics evidence. Thompson's conclusions: there had been three shooter locations (the grassy knoll, the roof of a government building on Houston Street, and the sixth-floor window of the Texas School Book Depository); President Kennedy and Governor Connally had been wounded in the back by separate shots; and Kennedy had been killed by two shots to the head, one fired from the rear and one from the right front. Sylvia Meagher, a career administrator for the United Nations, who had turned out a valuable *Subject Index to the Warren Report and Hearings and Exhibits* in 1966, did much the same, though in narrative form, for all the arguments of the critics in *Accessories after the Fact*. Her purpose, as stated in a foreword, was to examine the correlation between *The Warren Report* and the hearings and exhibits: "The first pronounces Oswald guilty; the second, . . . creates a reasonable doubt of Oswald's guilt and even a powerful presumption of his complete innocence . . ."

From the standpoint of public perception, the most damaging evaluation by a critic of the Warren Commission was initially a master's thesis by Edward J. Epstein, a political science student at Cornell. Epstein's thesis was published in 1966 as *Inquest: The Warren Commission and the Establishment of Truth*. The central point of the book — not unexpectedly for a graduate student in government — was that the Warren Commission had sought, not "truth," but "political truth," and the process by which it arrived at its conclusions was as much a worthy subject of study as the conclusions themselves. The chief significance of the book, however, was its primary source: documents that had been obtained by Epstein, mostly from Wesley J. Liebeler, a former assistant counsel for the Commission, including the FBI Summary Report that had been submitted to President Johnson and was forwarded to the Commission on December 9, 1963, and a supplement to that report, sent to the Commission on January 13, 1964. Epstein also reviewed the importance to the lone-assassin conclusion of a hypothesis that the bullet that wounded Connally had first passed through Kennedy's neck, attributing to Commission Assistant Counsel Norman Redlich the statement: "To say they were hit by separate bullets is synonymous with saying that there were two assassins." Redlich's conclusion was based on an analysis of the Zapruder film, which showed that only about a half-second elapsed between the visible reactions of the two men to being hit, and FBI tests that indicated it would have taken 2.3 seconds for a single gunman to have fired two well-aimed shots with the Mannlicher-Carcano. Taken together, these studies meant that what Epstein called the "threshold question of conspiracy" hinged on the autopsy: if it showed that the bullet that had struck Kennedy in the back had exited from his throat, then it was quite likely it had also struck Connally. Epstein went on to quote a part of the Commission's report on the autopsy of the President, which confirmed that the bullet did exit the throat, that is, it "made its exit through the anterior surface of the neck." But he then cited a contradicting statement from the FBI report of December 9:

> Medical examination of the President's body revealed that one of the bullets had entered just below the shoulder to the right of the spinal column at an angle of 45 to 60 degrees downward, that there was no point of exit, and that the bullet was not in the body.

Epstein made it clear that the FBI had not shifted its position by January 13, quoting from the supplemental report: "[T]he bullet which entered his back had penetrated to a distance of less than a finger length." Epstein's deduction that either the FBI investigation was fundamentally flawed, or else the autopsy evidence was misrepresented by the Commission, was an overstatement by a young scholar who was unfamiliar with the full FBI investigation and unaccustomed to the ways of government, but it had a tremendous impact. For that matter, it started a debate over the Warren Commission's work in general, and the autopsy by the Navy in particular, that would last at least until our panel of medical experts had an opportunity to examine autopsy X-rays and photographs that the Commission did not see. Epstein also unlatched a Pandora's box of conspiracy suspicions, many of which he just mentioned in passing: eyewitness reports of shots from the grassy knoll that, in Epstein's view, were not investigated adequately by the Commission; the "nearly whole bullet" (Commission Exhibit 399) reportedly found on Connally's stretcher at Parkland Hospital and assumed to be the one that had wounded both men, although an expert in forensic medicine and wound ballistics testified that more metal had been found in Connally's wrist than was missing from the bullet; and the testimony of Silvia Odio, the Cuban woman who placed Oswald at her home in Dallas at a time when he was supposed to have been on his way to Mexico City.

Epstein charged that the Commission, rather than conducting an impartial inquiry, had assembled the evidence against Oswald in a fashion that, according to Liebeler, had made its report read "like a brief for the prosecution." He quoted at length from a twenty-six-page memo by Liebeler that criticized an original draft, not much of which was changed before its publication as Chapter 4 of *The Warren Report.* (When we talked to Liebeler in 1977, he explained that the memo represented little more than a difference of opinion on how the Commission's conclusions should be phrased — in bare conclusionary form, or with reservations laid out before judgments were reached. He said he did not disagree with the basic conclusions, "including the conspiracy question. . . .")

The publication of *Inquest* inspired a surge of assassination-related activity, not only by "buffs," but by investigative journalists and other members of the press, which had, to then, applauded *The Warren Report* as the final word. Epstein had academic credentials, he was not considered biased (as were Mark Lane and other critics), his book was accompanied by an introduction by Richard H. Rovere, the respected *New Yorker* writer, and it was favorably reviewed and widely read. Soon the popular press began to pick up the beat: in July 1966 *Look* featured an article, "The Warren Commission Report on the Assassination Is Struck by a Wave of Doubts"; *Life*, in November, produced "A Matter of Reasonable Doubt," an evaluation of the single-bullet theory based on Governor Connally's analysis of the Zapruder film; and on December 2, 1967, the *Saturday Evening Post* printed an excerpt from

Thompson's *Six Seconds in Dallas,* "The Cross Fire that Killed President Kennedy."

When they had exhausted arguments over flaws they found in the physical evidence (the conflicting autopsy reports, the "pristine" bullet found on Connally's stretcher) and over the interpretation of eyewitness testimony (in particular, that which had to do with the origin of the shots), the critics turned to events in Oswald's career that might demonstrate he had been either an unwitting dupe or a willing participant in a conspiracy. The idea of Oswald as a dupe or "patsy" was fostered by conjecture, originating with a philosophy professor named Richard Popkin in 1966, that inconsistencies in Oswald's activities could be explained by an imposter, an Oswald double, who had appeared at rifle ranges and gun shops (at times in the company of a Marina stand-in) in order to incriminate him in the crime. (In the absence of photographic evidence of Oswald's visit to the Soviet Embassy, critics found the theory of an impersonator in Mexico City in September 1963 very compelling.) On the other hand, if it was Oswald who was sighted in the summer and fall of 1963, using a rifle other than the Mannlicher-Carcano or receiving funds, then it was likely that he had played a role in a plot of some kind. This is why, the critics contended, the Commission disputed the sightings.

The sightings, along with arguments for their authenticity, were summarized in *Accessories after the Fact* by Sylvia Meagher, who maintained her intention was not to suggest there actually had been a conspiracy but to raise doubts about the caliber of the FBI investigation and the "competence and good faith" of the Warren Commission. It was a somewhat deceptive disclaimer, since she titled the chapter, "No Conspiracy?" and chose as a subtitle for a climactic section, in which she took the Commission to task for its treatment of the celebrated Odio incident, "The Proof of the Plot." Silvia Odio, a twenty-six-year-old Cuban exile active in the anti-Castro movement in Dallas, fainted and was taken to a hospital when she heard the news of the assassination, having recalled the visit of three men to her apartment in September, one of whom had remarked that Kennedy deserved to be assassinated. Two of the men looked Cuban or Mexican, one calling himself "Leopoldo" and the other, something like "Angelo." The third, an American, was introduced as "Leon Oswald," who, according to Leopoldo in a telephone call the next day, was a "loco" former Marine, a crack marksman, who felt Kennedy should have been shot for the failure of the Bay of Pigs invasion. After Oswald was arrested and his picture appeared on television, Odio recognized him as the same Leon Oswald, as did her sister, Annie, independently. The Commission did not question Odio's encounter with the three men, but it rejected the notion that Oswald was among them, for during the period Odio thought the visit had occurred (September 26 or 27), Oswald was en route by bus, according to the Commission, from Houston to Mexico City. (Meagher did a time and distance study of her own, using the Commission's data: Oswald would have had 18 and a half hours — from 8 A.M., September 25 to 2:35 A.M., September 26 — to get from New Orleans to Dallas to Houston, a total distance of 747 miles.)

Prior to the meeting at the Odio apartment, Oswald had been seen in the company of Latin-looking men in New Orleans — at least that was the testimony to the Commission of a lawyer named Dean Andrews, who testified that Oswald had come to his office several times in the summer of 1963 for legal advice and that each time he had been accompanied by a Mexican. Additionally, according to Meagher, Andrews's claim that Oswald had appeared with a Mexican companion was consistent with the assertion of Evaristo Rodriguez, a New Orleans bartender, that he had served two men who came in to the Habana Bar together in the summer of 1963. ". . . the one who spoke Spanish ordered the tequila. . . . Then the man I later learned was Oswald ordered a lemonade," Rodriguez testified. Oswald's alleged association with mysterious young men, usually Latins, did not end when he returned to Dallas in October: a Western Union clerk reported that he had collected small money orders on several occasions, and another Western Union employee, though he did not identify Oswald, recalled transactions with a man who used a Navy I.D. card and a library card as credentials, and who had been accompanied by a man of Spanish descent. Finally, a Dallas dentist, who was certain he had seen Oswald at a firing range on Saturday, November 16, a day Oswald specifically had not visited his family in Irving, testified that he had watched him drive off "with a man in a newer model car," the other man driving.

The Garrison "Case"

In July 1966 the district attorney of Orleans Parish, Louisiana, Jim Garrison, launched an investigation of the Kennedy assassination that would momentarily galvanize the critics, for here was a duly elected public official, eager to listen to their conspiracy theories, who had the authority to act on them. Garrison, a political prosecutor who attracted worldwide attention when he took his case to the public in early 1967, became, as he put it, the "wagon boss of the buffs," but in time, he would do their cause irreparable harm. He would fail to prove a plot in a loud and outlandish fashion, and even if there was bona fide evidence in this array of charges, he stigmatized it by his conduct. It would require the surprising disclosure of the findings of a Senate committee on intelligence in 1976 to prevent Garrison's probe from effectively ending any hope that the federal government would take a second look at the work of the Warren Commission. In short, the Garrison case was a fraud. It did not begin that way, for Garrison had a reasonable premise: if there had been a conspiracy, it might well have been rooted in New Orleans, which had been Oswald's home as a youth and from April to September 1963. It appeared to Garrison that during that summer, Oswald had behaved in an uncharacteristic way for the introvert the Commission portrayed him to be. He had tried, for example, to join, or perhaps to infiltrate, a Cuban exile organization dedicated to the overthrow of Fidel Castro, and then he had flaunted his support for the Cuban Premier in the face of the exiles by handing out ''Fair Play for Cuba'' leaflets on public streets. The fight that ensued cost Oswald a night in jail, a $10 fine, and enough notoriety to be asked to debate the Cuban issue on the radio, which he did. New Orleans was also the city where Oswald, accompanied by a Mexican, sought advice on what to do about his less-than-honorable discharge from the Marines, according to the lawyer, Dean Andrews.

Garrison's office was informed on the day after the assassination of another Oswald association, which was even more intriguing, if true: he had been taught to fire a rifle by David W. Ferrie; at least that was the substance of a tip from Jack S. Martin, a private detective. An accomplished pilot, who had been fired by Eastern Airlines for homosexuality, Ferrie was an anti-Castro activist as well as an investigator for the lawyer of Carlos Marcello, the leader of the underworld in Louisiana. Ferrie's anti-Castro confederates included Sergio Arcacha Smith, the chief New Orleans delegate of the Cuban Revolutionary Council until 1962, and W. Guy Banister, a former FBI agent and ardent anti-Communist, who had opened a private investigations agency and had employed, from time to time, both Ferrie and Martin. Arcacha and Banister each had occupied offices at 544 Camp Street, which was at least tenuous corroboration of a link to Oswald, since he had in 1963 stamped that address on some of his ''Fair Play for Cuba'' leaflets.

On November 22, 1963, Ferrie was in a federal courtroom in New Orleans, where Marcello, who was of Sicilian parentage, was found not guilty of conspiracy to defraud the United States by obtaining a false Guatemalan birth certificate. According to the FBI, that Friday night Ferrie drove with two friends from New Orleans to Houston and, on Saturday, to Galveston, and then back to New Orleans on Sunday. Before reaching New Orleans, Ferrie learned by telephone from the Marcello lawyer who employed him, G. Wray Gill, that Martin had implicated him in the assassination. When he got to his home, Ferrie did not go in, but sent in his place one of his companions on the trip, who, along with Ferrie's roommate, was detained by Garrison's officers. On Monday, Ferrie turned himself in and was placed under arrest for suspicion of having been involved in the assassination, which he denied, claiming that his time in the days just preceding the assassination had been spent in his work for Gill on the Marcello fraud case, and his trip to Texas over the weekend had been for relaxation. The Secret Service and the FBI wrapped up their investigations of the alleged Ferrie-Oswald link in a matter of days, concluding that Martin's accusation was "without foundation" and closing the Ferrie file for lack of evidence.

In December 1966 Garrison was telling newsmen "for background" that he had a suspect in the Kennedy assassination and that an arrest was imminent, even though it was premature and improper for him to be divulging the details of his investigation. "Garrison never lets the responsibilities of being a prosecutor interfere with being a politician," was how Aaron M. Kohn, the managing director of the Metropolitan Crime Commission at New Orleans characterized Garrison's thirst for publicity. National headlines were what he was after when he agreed to brief representatives of *Life* and CBS on his case, "the Smith case," as he liked to call it. "Smith," the suspect, was David Ferrie: "He may not be the assassin, but he'll do," Garrison would say, as he proffered a mug shot of Ferrie taken after a February 1962 arrest as a fugitive from justice. It showed an ordinary-looking middle-aged man, except he had lost all his hair, the after effect of a rare disease, and wore a homemade wig and eyebrows made of mohair. What did Garrison have, other than the record of Ferrie's arrest by his own office, on the strength of Jack Martin's tip, and the FBI and Secret Service reports of his arrest and questioning in 1963? Not a lot, it seemed. There was a background file on Ferrie that had been prepared by a private investigative agency as grounds for his dismissal by Eastern Airlines in 1963, as well as three witnesses, each evasive and of questionable reliability: the tipster, Martin, an alcoholic who, according to the FBI, had acknowledged his Ferrie-Oswald connection had been imagined; Dean Andrews, the lawyer, who was telling Garrison no more than he had told the Warren Commission about the call he had received from a mysterious Clay Bertrand soon after the assassination, asking if he would represent Oswald; and G. Wray Gill, the Marcello lawyer, who had supplied Garrison with his 1963 telephone records, indicating which calls Ferrie had placed, though the calls for November were missing. Garrison did have, however, what we determined in 1978 to be a sound report that Oswald, as a teenager, had served in a Civil Air Patrol unit that Ferrie commanded. Garrison was also certain, or so he said, of the validity of reports that Ferrie met with Oswald in Guy Banister's office in the summer of 1963.

It was quite plain that Ferrie had not been in Dealey Plaza on November 22, 1963 — his presence in a federal courtroom in New Orleans was an airtight alibi, but that did not faze Garrison: "He knew it was going to happen, and he was involved." Ferrie was aware he was a suspect, since he had been called in for questioning, and he kept abreast of the case by contacting Garrison's former chief investigator, Pershing Gervais, to whom Ferrie offered his own theory, based on his knowledge of ballistics, that there had been a second assassin. On February 11, 1967, Garrison expressed a prophetic fear: "He talks a lot about not having long to live. He's a sick man, and it's obvious to him we're not stopping." When Ferrie did die just eleven days later, Garrison termed it suicide by "one of history's most important men," although the coroner listed it as death due to natural causes.

Garrison had been asked in January if he knew the identity of Clay Bertrand. "He is a man who lives in the French Quarter," he said. "His real name is Clay Shaw, but I don't think he is too important." The reply was purposely misleading, since Garrison had been suspicious enough of the retired director of the New Orleans Trade Mart to have had him questioned by an assistant on December 23. Shaw was asked if he had ever met Oswald (he said he had not) and where had he been on the day of the assassination (en route to San Francisco). That was it for the time being, but with Ferrie's death, Garrison's passive interest in Shaw turned aggressive, and three days later, on February 25, he was preparing to issue a subpoena for Shaw's appearance before the grand jury. There was no apparent reason for Shaw's elevated prominence in Garrison's perception of the conspiracy. In fact, Dean Andrews, the only witness to have mentioned a Clay Bertrand, was becoming more and more vague about the man, confiding to Garrison at one point that Bertrand might not even exist. That did not deter Garrison from doing his utmost to prove that Shaw and Bertrand were one and the same. As luck would have it, on the very day Garrison was mapping his grand jury strategy, one of his assistants, Andrew Sciambra, was in Baton Rouge taking a story from a twenty-five-year-old insurance salesman, Perry Raymond Russo, that would enable Garrison to begin to conduct a case against the hapless Shaw. Russo said he had known Ferrie in the summer of 1963 as a man who hung around with tough-looking Cubans and who had a roommate, "a man in his middle twenties with dirty blond hair and a scruffy beard, a typical beatnik type." He said he often heard talk about assassinations and that the assassination of President Kennedy was discussed at a meeting in Ferrie's apartment in September. Shown a picture of Oswald, Russo said he looked like the roommate, once a beard was drawn on the face; shown a picture of Shaw, he said it reminded him of a man he had seen on two occasions, once when Kennedy had delivered an address at the dedication of the Nashville Street wharf, and again at a service station with Ferrie, though he did not know the man's name. Two days later, under sodium pentothal, Russo was questioned again by Sciambra. This time he remembered the roommate had been named "Leon," and while the name Clay Shaw meant nothing, he had met Clay Bertrand at Ferrie's apartment. (Garrison would insist later that Russo told of having met "Bertrand" at Ferrie's apartment in his first interview with Sciambra, when he was not under sodium pentothal, but we knew better. On assignment for *Life* in 1967, Billings witnessed a meeting of Garrison, Sciambra, and Russo, at which Russo said he did not have, even then, a conscious recollection of the meeting, but having been reminded, he remembered it under the truth drug, and testified to it, as though he did remember.) Bertrand was also the man, said Russo, whom he had seen at the wharf dedication and at the service station with Ferrie. Garrison was not bothered by the substantial flaws in Russo's account: Why had he been permitted to sit in on the planning of a conspiracy to which he was not a party? Why had he not recognized Oswald as Ferrie's roommate when he was arrested for the assassination and come forward then? And since Russo was unable to recall the name Bertrand when no longer under the influence of sodium pentothal, the only proof that he recognized the name was the word of Sciambra. Russo's testimony was, however, sufficient for Garrison to have Shaw indicted.

The evidence of Shaw's participation in a conspiracy was flimsy, and from his indictment to eventual acquittal in 1969, the course of the investigation was downhill to disaster. Garrison's response was to flail at any number of presumed conspirators, as Edward J. Epstein pointed out in his second book on the Kennedy assassination, *Counterplot:*

> In the early stages of the investigation, Garrison had told Senator Russell Long (of Louisiana) that only a few insignificant men were involved. Then, after Ferrie's death, Garrison began to specify the guilty parties, identifying them as a band of perverts and anti-Castro Cubans. With the arrival of the demonologists, however, the conspiracy was rapidly escalated to include Minutemen, CIA agents, oil millionaires, Dallas policemen, munitions exporters, "the Dallas Establishment," reactionaries, White Russians, and certain elements of the invisible Nazi sub-structure.

The principal villain, however, was the federal government. It had covered up the truth: "Even before the Warren Commission was appointed, the command of the FBI and the President of the United States had to know that there were a number of people shooting at President Kennedy and that the Dallas police scenario was completely false," Garrison proclaimed. It had in fact been agents of the government who had committed the murder: "The main function of the Warren Commission was to conceal the assassination of the President by an ambush of CIA employees . . . ." In 1967, Garrison charged, the same federal forces, led by FBI Director Hoover, were resorting to character defamation to thwart him: "They've convinced LBJ I'm a drunk, and I'm committed to Marcello." Garrison's drinking habits were of no apparent interest to the bureau, but there was more than a little evidence to support the second part of that statement. In early 1967, we learned, Garrison took a brief vacation in Las Vegas, staying at the Sands, which at the time was owned, at least in part, by underworld figures, and the casino manager there, Mario Marino, was a Marcello man from Louisiana. According to federal authorities, Marino gave Garrison a $5,000 gambling credit and picked up his hotel bill. Garrison denied any wrongdoing when confronted in August 1967, but if there was truth to the allegation (Garrison was tried, but acquitted in 1971 on federal charges of taking payoffs from underworld pinball operators, despite evidence that included incriminating tape recordings of Garrison and the seizure of $1,000 in marked money from Garrison's home), it would have served to explain the most baffling aspect of his investigation. Why, with all the evidence that he claimed implicated Ferrie in an assassination plot, did Garrison not suspect that Marcello himself was also involved? There was more to the Ferrie-Marcello connection than the fact that Ferrie had worked as an investigator for Gill. When his roommate, Layton Martens, and his Texas traveling companion, Alvin Beauboeuf, were detained by Garrison's men on the night of November 24, 1963, they each had in their possession a document signed by Jack Wasserman, Marcello's Washington attorney. An even more intriguing fact came to light after Ferrie died and Garrison confiscated his papers. Among them was the record of a franchise for a service station that Ferrie operated beginning in early 1964, with Marcello listed as his sponsor. Garrison never indicated a bit of interest in the answer to why, just a few months following the assassination, Ferrie would gain such a benefit. Garrison's tendency to look the other way when organized crime complicity in the assassination was suggested fell into his pattern of conduct as a prosecutor, which was addressed by Aaron Kohn of the Crime Commission, in an interview with Clark R. Mollenhoff, the veteran investigative reporter: ". . . we have been in repeated public conflict with . . . Garrison, who denies the existence in our city of probable organized crime," Kohn said. "He and his staff have blocked our efforts to have grand juries probe the influence of the Cosa Nostra and other syndicate operations. Prosecutive trickery and public deception have successfully prevented grand jury action on the pinball gambling racket, suspected liquor license irregularities, bookie operations, and numerous others."

There seemed to be no doubt that Garrison was a creature of publicity, and it made no difference that ultimately the publicity was bad. As Epstein noted in *Counterplot*:

> To . . . [Garrison] even the most vocal censure, however adverse its ostensible effect, represent[ed] useful publicity, for the more rigorously he . . . [was] assaulted by the press, the more prominently he figure[d] in the popular imagination. A false charge has to be repeated if it is to be refuted, and if the charge happens to be more appealing than the truth, it is entirely possible that it, rather than its refutation, will win general credence.

But just as the press created Garrison, so it was the press that finally turned against him and destroyed him. The first full-scale attack came in the last week of April 1967 in James Phelan's "Rush to Judgment in New Orleans," published in the *Saturday Evening Post*. It was soon followed by a major piece of investigative journalism done for NBC by Walter Sheridan, a former aide to Robert Kennedy in the Department of Justice.

Garrison's discrediting may have been a case of "overkill." As Epstein noted, "[T]he fact that Garrison expressed his ideas in a paranoid style [did] . . . not of itself rule out the possibility that there [was] . . . substance to his claims." In fact, historian Arthur M. Schlesinger, Jr., in *Robert Kennedy and His Times*, recorded a conversation he had had with Robert Kennedy on October 30, 1966, in which the senator wondered how long he could continue to avoid commenting on *The Warren Report*. Kennedy's reservations were shared by some responsible critics. Alexander Bickel, a distinguished professor of law and legal history at Yale, wrote a review of the work of the Commission and its critics, particularly Epstein, in the October 1966 issue of *Commentary*. Bickel observed first that it was "no longer possible . . . simply to love the Warren Commission for the enemies it . . . [had] made." In fact, the Commission "did not satisfactorily investigate the assassination. It did not," he observed, "fit the established facts into a narrative consistent with all of them." Bickel called for a new inquiry by the Congress or the President to reexamine the assassination, saying that "a President of the United States was wantonly shot down, and if there is such a thing as national honor, we must know all that can be known of the truth of [that] . . . terrible affair." Bickel's view was not universally shared. A. L. Goodhart, in the *Law Quarterly Review*, a British journal, wrote in January 1967 an impressive defense of the Commission. For Goodhart, the only mystery about the assassination was that there was so much mystery attached to it. The chance that "something new will turn up" in Goodhart's opinion, was "nil." Each critic had nothing to say, and it had to be remembered "that however many zeroes . . . [were] added together, the result . . . [would] still be zero." (That Goodhart undertake to review the criticism of the Warren Commission was suggested to him by the cultural attache of the American Embassy in London.) John Kaplan, a law professor at Stanford, wrote a piece in the May 1967 issue of the *Stanford Law Review* in which he also reviewed a number of the books of the critics. At worst, he wrote, the critics had established only that the Commission was incompetent, not wrong. The crucial issue, he suggested, was not Oswald's guilt, but the existence of a conspiracy, and the Commission, no matter how competent, could never prove a negative with certainty. As for the work of the major critics, Kaplan found Epstein's book the most interesting, but he reserved judgment in light of allegations by former Warren Commission lawyers that they had been flagrantly misquoted. Lane, Kaplan suggested, was essentially dishonest and guilty of fallacies in logic. Because the single-bullet theory was improbable, for example, it did not follow it was impossible, as Lane would let us believe. But in spite of what he called the "abysmal quality of the thought and integrity" of the critics, Kaplan was unwilling to conclude they had attracted so much attention simply by showmanship. Part of the blame, he wrote, had to be shouldered by the Warren Commission, whose work was "rushed out." *The Warren Report*, said Kaplan, was written not from the perspective of "an impartial historian, but in many places, as an advocate," and without a full disclosure of "all the evidence before it."

The Castro Assassination Plots

There is little doubt that *The Warren Report* would have withstood the critical barrage, which by the mid-1970s had diminished to tedious nitpicking, were it not for the Senate Select Committee to Study Governmental Operations with Respect to Intelligence Activities and its investigation of plots by the U.S. government to assassinate foreign leaders, in particular Fidel Castro of Cuba. The Senate Committee concluded that the CIA had actually enlisted the help of the Mafia in plotting Castro's murder, and while there were hints, beginning with two columns in March 1967 by Drew Pearson and Jack Anderson, that Kennedy had been killed in retaliation for such CIA actions (an interpretation the Senate Committee ultimately rejected), they were not taken seriously at first. There was quite a different reaction in 1976 however — for two reasons: the Senate Committee dramatically disclosed that top government leaders, including President Kennedy, had not been fully briefed by the CIA officers responsible for the plots; and the Warren Commission had been kept in the dark about them, even though one of its members, Allen W. Dulles, had been Director of Central Intelligence when the plots were conceived. We tested the conclusions of the Senate Committee against the results of our own investigation, confirming to our satisfaction the basic accuracy of an account of the plots published in November 1975 in the *Interim Report* of the Senate Committee.

According to the richly detailed, 346-page *Interim Report,* the CIA was involved in several schemes to eliminate Castro, but two had received particular attention: in one, the agency teamed up with leading organized crime figures who had their own reasons to oppose Castro, since he had closed down their gambling operations in Havana; in the other, the CIA plotted with a Cuban government official, code name AM/LASH, who had professed a desire to orchestrate a coup d'etat that would depend on Castro's death. On December 11, 1959, J. C. King, the head of the Western Hemisphere Division of the CIA, wrote a memorandum to Dulles that the "far left" dictatorship in Cuba posed a threat to U.S. holdings in other Latin American countries, and ". . . consideration should be given to the elimination of Fidel Castro." Dulles concurred, as did his Deputy Director for Plans, Richard M. Bissell, Jr. On March 10, 1960, at a meeting of the National Security Council, Admiral Arleigh Burke, Chairman of the Joint Chiefs of Staff, commented on a Dulles advisory that a covert action plan for Cuba was being prepared: ". . . any plan for the removal of Cuban leaders should be a package deal, since many of the Cuban leaders around Castro are even worse. . . ." Then, at a March 14 meeting of the Special Group, a Cabinet-level strategy-planning body, there was a discussion of the impact on the Cuban nation if Castro, his brother Raul, and Che Guevara should all disappear simultaneously. Not all of the early schemes to dispose of Castro necessarily entailed his murder — some were designed to undermine his charismatic appeal to the Cuban people by, for example, spraying the studio from where he was to broadcast a speech with an LSD-like chemical. Such exotic ideas were merely food for thought, but, by July 1960, the effort became deadly serious. A Cuban, who had volunteered to gather intelligence, told his case officer in Havana he would probably be in touch with Raul Castro. The information was relayed to Washington, prompting a cable to the Havana station from CIA headquarters, based on instructions from King and Bissell's deputy, Tracy Barnes: "Possible removal of top three leaders is receiving serious consideration at HQS."

In August 1960 the CIA took its initial steps to enlist the underworld in a Castro assassination plot. Bissell told the Senate committee the idea originated with King and Colonel Sheffield Edwards, the director of the Office of Security. The chief of the Operational Support Division under Edwards (the Committee agreed not to identify him, referring to him only as the "support chief") asked Robert Maheu, a former FBI agent who, as a private detective, had developed Mafia connections, to contact John Roselli, a Las Vegas underworld figure and determine if Roselli would participate in a Castro-assassination plot. After a preliminary meeting, Maheu, Roselli and the "support chief" met with two top members of the national crime syndicate, Sam Giancana, the head of the Chicago Mafia, and Santo Trafficante, Jr., of Tampa, a Florida leader, whose domain had included gambling in Havana until he was jailed and then ousted from Cuba by Castro. (The FBI learned in October that Maheu was up to something with Giancana, because the bugging of an apartment in Las Vegas, arranged by Maheu as a favor to Giancana, was botched and traced to Maheu.)

In late November 1960, President-elect Kennedy was briefed by Dulles and Bissell on the operation that would become the Bay of Pigs invasion of April 17, 1961, but he was not told about the assassination plot, according to Bissell's testimony to the Senate Committee. Kennedy was also not to be let in on all aspects of an assignment given to CIA officer William Harvey in early 1961. Harvey, who was to become chief of Task Force W, the Cuban covert action unit, was ordered to establish the general capability of disabling foreign leaders, with assassination as a last resort. The executive action project was to be called ZR/RIFLE. At the same time that Harvey was devising his method of execution, which was to be poison pills, a CIA official was meeting with AM/LASH, to determine if the Cuban official was willing to cooperate in an effort to overturn the Castro regime. The AM/LASH plot was kept separate from the Mafia plot.

On February 13, 1961, the "support chief" delivered the pills to Roselli, who reported, in late February or early March, that they had been passed to a Cuban official close to Castro. But they had been returned, perhaps because the official had lost his position in the government and, therefore, his access to Castro. As failure followed failure, Maheu informed the FBI on April 18 that the CIA had been involved in the Las Vegas wiretap, suggesting the bureau contact Edwards, who, in turn, proposed that prosecution of Maheu might expose sensitive information related to the aborted invasion of Cuba just the day before. On April 19 President Kennedy held a Bay of Pigs postmortem with a group of Cuban exile leaders, at which he took sole responsibility for the failure. Included among the Cuban leaders at the meeting was the one who had taken the poison pills from Roselli, a man whose anti-Castro activities were being financed by racketeers like Trafficante, who hoped to regain their monopoly of Cuban gambling in the event of a Castro overthrow.

On May 22 Hoover sent Attorney General Kennedy a memorandum on the Las Vegas wiretap incident with an attachment quoting Edwards to the effect that Bissell had briefed him (Kennedy) on the use of Giancana in connection with the Bay of Pigs. Hoover wrote that Edwards had acknowledged the use of Maheu and hoodlum elements by the CIA in anti-Castro activities but that the purpose of the wiretap had not been determined. Edwards had told the FBI on May 3 that Giancana had been relied on because of his contacts with gambling figures who might have valuable sources; that he had had no direct contact with Giancana and that no details about the methods of Maheu or Giancana had been reported to him. On August 16, 1961, an assistant U.S. attorney in Las Vegas reported he was reluctant to proceed on the wiretap case out of concern that the CIA's role might become known, and in September, when the FBI concluded its investigation, prosecution of the case was halted.

In the fall of 1961 Dulles was fired for the failure of the Bay of Pigs invasion. From September to November he briefed his successor, John A. McCone, ten or twelve times, though it was apparent from the Senate Committee's investigation, that the subject of a Castro assassination was never brought up. McCone was not told about the plots by Bissell, or by Richard Helms, who would replace Bissell in February 1962, or by anyone. There were growing indications, beginning in October, that the White House, while still in the dark about the ongoing plots, was coming to its own conclusions as to what to do about Castro. On November 2, Richard N. Goodwin, a presidential assistant who specialized in Latin American affairs, addressed a memo to the President suggesting an operation, to be named MONGOOSE, that would serve to coordinate activities with respect to Cuba, such as intelligence collection, guerrilla strikes, and propaganda. At about the same time, Goodwin asked *New York Times* reporter Tad Szulc to meet with the Attorney General for an "off the record" discussion of Cuba, which Szulc did on November 8, and the next day he met with the President for over an hour. Kennedy, according to Szulc's testimony to the Senate Committee on June 10, 1975, asked him what he thought about assassinating Castro. Szulc replied that an assassination would not necessarily cause a change in the Cuban system, and he was personally opposed to political murder. The President responded: "I agree with you completely."

That was the theme the President carried to the University of Washington where, in a speech on November 16, he said, "We cannot, as a free nation, compete with our adversaries in tactics of terror, assassination, false promises, counterfeit mobs, and crises." At the CIA, however, just a day before that speech, moves were made that were intended to lead to action quite counter to the President's declaration. On November 15 Harvey was asked by Bissell to take over the crime syndicate operation from Edwards, and there was then a discussion of how to apply ZR/RIFLE to Cuba. Also on November 15 Major General Edward G. Lansdale, a guerrilla warfare expert who had been assigned the task of coordinating CIA MONGOOSE activities with the Departments of State and Defense, sent an outline of action alternatives to Robert Kennedy, noting that "... a picture of the situation has emerged clearly enough to indicate what needs to be done and to support your sense of urgency about Cuba." The CIA component of MONGOOSE was Harvey's Task Force W, which employed some four hundred operatives at CIA headquarters and at the Miami station. Harvey, along with Director McCone, was the principal CIA participant in MONGOOSE, although Helms, as Deputy Director for Plans, attended seven of the forty MONGOOSE meetings and, according to his testimony to the Senate Committee, was just as interested in the project as were Harvey and McCone.

As the first year of Kennedy's term came to an end, Castro compounded the problem of U.S. Caribbean security by announcing officially that he was a Marxist-Leninist. On January 18, 1962, Lansdale designated thirty-two planning tasks for agencies participating in MONGOOSE, sending a list of them to the Attorney General with a handwritten note that read: "... my review does not include the sensitive work I have reported to you; I felt you preferred informing the President privately." When he testified before the Senate Committee on June 8, 1975, Lansdale insisted his "sensitive work" had not been an assassination plan. He said he had never discussed an assassination with either the Attorney General or the President, and he imagined that what he had omitted from the note had to do with a secret trip he had taken to Florida to meet with Cuban exile leaders. The Senate Committee did note, although it was unable to establish the significance, that Lansdale had dealt directly with the Kennedys on his "sensitive work," bypassing General Maxwell Taylor, who was chairman of the SGA (Special Group Augmented). It also noted that the Attorney General had begun in early 1962 to take command of MONGOOSE, citing a meeting of the principal participants in the operation held in Kennedy's office on January 19. On January 27, in a memo to Robert Kennedy, Lansdale wrote, "... we might work the touchdown play independently of the institutional program we are spurring." Lansdale told the Senate Committee the touchdown play he had referred to was "a revolt by the Cubans themselves ... a revolution ... that would break down the police controls and ... drive the top people out of power ...," not an assassination attempt. He did say, however, that at one point he had asked Harvey for an assassination plan, though he did it on his own:

Senator Baker: *Did you ever discuss it with Robert Kennedy?*

Lansdale:	*No, not that I recall.*
Senator Baker:	*With the President?*
Lansdale:	*No.*

On January 29, 1962, the head of the Administrative Regulations Division of the Justice Department sent a note to the first and second assistants in the Criminal Division (one of whom was Howard Willens, later a Warren Commission assistant counsel): "Our primary interest was in Giancana . . . apparently detective [Maheu] has some connections with Giancana but he claims this was because of CIA assignment in connection with Cuba. . . ." Then on February 7 the FBI reported to Assistant Attorney General Herbert J. Miller, Jr., that Sheffield Edwards had been contacted about possible prosecutions in the Las Vegas wiretap case, and he had objected.

The Senate Committee obtained evidence that a "close friend" of President Kennedy, one who had been in frequent contact with him since early 1960, was also an intimate associate of John Roselli and Sam Giancana and had seen them often over the same period. (The Senate Committtee learned the identity of the friend but carefully concealed it.) White House telephone records indicated seventy instances of contact, and the friend, in testimony, confirmed frequent telephone conversations with President Kennedy. Both the friend and Roselli testified that the friend knew nothing of the assassination plots or of the Las Vegas wiretap case; Giancana was murdered before the Senate Committee was able to take his testimony. Details of the friend's relationship with the President were contained in an FBI memorandum preparing Hoover for a meeting with the President on March 22 (the FBI Director had notified the Attorney General and Presidential Assistant Kenneth P. O'Donnell on February 27 that the President's friend was also seeing Roselli and Giancana). There was no record of what transpired over Hoover's lunch with the President on March 22, but the telephone logs showed that Kennedy's last contact with the friend occurred a few hours later. By March 22, 1962, FBI files contained references to Giancana's link to the CIA and his participation in assassination plotting, leading the Senate Committee to ponder whether Hoover had advised the President to that effect at the luncheon. If so, it would have been logical for Kennedy to call for an explanation from the CIA, which was at least implied by notations on the presidential calendar of meetings between February 27 and April 2 with most of the CIA officials who were aware of the plots. They all testified, however, that the question of a Castro assassination was not raised at those meetings. Nevertheless, the Senate Committee presumed that Roselli and Giancana were a topic of conversation at the Kennedy-Hoover luncheon, which probably explained why, on the following day, March 23, Hoover inquired again about pursuing a prosecution in the Las Vegas wiretap case. The CIA, of course, did object, and on April 10 Hoover summarized Edwards's reply in a memo to Assistant Attorney General Miller, who ran the Criminal Division:

> . . . he has now advised that he has no desire to impose any restriction which might hinder efforts to prosecute any individual, but he is firmly convinced that prosecution of Maheu would lead to exposure of most sensitive information relating to the abortive Cuban invasion in April 1961, and would result in most damaging embarrassment to the U.S. Government.

On April 24, having met with CIA General Counsel Lawrence Houston the previous week, Miller advised the Attorney General that the national interest ruled out prosecution of the wiretappers, and following a final meeting between Kennedy and CIA representatives, the decision was made not to proceed with a prosecution.

In early April, acting on what he told the Senate Committee were "explicit orders" from Helms, Harvey asked Edwards to put him in touch with Roselli. A meeting in Miami was then arranged by the "support chief," at which Harvey told Roselli to maintain his Cuban contacts but not to deal with Giancana or Maheu, who were considered unreliable. On April 18, according to a notation in the files of the CIA's Technical Services Division, four poison pills were issued to the "support chief," who passed them on to Harvey. Harvey arrived in Miami on April 21 to find Roselli already in touch with the same Cuban exile leader who had sent "the medicine" to Havana in April 1961, only to have it returned. Roselli told the Senate Committee on June 24, 1975, that when Harvey gave him the poison he informed him that the Cubans intended to use it not just on Castro, but on his brother, Raul, and on Che Guevara as well, and Harvey had approved. When he was interviewed in 1967 in connection with an Inspector General's report on the Mafia plots, which had been requested by President Johnson, Harvey said that he had advised Helms of his first meeting with Roselli, and "thereafter he regularly briefed Helms on the status of the Castro operation." Helms was pressed by the Senate Committee to tell why he had not sought clarification from the SGA or the Attorney General as to whether the policy of the government was to kill Castro. "I don't know . . . ," he replied. "There is something about the whole chain of episodes in connection with this Roselli business that I am simply not able to bring back in a coherent fashion."

On May 7 President Kennedy was briefed by General Taylor on Cuba, but there was no mention of Harvey's contacts with Roselli or the delivery of poison pills and weapons to the exiles. (Taylor swore to the Senate Committee on July 9, 1975, that he never heard of Harvey's passing pills to poison Castro.) It was also on May 7 that Attorney General Kennedy was briefed by Colonel Edwards and CIA General Counsel Houston, who informed him of the operations involving underworld figures, but they said they had been terminated, which was a lie. They said that Roselli and Giancana had been offered $150,000; that senior CIA officials in the Eisenhower administration had approved the project orally; and that knowledge of the operation extended to only six persons within the agency. (The 1967 Inspector General's report indicated it was known to thirteen CIA officials, including ex-Director Dulles.) Edwards testified to the Senate Committee on May 30, 1975, that at the time of the Kennedy briefing he had not known the CIA was still dealing with the underworld, but the Senate Committee chose not to believe him, citing the 1967 I.G. Report and Harvey's testimony of July 25, 1975, in which he said Edwards knew full well that the operation was proceeding on track when he told him about briefing the Attorney General. Houston described the Attorney General's reaction at the briefing to the Senate Committee: "If you have seen Mr. Kennedy's eyes get steely and his jaw set and his voice get low and precise, you get a definite feeling of unhappiness." Kennedy met on May 9 with Hoover, who described the Attorney General's displeasure in a memo. First, the CIA was in a position where "it could not afford to have any action taken against Giancana or Maheu." Second, ". . . as he well knew, the 'gutter gossip' was that the reason nothing had been done against Giancana was because of Giancana's close relationship with [Frank] Sinatra who, in turn, claimed to be a close friend of the Kennedy family." (The Senate Committee took pains to point out it was not Sinatra whose friendship with the President had been discussed at the March 22 Kennedy-Hoover lunch.) On May 14 Edwards and Houston prepared two memos: one that recorded their briefing of the Attorney General; and one for the record, stating falsely that the Roselli operation had been terminated. That same day Harvey told Helms of the Edwards-Houston meeting with the Attorney General. He advised against briefing McCone or General Marshall S. Carter, the Deputy Director, and Helms, according to Harvey, agreed. In late May Roselli reported to Harvey that "the medicine" and the weapons had arrived in Cuba.

On August 8, 1962, Lansdale proposed to the SGA a stepped-up Course B that would ". . . exert all possible diplomatic, economic, psychological, and other overt pressures to overthrow the Castro-Communist regime." (Harvey attended the SGA meetings, though he never mentioned assassination, and the one time the option of killing Castro was briefly discussed, and firmly rejected, it was not with respect to the current CIA plots.) The Lansdale plan was rejected in favor of a CIA variant, offered by McCone, that would seek a split between Castro and "old-line Communists" rather than his overthrow. Nevertheless, Lansdale directed Harvey on August 13 to draft an option for the "liquidation of leaders," leading the Senate Committee to press him on July 8, 1975, as to why, if the assassination idea had been rejected by the SGA, he had gone ahead with the directive to Harvey. Lansdale said he could not recall the reason. On July 11, 1975, Harvey told the Senate Committee of a proposal by Secretary of Defense McNamara at an SGA meeting on August 10, 1962, that the elimination of Castro should be considered. Harvey said he had discussed it with McCone the next day: "I expressed some opinion as to the inappropriateness of this having been raised . . . , at which point Mr. McCone stated in substance that he agreed. . . ." McCone, in fact, was so opposed to the idea of assassination that he telephoned McNamara and insisted that the Lansdale directive to Harvey be withdrawn. McCone testified to the Senate Committee on June 6, 1975, that McNamara had agreed that the Lansdale memo should be withdrawn. The Senate Committee wondered why, with this flurry of assassination discussion by the nation's leaders, Harvey and Helms had continued to withhold the Roselli operation from the CIA Director. It was, after all, documented in the 1967 Inspector General's report that as of August 1962, "the medicine" was in Cuba and the plot was very much alive. Harvey himself had confirmed this by meeting with Roselli in Miami from September 7 to 11, at which time he was told that another three-man team had been dispatched, with orders to penetrate Castro's bodyguard.

On August 20 General Taylor told President Kennedy in a memo that the SGA, deeming Castro's downfall unlikely without direct U.S. military intervention, was recommending a more aggressive MONGOOSE program; on August 23 McGeorge Bundy, the national security assistant, issued NSC memorandum 181, a presidential directive calling for immediate implementation of MONGOOSE Phase B; and on August 30 the Special Group ordered the CIA to submit a list of sabotage targets in Cuba. In September and early October the SGA approved a number of options, including stepped-up sabotage and provocation of incidents designed to create tensions between Cubans and Soviet military personnel. Then, on October 4, it was decided that the Attorney General would act as chairman of the SGA "for the time being" (the decision was apparently not intended as a rebuke to General Taylor, who was named Chairman of the Joint Chiefs of Staff in November), and Kennedy promptly declared he would take a personal hand in achieving "massive (MONGOOSE) activity."

In 1963 the schism between the Kennedy administration, which was starting to move toward reconciliation with Cuba, and the hardliners at the CIA widened, although the White House probably did not know it, since it was not being kept abreast of the covert operations. The President and his brother did not know, for example, that in January Harvey paid Roselli $2,700 for expenses that his Cuban agent had incurred. This relatively minor event, one of Harvey's last acts as chief of Task Force W, foreshadowed the end of the CIA-Mafia plots. In January Harvey was replaced by Desmond Fitzgerald, and the name of the covert Cuban operations unit was changed to Special Affairs Staff. Fitzgerald's pet project, however, was the AM/LASH plot, and he would be in contact with the disloyal Cuban official — literally — right up to the moment of President Kennedy's assassination.

The ambivalence of the country's Cuba policy became more and more evident by mid-1963. While Bundy declared at an SGA meeting on April 3 that no sabotage raids were underway because the SGA "had decided . . . that such activity is not worth the effort expended on it," and while Rusk opposed such raids because of their "high noise level," a sabotage program was approved by the President on June 19. The CIA approach to assassination was no more consistent: while the Helms faction was still determined to kill Castro, and was plotting ways to do it, a study by the agency's Office of National Estimates indicated the futility of assassination. ". . . [The] odds are," the study concluded, "that upon Castro's death, his brother Raul or some other figure in the regime would, with Soviet backing and help, take over control," and in the event of Castro's death by other than natural causes, "the U.S. would be widely charged with complicity."

On August 16 *The Chicago Sun-Times* broke the news of a CIA connection with Giancana for the purpose of gathering intelligence on Cuba (the article was written by Sandy Smith, many of whose inside stories were based on information obtained from the FBI). McCone demanded an explanation from Helms, who produced a copy of the Edwards-Houston memo on the May 1962 briefing of the Attorney General, adding the notation: "I assume you are aware of the nature of the operation discussed in the attachment." On the contrary, McCone told the Senate Committee, the first he had heard of an assassination plot was "that day in August" when Helms informed him.

If the Warren Commission, save one member, who kept it to himself, knew anything about the CIA-Mafia plots, it left no record of it; none of the members or staff counsel we talked to acknowledged that they did, so the plots would have had no effect on their deliberations. No wonder their subsequent revelation stirred new interest in the assassination of President Kennedy.

4

Congressional Inquiry: 1976-1978

*It is the proper duty of a representative body to look diligently into
every affair of government and to talk much about what it sees. It is
meant to be the eyes and the voice . . . of its constituents.*

Woodrow Wilson
Congressional Government

An Investigation Initiated

Thomas N. Downing, the congressman from Tidewater Virginia, never
believed that one man could have fired all the shots Oswald was supposed to have fired that accurately, and when he was shown a visually
enhanced version of the Zapruder film (in which President Kennedy's
head appears to snap back and to the left, as if driven in that direction by
a shot from the right front), his doubts were confirmed. Downing
immediately became the focal point of the lobbying efforts of the Warren Commission critics, who urged him to draft a resolution calling for a
congressional investigation and supplied him fact sheets, appropriately
flavored with their views, that he could use to argue for its passage.
Downing's resolution was offered in April 1975. It was not the first, for
earlier in the first session of the 94th Congress, Henry B. Gonzalez of
San Antonio tendered a resolution that called on the House of Representatives to reopen not just the JFK case, but to investigate anew the
murders of Dr. Martin Luther King, Jr., and Senator Robert F. Kennedy, as well as the attempted assassination of Governor George C.
Wallace of Alabama.

Downing's cause got a boost when FBI chicanery in the Dallas investigation was revealed for the first time. According to the Senate Select Committee on Intelligence Activities, a newsman confronted FBI officials in July 1975 with a report that Lee Harvey Oswald had visited the Dallas FBI office shortly before the assassination and had left a threatening note for Special Agent James P. Hosty, Jr., who had been conducting a bureau investigation of Oswald. It developed from further checking by the Senate Committee that about two hours after Oswald was pronounced dead on November 24, 1963, Hosty, on instructions from a superior, destroyed the note by flushing it down a toilet, and the incident had been concealed for over twelve years. By the end of 1975 Downing had some one hundred colleagues lined up behind his resolution, but when, in the early months of the second session of the 94th Congress, an attempt was made to move it out of the Rules Committee, it failed in a tie vote.

Downing had about given up hope by the summer of 1976, believing that support for a new investigation had peaked. He had decided not to seek reelection in November, so he thought it was fitting to announce he was not a candidate for chairman of an assassinations committee, even if there was to be one. Then, unexpectedly, he got a call one day in early September from Speaker of the House Carl Albert, inviting him to a meeting with Coretta Scott King, Dr. King's widow. Mrs. King had come to Washington to tell the Congressional Black Caucus of new evidence in her husband's death in 1968 that she believed to be significant, and Albert was proposing that Downing get together with Gonzalez and Walter E. Fauntroy of the District of Columbia, a Black Caucus leader, to draft a new resolution that would create a 12-member committee to investigate the deaths of President Kennedy and Dr. King. Albert asked Downing to be chairman for the balance of the year, realizing Gonzalez would succeed him when Congress returned in 1977.

H.R. 1540 was introduced on September 14, and it came up for a vote on the floor of the House on September 17 as Congress was getting ready to adjourn. In the debates, Downing said he was certain of a conspiracy in the murder of President Kennedy, and he cited several suspicious developments in the case that deserved looking into, including: the CIA-Mafia plots to kill Castro, which had been withheld from the Warren Commission; the murders of Sam Giancana and John Roselli; and the FBI cover-up of the Oswald note to Hosty. Downing asserted that the American people did not believe the Warren Commission, offering as proof a *Detroit News* poll indicating 87 percent of the population had been recorded as doubters. He had backing from all factions, liberals and conservatives, Democrats and Republicans. John B. Anderson of Illinois was impressed by the import of the matter at hand, urging members "to put aside their doubts and support the adoption of the resolution." Charles Thone of Nebraska sounded Shakespearean: ". . . sinister conspiracy aspects loom larger and larger." More than any single factor, though, its sponsorship by the Black Caucus led to the passage of H.R. 1540 by an overwhelming 280 to 65 vote, and on September 30, 1977, the House passed H.R. 1557, to fund the House Select Committee on Assassinations with $150,000 for the rest of the year.

Initially, Downing preferred Bernard Fensterwald, Jr., a Washington attorney and founder of the Committee to Investigate Assassinations, for the position of chief counsel and staff director, while the Black Caucus was leaning to Mark Lane, the "defense attorney" for Oswald, who had turned his attention to the King assassination and written a book, *Code Name "Zorro,"* which contained allegations of government complicity in a conspiracy that led to the slaying of the civil rights leader. Lane, however, recommended Richard A. Sprague, a Philadelphia prosecutor, contending that it would be unwise to hire an advocate whose name was identified with the assassination issue, and Fensterwald agreed. Sprague, who was best known for conducting the trial that resulted in the murder conviction of United Mine Workers President Tony Boyle, met with Downing, who named him acting chief counsel in early October with the proviso that his permanent appointment would be put before the Committee at a meeting on November 15. Sprague went to work, as though his confirmation were a mere formality (he was right), assembling a staff of 170 lawyers, investigators, and researchers, and preparing a budget for 1977. He was a man of action, not reflective or cautious, who told a newsman in early December that he had not yet read *The Warren Report* or any of the critical books, because he wanted to keep an open mind. (Sprague told George Lardner of *The Washington Post* he had never discussed the Kennedy assassination with his old boss, former Philadelphia District Attorney Arlen Specter, who had been an assistant counsel for the Warrren Commission.) "I think Sprague is a remarkably fair-minded and tough-minded investigator," was the size-up of Sprague that Lardner got from Richardson Preyer of North Carolina. Preyer was a highly respected congressman, and former federal judge, whose presence on the Committee added to its stature. Unfortunately, fairness and toughness would not make up for Sprague's shortcomings. It took him no time at all to get into hot water, although the Committee at first preferred not to interfere. On December 8 Sprague submitted a 1977 budget of $6.5 million. "It blew my hat off too," Downing told *The Washington Post.* (Lardner noted that the Nixon impeachment investigation by the House Judiciary Committee in 1974 had cost less than $2 million.) Then, on December 15, *The Los Angeles Times* reported that Sprague had said he would make extensive use of two types of lie detectors, the standard polygraph and a product of more recent technology, the stress evaluator, which, he said, was capable of determining the veracity of tape-recorded statements. Sprague also planned to furnish his investigators with tiny transmitters that would enable them to record a witness's testimony without his knowledge. The combination of stress evaluator and "bug" would, therefore, enable the Committee to take secret lie detector tests. A story on December 30 in *The Philadelphia Bulletin* signaled the opposition of Frank Thompson, Jr., of New Jersey, the Chairman of the House Administration Committee, which controlled the purse strings. Describing himself as a fiscal conservative and civil libertarian, Thompson said the Committee would have to justify every nickel of the $6.5 million. As for the invasion of privacy implications of secret lie detector tests, he said he would not let Sprague "run amok."

In a long Sunday piece on January 2, 1977, David B. Burnham of *The New York Times* reported on evidence that Sprague's past as a prosecutor in Philadelphia was somewhat questionable, including an allegation that he had mishandled a homicide case involving the son of a friend. On January 6, *The Times* reported, Don Edwards of California, Chairman of the House Judiciary Subcommittee on Civil and Constitutional Rights, warned that the investigative techniques proposed by Sprague were "wrong, immoral and very likely illegal." Gonzalez rose to Sprague's defense in a letter to Edwards that he inserted into the *Congressional Record* on January 10, which laid the blame on Downing for failure to establish guidelines. Gonzalez vowed that as chairman he would keep a tight rein on Sprague and his staff, leading *The Philadelphia Bulletin* on January 7 to detect "a hint of trouble brewing." The drift of the debate prompted *The Washington Post* to predict that a stiff budget cut was in the offing. (Robert E. Bauman of Maryland, a conservative, castigated Sprague for his high-handed ways and his "checkered career," but he was most enraged by the excesses he found implicit in a $13 million two-year budget.)

The controversy over Sprague, his methods, and his proposed budget forced the Democratic leadership of the House to postpone a vote to reconstitute the Committee in the 95th Congress, which had convened on January 4, 1977. The House Administration Committee had ruled that under a continuing resolution monthly expenditures could not exceed what the Committee had spent in December 1976, or $84,337.12, which was not enough to cover salaries, let alone other expenses. (Sprague assured his staff he would make up for lost income with raises once a new budget was approved.) House Resolution 222, which would breathe life into the Committee, was passed on February

2, but it was clear from the debate that resistance to the inquiry was mounting. Richard Kelly of Florida called it a "multimillion-dollar fishing expedition for the benefit of a bunch of publicity seekers"; and Eldon J. Rudd of Arizona, a former FBI agent who had worked on the assassination investigation, declared the Committee had "already fanned the flames of rumor, distortion and unwarranted distrust of law enforcement agencies." Paul Simon of Illinois insisted it would be better to honor President Kennedy and Dr. King "by fighting for the things they stood for, such as getting jobs for people who are unemployed"; and Bauman of Maryland reminded his colleagues that ". . . these matters have been dealt with by official forums at great length."

The members of the Committee were its most vocal supporters. Samuel L. Devine, the ranking Republican, had not voted for H.R. 1540, but since it had been "the will of this House by a substantial vote to go forward," then it only made sense to provide "sufficient funds to do a thorough and efficient job to settle the problems having to do with these assassinations." Walter Fauntroy, Chairman of the King Subcommittee, maintained that "threshold inquiries by a thoroughly professional staff . . . in the last three months have produced literally a thousand questions unanswered by the investigations of record. . . ." Richardson Preyer, who had taken charge of the Kennedy investigation, put the issue in perspective. He understood why there had been a pronounced shift from enthusiasm for the investigation in September 1976 to skepticism in February 1977: it was based, he said, on a natural inclination to look toward new beginnings, not the nightmares of the past. But, he contended, ". . . we are not out to tear the nation apart. We are out to restore credibility, just as the Watergate hearings . . . restore belief in our government. Mr. Speaker, this question is not just one of the murders of two men. It is one of assassination, or regicide in President Kennedy's case. . . . Assassination is a peculiarly horrible crime. It arouses our deepest fears. It is going to continue to raise questions . . . unless we answer this matter once and for all."

H.R. 222 passed by a margin of 237 to 164. It contained the Committee's mandate (beyond determining who murdered Kennedy and King and evaluating previous assassination investigations, the Committee was charged with deciding whether the laws of the land that deal with assassination were adequate and whether responsible government agencies had disclosed all pertinent evidence), but it did not solve the money problem. Until a new budget could be agreed on, the Committee had to get along on its $84,000-a-month stipend, a large amount if the frame of reference is a personal bank account, but not enough to cover the Committee payroll and other expenses. On February 2 Gonzalez was named chairman by Speaker Thomas P. O'Neill, Jr., and he

promptly ordered Sprague to cut expenses by firing twenty-three people. When Sprague refused, Gonzalez dismissed him. Sprague was
defiant, however, claiming that only the full Committee had the authority to fire him. He was supported by Fauntroy, who contacted the
other ten members by phone (it was the first day of the George Washington's Birthday recess, and the members were all in their districts),
and they decided to defy their chairman and try to retain their chief
counsel, which was unprecedented for a congressional committee. On
February 16 the Committee met in secret session but adjourned without resolving the conflict, although it was apparent that Sprague's days
were numbered. Gonzalez was in Texas, down with the flu, but he was
well enough to present his case against Sprague in a blistering attack
that he had inserted in *The Congressional Record*. Gonzalez reviewed
the Committee's financial difficulties, attributing them to Sprague's
decision to hire twenty-three persons effective January 1, "without my
knowledge, consent or approval." Then, when ordered to come up with
a plan for cutting expenses, Sprague blithely suggested that further belt
tightening and expeditious approval of a new budget was all that was required. "It is hard to imagine anything less responsive than that," said
Gonzalez. What is more, Sprague assumed he had the authority of a
member of the House, even a committee chairman, and by assuring the
staff that he was in complete charge, he was guilty of insubordination
and usurpation. "Let me simply say that when I see a rattlesnake on the
doorstep, I don't hesitate, I stomp on it. . . ." On March 1 Gonzalez
submitted his resignation, calling Sprague "an unconscionable
scoundrel." On March 8 his resignation was accepted by a vote of 296 to
100, and the following day, Speaker O'Neill named a new chairman,
Louis Stokes of Ohio. Stokes was a realist, who knew that if he did not
get rid of Sprague the Committee would go out of business on March
31. After a late-night session with Stokes on March 29, Sprague resigned, and on March 30, by a vote of 230 to 181, the House passed
H.R. 433, which extended the investigation to the end of 1978. On
April 28 funding for 1977 was approved, though at $2.5 million it had
been scaled down considerably.

There were worthy lessons to be learned from Sprague's experience.
Granted, he had many shortcomings, so his dismissal was fitting. He
was egotistical and arrogant to the extent that he believed he did not
need to pay attention to the work that had been done by the FBI and the
Warren Commission (he was literally calling witnesses — gangsters, ex-
CIA officials — without the benefit of full background briefings). He insisted that his investigation be kept independent of individuals who had
been "tainted" by experience — federal agency officials, critics, and

politicians (this would seem even to include members of the Committee). Sprague apparently forgot he was conducting a congressional investigation. To him, the Kennedy and King assassinations were everyday murders, which explained why he staffed the Committee with attorneys and investigators from metropolitan homicide bureaus. The approach was doomed from the start, for it was predicated on the single objective of apprehending and prosecuting the killers, an unconstitutional undertaking for a congressional committee. (Even if he had developed evidence against named conspirators that met trial standards, it would have been up to the Department of Justice, not the Committee, to act on it.)

It is only fair to say, however, that Sprague came to terms on the conditions of his appointment with Downing, and Gonzalez switched the signals. Sprague understood, for example, that he had full authority to hire and fire, and he understandably resented the public way that Gonzalez took it away from him. He also resented having to justify his stewardship once Downing had departed, and he objected strenuously to being forced to go hat-in-hand before other congressional committees for funding. Sprague confided to associates that he had thought, when he accepted the job, that all he had to do was put together a staff, prepare a budget, and proceed to solve the cases. Thus, he betrayed a misunderstanding of Congress, for if it is nothing else, Congress is a political institution accustomed to granting nothing that is not inveigled from it by the lobbying process that Sprague resented. Congress also draws a sharp distinction between elected and appointed power — committee staff members, even a chief counsel, are expected to know their place.

An Investigation Reconstituted

Following the firing of Sprague, the Committee lay dead in the water for three months. What direction there was came from a succession of acting chief counsels who lacked either authority or motivation, or both. Staff morale sagged to zero, as make-work exercises were devised. By July the state of the investigation had gone from bad to abysmal. First, there were the realities of the Kennedy case: the trail had not just cooled over the years, it had been trampled into a state of confusion by amateur sleuths; witnesses had died, and the memories of those who were still around had been altered by secondhand perceptions (witnesses, too, read the critical books) and dimmed by the passage of time; and evidence had been misplaced or destroyed. There were also hindering limitations that had been set by Congress when it reluctantly agreed to let the Committee proceed: its life was limited — in eighteen months, January 1979, it would be disbanded; and its resources were tightly restricted — a twelve-month budget of $2.5 million for both investigations (in 1977 dollars, the Warren Commission spent $10 million in nine months), with no assurance of funding for 1978. Finally, there were the self-imposed burdens, the legacy of Sprague's management approach. The Committee was clearly not equipped to conduct a sophisticated investigation. It had not laid plans or set priorities; it had not even come to agreement with the FBI and the CIA on a procedure for reviewing classified files. Even though it was apparent from the start that there were many technical issues to be settled — in the fields of forensic pathology, ballistics, photography, handwriting and fingerprinting analysis, to name a few — not a single qualified consultant had been retained. And the staff was young and inexperienced in many instances, unqualified and incompetent in others. (On the other hand, it consisted of some exceptionally well-qualified, energetic, and loyal individuals whose decision to stay on after Sprague departed made the difference between a boat that was dead in the water and one that had sunk.)

The period from July 1977 to January 1978 was one for rebuilding the staff; mastering the literature, the work of the Warren Commission and its critics; establishing working relationships with the investigative agencies, not only the FBI, CIA, and others in Washington, but authorities in Dallas, some of whom were defensive and leery of leveling with us; devising a fact-finding format and a public hearing policy; conducting a preliminary file review; doing exploratory fieldwork; and, most important, preparing a comprehensive investigative plan for the balance of the life of the Committee. The plan was a prerequisite, because we could not, even with infinite resources, expect to answer every question that could be asked. We had to choose carefully from the alternative courses of action open to us, hoping to achieve a balanced approach to the requirements of our congressional mandate and not to succumb to the temptation to concentrate on the question of conspiracy to the exclusion of other tasks. It was a matter of assessing and assigning the proper priorities. We decided to rely primarily on the hard data of science and technology, because the physical aspects of the evidence had not been as affected by time as had human testimony. Further, we stood to gain from scientific advances that would enable our experts to apply testing techniques that were not available to the Warren Commission, an advantage of particular relevance, we were to find, with respect to the acoustical evidence. There was no new physical evidence in the case, as far as we could tell, but there might be new ways to read it. In this respect, we possibly could put the passsage of time to advantage.

We realized that we — and therefore the nation — were running a risk. If we were able to answer the questions before us in a fashion consistent with the results of previous investigations, doubts about those investigations might be laid to rest. If, on the other hand, our answers were inconsistent with the official position, and in the process, we raised new questions, new doubts would be created, for we might not have the time or resources to conduct further investigation. While the risk was real, it seemed a small price to pay for a chance to learn the truth.

5

The Warren Commission Evaluated

[T]ruth is on the march, and nothing can stop it. . . . When truth is buried in the earth, it accumulates there, and assumes so mighty an explosive power that, on the day when it bursts forth, it hurls everything into the air.

Emile Zola
J'Accuse

Critical Analysis

A critical evaluation of the work of the Warren Commission was a first order of business. Our basic approach was to study the 1964 investigation and question closely the members of the Commission (three of whom, Gerald R. Ford, John Sherman Cooper, and John J. McCloy, were still living) and the staff counsel. On the question of conspiracy, these men had stood firm over the years. There were no facts to support a plot, Earl Warren wrote not long before he died in 1974, and he added, perhaps overstating his case:

Practically all the Cabinet members of President Kennedy's Administration, along with Director J. Edgar Hoover of the FBI and Chief James Rowley of the Secret Service, . . . testified that to their knowledge there was no sign of conspiracy. To say now that these people, as well as the Commission, suppressed, neglected to unearth, or overlooked evidence of a conspiracy would be an indictment of the entire government of the United States. It would mean that the whole structure was absolutely corrupt from top to bottom.

71

Norman Redlich, a New York University law professor who was one of two top assistants to Commission General Counsel J. Lee Rankin, was not so defensive when he appeared at an executive session of our Committee in November 1977, but he was just as certain: ". . . there are simply a great many people who cannot accept what I believe to be the simple truth, that one rather insignificant person was able to assassinate the President of the United States."

First, we considered the purpose of the Warren Commission in the view of men who had staffed it. At the initial staff meeting, on January 20, 1964, Chief Justice Warren discussed the role of the Commission, and his remarks were the subject of a memorandum by Melvin A. Eisenberg, a staff attorney. Warren emphasized that the Commission had to determine "the truth, whatever that might be," but we were aware of allegations of certain pressures that might have inhibited the truth-seeking process. There was, for example, the question of whether sufficient time had been allotted for a thorough investigation. It had been widely reported that there was immense pressure on the staff to finish the job — pressure from high government officials, including the Chief Justice, who were convinced that the case against Oswald was open and shut and could be wrapped up in short order; and pressure from the White House, because President Johnson feared that a prolonged investigation would turn the assassination into a presidential campaign issue. We knew, of course, that a plan to wind up in advance of the presidential nominating conventions had proven unrealistic, but the Commission had nonetheless kept to a tight schedule: it was created on November 29, 1963; the staff had been assembled by the end of January 1964; hearings lasted from February 3 to June 17; the summer was spent in writing and editing the report, which was submitted to President Johnson on September 24. Most of the staff had been told, however, that the investigation would last no longer than six months. Accordingly, the original schedule called for winding up the investigation by May 1, a draft report by June 1, and a final report by July 1.

Rankin explained how the deadline kept slipping and how he prodded the staff: "I was told that it would take only three months . . . , and then we were going to try to get it out in six months and that seemed obviously impossible soon after I got there. . . . So I did exert considerable pressure about not dilly-dallying." W. David Slawson, for one, resented "being pushed to work at such a rapid pace," and Burt W. Griffin sensed there was more to the pressure than presidential politics, that there were fears of a witch hunt, since the memory of Senator Joseph R. McCarthy was still vivid: "There was a great deal of concern that we not conduct an investigation that would have overtones of . . . McCarthyism." In addition, there was pressure that stemmed from

Warren's impatience, said Griffin, who told us that the Chief Justice was very impressed with the FBI investigation, ". . . and if we had not found anything . . . more than already seemed to be the conclusions, there was not anything there to be found." Howard P. Willens, who like Redlich was a principal Rankin assistant, denied Griffin's suggestion that Warren had importuned the staff to reach conclusions comparable to the FBI's. Was there pressure in the form of reminders to the staff of the need to allay public fear and to effect a smooth governmental transition? we asked Willens. Were there concerns about international relations or about the investigation being turned into a witch hunt? He acknowledged the constraints had existed, but not in such a way that they "affected either the scope of the investigation or the substance of our findings." The international concerns were the most troubling to Willens: "[T]here was considerable speculation and apprehension arising from the fact that the apparent assassin . . . had lived for several years in the Soviet Union and had married a citizen of the Soviet Union." That being said, Willens insisted it did not stop the Commission from taking a hard, though admittedly limited, look at the possibility of a foreign conspiracy. But what did Willens have to say about a December 9, 1963, communication from Deputy Attorney General Katzenbach to Chief Justice Warren urging immediate release of a statement that would establish beyond a reasonable doubt that Oswald assassinated the President and there was no evidence of a conspiracy?

Blakey: *Would it be fair to characterize this letter as an example of the kind of outside pressures that were put on the Commission with an apparent design to shape its work?*

Willens: *Well, I do have some difficulty with your use of the word "pressure." The letter, I think, is an effort to inform the Chief Justice of a possible course of action for his consideration. . . .*

At the very first meeting of the Commission, on December 5, 1963, Warren announced his belief that the Commission needed neither its own investigators nor the authority to issue subpoenas and grant immunity from prosecution to witnesses if they were compelled to testify, after first having chosen to take the Fifth Amendment on grounds of self-incriminaton. The Chief Justice was overruled by the Commission on the subpoena and immunity authority, though immunity was never used; but he held sway on his insistence that evidence that had been developed by the FBI would form a foundation for the Commission investigation. It was not a decision to be accepted without debate. "How much . . . does the FBI propose to release to the press before we present the findings of this Commission?" Senator

Russell demanded. And when the bureau's initial report was presented to the Commission on December 9, it left a lot to be desired: it was difficult to decipher and, in the opinion of Congressman Boggs, there were "a million questions" still to be answered. Rankin endorsed the decision to forgo an independent investigative staff, saying it would require an inordinate amount of time to put it together, and advising it would be more prudent "to use the intelligence facilities that the government had at hand." Rankin had another reason for his belief that there was more to be lost than gained from hiring an independent detective force: "[T]he whole intelligence community in the government would feel that the Commission was indicating a lack of confidence in them . . ." Rankin's viewpoint did not, however, meet with the unanimous approval of his staff. Griffin, for one, had lost respect for the FBI while serving as a federal prosecutor in Ohio. "I frankly didn't think they were very competent, . . ." he told us. "I felt then, and I still feel that they have a great myth about their ability, but they are not capable . . . of ever uncovering a serious and well-planned conspiracy. They would only stumble on it." Redlich was also critical. "I thought the FBI report was a grossly inadequate document," he said. "In fairness . . . , they apparently decided to produce something very quickly, but based upon what I feel I know and remember about the facts of the assassination, . . . it was a grossly inadequate document."

Willens was asked about the use of immunity — specifically, the failure to use it — since we had been unable to find any indication that a witness before the Commission found it necessary to claim the privilege of self-incrimination and consequently be granted immunity.

Blakey: *Should we draw . . . the inference that it was the policy . . . not to call any witness . . . whose testimony could only be secured on a grant of immunity?*

Willens: *No, I don't think you can draw that conclusion. I have a recollection of one or two witnesses who advised the Commission or the staff that they might invoke their constitutional privilege. . . . [But] I agree with your recollection that no witness did in fact invoke the Fifth, . . . and there were no instances where immunity was granted.*

We also asked Willens if the Commission staff at times tended to assume an advocacy role, rather than act as the support unit of an objective fact-finding panel. It was a statement by Willens, in a memo to Rankin reviewing a chapter of the report on Oswald's guilt, that raised the question. He had written:

I still have a question about the validity of including as a minor finding

Oswald's capability with a rifle. I think our case remains the same even if Oswald had limited or negligible capability with a rifle. In a way, we are emphasizing an argument we don't particularly need, which prompts controversy and may tend to weaken the stronger elements of our proof.

Thus, our question:

Blakey: *. . . the memorandum employs words like "case," "argument," "weaken." Aren't these words appropriate to a brief, a legal brief?*

Willens: *These are words that come naturally to a lawyer reviewing a written product.*

Self-Imposed Limitations

Certain strategic decisions by the Commission, including controversial ones, were the product of clearly defined, at times hotly debated, policy. Perhaps the most questionable of these was an edict that deprived the Commission of crucial evidence. At Warren's insistence, the Commission did not inspect the X-rays and photographs taken of the President's body during an autopsy at the U.S. Naval Hospital in Bethesda, Maryland. The decision was based on a dual conviction of the Chief Justice, according to Redlich: he wanted everything that was viewed by the Commission to be part of the published record; and he "felt publication of the autopsy film . . . would be a great disservice to Mrs. Kennedy and the Kennedy family." Warren was also known to believe there was ample other evidence to substantiate conclusions about Kennedy's wounds — the clothes he had been wearing, bullet fragments, and the testimony of the autopsy doctors.

Warren was also widely criticized for making it a matter of Commission policy — at least that is the way it appeared — to go easy on Marina Oswald. It was no doubt a well-intentioned decision on the part of the courtly Chief Justice, but it caused the one run-in Redlich had with the chairman. Warren was unhappy with the way Redlich had taken testimony from James H. Martin, who was Mrs. Oswald's business manager following the assassination, in which Redlich described her as "cold, calculating, avaricious, scornful of generosity and capable of an extreme lack of sympathy in personal relationships." Redlich explained to us that he had intended to cast Marina Oswald in an unfavorable light since the Commission had an obligation to pursue all possible motives. "One of the motives could have been," he said, "that Mrs. Oswald, through the kind of person that she was, drove Lee Harvey Oswald to the assassination."

Dependence on the FBI and the CIA

Because the Warren Commission was so totally dependent on the intelligence agencies, the FBI and CIA, for its information, its success or failure hinged on the state of its relations with the agencies. This was so even if the investigative work of the agencies had been flawless (a rather big *if*, in the collective judgment of the Commission and its staff, given the dubious quality of the December 9, 1963, FBI report). Nevertheless, the Commission was at first willing to trust and rely on the FBI; only later, when there were indications of hostility by J. Edgar Hoover and his top assistants, did this faith begin to erode. As for the CIA, the Commission was reluctant to use CIA facilities, and when it did it only expected answers to specific queries, which, it turned out, was all the agency intended to give. Consequently, the Commission and the staff were generally satisfied with the performance of the CIA, though this assessment would lead to deep disillusionment when it was too late to do anything about it.

The Commission staff, on the whole, was predisposed to an uncritical acceptance of the FBI, based on its reputation as a top-notch law enforcement organization. Rankin did say, however, that the listing in Oswald's address book of the name of Special Agent James Hosty, which was not promptly forwarded to the Commission, and the rumors of an Oswald connection to the bureau that required a personal denial from Hoover, had a chilling effect on the relationship. What if he had known during the investigation about the note from Oswald to Hosty that Hosty had destroyed? we asked Rankin. "There is an implication from that note and its destruction that there might have been more to [an Oswald-FBI connection]," Rankin replied, "and that the Bureau was unwilling to investigate whatever more there was and never would get the information to us." Rankin would have had even greater reason to be concerned about the FBI had he known in 1964 what had come to light by 1978, for the Hosty incidents did not constitute all of the information that was withheld. It was never revealed to the Commission, for example, that Hoover had disciplined several of his subordinates, including senior FBI officials, for deficiencies in the security investigation of Oswald prior to the assassination.

J. Edgar Hoover's attitude toward the Commission was addressed in 1976 by the Senate Select Committee on Intelligence Activities, whose key witness was former Assistant FBI Director William C. Sullivan. Bearing in mind that Sullivan may have been embittered by a falling-out with Hoover, we reviewed his testimony and found it informative. (We were unable to call Sullivan as a witness, since he died in a deer-hunting accident in 1977.) "Hoover did not want the Warren Commission to conduct an exhaustive investigation for fear that it would discover

important and relevant facts that we in the FBI had not discovered,''
Sullivan said. One Hoover tactic, according to Sullivan, was to take
advantage of the presence of a friend of the FBI on the Commission —
Gerald R. Ford. ''He was our man on the Commission,'' said Sullivan.
''It was to him that we looked to protect our interest and keep us fully
advised of any development that we would not like, . . . and this he
did.''

When former President Ford appeared before the Committee in September 1978, he was asked by Congressman Devine about two FBI
documents that seemed to support Sullivan's charge. They were memos
from Assistant to the Director Cartha D. DeLoach to Director Hoover,
dated December 12 and 17, 1963, which described meetings in Ford's
office. ''He asked that I come up to see him,'' DeLoach wrote. ''Upon
arriving he told me he wanted to talk in the strictest of confidence. This
was agreed to.'' At the first meeting, according to DeLoach, he and
Ford discussed Warren's intended appointment of former Assistant
Attorney General Warren Olney as General Counsel, the objection to
Olney by Ford, Boggs, and Dulles (though no reason was given), and
the compromise choice of Rankin. (The objection to Olney, based at
least to some degree on Hoover's feelings about the former Assistant
Attorney General, was unfortunate, in light of our conclusions about
organized crime's role in the assassination. Olney had been counsel to
the Special Study Commission on Organized Crime, which was established by Warren when he was Governor of California, and he was
regarded as an authority on the underworld.) Ford mentioned a visit he
had been paid by CIA Director John A. McCone, the purpose of which
was to acquaint him with a CIA report that Oswald had received money
in Mexico City from a Cuban, to which DeLoach replied that ''the CIA
source was either unstable or somewhat of a psychopathic liar.'' Finally,
DeLoach wrote, ''Ford indicated he would keep me thoroughly advised
as to the activities of the Commission. He stated this would have to be
on a confidential basis. . . .'' At the second meeting, still according to
the DeLoach memos, Ford made good on his promise by briefing
DeLoach on developments at the Commission.

Ford's explanation of the meetings to us in public testimony in September 1978 was that he had been fearful that Warren, by appointing
Olney, was ''moving in the direction of a one-man Commission,'' so he
had decided to enlist support for his opposition to Olney from the FBI.
(In view of Hoover's own antipathy toward Olney, Ford's answer was
less than credible. We found it more likely that it was the other way
around, with Hoover initiating the opposition.) Ford said that the meetings with DeLoach were terminated after the one on December 17.

James R. Malley, the FBI official who was the liaison to the Warren
Commission, described the relationship as strictly business, not friend-

ly but "never any animosity shown." Malley's assurances were hardly consistent with the testimony of former Deputy Attorney General Katzenbach (he became Attorney General when Robert Kennedy resigned in August 1964 to run for the Senate from New York), who related to us how Hoover had refused to send a representative to the first Commission meeting. Katzenbach was also convinced that the FBI hierarchy would have been deeply troubled if the Commission had developed evidence that contradicted its conclusion that Oswald had been a lone assassin. At the Commission itself, we found, there was sympathy for the bureau's misgivings. Howard Willens, for one, did not believe the FBI was any less cooperative because of its anxieties, commenting that it was "completely understandable" that there was concern over the possibility that the Commission might disprove one or more of the FBI findings. Willens, however, was bothered by the bureau's tendency to be less than candid. When it was learned, for example, that the Hosty entry in Oswald's address book had been deleted from a transcript submitted to the Commission, he and others on the staff were "generally upset." As for the destruction of Oswald's note to Hosty, Willens told us in 1978 that it was "the saddest possible commentary on the mentality that apparently prevailed . . . at the FBI."

W. David Slawson was the Commission counsel (along with William T. Coleman, Jr.) assigned to probe the possibility of a foreign conspiracy, which meant he had to depend heavily on the CIA. In fact, it occurred to Slawson, as he dug deeper into evidence that foreign agents might have had a hand in the assassination, that he was at the virtual mercy of the CIA. The agency was, after all, the Commission's only source of information, other than the governments of suspected nations, whose reliability could not be trusted. Neither could the CIA's, it turned out.

From a detailed study of the record, we found that, at least for the sake of appearances, the Commission's relations with the CIA were perfect, as might be expected with a former Director of Central Intelligence serving on the Commission. As Allen Dulles had suggested it would be, the agency was indispensable in areas where it had exclusive access to information, such as Oswald's defection to the Soviet Union. Raymond Rocca, the Chief of Research and Analysis in the Counterintelligence Division, was assigned as "point of record" officer, and he produced an exhaustive analysis of the period Oswald lived in Russia. The agency came up with nothing comparable concerning Oswald's contacts with Cubans in the United States and Mexico, however, although Rocca did call Slawson's attention to Castro's reported warning to American leaders just two months before the assassination. Rocca was not, we learned, really the key man in CIA-Commission contacts, nor was his immediate superior, Counterintelligence Chief James J. Angleton. The official in charge was Richard M. Helms, Deputy Director for Plans, though he often communicated with the Commission through an assistant, Thomas Karamessines. Helms, of course, knew all about the CIA-Mafia plots to assassinate Fidel Castro, but he volunteered nothing and provided the Commission with information only as it specifically requested it. Since the Commission did not ask, it did not learn about the agency's transactions with Mafia figures John Roselli, Sam Giancana, and Santo Trafficante. If nothing else, the proximity of the period of the Castro plots (Roselli's last-known meeting with CIA officer William Harvey was in June 1963) to the assassination implied a degree of significance that might have altered the course of the Commission's investigation, if not its ultimate outcome. We put the question to Redlich: Would knowledge of the plots have made a difference? "I think it would have affected it, . . ." he replied. "I think that an important fact like that might have led to additional inquiry as to whether the Cuban government might have tried to retaliate." The Commission considered an Oswald-Cuban connection, Redlich said, but ". . . it is possible that this additional fact might have led to additional inquiry." Slawson told us, however, that it would not have altered his approach that much, since he already had suspected some sort of Cuban complicity; but Willens believed an awareness of the CIA's Mafia sources would have "prompted a specific investigative request to the CIA to utilize those . . . sources to find out what Cuban involvement" there might have been in the assassination. Would it also have prompted a wider effort to trace telephone toll records, as had been urged by Assistant Counsel Leon D. Hubert, Jr., and Burt W. Griffin? "Yes," Willens replied, but in a more focused way than had been suggested by Hubert and Griffin, concentrating on particular organized crime figures at times when they might have been in Cuba or in touch with people in Cuba.

The FBI knew about the Castro plots at least from the time Director Hoover met with Attorney General Kennedy, which was on May 9, 1962, two days after Kennedy was briefed by CIA officials. The bureau had its own file on Giancana's CIA connection, pertinent bits of which were leaked to Sandy Smith, a reporter for *The Chicago Sun-Times,* whose article on August 16, 1963, quoting "Justice Department sources," indicated Giancana was playing the CIA along in order to stay out of prison. The FBI, then, did make the CIA-Mafia relationship public, so it was all the more ironic that the Commission did not take it into account. On the other hand, there was an instance in which the FBI possibly prevented the Commission from learning about the plots, asserting that the allegations of a witness who may well have known about them were not to be believed. The witness was John Martino, a former gambling casino employee in Havana who in 1963 was living in Miami, having been released after 40 months in a Cuban prison. Martino had ties to both the Mafia and Cuban-exile activists, and, in June 1963 he was involved in the infiltration of a band of heavily armed anti-Castro guerrillas into Cuba, which was supported indirectly by the CIA. (We were able to document the Martino mission from firsthand experience, since Billings, on assignment for *Life*, witnessed the operation up to the drop-off of the Cuban guerrillas five miles from the Cuban coast.)

After the assassination, Martino contacted the Commission and told a story that was hauntingly similar to the one John Roselli told more than twelve years later: the Kennedy assassination had been an act of retaliation for an anti-Castro plot, according to a source "high in the Cuban government" whose identity Martino refused to reveal. In a memo to Rankin on April 1, 1964, Slawson urged that Martino be called as a witness; but on April 24 he reported that the FBI had interviewed Martino and determined that his story did not stand up, so Slawson recommended that "we let the whole thing drop." (As Martino had died by the time of our investigation, we were not able to take his testimony.)

We asked Rankin if, in his judgment, ample time had been devoted to the Commission investigation. "Certainly," he replied, "it would not have been adequate if we had gotten this information . . . about the CIA's activity [with the Mafia] and the FBI's knowledge of it. . . . I am sure there would have been quite a serious upheaval. . . ." Rankin also compared relations with the FBI and the CIA: with the bureau "we were partners of convenience rather than enjoyment, . . . but I really don't think that the bureau was withholding generally, and to me what the CIA withheld is of major importance. . . ." Had the Commission known about the CIA-Mafia plots, what then? ". . . [W]e certainly would have followed every lead down," Rankin declared. "I don't want to claim that we would have found something, or that we would have broken . . . the underworld shield . . . but at least we ought to have had the opportunity to try."

Slawson told us that he had developed an "especially strong" interest in anti-Castro Cubans because they seemed to have the most motivation.

[T]he anti-Castro Cubans, we knew, were very angry with Kennedy because they felt they had been betrayed with the Bay of Pigs. Oswald, on the other hand, was identified publicly with Castro. . . . So, we felt that if somehow the anti-Castro Cubans could have got Oswald to do it, or [had] done it themselves but framed Oswald, either way, . . . that they would achieve two objectives. . . . One was revenge on Kennedy and the second would be to trigger American public opinion strongly against Castro and possibly cause an invasion of Cuba. . . . As I say, this made a lot of sense to me. . . . It was a hypothesis I held in mind for quite a while, trying to see if the facts would fit it. Ultimately, they didn't.

In the waning days of the investigation, however, Wesley J. Liebeler, in a memo to Rankin, listed four pieces of evidence that tended to support Slawson's hypothesis: the testimony of Dean Andrews, a New Orleans lawyer, who claimed that Oswald had come to his office several times in the summer of 1963, accompanied by a man who appeared to be Mexican; the statement of Evaristo Rodriguez, a New Orleans bartender, who said he had seen Oswald in the Habana Bar in August 1963 in the company of a man of Spanish descent; a photograph of Oswald handing out "Fair Play for Cuba" leaflets in New Orleans in August 1963, assisted by a young man with Latin features; and the alleged visit to Silvia Odio's home in Dallas by "Leon Oswald" and two men who appeared to be either Cuban or Mexican. The common thread, of course, was Oswald's Latin companion or companions whose identity would never be learned by the Commission. In November 1977 we asked Liebeler if there had been adequate time to complete a thorough investigation. He said, yes, with one exception: ". . . the FBI was still trying to . . . corroborate or discredit, to determine the truth or falsity of some testimony that had been given by Silvia Odio to the effect that Oswald had been in her apartment in Dallas sometime in either September or October 1963."

| Cornwell: | *The Silvia Odio incident was never resolved to your satisfaction, was it?* |
| Leibeler: | *No, not really.* |

The Ruby Investigation

The relative unimportance of Jack Ruby, so far as the Commission was concerned, was reflected in the way the staff was organized according to subject area: four areas treated Oswald as the primary figure, while only one was devoted to Ruby. In addition, we learned, there was nothing to indicate that the possibility that Ruby was a party to a conspiracy, without having been connected to Oswald, was ever seriously considered.

Griffin, a former assistant U.S. attorney in Ohio, was assigned to the Ruby investigation along with Leon D. Hubert, Jr., who had been a prosecutor in New Orleans, so the team was not lacking in experience. (Hubert had died by the time of our investigation; Griffin, in 1975, was elected judge of the Court of Common Pleas in Cleveland.) Given their backgrounds, it was inevitable that conflict would arise when Hubert and Griffin were handed the FBI's ready-made solution, especially since all the pieces did not fit. Griffin had distinct misgivings within a couple of months: "Hubert and I began to feel . . . that perhaps there was not a great deal of interest in what we were doing, that they looked upon the Ruby activity as largely peripheral."

On May 14 Griffin and Hubert indicated in a memo to Rankin that they were far from finishing their investigation. They had not been able to determine why Ruby had murdered Oswald: Had Ruby been an associate of the assassin of the President? Had he acted under orders from someone? Faced with an impossible June 1 deadline, they wrote that much of what Ruby was up to in the period leading to the assassination had not been accounted for; some forty-six persons known to have been in contact with Ruby between November 22 and 24, 1963, had not been interviewed; and those who had been interviewed had not been fully checked out. In fact, Hubert and Griffin were forced to concede, much of what the Commission had learned about Ruby had come from four close associates, whose testimony had not been corroborated. Arguing that further investigation was required, they noted that Ruby had "long been close to persons pursuing illegal activities," including Lewis J. McWillie, a Las Vegas racketeer who, while managing a gambling casino in Havana in 1959, had been paid an extended visit by Ruby. "In short, we believe that the possibility exists, based on evidence already available, that Ruby was involved in illegal dealings with Cuban elements who might have had contact with Oswald." This was just a guess, they admitted, since their investigation had not addressed Ruby's criminal connections. We found the suspicions expressed in the memo very significant, and we questioned Griffin closely about the response it got. We asked if the FBI had responded to the several specific investigative suggestions that were listed. Griffin thought not, but, he volunteered, the real question had to do with Rankin's response. He remembered being told the recommendations were being tacitly accepted, but not with enthusiasm: "[W]e were, in a sense, given a light to go ahead, but they still made it clear that we had these deadlines." What about something as general as Oswald's and Ruby's respective Cuban connections — did the FBI explore them further? "In fairness to the bureau," Griffin replied, "I don't think they had much of a request to explore them. . . . We did not pursue these matters in a manner I felt at the time, or have ever felt, was satisfactory." We referred Griffin to a statement on page 365 of *The Warren Report*, which read:

> In addition to examining in detail Jack Ruby's activities from November 21 to November 24, and his possible acquaintanceship with Lee Harvey

Oswald, the Commission has considered whether or not Ruby had ties with individuals or groups that might have obviated the need for any direct contact [with Oswald] near the time of the assassination. Study of Jack Ruby's background . . . leads to the final conclusion that he had no such ties.

Griffin said, "If this phrase, 'individuals or groups that might have obviated the need,' if that is read to mean Cuban groups or any people interested in dealing with Cuba, I would say no, I would not agree. . . ." We then called his attention to the Commission's conclusion that "the evidence does not establish a significant link between Ruby and organized crime." "Right," said Griffin. "I think the key words are 'significant link,' and the question was: Where did Ruby stand in the organized criminal hierarchy? Was he a big fish, or was he on the periphery?"

Blakey:	*In your professional judgment, did you adequately explore the relationship between Ruby and McWillie and possible connections with organized-crime figures?*
Griffin:	*If we were conducting . . . a no-time-limit, no-stops investigation into . . . a conspiracy . . . that involved the underworld, and if we had one bit of information that would show that the underworld . . . had a motive . . ., my answer would be that this was not adequate.*

Griffin explained that the Commission missed the significance of Ruby's alleged Mafia ties because it had not been aware of the CIA-Mafia plots to assassinate Castro. He could not recall if he had known that in May 1960 Ruby's friend McWillie had gone to work for a casino in which organized-crime figures reportedly had an interest, but ". . . that kind of information would not have significantly affected our decision unless we knew two things at least: that . . . underworld types were being used by the CIA . . . [and] there was an effort [by] . . . people in our government to assassinate Castro." Griffin's familiarity with underworld operations in the Caribbean in the 1950s and 1960s was not extensive however (more the pity, we decided, that Warren Olney had not been named Commission General Counsel). Griffin had heard of Meyer Lansky and his brother, Jake, but names of other well-known gamblers such as Dino Cellini and Ed Levinson meant nothing to him, and when we asked him if the names Santo Trafficante and Carlos Marcello rang a bell, he said they did not. (By 1964 the FBI had determined that Trafficante and Marcello were the organized-crime leaders in Florida and Louisiana, respectively.)

Griffin acknowleged that in 1964 he had been aware that, under Attorney General Kennedy, the Justice Department had embarked on a vigorous drive against organized crime, but he had made no connection between that and the assassination. "You see, the difficulty with making that leap was that . . . Oswald was the person who assassinated the President. There was no showing that Oswald had any connection with organized crime. Therefore, there was no reason to think that, simply because Ruby was involved in organized crime, that that would have been linked to the assassination. . . ." He did admit, however, that knowledge of the CIA-Mafia assassination plots would have altered his perspective.

Griffin was convinced that Oswald had murdered the President, and he agreed with a central conclusion of the Warren Commission that no evidence of a conspiracy had been found. When we asked him, however, if he was satisfied with the investigation that had led to that conclusion, he said he was not. A particular reason for his discontent was the response he and Hubert got to a memo dated February 24, 1964, to Howard Willens, recommending a thorough FBI examination of all phone calls by Ruby, his family, and his associates, and a request to phone companies in Texas, Nevada, Los Angeles, San Francisco, Chicago, Detroit, Boston, New York, Washington, Miami, and New Orleans to freeze all records until June 1, 1964. It was Griffin's recollection that, while the FBI did compile some telephone information, it was not the comprehensive check he had requested, and "no request to freeze records was made to telephone companies." (Following his testimony, Griffin reviewed his records and told us by letter that he had found a memorandum, dated June 1, 1964, in which he and Hubert told Willens that they believed that investigative requests, based on a compromise reached after they had written a follow-up to their February 24 proposal, "will serve to correct all of the matters specified in our memorandum of May 14." "In light of that statement, I don't see how I can now complain . . . ," he wrote. While Griffin may have felt bound by his 1964 memo, we disagreed. The compromise that was reached was unfortunate, for its effect was to permit the destruction of potentially valuable evidence.)

We asked Willens about the telephone records check, telling him of Griffin's testimony to the effect that, while some of the suggestions were followed, a general freezing of the records was not attempted, and no effort was made to ascertain how complete the compilation of data by the FBI had been. Why?

Willens: *My recollection is that the broad-based request here was not implemented . . . but that throughout the remaining months of the investigation some of the specific inquiries . . . were made and reports produced. . . . I think that the reason the broader*

> *requests were not taken is anticipated very neatly by Mr. Hubert's and Mr. Griffin's second paragraph, which I quote: "Some of the suggestions made impose burdens on private parties which are not justified by the possible results to be obtained. If so, they should be rejected. . . ."*

Blakey: *Mr. Willens, there are obviously only a limited number of ways in which conspiracy allegations can be pursued. There was not available to the Commission sophisticated electronic surveillance techniques that would deal with . . . conspiracy. It is doubtful that physical records would be in existence or that the Commission had . . . search warrant authority to seize them. Basically, all you could do was engage in field interrogation and depositions. I wonder why you would have foregone the opportunity to examine long distance call records in pursuit of the conspiracy allegation. Had you done so and . . . developed a pattern of preassassination communications between . . . individuals . . . who were associated with Mr. Ruby and perhaps even with Mr. Oswald, it might have been possible to pursue these associations and precipitate Commission interrogation.*

Willens: *I would not accept that characterization. If your investigation discovers that it did have those consequences, then I think that is an important conclusion for you to report. . . .*

We turned to the subject of electronic surveillance. Was Willens aware, we asked, that during the period surrounding the assassination — roughly 1959 to 1964 — the FBI, albeit illegally, had engaged in an extensive program that targeted major organized-crime figures. As we understood it, the bureau had placed up to a hundred listening devices in the homes and offices of major underworld figures in the metropolitan areas of such cities as New York, Chicago, Buffalo, Philadelphia, Detroit, Los Angeles, and San Francisco, and there were in existence in 1964 literally hundreds of volumes of logs based on the eavesdropping.

Blakey: *Was either the existence of this program or [its] products ever brought to the attention of the Warren Commission?*

Willens: *I do not recall. I was aware that an extensive investigative program was underway with respect to organized crime. I had every reason to believe that the FBI and Criminal Division, which had responsibility for the overall prosecutorial effort, would bring to the attention of the Warren Commission any information developed by any source that pertained to the work of the . . . Commission. . . .*

Blakey: *To your knowledge, was there any effort made by the Commission, by the Department of Justice, or the Bureau to survey that electronic surveillance to determine whether there was any in-*

> *dication in it, either direct or circumstantial, that any of the*
> *major figures of organized crime might have had motive,*
> *opportunity, or the means to assassinate the President . . .?*
>
> Willens: *I do not know whether any effort of that kind was made. I do*
> *not believe it was made. . . .*

We also put the question of Mafia participation in a conspiracy to General Counsel Rankin: Had that possibility been thoroughly investigated by the Commission? "Yes," said Rankin, "I think that we examined that to a considerable extent in regard to Ruby because . . . he had some background with underworld connections, and we tried to follow that out. . . . It didn't seem to reveal anything as far as conspiracy was concerned, and, except for his ability to kill Oswald, Ruby didn't demonstrate any characteristics [of] . . . the type of person that the Mafia would select to be one of their men. . . ." Had Rankin known about the FBI's electronic surveillance of La Cosa Nostra, as the underworld referred to itself? "I was not aware of that at all . . . ," said Rankin, whose tenure as solicitor general ended in 1960, after the FBI surveillance program had been initiated. "I had been assured by Mr. Hoover, . . . that there were no domestic wiretaps. . . ." While he was Warren Commission General Counsel, had he inquired whether there had been any domestic surveillance? "No, I had not. I thought it was illegal, and I assumed that they were not doing illegal acts."

Finally, we asked Rankin if, in hindsight, he wished he had concentrated more of his resources on any of the conspiracy theories that had been proposed. He harked back to the CIA-Mafia plots and what an awareness of them in 1964 might have meant: "[I]t would have bulked larger, the conspiracy area, . . . and we would have run out all the various leads and probably, it is very possible . . . we could have come down with . . . a lead . . . to the underworld. . . ."

6

Dallas in Light of Modern Science

For murder, though it have no tongue, will speak
With most miraculous organ.

Shakespeare
Hamlet

The Witnesses in the Plaza

The crowd had begun to thin out as the President's motorcade entered Dealey Plaza, turned right from Main Street, and headed north on Houston Street toward the Texas School Book Depository at the corner of Houston and Elm. Estimates put the number of people in the Plaza, including onlookers, the presidential entourage, police, and the press, at over 250. The statements of 171 witnesses were available to the Warren Commission in 1964. Summarized, they indicated that from two to four shots were fired: 76 witnesses said they did not know what direction the shots came from; 46 said they came from the Book Depository; 29 said they came from some place other than the Book Depository or the grassy knoll (an area west of the Book Depository and north of Elm Street); and 20 said they came from the knoll. The Warren Commission, for its part, found that "the physical and other evidence" compelled the conclusion that two shots were fired. The Commission had relied principally on the autopsy and ballistics evidence, which showed that the President, as his car moved west on Elm Street away from the Book Depository, was struck by two bullets fired from above and be-

87

hind him. Nevertheless, because three cartridge cases were found near the sixth-floor southeast window of the Book Depository and since witnesses said they heard more than two shots, the Commission concluded that at least three shots were fired. The Commission then observed that there was "no credible evidence to indicate shots were fired from any place other than the Texas School Book Depository."

Our reexamination of the Commission's conclusions began with an analysis of evidence that was available to the Warren Commission, which indicated other shooter locations, in particular the grassy knoll, a landscaped hillock that stood to the right front of the President's limousine as it traveled west toward the triple underpass at the time of the shooting. The statistics did not convey a full impression of the character of the testimony on the issue of the direction of the shots. It was enlightening, therefore, to review the testimony, especially that which the Commission chose to disregard, saying it was "not credible." A Dallas police officer, Bobby W. Hargis, was, for example, riding a motorcycle to the left and slightly to the rear of the President's limousine. On April 8, 1964, he gave the Commission a deposition:

> I was next to Mrs. Kennedy when I heard the first shot, and at that time the President bent over, and Governor Connally turned around . . . . [W]hen President Kennedy straightened back up in the car the bullet [hit] him in the head, the one that killed him and it seemed like his head exploded, and I was splattered with blood and brain.

When asked about the direction of the shots, Hargis replied:

> Well, at the time it sounded like the shots were right next to me. There wasn't any way in the world I could tell where they were coming from, but at the time there was something in my head that said that they probably could have been coming from the railroad overpass, because I thought since I had got splattered. . . . I had a feeling that it might have been from the Texas Book Depository, and these two places was [sic] the primary place that could have been shot from.

Hargis also testified that he remembered seeing a man, accompanied by a woman and holding a child, fall to the ground at the base of the grassy knoll and cover the child. From photographs of the scene that showed them lying on the ground, the couple was identified as William and Gale Newman. William Newman told the sheriff's office on November 22, 1963, that he was standing at the edge of the curb on Elm Street when there was a sudden loud noise, like a firecracker. The President jumped in his seat. Newman said he was looking right at the President when he was hit in the head by another shot. He said that he and his wife "fell down on the grass as it seemed that we were in [the] direct path of fire." Newman amplified his point:

> I thought the shot had come from the garden directly behind me that was on an elevation from where I was . . . on the curb. I do not recall looking toward the Texas School Book Depository. I looked back in the vicinity of the garden.

We did not contact Hargis, who was ill at the time of our investigation, but we did talk to the Newmans, who said that they heard three, possibly four, shots. The first two shots sounded like firecrackers; they did not react to them. But then they saw the President react and Governor Connally start to bleed. Next, they heard a loud "boom," and the President's head exploded. They also heard Mrs. Kennedy say, "Oh, my God, no! They've shot Jack!" Fearing that they were in the line of fire and positive the third shot had come from behind them, they dropped to the ground (Newman saw combat in the Korean War). If all the shots came from the Book Depository, they asked rhetorically, why did they not drop to the ground when they heard the first two?

Abraham Zapruder was standing with his eight-millimeter motion-picture camera on a concrete abutment on the grassy knoll. On July 22, 1964, in an emotional deposition (he actually broke down and cried), he told the Warren Commission he thought he heard two, perhaps three, shots. He was not sure of the number. It was, he said, too upsetting. He said that he believed that one shot "came from right behind" him, but he added, "[I]t could [have] come from anywhere. . . ." He did, however, distinguish between the shots. The first was like "a backfire," but the other, assuming there were only two, had "an echo" that gave him "a sound all over." There was, he said, a great deal of "reverberation," from the other shot. We were unable to interview Zapruder, because he died before our investigation got under way.

Secret Service Agent Paul E. Landis was riding on the right running board of the follow-up car, a big armored convertible that carried eight bodyguards. In a statement he wrote a week after the assassination, Landis said that the first shot sounded like the report of a high-powered rifle from behind, over his right shoulder. He was not certain about the second shot, but his "reaction . . . was that the shot came from somewhere toward the front, right-hand side of the road." Landis confirmed to us that his written statement represented his best recollection at the time; that it was not based on anything he had heard from other agents or had read in the newspapers; and that, yes, he understood the implication of writing that shots had come from two directions. Still, based on the different character of the sounds, he was able to distinguish the directions of the shots.

S. M. Holland, a railroad supervisor, was inspecting signals along the tracks that crossed the triple underpass, when he stopped to watch the presidential motorcade. He heard four shots, he told the Warren Commission in a deposition on April 8, 1964. After the first shot Governor Connally turned around. Then another shot, and both the President and the governor were hit. The first two shots had come from the upper part of Elm Street. Then two more shots — they were close together, and the first of them, the third of the volley, was not as loud as the others. It apparently caused a puff of smoke to curl from the trees along the picket fence on the grassy knoll, which was to Holland's left. Down on Elm Street, in the follow-up convertible, a man stood up. He was holding an automatic rifle. (Holland's testimony about a Secret Service agent holding a weapon was confirmed by photographs.) Holland ran, he told the Warren Commission, to the end of the overpass and around the picket fence, but all he could see were rows of automobiles parked in a lot. When he reached the corner of the fence where he had seen the smoke, a number of policemen were already there. He helped them look for empty shells. (None was found.) He remembered that there was a station wagon backed up to the fence and that there was a spot, about three feet by two feet, that looked to him like somebody had been standing there for a long time. (It had been raining earlier that day.) There were about a hundred foot tracks on the spot, and there was mud up on the bumper of the station wagon, as if someone had cleaned his foot or had stood up on the bumper to look over the fence. (We were unable to take Holland's testimony, since he had died, but Billings interviewed him in December 1966, while on assignment for *Life*. Billings found Holland to be sincere and his story to be credible.)

One of the first policemen to run to the area behind the picket fence was Patrolman J. M. Smith, who had been directing traffic on the eastern side of Houston Street, where Elm crosses Houston. He gave the Commission a deposition on July 23, 1964. His back, he said, was to the Texas School Book Depository when he heard the shots, and he had no idea where they came from because of the echo effect. A woman came up to him and screamed, "They are shooting the President from the bushes," so he immediately ran down the street in front of the Book Depository, checking the bushes and the cars in the parking lot. When he reached the area behind the picket fence, he said, he encountered a Secret Service agent:

> I felt awfully silly, but after the shot and this woman, I pulled my pistol from my holster and I thought, this is silly, I don't know who I am looking for, and I put it back. Just as I did, he showed me that he was a Secret Service agent. . . . [H]e saw me coming with my pistol and right away he showed me who he was.

(We checked out Smith's story about a Secret Service agent behind the fence; none was in the area *at any time* that day.)

Lee E. Bower, a railroad workman stationed in a glass-walled fourteen-foot tower about fifty yards north and west of the Book Depository, gave the Warren Commission a deposition on April 2, 1964. He said there were several unfamiliar automobiles in the parking lot near his tower just before the shooting. He noticed them, he said, because he recognized the cars that were parked in the lot regularly. One of the unfamiliar ones was a blue and white 1959 Oldsmobile station wagon; another was a 1961 or 1962 Impala. Both were dirty and had out-of-state license plates — white background with black numbers — and both had single, white male occupants. (We were unable to talk to Bower, for he, too, was deceased.)

Scientific Analysis

As had the Warren Commission, we recognized that human testimony labored under "the difficulty of accurate perception," so we sought to base our conclusions, wherever possible, on physical evidence that could be subjected to scientific tests: the autopsy X-rays and photographs, weapons, bullet fragments, cartridge casings, photographs and motion picture film, fingerprints and handwriting samples. By and large, the "hard" evidence available to us had been examined already by the Warren Commission, so we could do little more than double check the results of the 1964 investigation, although we were able to do some sophisticated computer enhancement work on the photographs, using techniques not available in 1964. There was, however, one significant exception, a Dictabelt and tape, which were brought to our attention at a conference of Warren Commission critics that we convened in Washington on September 17, 1977.

We had substantial misgivings about the conference. While many of the critics were motivated by honest doubts, there were some who had played on the emotions of a dispirited American public, writing books or articles for profit, with scant regard for the truth, and we were reluctant to dignify that kind of conduct, even by implication. We knew, too, that our dealings with the critics could not be on a two-way street. We were willing to listen to their theories attentively, though skeptically, and we were anxious to receive hard facts and any likely leads; but we had nothing to give in return, since it was our strict policy to divulge nothing about the investigation while it was in progress.

We sat with the critics for two days at the Committee offices in House Annex Number Two (an FBI building originally), recording the conference for future reference. Among those we invited was Mary Ferrell, a Dallas woman, who had tirelessly devoted much of her life to learning all she could about the assassination. The first day of the meeting lasted from 9:30 A.M. until 4:30 P.M. Just as we were about to break up, Mrs. Ferrell said, almost as an afterthought, "I wanted to drop one thing in." She went on to say that she had obtained a copy of the radio dispatch tapes made by the Dallas Police Department on November 22, 1963. Evidently, a police motorcycle in Dealey Plaza had had its transmit button depressed during the time of the assassination. Mrs. Ferrell said that she and another critic, Gary Shaw, had taken the tape to Larry Darkel, the program director of Radio Station KFJZ in Fort Worth, and Darkel thought he could detect seven shots. Mary Ferrell's offhand remark was the beginning of a process that would reverse the verdict of history.

We immediately obtained Mrs. Ferrell's dispatch tape, and we contacted the Acoustical Society of America to ask for recommendations of the top scientists or firms in the field. Of the five we selected initially, Bolt, Beranek, and Newman, Inc., of Cambridge, Massachusetts, was at the top of the list. Dr. Richard Bolt, a founder of BBN, had been the chairman of an acoustics panel appointed by Judge John J. Sirica to examine the mysterious eighteen-minute gap on a tape in the Watergate case. The firm had also been engaged by the Department of Justice to analyze a tape made during the shooting of the Kent State University students by Ohio National Guardsmen in 1970.

A senior staff attorney, John Hornbeck, went to Cambridge on October 5, 1977, to speak with the BBN people, and they said they thought that if they were given "a good enough" tape, recorded at the time of the assassination, they could resolve a number of the questions concerning the number of gunshots, the intervals between them, and their direction. In a meeting with BBN in Washington on October 9, 1977, the outlines of the project were developed: if we could obtain a tape, they would "clean up" the extraneous noise and convert the sound on the tape into a graph showing loudness and time. Next, it would be necessary to recreate the sounds of the shots in Dealey Plaza, making a test tape to see if it matched the original tape. We would be, the scientists said, looking for, and trying to match, "shapes of sound" similar to shapes of fingerprints.

Mary Ferrell's copy of the dispatch tape was not good enough for the BBN scientists, so we assigned Jack Moriarty, a resourceful Committee investigator who had been a District of Columbia homicide detective, to continue the search in Dallas. He located Paul McCaghren, a retired senior officer in the Dallas Police Department. McCaghren told Moriarty on February 11, 1978, that Police Chief Jesse E. Curry had put together a group of four or five lieutenants following the Kennedy assassination to look into the shooting of officer J. D. Tippit and the security breakdown that had enabled Jack Ruby to gain entry into the basement of police headquarters. Following the investigation the reports and other materials it had produced were gathered together and given to Chief Curry. In 1969 Chief Charles Batchelor found them in a cabinet and turned them over to McCaghren, who was then director of the Intelligence Division. McCaghren had kept them at the department until 1971, at which time the Ford Foundation sent a team to Dallas in preparation for a possible grant for the department. McCaghren, not trusting the Ford Foundation people, removed the files to his home, where he had them at the time he met with Moriarty. They were contained in a small box, two and a half by one and a half feet, twelve inches deep; it was two-thirds full of file folders and other material, including a Dictabelt and a tape of KKB-364, Channel One, the Dallas Police Department dispatcher, covering from 10 A.M. to 2:15 P.M. on November 22, 1963. They were logged in as JFK 007415 in the Committee files.

Arrangements were made for the BBN scientists to analyze the belt and tape. After a quick look, James Barger, the firm's chief scientist, a tall, thin perfectionist with an applied physics Ph.D. from Harvard, spoke in his characteristic measured manner. He was not hopeful about the prospects of recovering anything from the tape. (We had decided to work with the tape because it was in better shape than the belt.) Dr. Barger recognized, however, that it was as important to us to find nothing on the tape as it was to find any set number of gunshots. He suggested, therefore, that after he had made an effort to clean it up, he would conduct a series of tests that would prove that there were no gunshots recorded on it. If that proved to be the case, it obviously would not be necessary to do the acoustical reconstruction in Dallas, and the Committee would be saved both time and expense. We committed $40,000 to the project, reserving another $20,000, just in case.

In March the Committee was refunded for the year. We had asked for $3 million, noting that certain scientific projects might cost more and require a supplemental appropriation. The House Administration Committee, however, cut us to $2.5 million. The reduced budget forced us to face unattractive alternatives: it was enough to keep the full staff through December, but not travel; it was also enough to keep the full staff through July and still travel, but then, to make it to the end of the year, we would have to cut the staff in half, which would effectively shut down both the Kennedy and the King investigations. We decided to take the risk. If we got a break in either case before the end of July, we could get more funds; if not, no one would really care if we shut down.

On July 13, at 10 A.M., we met with the Committee to review our funding needs. There had been a break on the King side; we had developed evidence of a conspiracy. We had a chance, therefore, to get additional funds, and we needed them. Even though we had cut thirty people from the staff, it was still going to be necessary to seek new funding, in the amount of $790,000, if the Committee was to hold hearings and write a final report. Without the supplemental appropriation, we would run out of money on September 15, which would be right in the middle of public hearings in the Kennedy investigation. The Committee agreed at the July 13 meeting to seek the additional funds. That same day, at 1:55 P.M., Barger called from Cambridge. He said he was fully aware of the significance of what he was about to say; in fact, he even felt a little sick to his stomach, for he found himself in the embarrassing position of being unable to prove that nothing had been recorded on the tape. Further, he had not only found sounds on the tape that appeared to be recorded gunfire, but — and this was what troubled him — he had found more shots than the three that the Warren Commission had thought had been fired. Barger's interim report arrived the next day. His attention had been directed to the segment of the tape lasting from 12:28 to 12:33 P.M., since the President had been shot at about 12:30. A cursory examination had revealed no identifiable sounds of gunfire, but Barger could hear sounds that were apparently transmitted by the radio of a police motorcycle with its microphone talk button stuck in the "on" position. Then, when the segment of the tape was studied after it had been filtered to eliminate the sound of the running motorcycle, there were three groups of sounds, two of which seemingly had subgroups, which merited closer analysis. Barger concluded that each of the groups and subgroups of closely spaced impulses on the tape could have been caused by the sound of a bullet and its echoes, although the sound of a bullet and its echoes could only be reliably identified by recreating it in the same environment. We had, in short, three to five shots, and the only way we were going to be able to find out precisely how many and from where they had been fired was to go to Dealey Plaza and reconstruct the sounds of the assassination.

The impact on the staff and the Committee was dramatic. Curiously, some staff members, who had argued vigorously for conspiracy, now recoiled; they were troubled. Could it really be? It was not something merely to argue or speculate about anymore; it looked like we were really going to prove it. Could the country actually have been wrong all these years? Others were elated, and they began to greet each other in the hall with a five-finger salute and a smile. The acoustics were dubbed "Blakey's Problem." More than one staffer was heard to say, "Let's see if the professor can talk his way out of this one." The integrity of the "main office" would now be put to the test.

Barger had called on a Thursday afternoon. Chairman Stokes asked us to arrange to have him come to Washington for an extensive briefing of the Committee on the following Monday and Tuesday. He brought the rolls of paper on which the tape had been turned into a graph that extended for more than twenty-three feet. The key segments were spread out on the green felt-covered tables in a meeting room just off the House floor in the Capitol. It was an exciting but sobering meeting, particularly for Chairman Stokes and Subcommittee Chairman Preyer. Stokes had been a trial lawyer in Cleveland; Preyer, a federal judge in North Carolina. They each looked at the evidence in front of them, but they saw more than the rolls of paper. They knew then, as we knew, that we were pulling on a piece of thread from an intricate tapestry that was the Kennedy assassination, as it had been understood since 1964. If we pulled hard enough, it might all unravel.

The Acoustical Reconstruction

We made plans for the Dallas reconstruction. More was involved than getting permission from the Dallas authorities, which went very smoothly. "I'll do anything you want," Dallas Police Chief Con Byrd said. "If you want us to reenact it down to the minute, [I'll] stop traffic on a Friday afternoon, rope it off — that's how we will do [it]." We appreciated his offer but knew that the tests did not need to be that realistic to be scientifically valid. Besides, we were concerned about safety, as well as avoiding unseemly sensationalism. We were particularly concerned about the sensibilities of the Kennedy family; Chairman Stokes wanted Senator Edward M. Kennedy briefed immediately. (It was not our first contact with the family. In preparing our presentation of the autopsy evidence, we had worked closely with Burke Marshall, who was in charge of the Civil Rights Division under Attorney General Robert F. Kennedy. He had since joined the faculty of the Yale Law School but still represented the Kennedy family.) It seemed only appropriate that the senator learn the details of the acoustics study in advance, which he did when we met with him on August 2 in his Capitol office. Kennedy was visibly shaken. "That brings it all up again," he said. He wanted to know if we were sure that the Dallas trip was necessary. Had we gotten a second opinion? He was assured that everything was being done in a step-by-step, well-planned way. As for the second opinion, we had, in fact, gone back to the Acoustical Society of America, once we had received Barger's interim report, for recommendations of experts who might review the BBN study. From this list, we chose Mark Weiss, a professor of computer science at Queens College, City University of New York (Weiss, like Richard Bolt of BBN, had served on Judge Sirica's expert panel in the Watergate case) and his assistant, Ernest Aschkenasy. Weiss and Aschkenasy studied the work that BBN had done, including the proposed reconstruction, both theoretically and practically. They told us we had no choice; it was necessary to go to Dallas. We made the decision to go ahead, committing our cash reserve of $20,888 — and began preparations for the reconstruction, which we had scheduled for Sunday, August 20.

Our supplemental budget hearing before the House Administration Committee came on August 8 and 9. We outlined to a skeptical panel what we had done, what we had learned, and what we needed to do. The Committee seemed ready to support us by the end of the first day's session, but then we were dealt a setback in the King case. At the urging of James Earl Ray's lawyer, Mark Lane, a witness in St. Louis had accused the Committee of surreptitious tape recording (which was in violation of our own rules) and illegal spying on the Ray family, charges that subsequently proved to be without foundation. Nevertheless, the Administration Committee abruptly changed its mind and postponed consideration of our request for supplemental funds until after the August recess. We were stunned. All of our work was now put in jeopardy by a Mark Lane press conference, right when it seemed as if we were turning a corner.

To add to our trouble, what Chairman Stokes feared might happen, did: the results of the acoustics study were all over the newspapers right after our briefing of the Administration Committee. On August 9 *The Dallas Morning News* headlined, "JFK Report Backs 2-Gun Theory." The story that followed was a little more accurate, and it contained a note of caution: "Blakey is warning everyone that it could still fall through somehow." Nevertheless, the startling possibility of too many shots, resting on a scientific test, was out. But there was a positive aspect of the publicity; it was beginning to stir excitement. Jack Moriarty, while meeting with the range master at the Dallas police shooting range in an effort to set up the reconstruction, for example, found himself surrounded by policemen, who all joined in an enthusiastic discussion of the building of sandbag traps to receive the gunfire.

Barger had given us another puzzle to ponder. He had found on the tape the eerie sound of what appeared to be a bell, faintly tolling, right after the President was shot. He told us that locating that bell would help him pinpoint the position of the motorcycle with the stuck mike. We got aerial maps of Dallas and then contacted every person within miles of Dealey Plaza who might be associated with bells — bell manufacturers, pastors, priests, but we could not find it. It was as ghostly as it was eerie. We concluded that the sound of the bell had been picked up, not by the stuck mike on the motorcycle, but by a microphone in some other part of Dallas, whose stronger signal had captured the dispatcher's receiver. We were satisfied with that answer, but it had been a frustrating search.

Every effort was being made to identify the motorcycle officer whose radio had been transmitting. We believed he had been riding escort, so we secured a list of motorcade assignments and talked to the officers named on the list. None recalled that his mike switch had stuck, though most acknowledged that this malfunction was common on the radios mounted on the Harley Davidson motorcycles in use in 1963. We also talked to the chief dispatcher, Gerald D. Henslee, who recalled the jamming caused by a stuck mike on Channel One. He thought, he said, that the transmitter in question was "mounted on a two-wheeler." He said that on the last segment of the transmission he could hear sirens, so he concluded that the mike was mounted on an "escort traveling at high speed on Stemmons Highway" on the way to Parkland Hospital.

As we still had not identified the officer in question by August 20, we had to go ahead with the experiment without a fixed position for the motorcycle. A crowd started to gather in the Dealey Plaza area at about 5:30 A.M. The police had announced that no one would be permitted in the area, so only about 200 people showed up — mostly media representatives, but also assassination buffs, amateur photographers, night-shift taxi drivers, and tourists. The official contingent was comprised of four Committee staffers, seven acoustical experts, one photographic consultant and thirty-three Dallas police officers. The day started off cool, around 73 degrees, but it climbed to 90 by noon, and the sun was shining. The weatherman was on our side.

The position of the radio that was transmitting at the moment of the assassination was crucial to achieving our objective, which was to identify the number, time interval, and origin of the shots. But we would have to approximate its location; we would have to look for the radio the hard way. It could have been anywhere in Dealey Plaza — or somewhere else altogether. Barger constructed a test designed to locate it. Microphones were placed on tripods at eighteen-foot intervals along the last two blocks of the motorcade route along Houston and Elm. Since the roadway was about forty feet wide, the transmitting microphone, assuming it was on an escort motorcycle, would have to have been not more than eighteen feet from its center. We could not, except by sheer luck, place our microphones exactly along the path of the motorcycle, but we knew we would not be more than eighteen feet from it at any given time. Shots would be fired from the sixth-floor southeast window of the Texas School Book Depository and from the grassy knoll near the corner of the picket fence, the sources of gunfire, according to most on-the-scene witnesses. A rifle like the one Lee Harvey Oswald allegedly had used would be fired from the Book Depository window, and a rifle and a pistol would be fired from the grassy knoll, since it was not known what type of weapon, if any, had been fired from there. The selection of the four target locations along the motorcade route was based on a study of the Zapruder film and a preliminary analysis of the tape. There had been no major structural changes in the Plaza since 1963, so the test firing would produce an acoustical replica of the 1963 tape, and we would get our chance to match the "sound fingerprints." Because of the uncertainty of the location of the motorcycle microphone, there would, however, be a measure of uncertainty in our results; it would amount to plus or minus eighteen feet. We had to live with it.

For five hours, Barger, his staff and ours, and the Dallas police orchestrated a slow drum roll of fifty-seven gunshots that broke the still of the morning, each slamming harmlessly into sandbags and echoing into an array of microphones spotted along the path of the 1963 motorcade. Jerry Compton fired from the Book Depository window, kneeling as Oswald reportedly had, and Clint L. Metcalf shot from the grassy knoll. Neither marksman used a telescopic sight. The open iron sights were adequate, they said, and for safety purposes they wanted to be able to see all around the target. Barger and his assistants had covered the pavement with hundreds of feet of cable leading from the microphones to a rented trailer filled with sensitive electronic equipment. The test took about two-and-a-half hours longer than expected, but the marksmen and the scientists had worked well together.

Crowd reaction to the tests actually addressed the assassination itself. Tony Piccola, a night security guard, said, "I always felt Oswald acted alone — but with Castro in mind." John Ruiz, a steelworker from Crown Point, Indiana, attending a Veterans of Foreign Wars convention, commented, "I've never really accepted the idea that Oswald was alone." Mrs. Geraldine Walker, a cabdriver just off work, said, "I think Oswald was killed to keep him from talking. There was a lot he could have told us." Another conventioneer, Milo Hazen, from Nebraska, said, "I don't see why they keep fiddling with it. They've solved all they'll ever solve. . . ." But a Venezuelan military officer, touring Dallas with his family, agreed that the test was valuable. "It is very important for us," he said in Spanish, "to know what happened. This . . . is important."

On August 25, 1978, Dan Sullivan, the BBN accounting officer, called. They were, he said, running into a cost overrun; it might be as much as $20,000. We told him we had no additional money; we had committed every cent through September 15, when our funds would run out. Subsequently, the firm agreed that because of the "national importance" of the project, they would continue the work. We were duly grateful.

On August 30, 1978, at 4:40 in the afternoon, Barger called to say they had found four shots, the third of which had come from the grassy knoll. He would fill us in with the details when he came to testify at a Committee public hearing, which was scheduled for September 11. When did we want him to come down? We suggested he come the day before he was to testify. The Sunday evening he arrived, as we reviewed his testimony in detail, he looked as if the whole world rested on his shoulders. Congressman Floyd J. Fithian of Indiana, who was scheduled to carry the main burden of questioning for the Committee, stayed with Barger late into the night, going over the questions. On Monday Barger was the lead-off witness, and his testimony would consume most of the day. Chairman Stokes, in an opening statement, tried to put what he expected Barger to say in context: he noted that the evidence presented the previous week had "tended to support . . . the Warren Commission, which had concluded that Lee Harvey Oswald was the lone assassin of the President." Now we were coming to the number, direction, and timing of the shots — evidence, Stokes suggested, that "would be troubling to some persons." But he warned that it was too early to draw "sensational conclusions" and that "final resolution of the questions . . . raised by . . . [the] evidence [would have to] . . . await the conclusion of our hearings and the submission of our final report. . . ." The caution was unnecessary. Barger turned out to be not very persuasive. All of the virtues that made him a fine scientist worked against him as a witness. He was too precise. His answers were too qualified. The Committee, the audience, and the press wanted clear-cut answers. When Barger told them the truth, including the elements of uncertainty, the impact of his testimony was lost.

Congressman Robert W. Edgar of Pennsylvania spoke for most of the people in the hearing room when he asked Barger how he might explain the acoustics evidence to his son, a seventh grader. Barger made a valiant effort to state his findings in simple language. "There was," he said, "by a considerable measure of chance, a motorcycle in the motorcade with its radio in an operating condition, but with the motorcycle policeman not speaking into it. . . . Over that radio was [heard] . . . sounds, including the motorcycle, including other radios, and including the possibility of the sounds of the assassination of the President. What you were observing today," Barger continued, "was the description of a test that was made on that tape to see if it was statistically likely to have contained the sounds of gunfire. You found out that it was possible . . . to locate the position of the motorcycle with a good deal of confidence. . . . It turned out that the motorcycle was about ten feet short of the [Houston and Elm] corner at the approximate time of the first gunfire. . . . You found out also that the motorcycle was in a position, . . . when the first shot was heard, that corresponded to the limousine being . . .

where it was at approximately the time of the first shot." Barger, therefore, was generally confident that the location of the motorcycle had been determined and that a series of shots had been correctly detected. "There is less confidence in questions of increasing detail," he cautioned.

Barger got into difficulty by attempting to quantify for the Committee a measure of confidence in the acoustical results: the degree of that measure of confidence was directly related to the uncertainty that had resulted from the eighteen-foot spacing of the microphones. The determination of the number, time interval, and origin — or direction — of the shots had been based on approximate matches of impulse patterns produced by the 1963 tape and the tape of the 1978 reconstruction. (Barger had finished going over his data shortly before his testimony. He had done 2,592 calculations, involving 432 combinations of rifle shots and microphone locations. He did not complete the task until September 6, although he had been able to give us his preliminary results on August 30.) Barger had found three close matches for shot number one from the Book Depository; three close matches for shot number two from the Book Depository; one close match for shot number three from the grassy knoll; and two close matches for shot number four from the Book Depository. From the way the matches lined up with the probable path of the motorcycle, however, it was possible to predict that any one of them had a 50–50 chance of being wrong. Statistically, that broke into an 87.5 percent chance (50–50 over three) of being right on shots one and two; a 75 percent chance (50–50 over two) of being right on shot number four; and only a 50 percent chance (50–50 over one) of being right on shot number three. Consequently, the answer to the crucial question of the third shot from the grassy knoll had but a 50–50 chance of being right — the flip of a coin.

Barger had located the motorcycle in Dealey Plaza moving at about eleven miles per hour about 120 feet behind the presidential limousine on the left-hand side of the street. He had determined the number, timing, and direction of the shots. But the uncertainty factor of plus or minus eighteen feet that had been built into the Dealey Plaza reconstruction by the placing of the microphones had left the Committee in doubt about the question that mattered most: had there been a shot from the grassy knoll? By this time, we could not help feeling competitive and thinking in terms of winning or losing. We had been led by the evidence to date to suspect an event that we had come to want to prove. Using the inevitable football analogy (inevitable, certainly, if you had gone to Notre Dame, as Blakey had), we had reached the goal line, owing to Barger's brilliant effort, but we had not scored.

A Refined Analysis

Before the sun had set on September 11, 1978, we were mapping our strategy. It was obvious what we had to do. We had to figure out how to reduce the uncertainty factor, for it would be irresponsible to allow the question of the nature of the President's death — the question of con-spiracy — to turn on what amounted to the toss of a referee's coin. We knew it would help enormously if we could prove, independent of the acoustics project, that there had been a motorcycle where Barger's tests put it. We had reviewed film clips and photographs prior to Barger's ap-pearance, but none had been taken at the time and place we expected to find the motorcycle in question. We decided to keep looking, and we also placed a call to Mark Weiss and Ernest Aschkenasy and asked if they would take a fresh look at Barger's work. Up to this point, Weiss and Aschkenasy had directed their attention to the theoretical sound-ness of the Barger project. When asked if they could go further, they were not at all optimistic that anything more could be extracted from the data. Nevertheless, after consulting with Barger, Weiss and Asch-kenasy conceived a mathematical extension of the BBN analysis. Be-cause an approximate position of the motorcycle had been established, it might be possible, they reasoned, to assume that the microphone and a shooter were in certain locations, and then test mathematically to see if those locations would produce "sound fingerprints" that corre-sponded to the 1963 tape. The "sound fingerprints" would be com-posed of the time delays between the arrival at the microphone of the sound of a muzzle blast and the arrival of echoes created by the major structures, or acoustical features, in Dealey Plaza. Given our tight deadline, Weiss and Aschkenasy were not hopeful that much could be accomplished, but they agreed to try. Each location for the microphone and a shooter would have to be tested by trial and error, with reference to twenty-two major acoustical features that had been identified. Since the distances were known, and the speed of sound at a particular air temperature was constant, the calculations were possible, albeit time-consuming. No one was more surprised with the results of their efforts than Weiss and Aschkenasy themselves. As they put it when it was their turn to testify before the Committee, the numbers just "would not go away." Shot number three from the grassy knoll was there, no doubt about it, and they were able to locate the motorcycle microphone along the eleven-mile-per-hour path that Barger had charted with impressive precision, reducing the margin of error to plus or minus one and a half feet. They also fixed the position of the gunman behind the picket fence on the grassy knoll to within plus or minus five feet. Weiss and Asch-kenasy told us they were willing to testify, to a 95 percent degree of con-fidence, that a shot had been fired from behind the picket fence.

Weiss and Aschkenasy also learned more about the motorcycle. The strength of the echoes indicated that its microphone was located on the left side and was facing downward. In addition, they could tell that the motorcycle had a windshield that also acted as a "soundshield." When the first two shots were fired from the Book Depository — as the motorcycle was heading north on Houston Street — the windshield was in-between the shooter and the microphone. When the third shot was fired from the grassy knoll — as the motorcycle was proceeding west on Elm Street — the windshield again was in-between the shooter and the microphone. But when the fourth shot was fired from the Book Depository — with the motorcycle still moving west on Elm — the windshield no longer was in-between the shooter and the microphone, and the sound graphs showed the sound of the shot traveling directly to the microphone.

We asked Barger to review the work of Weiss and Aschkenasy. Was it valid? Did it eliminate some of his uncertainty? Barger reported that he would be willing to testify with Weiss and Aschkenasy that there was, in fact, a 95 percent degree of certainty of a shot from behind the fence on the grassy knoll.

We presented Weiss and Aschkenasy, as well as Barger, to the Committee in an executive briefing on December 18, 1978. We had planned to review a draft of the final report that had been prepared shortly after Barger's testimony on September 11. The draft was based on our assumption that the scientific evidence could not be made more definite: it was our only option, so it seemed at the time, since the Committee was due to go out of existence at the end of the year. As it turned out, the day and evening were largely spent reviewing the dramatic turn of events. Most of us had seen it coming, but it was no less startling when it happened. The Committee members took turns questioning the scientists. There was nothing complicated about the experimental process (Weiss testified that the only tools required were a survey map, a long ruler, a hand calculator, and an oscilloscope), and there was nothing arcane about the acoustical principles from which the proof of the four shots had been derived. Nevertheless, Congressman Harold S. Sawyer had trouble grasping it, and he raised a number of questions. Finally, he conceded, "Well, I do understand it now. . . ." Barger summed up the feelings of the scientists when he commented toward the end of the meeting:

The result . . . [was] for me quite a revelation . . . . I proved to myself beyond a reasonable doubt that there was gunfire on that tape when my scientific hypothesis . . . [was] that there was not. . . . I personally never had . . . [a] situation . . . [so] completely reversed so clearly by scientific tests. . . .

For nearly a year and a half, the Committee members had held firm on the no-leak policy, but Congressman Sawyer, on a radio program on December 20, 1978, in Grand Rapids, Michigan (Sawyer was from the Fifth District of Michigan, which for twenty-five years was represented by Gerald R. Ford), inexplicably broke silence, noting he was "probably in hot water" for disclosing the contents of an executive briefing. He said we were 95 percent sure of the third shot from the grassy knoll, and he added: "I don't know how in the name of heaven we are going to handle this. . . ."

The news spread quickly. *The Washington Post* headlined across the top of page one the next morning: "JFK Panel Gets Evidence of Conspiracy." *The Washington Star* followed that afternoon: "Hearing Set on New JFK Evidence." Both papers missed a key point. We had had the evidence since July. What we now had done was develop a higher level of confidence in that evidence. Editorials, too, appeared. The *Post* called for "objective analysis." The *Star* wondered if there could be "undetected flaws in the esoteric science." *The Philadelphia Inquirer* noted that the finding had come as the Committee "was about to close up shop," and commented that the evidence was "unfortunate" in its "timing," but that was not to the "discredit of the Committee." The *Inquirer* called for a continuation of the probe, which was out of the question. It could have been worse. As Congressman Fithian put it, "Better a week before the end than a week after . . . !"

There was work yet to do. We needed to confirm the existence of a motorcycle in the position the scientists had placed it. From the list of motorcycle assignments, we had determined the most likely candidate to be Officer H. B. McLain, who was riding motorcycle 352 to the left rear of the presidential limousine. We sought photographic substantiation. We located a photo of a police motorcycle parked in front of the Book Depository, but its microphone was mounted on the right side. Eventually, we found several film clips which, when put together, showed motorcycle 352 going up Main Street and then turning down Houston Street at the right time. McLain was our man. We were across the goal line. (Later, after the Committee had completed its hearings, and it was too late to introduce new evidence, we located photographs of McLain rounding the corner of Houston and Elm at the precise time the acoustical analysis put him there.)

The Proof of Conspiracy

On Friday, December 29, 1978, the Committee met in a crowded caucus room of the Cannon House Office Building for its final public hearing, which was covered live by television. We sensed an atmosphere of expectation. First, we reviewed the witness testimony as to the number, interval, and origin of the shots that the Warren Commission had rejected as "not credible." We then called, in turn, Weiss and Aschkenasy, H. B. McLain (still a Dallas police officer), and Barger.

In clear and forceful terms, Weiss and Aschkenasy reviewed their work. They had become involved at first only to review Barger's proposed test in Dallas in August. After Barger's September testimony, they had been asked to try to move the uncertainty off center "either way." They started their work in October and finished in late December. The result was "a probability of 95 percent or better [that] there was indeed a shot fired from the grassy knoll." They were, they said, able to place the shooter within a five-foot "circumference." They could pinpoint the location of the microphone to within a foot and a half. They knew that the weapon had fired a supersonic bullet, since a shock wave had preceded the sound of the muzzle blast (they could detect both phenomena on the tape). The weapon could have been a rifle or a pistol, since either could fire supersonic ammunition. They explained how they knew the microphone had been shielded at various points by the windshield of the motorcycle. In their calculations, they had made allowances for possible small error on the scale map they had used (less than one foot); air-temperature and humidity variances; and the characteristics of the type of radio equipment used by the Dallas police in 1963. They had double-checked their calculations, and, yes, they were satisfied with their conclusions "beyond a reasonable doubt." In addition, the scientific principles they had employed were little more than "high school physics and geometry." Anyone who had heard an echo could understand what was involved. No, the sound could not have been a motorcycle backfire since it was preceded by the supersonic shock wave. In any event, there was no motorcycle behind the picket fence. Obviously, the bell tolling on the tape had come from somewhere other than Dealey Plaza. Could the sound of the grassy knoll shot also have come from a different area? Only if the other area were an exact acoustical replica of Dealey Plaza, and shots had been fired there too. "If somebody were to tell me that the motorcycle was not in Dealey Plaza," Aschkenasy noted, "[that] he was transmitting from some other location, . . . I would ask to be told where that location is, . . . I would go there, and, . . . I would expect to find a replica of Dealey Plaza. . . ." The shot had not been fired up in the air, they said, but at the presidential limousine. No, the sound of the grassy knoll shot could not have been an acoustical mirage. The distance was too short, and the sequence of echoes was inconsistent with a mirage. The conclusion was, they said, inescapable; it was not a matter of interpretation; there "didn't seem to be any way to make those numbers go away, no matter how hard . . . [they] tried."

Officer McLain appeared next. He recognized himself on his motorcycle in the photographs showing him at the right time and place. But he
said that he had heard only one shot. (He had said two in an earlier interview.) His radio was normally on Channel One, but he had no memory of using it that day. McLain could not testify that it was his
microphone that had stuck because he did not remember, but it was a
common problem with his equipment. After the shots were fired, the
presidential limousine took off for the hospital. McLain left too, but he
did not catch the limousine until it was on Stemmons Freeway. (Back in
Dallas after the hearing, McLain told a CBS newsman that he believed it
was not his microphone that had recorded the sounds. He cited the
sound of sirens on the tape, saying be believed he had turned his siren
on while he was still in Dealey Plaza. Ultimately, the Committee
decided that the tape, not McLain's memory, was correct.)

Barger rounded out the testimony for the day. He told how the pattern of sound (muzzle blast and echo) received by the microphone for
each rifle location was "unique." He described how he was able to
determine that the microphone was to the left and to the rear of the
presidential limousine, where the photographs ultimately placed
McLain. He explained the sound of the sirens on the tape (that had
troubled McLain). While McLain's motorcycle was running, his radio
microphone could not pick up any siren more than three hundred feet
away. The evidence indicated that McLain did not turn on his siren
right away, and he did not catch up with the other vehicles in the motorcade, whose sirens were sounding, until he reached Stemmons Freeway. (The necessary implication of Barger's testimony was that if
McLain remembered that he had turned on his siren immediately, the
tape indicated he was mistaken.) Barger noted that there was no evidence on the tape of a supersonic shock wave accompanying the first
two shots, even though the ballistic tests indicated Oswald's rifle fired
supersonic ammunition. This was so, he explained, because McLain's
motorcycle at the time of the first two shots was outside the area where
the shock wave would have been picked up by his microphone. At the
time of the third and fourth shots, McLain was in a position to have
picked up the shock waves, and they did appear on the tape. Barger
repeated his statistical analysis of the confidence level — 95 percent or
better — and then added, in plain language, that he was "quite confident" he had measured "gunshots."

We concluded the hearing by showing the Zapruder film with the
tape-recorded sounds of shots from the Barger reconstruction in August
1978 dubbed in at the points in time when they were fired on November
22, 1963. It was as if we had all been returned to Dealey Plaza to hear, as

well as see, the assassination. The effect was awesome. Our hearings had begun with Governor and Mrs. Connally testifying to what they remembered; our hearings ended with a demonstration of what modern science had proved. That night, after extended discussion, the Committee came to its historic conclusions. First, it reviewed the evidence of what had occurred on November 22, 1963, principally as it had been developed by our scientific projects in the fields of photography, forensic pathology and dentistry, ballistics, neutron activation analysis, and acoustics. The evidence wove a coherent and compelling scenario of the basic facts of the assassination.

The Assassination Reconstructed by Science

The President's limousine turned left from Houston Street onto Elm Street in front of the Texas School Book Depository at approximately 12:30 P.M. Central Standard Time. It was, according to the weather bureau, a clear and sunny day, about 65 degrees, with a light wind blowing. Forty-seven seconds later, a shot rang out from the window on the southeast corner of the sixth floor of the Book Depository. (The time and direction of the shots were fixed by the acoustics evidence.) The shot would have been heard in the limousine at frames 157–161 of the Zapruder film; it missed the limousine and its occupants. Three expended shell casings found on the sixth floor of the Book Depository were determined by a panel of ballistics experts to have been fired from a 6.5 millimeter Mannlicher-Carcano rifle, which was identified as belonging to Lee Harvey Oswald. At the time of the shot, according to the acoustics evidence, the weapon was 143 feet from the limousine. The radio on Officer H. B. McLain's motorcycle, which transmitted the sound of the shot to police headquarters where it was recorded, was located on Houston Street, approximately 215 feet north of the corner of Houston and Main. Three seconds earlier, McLain had slowed his motorcycle to ten miles per hour, preparing for the left turn onto Elm Street. An examination of the Zapruder film at frames 162–167 by a panel of photographic experts determined that Governor Connally, who had been looking to his left, began a rapid motion to his right, an action consistent with Connally's testimony that he was not hit by the first shot and that he turned to his right when he heard the shot. The Zapruder film also showed a young girl, who had been running on the grass on the south side of Elm Street, suddenly stop, turn sharply to the right and look up the street, indicating that she too had just heard a shot.

After a lapse of 1.6 seconds, at Zapruder frames 187–190, a second shot was fired from the sixth-floor window of the Book Depository. The leaves of an oak tree had obscured the view of the limousine from the window, but at Zapruder frame 186 there was a break in the foliage. The weapon was at this point 165 feet from the limousine. A panel of forensic pathologists made these determinations with respect to the second shot: it struck President Kennedy in the upper right part of his back and exited from his throat; it then hit Governor Connally in the back, entering just below his right armpit and exiting below the right nipple of his chest before it struck and shattered his right wrist and caused a superficial wound to his left thigh. Neutron activation analysis, a metal-matching process, established that the bullet that left fragments in Connally's wrist was the one found on Connally's stretcher at Parkland Hospital, the so-called pristine bullet. The ballistics panel linked this bullet to Oswald's rifle. It was determined from the photographic evidence and a trajectory analysis performed by a National Aeronautics and Space Administration engineer that President Kennedy's back and neck and Governor Connally's back, wrist, and thigh all were aligned with the course of the second shot from the Book Depository. While FBI tests with Oswald's rifle in 1964, using a telescopic sight to aim the weapon, indicated it could not be fired, reloaded, aimed, and fired again in less than 2.25 seconds, tests by the Committee showed that if the open sights were used, it could be fired, reloaded, pointed, aimed, and fired again in as little as 1.2 seconds.

Six seconds after the second shot, a third shot was fired from the grassy knoll by a weapon that fired a supersonic bullet. The shot would have been heard in the limousine at Zapruder frames 295–296. Since only one shot was fired from the knoll, there was no need to eject a shell casing, and none was found. According to the forensic pathology panel's analysis of autopsy X-rays and photographs (which were authenticated by the photography panel), the shot from the grassy knoll did not hit the President (nor was there evidence that it hit the limousine or any of its other occupants). The weapon fired from the grassy knoll was 111 feet from the limousine at the time of the shot.

Seven-tenths of a second after the third shot, a fourth shot was fired; it was the third shot fired from the sixth-floor window of the Book Depository. It would have been heard in the limousine at Zapruder frame 312, and the President's fatal head wound was recorded in Zapruder frame 313. The weapon was 266 feet from the limousine. The forensic pathology panel determined that the shot entered at the right rear of the President's head and exited from the right side of the head toward the front, causing a massive wound that was visible in the Zapruder film. Neutron activation analysis established that bullet fragments found in the front seat of the limousine were part of the bullet that struck the President in the head, and the ballistics panel linked these fragments to Oswald's rifle. From data supplied by the photographic panel and the forensic pathology panel, a trajectory was plotted from the wound back to the Book Depository.

The evidence convincingly established that Oswald was the President's assassin. It was his rifle that fired the fatal shot: his handwriting showed that he ordered it, although he used an alias; he was photographed with it by his wife, and he gave an autographed copy of the photograph to a friend; he left his palm print on the rifle, and his palm print and fingerprint on a carton that had been used to construct a sniper's nest, as well as on a paper bag that was found in the sniper's nest; and he left the rifle and his book-order clipboard within a few feet of each other on the sixth floor of the Texas School Book Depository — where he was seen by a fellow employee shortly before the assassination, and where he was identified as having been at the time of the assassination by at least one witness outside the building. (Others, although they could not positively identify Oswald, saw a young white male who fit Oswald's description in the sixth-floor window moments before the assassination.) Oswald fled the scene and resisted arrest when he was caught; he then lied to police about owning the rifle and having been photographed with it. Oswald's willingness to engage in violence was demonstrated by his murder of a Dallas police officer, J. D. Tippit, during his flight following the assassinaton of the President, as well as his attempt in April 1963 to murder General Edwin A. Walker. To be sure, there were points in the evidence that a shrewd defense counsel could have raised in Oswald's behalf, had he stood trial. Many of the witnesses, including Dallas police officers and FBI agents, could have been subjected to a telling cross-examination. But the effect of the prosecution would have been to demonstrate overwhelming evidence of guilt.

On the question of conspiracy — that is, the involvement of others with Oswald — the evidence was also compelling. The Warren Commission and the FBI investigations of conspiracy were so seriously flawed that their conclusions of no evidence of conspiracy could not be given any weight. But most important, there was scientific evidence, as well as human testimony, of two gunmen shooting at the President in Dealey Plaza. The Committee was also aware that the most plausible explanation for the murder of Oswald by Jack Ruby within forty-eight hours of the assassination was to silence him, and it took into account the evidence of significant associations of both Oswald and Ruby with groups and individuals with strong motivation to assassinate the President. While it could not identify the other conspirators, the Committee voted to reverse the verdict of history. It found that President John F. Kennedy was killed as a result of a conspiracy.

7

A Message from the Soviet Union

[T]he contemporary Soviet concept of dezinformatsiya or disinformation [is] defin[ed] as the dissemination of false and provocative information. As practiced by the KGB, disinformation is . . . used variously to influence policies of foreign governments, . . . and, at times, simply to obscure depredations and blunders of the KGB itself.

John Barron
KGB

Soviet-American Relations

John F. Kennedy came to power at the height of the cold war. As the United States and the Soviet Union stood poised either to obliterate each other or to coexist, his own militant oratory during the 1960 campaign made mutual obliteration seem to be the more likely alternative. Once elected, Kennedy followed through on his emphasis of the need for more military might by adding $4 billion to a defense budget that had been approved by his predecessor, Dwight D. Eisenhower; and he ordered the biggest buildup of armed force in the peacetime history of the nation. At the same time Kennedy seemed to be committed to negotiation. He doggedly pursued a nuclear arms limitation treaty, finding no contradiction in his approach to foreign policy, since he considered military preparedness to be the foundation of peaceful solutions. "We are ready and anxious to cooperate with all who are prepared to join in genuine dedication to the assurance of a peaceful and more fruitful life for mankind," Kennedy told Nikita Khrushchev, in response to a congratulatory note he received from the Soviet Premier when he was inaugurated in January 1961. Nevertheless, when Lee Harvey Oswald was arrested in the assassination of President Kennedy, there was speculation about his defection to the Soviet Union from October 1959 to June 1962. There also was a report that, on a visit to Mexico City in September 1963, Oswald met with the Soviet consul, Valery Vladimirovich Kostikov, a KGB officer, who was thought to be a member of Department 13, the sabotage and assassination section of the Soviet intelligence agency. (Kostikov was one of several KGB officers who was recalled to the Soviet Union in 1971 after Oleg Adolfovich Lyalin, a key member of what was then Department V, was granted protective custody by the government of Great Britain.) It was up to us, as it had been up to the Warren Commission, to determine whether the Soviets chose neither mutual obliteration nor coexistence, but elimination of a free world leader. The state of U.S.–Soviet relations as of November 1963 was, therefore, relevant.

In the first two years of Kennedy's term, confrontation rather than cooperation was the dominant theme of dealings between the two superpowers, and the first sign of it the new President would encounter was a Communist government in Cuba. On January 2, 1961, just eighteen days before Kennedy took the oath of office, the United States broke with the regime of Fidel Castro. It was the culmination of a year of deteriorating relations: more than $700 million in U.S. property had been expropriated; the Cuban sugar quota had been cut to zero by President Eisenhower; and a prominent Cuban leader, Ernesto "Che" Guevara, had proclaimed the revolution to be on a course set by Karl Marx. That Castro was becoming increasingly dependent on the Russians was indicated in February 1961, when Deputy Prime Minister Andrei Gromyko visited Havana and promised massive military and economic aid.

On March 17, 1960, Eisenhower had quietly authorized the CIA to organize, equip, and train a guerrilla force of Cuban exiles to overthrow Castro. On April 17, 1961, after Kennedy had given his permission, Brigade 2506 was put ashore by American landing craft at the Bay of Pigs on the southern coast of Cuba. U.S. intelligence agencies had, however, underestimated Castro's popular support; an anticipated internal uprising never materialized; and the invasion resulted in a humiliating defeat. The Bay of Pigs disaster was followed by a confrontation with the Soviets in Berlin, which was the subject of twelve hours of fruitless talks in Vienna in June. Khrushchev threatened to end four-power control of the former German capital by signing a treaty that would give East Germany control of access routes to West Berlin. Kennedy reported to the American people on his return from Vienna that he had told Khrushchev: "[T]he security of Western Europe, and therefore our own security, are deeply involved in our presence and in our access rights to

West Berlin; that those rights are based on law and not on sufferance; and that we are determined to maintain those rights at any risk. . . ." In response to Khrushchev's demand that the allies get out of Berlin by the end of the year, Kennedy ordered a doubling of the draft and got authority from Congress to call up the Reserves and National Guard. In August the crisis was intensified by the building of a wall to prevent East European refugees from entering West Berlin, and the United States sent troops and tanks to the beleaguered city. The situation was tense, and war seemed a distinct possibility, but in late 1961 Khrushchev decided not to sign the treaty with East Germany, and in January 1962 the U.S. armored units were pulled out of Berlin. Meanwhile, the nuclear arms race was escalating, as the Russians resumed testing on August 30, 1961, and exploded fifty devices during the fall. After Khrushchev turned a deaf ear to Kennedy's call for a moratorium on atmospheric detonations, the United States resumed nuclear testing in March 1962 with a series of blasts over Christmas Island in the Pacific Ocean.

The Cuban missile crisis of October 1962 was the most dangerous clash with the Soviet Union of Kennedy's presidency. It came about after actions by Soviet secret agents in the United States, who were under FBI surveillance, led to a suspicion that the Russians were engaged in a high-risk operation in Cuba. Reconnaissance flights over Cuba were resumed, and, on October 14, U.S. intelligence analysts detected in aerial photographs of the San Cristobal area installations that were verified as offensive nuclear missile sites. On October 20 Kennedy returned abruptly to Washington from a political trip on the pretext that he had a cold, and on October 22 he declared that the United States had verified from the photos that the Soviet Union had deployed ballistic missiles and Ilyushin-28 bombers in Cuba. He announced that he had ordered an air and sea blockade of Cuba, and he vowed drastic action if the missiles and bombers were not promptly withdrawn. Kennedy put U.S. forces on "maximum alert" and grimly warned the Soviets that we would intercept any arms-carrying vessel. He said the United States would retaliate against the Soviet Union if an attack was launched against any nation in the Western Hemisphere. After six tense days Khrushchev backed down and said he would remove the missiles and bombers in return for a pledge by Kennedy not to invade Cuba. It was applauded around the world as a cold war victory for Kennedy.

The third point of confrontation with the Soviets during Kennedy's brief term was South Vietnam, where there had been a U.S. commitment to support the government of Ngo Dinh Diem since 1956. In 1961 Vietcong guerrillas, with the backing of Communist North Vietnam and the Soviet Union, mounted a series of attacks that put the Diem regime in jeopardy. Kennedy responded by sending 4,000 military "advisers" to Vietnam, and, over the succeeding months, U.S. participation in the conflict steadily grew. Kennedy was following a military script that had been written by his national security staff, one that emphasized a varied capability that could be adapted to the jungle warfare tactics of an enemy such as the Vietcong, rather than a "massive retaliation" strategy based on a superior nuclear arsenal.

In two memorable speeches in June 1963 Kennedy enunciated a foreign policy that coupled toughness with a willingness to negotiate (though it appeared to some observers to combine contradictory approaches of bluster and appeasement). On June 26 he reasserted his pledge to go to war to defend Western Europe, as he stood in front of Berlin City Hall with a huge American flag in the background and declared, "*Ich bin ein Berliner*" ("I am a Berliner"). But on June 10, at American University in Washington, he had stressed a strategy for peace: "Let us focus on a peace based not on a sudden revolution in human nature but on gradual evolution of human institutions." Of the two choices, Kennedy much preferred the quest for peace, and in the summer of 1963 the term "detente" was applied for the first time to relations between the United States and the Soviet Union. A "hot line" between Washington and Moscow was installed, cultural exchanges were initiated, the sale of four million tons of surplus American wheat to Russia was approved, and on August 5 a treaty prohibiting nuclear tests in the atmosphere was signed in Moscow. CIA-sponsored raids on Cuba continued, however, even as Kennedy considered patching up differences with Castro, and the risk of the commitment of 16,000 troops to South Vietnam was underscored by a coup in Saigon in November 1963 that resulted in the assassination of President Diem and his brother, Ngo Dinh Nhu.

A Confrontation with the Soviets

We found it difficult to disagree with the testimony of Secretary of State Dean Rusk on June 10, 1964, which contributed to the Warren Commission's conclusion that there had been no participation by the Soviet Union in an assassination conspiracy: "I have seen no evidence . . . that the Soviet Union considered that it had an interest in the removal of President Kennedy or that it was in any way involved in the removal of President Kennedy." We believed, as the Warren Commission had in 1964, that the Soviet government reacted to the assassination with genuine shock and sincere grief. We were not being naive. We knew that assassination had been an instrument of Soviet policy since the formation in 1917 of the Cheka, a precursor of the KGB. (Assassinations, such as that of Leon Trotsky in 1940 in Mexico, were called *mokrie dela,* or wet affairs, since they involved the spilling of blood.) We knew, too, that under Khrushchev major operations of Department 13 were approved at the Politburo level, and they included the targeting of foreign leaders. Fidel Castro, for example, was marked for elimination twice — in 1961 and 1966. The KGB was, in addition, not the CIA. As John Barron noted, "The political controls [on it] are so strong and pervasive that . . . significant KGB actions may not be regarded as unauthorized aberrations." Nevertheless, we knew that after the public trial of Bogdan Stashinsky in Germany in 1962 for the prussic acid killing of Lev Rebet, a Ukrainian emigre, assassination had been downplayed and Department 13 had concentrated on sabotage. In addition, there was in Russia at the time of President Kennedy's death a visible concern that there would be war if it was attributed to a conspiracy conceived in Moscow. The concern led to a worldwide alert of Soviet armed forces, which was not rescinded until President Johnson gave personal assurance that the United States contemplated no rash action. Apart from Oswald's defection and his visit to the Russian Embassy in Mexico City, there was no sign of Soviet complicity.

There were, however, reasons to question the candor of the Soviets, and therefore their innocence, in the aftermath of the assassination. One had to do with information supplied with respect to Oswald's defection. While the Soviet government turned over to the Warren Commission 140 pages of documents, their authenticity could not be established, and they consisted merely of routine papers. There was no record of a KGB interview of Oswald, though one must have occurred, nor was there any indication that the KGB had kept Oswald under surveillance, although it was the judgment of senior Soviet specialists at the CIA that such surveillance of American defectors was standard procedure. The second — and far more disturbing — reason we mistrusted the Soviets was the defection to the United States in 1964 of Yuri Ivanovich Nosenko, a self-described officer of the KGB, who said he had information about Lee Harvey Oswald. To supplement the Warren Commission file on Oswald's defection, we hoped to secure permission to travel to the Soviet Union to interview Russian citizens who had come in contact with Oswald, and we hoped to obtain additional records from agencies of the Soviet government, particularly the KGB. As for Nosenko, whose defection to the United States the Warren Commission failed to comment upon, we went to great lengths to evaluate his Oswald story (he actually claimed to have been Oswald's KGB case officer) and to analyze the significance of his defection two months after the assassination in light of his lack of candor, if it turned out he had lied.

On May 8, 1978, we met for lunch at a Washington restaurant with

Ikar I. Zaurazhnov, the First Secretary of the Soviet Embassy. We outlined for him what we hoped to accomplish and the assistance we hoped
to secure. We explained that the Committee had to complete its work
by the end of the year and that we hoped for a response within the next
month, or month and a half at most. He said he would take it up at the
appropriate levels of his government. On June 1 we went to the Soviet
Embassy to discuss our request. Our appointment had been with
Zaurazhnov, but he called to tell us beforehand that Vladillen M.
Vasev, the minister-counselor, wanted to meet with us directly. When
we arrived at the embassy we were met by Zaurazhnov, who took us up
to see Vasev in his private dining room, which was dominated by an
enormous painting of late nineteenth-century Moscow in winter. One
look at the walled city frozen in snow and the elegant lunch before us,
and the thought occurred that the lunch was all we were going to get.
We were right.

After the usual pleasantries, we explained the Committee to Vasev.
We then told him that while the information provided the Warren
Commission had been useful, we had been reliably informed that
Oswald had been subjected to telephonic, mail, and neighborhood surveillance by the KGB when he lived in Minsk. We said we thought it
was ironic that the KGB probably had the most complete file on the alleged assassin of the President. We told him that access to that file just
might give us great insight into the Oswald character.

Vasev said he did not know "the final answer," but his government
"was prepared to speak frankly and bluntly on topics." Although its
decisions might sometimes be long in coming, "it was prepared to make
them and to accept the consequences of them." He said his willingness
to meet with us was a sign of his government's interest in the Kennedy
assassination as a matter of "historical truth." "Had we not been interested," he said, "we would have referred you to the State Department, and that would have killed your request with delay." He said the
Soviet government had not been involved in the President's death —
"obviously." He said that the Soviet people had felt a "great affection"
for President Kennedy, an affection exceeded only by that felt for
Franklin Delano Roosevelt. Nevertheless, the Soviet Union was a great
power. Other states might feel differently (we later learned, from talking to Cuban government officials, that he was referring to Cuba and
that the Cuban and Soviet governments were keeping each other
informed on our contacts with them), but it would be "inconsistent
with the dignity of the Soviet state to engage in a process where its
honor was implicitly, if not explicitly, called into question." Then, he
observed gravely, "If we answered some questions, other questions
would always be raised, and no one would be satisfied with whatever we
said anyway." Finally, he said, the situation in 1964 was unique: the re-

sponse of the Soviet government was a response "to the emotions of the event." He acknowledged he was "speaking only personally," but he did not believe that our request to travel to the Soviet Union or for access to files would be acted upon favorably.

Disappointed but not discouraged, we pressed our request. We considered asking the House of Representatives to pass a resolution calling on the Soviet government to cooperate, but we were persuaded by the House leadership and the State Department to submit through diplomatic channels a formal request to travel to the Soviet Union and for access to files. In due course, our request was denied, and, though frustrated, we understood the position of the Soviet government. By turning us down, it ran the risk that its denials of complicity in the assassination would not be believed. On the other hand, Vasev had a point: had his government complied, there would still have been doubts about the truthfulness of what we were told and the authenticity of documents provided to us. More important, turning over the KGB file would have been an admission that an American defector had been subjected to police state techniques.

As for Yuri Nosenko, we could proceed on our own. Nosenko contacted the CIA in June 1962 in Geneva, where he was serving as a security escort for a Soviet disarmament delegation. He offered to spy for the United States, though he said defection was out of the question. Agency officials were suspicious and decided to take a wait-and-see attitude. In January 1964 they heard again from Nosenko, who was back in Geneva again with the disarmament delegation. This time he demanded to be permitted to defect, and he revealed that he had personally handled Oswald's KGB file and had been assigned to review it after the assassination. He added an assurance that Oswald had not had any connection with the KGB. The CIA was still leery, possibly more than ever, because of the odd coincidence of Oswald's supposed case agent showing up when the Warren Commission investigation was just getting under way; but Nosenko was brought to the United States. He was questioned in January by the CIA, which also initiated the intricate process of checking his "bona fides," the proof that he was what he said he was and that his information was reliable. In February and March Nosenko was questioned by the FBI, which reported his story to the Warren Commission.

William T. Coleman, Jr., and W. David Slawson, the Commission staff counsel assigned to the area of foreign conspiracy, responded to the bureau's report by recommending that Nosenko be called to testify "as soon as the CIA has completed its evaluation of him." Coleman and Slawson said that Nosenko's statements, "if true, would certainly go a long way toward showing that the Soviet Union had no part in the assassination." They were, however, "struck by the rare coincidence between the sudden notoriety of Lee Harvey Oswald and the fact that a Soviet official who defects turns out to be a man with primary knowledge about Oswald." They added that if the CIA continued to have doubts about "the authenticity and sincerity of Nosenko," they would be forced "to face the vexing question of why the Soviet Union chose this method to place this 'information' in the hands of the United States." The CIA did, in fact, continue to have doubts, which were officially conveyed to Chief Justice Warren on June 24 by Deputy Director Richard M. Helms. Helms, who later became Director of Central Intelligence, told us in 1978:

> I told [Chief Justice Warren] . . . we were not able to satisfy ourselves that the man was what he was purported to be, that the jobs that he had held were the ones that he really did hold, that there were inconsistencies in his testimony, that what he had to say about the Oswald case didn't make sense to us, and that . . . I was sorry, but whatever the FBI had given him . . . [should be evaluated in light of] the fact that we could not vouch for his bona fides.

How to handle Nosenko was one of the most difficult problems the Warren Commission faced. General Counsel J. Lee Rankin explained to us in 1978 the decision not to call him to testify.

> [T]he CIA had told us that he was a fake and not a real KGB officer and that he was probably just planted on us. . . . [I]t was in light of that that we did not call him because we thought, the Commission thought, they would just be dupes of such a plan if that was true.

The Commission was nonetheless faced with the "vexing question" posed by Coleman and Slawson, and if it was not possible to determine what the Soviets were up to, how would the Commission treat the matter in its final report? On July 27, 1964, Rankin, Slawson, and Commission member Allen W. Dulles, himself a former Director of Central Intelligence, met with Helms and other CIA officials. According to a CIA memorandum, it was acknowledged that the agency's doubts about Nosenko raised the possibility that he would be "publicly exposed . . . sometime after the appearance of the Commission's report." If the Commission opted to mention Nosenko but note the CIA's doubts about him, there was an even greater risk: "the danger that his information [would] be mirror-read by the press and public, leading to conclusions that the U.S.S.R. did direct the assassination." The Commission decided, therefore, to reach its judgments about Oswald and the Soviet Union, as we were told by Assistant Counsel Howard P. Willens, without reliance on Nosenko.

Our effort to evaluate Nosenko's Oswald story drew us into the complex controversy over Nosenko's bona fides. It was an issue that had perplexed the CIA for years, splitting the agency at its highest echelons into two sharply divided camps. At that July 27 meeting with the Warren Commission, it was agreed that the CIA's "greatest contribution" would be to "break" Nosenko and get "the full story of how and why he was told to tell the story he did about Oswald." In fact, the CIA had decided in April to put Nosenko in isolation and subject him to hostile interrogation. He remained in isolation until October 1967, but the agency did not break him. Nor was he released because his credibility had been certified. The men who had conducted the hostile interrogation had not ceased to doubt his bona fides, but other senior CIA officials had taken a look at the same evidence and had come to a different conclusion. The evidence had not changed; just the faces of the people in charge.

Our task was further complicated in early 1978 by publication of *Legend: The Secret World of Lee Harvey Oswald* by Edward J. Epstein. George Lardner, of *The Washington Post,* whose stories on the Committee investigation tended to reflect his bias rather than the facts, was on target for once when he wrote in a review that was published on April 22: ". . . fascinating [but] essentially dishonest." *Legend* was, Lardner said, fascinating because it revealed a great deal about the Nosenko controversy at the CIA, but it was dishonest because Epstein was pretending to be objective, while he was in fact guilty of "demonstrable errors and inexcusable omissions." Epstein's book backed the losing side in the Nosenko debate; it was a brief for the CIA officials who had decided to subject Nosenko to hostile interrogation and never did become persuaded of his bona fides. (Though Epstein did not acknowledge it explicitly, it was quite apparent that his principal source was James J. Angleton who, as Chief of Counterintelligence in 1963, was in charge of the Nosenko assessment.) More than Nosenko's authenticity, however, was called into question by Epstein, who claimed that a principal link in the chain of analysis that led to finding Nosenko bona fide was another intelligence source, a defector code-named "Fedora," who supposedly reported to the FBI. If Nosenko was not bona fide, Epstein asked, then how could "Fedora" be bona fide? He was raising doubts about the judgment of the FBI, as well as that of the CIA.

The situation became all the more confused when, in April 1978, a senior Soviet diplomat, the Under Secretary-General of the United Nations, Arkady Shevchenko, refused to return to the Soviet Union, resigned his post, and sought political asylum in the United States. The press speculated that Shevchenko was "Fedora," whose cover had been blown by Epstein's book. When we asked the CIA to make Shevchenko available for an interview, we were told that he was in a delicate psychological state and was in seclusion. We were aware that Shevchenko's wife in the Soviet Union had reportedly committed suicide shortly after he defected, so we did not press the point until Shevchenko was suddenly in the news again. On October 9, 1978, a prostitute, Judy Chavez, who had been his companion on a ten-day trip to the Virgin Islands, made their liaison public in an interview with James Polk of NBC. Polk, an old friend, called in an effort to learn what we were doing about Shevchenko. Polk told us that Shevchenko's retreat was an apartment in northwest Washington, and he supplied the address. The Committee issued a subpoena, but Schevchenko would not accept it from our investigator, and twenty minutes later a CIA security officer arrived at the apartment house. The standoff ended finally when CIA legal counsel Lyle Miller told us (Blakey happened to be at CIA headquarters on other business), "We give up. Withdraw your subpoena, and we will arrange the interview." From the Shevchenko interview and other information, we were satisfied he was not Epstein's "Fedora" and had nothing to contribute to our investigation.

The Warren Commission decided that because it lacked the expertise to evaluate Nosenko's bona fides, it lacked as well the ability to make a judgment on his story about Oswald. We determined that the issues were distinct, that it was not necessary to be satisfied with his bona fides in order to believe what he had to say about Oswald. Besides, it was not in the Committee's mandate to answer the larger question. We believed further that we had before us a problem only a little more complicated than an assessment of credibility in a trial. While CIA officials with whom we were dealing had somewhat condescendingly suggested that the issue was too complex for a congressional committee to unravel, we were of the view that they had missed a simple point. Trial juries, relying on everyday experience, assess credibility regularly from the demeanor of witnesses testifying under direct questioning and cross-examination. Nosenko was, after all, available as a witness (he had asked insistently in 1964 to testify to the Warren Commission), so we decided to call him before the Committee, which, we were certain, was well suited to perform as a jury. It was, in fact, a uniquely qualified jury, since it consisted of respected elected officials from all over the country. It even was composed of the traditional number: twelve. We assigned as the head of the Nosenko interrogation team a senior staff lawyer, Kenneth Klein, who had served in the Homicide Bureau of the Manhattan District Attorney's office. Klein combed through the key CIA and FBI files on Nosenko, and he debriefed Nosenko himself. After carefully mapping our strategy, we scheduled an examination of Nosenko for two evening hearings on June 19 and 20, 1978. For security reasons, they were to be held in secret at CIA headquarters in Langley, Virginia. We were ready to face the "vexing question" the Warren Commission had avoided: had Nosenko told the truth about Oswald, and what did it mean if he had lied?

Nosenko Unmasked

In interviews and a deposition before the hearing at Langley and in the hearing itself, Nosenko painted a straightforward picture of himself. He said he was born in the town of Nokolayev in the Ukraine on October 30, 1927. His father, Ivan Isiderovich Nosenko, who died in 1956, had been Minister of Shipbuilding in the U.S.S.R. From 1945 to 1950, Nosenko said, he attended the Institute of International Relations; from 1950 to 1953 he served in the Far East and the Baltic region with Navy Intelligence. He then joined the MVD, the predecessor of the KGB, and was assigned to the First Department of the Second Chief Directorate, which was responsible for the surveillance and recruitment of U.S. Embassy personnel. In 1955 Nosenko was transferred to the Seventh Department of the Second Chief Directorate, which was formed to monitor the activities of tourists, but his assignment remained the same: surveillance and recruitment. In 1957 he was promoted to captain and made a member of the Communist Party, and in July 1962 he was named deputy of the Seventh Department, Second Chief Directorate.

When Nosenko first made contact with the CIA in Geneva, he offered to sell information to the CIA for nine hundred Swiss francs ($300), and the CIA agreed. He then promised to be back in touch the next time he traveled abroad, but on two conditions: he must not be contacted in the Soviet Union; and he should not be expected to defect, for he did not intend to leave his family. His CIA contact in Geneva was, therefore, surprised to learn on January 22, 1964, that Nosenko did desire to defect, giving as his reason disillusionment with his government. On February 4 Nosenko said that he had been ordered to return to Moscow. He said his life depended on his being permitted to defect at once, and the CIA again agreed. (He later admitted he had concocted the story of being ordered home to expedite his defection.) It developed from our investigation that Nosenko had been in the United States only a couple of months when officials at the CIA began to have doubts that he was an authentic defector. There were several reasons for their misgivings: much of what Nosenko had provided had been "giveaway" information; certain aspects of his background and events he had described seemed highly unlikely; and two other Soviet defectors were skeptical of him. One of the others, identified by Max Lerner of *The New York Post* as Anatoli Golitsin, went so far as to suggest that

Nosenko had come on a mission for the KGB. A fourth reason was of particular interest to us: information he had given about Oswald did not ring true; it seemed an afterthought to have been tacked on or to have been added. In two interviews with the FBI on March 4 and 6, 1964, Nosenko told of his knowledge of Oswald, since he had kept the file on him, and he said the KGB had not been in contact with Oswald. He offered to testify before the Warren Commission and seemed anxious that his offer be transmitted to the Commission.

On April 4, 1964, the CIA decided that Nosenko should be placed in isolation and subjected to hostile interrogation, but first he was given a rigged lie detector test. The agent who administered the test was instructed to inform Nosenko he had lied, whether he did or not. (He, in fact, did lie, although the CIA later changed the official reading to "inconclusive.") He was then placed in a room with sparse furnishings — a single bed and a light. Nosenko told us that he was not properly fed, he could not read or smoke, and he had no one to talk to. The CIA said he was given three meals a day, though his diet was periodically "modified," and he was provided with a limited number of books at the beginning and end of the period, though he had nothing at all to read from November 1965 to May 1967. The CIA acknowledged that he was under constant visual observation.

Nosenko was questioned about Lee Harvey Oswald three times in July 1964. He said he was with the section of the KGB that monitored American tourists when Oswald arrived in Moscow in 1959; he reviewed the KGB file on Oswald when Oswald attempted to renounce his U.S. citizenship and remain in Russia; he lost contact with Oswald when he was transferred to another government post; and he reviewed Oswald's file right after the assassination and was able to report that Oswald had neither been recruited nor contacted by the KGB. Nosenko was questioned again about Oswald when he was given a second polygraph examination in October 1966. The examiner found his assurances about Oswald to be untruthful, although the CIA interpretation of the test was: ". . . invalid or inconclusive because the conditions and circumstances under which it was administered are considered to have precluded an accurate appraisal of the results."

In February 1968 the Soviet Russia Division of the CIA submitted a 447-page report that enumerated discrepancies in Nosenko's story, leaving little that could be considered credible: he had not, as he had claimed, served in the Russian naval reserve; he had not joined the KGB at the time he claimed; he had been neither a senior case officer nor a deputy chief of the Seventh Department, Second Chief Directorate. The Soviet Russia Division's report was not the final word, however, for, while it was still being prepared, an officer in the Office of Security, who was identified by Robert G. Kaiser of *The Washington Post* as Bruce Solie, was assigned to do a critique of the Nosenko interrogation. Though he had never met Nosenko, Solie had been briefed on his previous statements, since it had been Solie's job to run down leads provided by defectors. Solie disagreed with the report of the Soviet Russia Division: Nosenko had not been thoroughly debriefed, nor had his leads been fully checked, so whether Nosenko was a bona fide defector was still an open question. Solie was directed to interrogate Nosenko further, which he did, and after nine months he came to the conclusion that Nosenko was authentic after all. Solie was not, however, able to learn more about Oswald. In January 1968, when he was asked to write down all he knew about Oswald, Nosenko did so in only three pages. Inexplicably, he was not asked why he knew so little about the man whose KGB file he claimed to have monitored; in fact, once the CIA had decided that Nosenko was a genuine defector, he was not interrogated further about Oswald.

At the end of the CIA investigation, on August 8, 1968, Nosenko was given a third polygraph test, one the CIA called "valid," as opposed to the first two, which it termed "invalid or inconclusive." We had our own panel of polygraph experts analyze the results, paying special attention to two questions that were related to information Nosenko had supplied about Oswald. Our experts assessed the validity of the answer to the first Oswald question as "atrocious," the second as "very poor." Of the three lie detector tests the CIA gave to Nosenko, our experts found the second, the one in which the examiner determined Nosenko was lying, to be ". . . the most valid and reliable."

In Solie's report, which was issued in October 1968, little attention was devoted to Nosenko's statements about Oswald (only 15 of 730 pages), but he did conclude that Nosenko was not dispatched to the United States by the KGB to give misleading information about the assassination. Three reasons were listed for this assurance: Nosenko's first contact with the CIA was a full seventeen months prior to the assassination; the "nature, scope, and content" of Nosenko's information were not sufficient to convince U.S. authorities of no Soviet participation in an assassination plot; and if the KGB *had* been behind the assassination, the Russians would have assumed that U.S. authorities would, in turn, believe that only a few senior KGB officials would be aware of it, and Nosenko would not be among them. We were concerned about how the CIA had handled the Oswald aspects of Nosenko's debriefing, so we took a deposition from the CIA officer who had interrogated him in July 1964 and learned he was not an expert on the KGB, nor had he worked with KGB defectors prior to the Nosenko interview. More important, from our standpoint, his knowledge about

Oswald was sorely lacking: "I cannot specifically recall having read any files pertaining to Lee Harvey Oswald," he testified, though he had heard a lot about him via the media, and he "may have had the opportunity to read some previous debriefings of Nosenko concerning Oswald." (Warren Commission General Counsel J. Lee Rankin told us he was "greatly surprised" when he learned how poorly prepared the CIA interrogator had been.) We asked Solie if he had spoken to Nosenko about Oswald. "No," he said, but he had read Nosenko's three-page summary of the KGB Oswald file. Had he not bothered to compare Nosenko's various statements on Oswald? He had not: "I did not have all the information on the Oswald investigation," he explained. "That was an FBI investigation."

What about the various statements about Oswald by Nosenko? In two interviews, one deposition, and those two secret night sessions at CIA headquarters, his account to us was consistent, if not overly detailed. It was in the fall of 1959, Nosenko said, that he first became aware of Lee Harvey Oswald, whose KGB file consisted of a questionnaire he had filled out when he entered the Soviet Union, his visa application, and reports from interpreters, tourist guides, and hotel employees. There was nothing in the file to indicate the KGB would have any interest in Oswald, so it was decided to refuse his request to remain in the country indefinitely. Nosenko next heard of Oswald when he slashed his wrists in a suicide attempt upon being told he would not be allowed to stay in the U.S.S.R. A psychiatric examination that found Oswald to be "mentally unstable" bolstered the resolve of the KGB to have nothing to do with him, so Nosenko was surprised when he heard that someone, he did not know who, had granted Oswald permission to stay in the Soviet Union. He believed the decision was based on a fear that the KGB would be accused of murdering an American tourist when the Kremlin was trying to relieve East-West tensions. When Oswald was sent to Minsk to work in a radio factory (Nosenko recalled his monthly stipend was seven hundred rubles), his file was sent to KGB headquarters in that city along with a letter directing that he be kept under surveillance, since a suspicion persisted that Oswald was an American spy. According to Nosenko, Oswald's phone was tapped, his mail was intercepted, and occasionally he was watched in his neighborhood by KGB agents.

Nosenko said he (Nosensko) was transferred soon after Oswald went to Minsk, and he did not hear of him again until 1963, when Oswald applied at the Soviet Embassy in Mexico City for a visa to return to Russia. He said he first learned that Oswald had married a Russian woman and returned to the United States when KGB headquarters in Moscow received a cable from Mexico City requesting guidance. (His department chief, he recalled, advised that Oswald should not be permitted to return to the Soviet Union.) When he learned that Oswald had been arrested in the Kennedy assassination, Nosenko said, he telephoned the KGB station in Minsk and requested that the Oswald file be sent to Moscow immediately. It was a bulky file, he recalled, consisting of seven or eight volumes. He examined the first one page by page, for it was the crucial volume, the one that would have indicated recruitment attempts by the KGB, if they had occurred (the others contained surveillance reports and transcripts). From his study of the first volume, Nosenko told us, he could say unequivocally that the KGB had not contacted Oswald. The last he heard of Oswald, Nosenko said, was a few weeks after the assassination when he was told the KGB had learned, from an investigation of Oswald's activities in Minsk, that he had belonged to a gun club and had occasionally gone on hunting trips. Members of the club reported that Oswald had been considered a poor shot. We asked Nosenko exactly why no KGB officer had contacted Oswald. "We did not consider him an interesting target," he said. But would not the KGB have been interested in a former marine who had served as a radar operator at a U-2 airplane base in Japan? Yes, it would, said Nosenko, but since the KGB did not contact Oswald, "it did not know that he had any connection with the U-2 flights." (We agreed with the deputy chief of the Soviet Russia Division of the CIA, who found it very hard to believe that the KGB had not questioned Oswald to the extent of learning about his having been a marine radar operator at the U.S. air base in Atsugi, Japan.)

Nosenko's testimony to us in 1978 sharply contradicted statements he made to the FBI and CIA in 1964, and we carefully brought out those contradictions at his hearing and gave him an opportunity to explain them. For example, he said nothing in his initial debriefings about the volumes of surveillance transcripts; in fact, he denied there had been any surveillance of Oswald. After an interview in March 1964, the FBI reported that Nosenko "opined that the only coverage of Oswald consisted of periodic checks at his place of employment, inquiry of neighbors, associates, and review of his mail." On July 3, 1964, he was specifically asked by the CIA if there had been physical or technical surveillance of Oswald. His repeated response: "No." When he appeared before the Committee, we asked him for an explanation, and he became flustered: "Sir, I cannot tell you what I stated. I was for quite a big period of time, quite a few years, interrogated by hours and in different types of conditions, including hostile conditions. . . ." We then produced the FBI report of the March 1964 interview. Nosenko read it, and we asked him why he had not told of the KGB surveillance of Oswald. "Maybe I forget," he answered. "It's not a big deal. . . ." We asked

Nosenko: If Oswald had met Marina Prusakova on March 17, 1961, in Minsk, how long would it have taken the KGB to learn about it. "In the same March, they would have had quite a batch of material on her," he testified, whereupon he was shown a statement he had made to the CIA in 1964. The KGB did not know of the acquaintance until the couple requested permission to marry (in April), he had said, because "there was no surveillance on Oswald to show that he knew her." He again blamed the inconsistency on the hostile method the CIA employed to interrogate him: "Better ask where I was in this period of time, what conditions I was kept, and what type of interrogations were going on." Nosenko told us that after Oswald tried to kill himself and was hospitalized in October 1959, the KGB assigned two psychiatrists to examine him, and their reports, which Nosenko said he had read, characterized Oswald as "mentally unstable." When he was questioned by the CIA in July 1964, however, Nosenko failed to mention the psychiatric tests, even though he was subjected to questioning that should have elicited the information, had he been trying to be candid. "Did the KGB make a psychological assessment of Oswald?" he was asked then. "No, nothing," Nosenko answered, "but at the hospital it was also said he was not quite normal. The hospital did not write that he was mad, just . . . not normal." "Did the hospital authorities conduct any psychological testing?" "I don't think so. There was no report like this." The FBI report of a March 5, 1964, interview also indicated Nosenko was telling a different story than he was telling us in 1978: "The hospital record also included an evaluation that Oswald's attempted suicide indicated mental instability. Nosenko did not know whether this evaluation was based on a psychiatric examination or was merely an observation of the hospital medical staff." When we pressed him on this inconsistency at the Committee hearing, Nosenko returned to a familiar refrain: he had been confused by the CIA's hostile interrogation techniques; he had not been able to understand the questions due to the language barrier; and he had been drugged. (In a sworn deposition, however, the CIA officer who had questioned Nosenko on Oswald's mental stability in 1964 told us that Nosenko was cooperative and spoke coherently, that when he did not understand a question, he asked for clarification, and he did not appear to have been drugged. In addition, the CIA assured us that no drugs were administered to Nosenko in 1964.)

The tension was mounting, and Nosenko's discomfort was showing. He had, he said somewhat defensively, indicated earlier to us that, had he been asked by the FBI and CIA, he would have told them about the surveillance of Oswald. We asked if the specific question had been put to him: "Was he (Oswald) physically surveilled?" and had he ever answered, "No, there was none." We then showed Nosenko a transcript of his July 3, 1964, CIA interview in which that exchange took place, and Nosenko replied: "I do not remember; it's not right, the answer." Our strategy was working. At first Nosenko was confronted with contradictions that had a built-in "out." A contradiction between his memory and a newspaper article was an honest mistake. A contradiction between his testimony and a document furnished by the Soviet government could be explained by Soviet duplicity. A contradiction between his testimony and an FBI report was written off because it was a report, not a transcript. And a contradiction between his testimony and a CIA transcript was due to his having been drugged. The final series of contradictions, however, were between his testimony and a CIA tape recording of a 1964 interview, which clearly showed by his tone that he was not drugged or suffering from strain. As we prepared to play the tape, Nosenko announced he would respond to no more questions about CIA interviews prior to 1967, since they had been hostile interrogations, conducted illegally, and were in violation of his constitutional rights. The Committee adjourned the hearing.

Committee Hearing on CIA–Nosenko

We summed up the evidence of our Nosenko investigation in a staff report that was sent to the CIA and FBI, which were asked if they wished to respond. The FBI deferred to the CIA, and it assigned John C. Hart, a twenty-four-year veteran of the agency, who had served as station chief in several countries overseas and had held senior positions at CIA headquarters, to testify at a public hearing the Committee had scheduled for September 15, 1978. Hart had retired in 1972 but had been recalled in 1976 to do a study of the Nosenko case and write a report for internal circulation. He was not very far into his hour-and-a-half prepared statement when we realized how deep a rift Nosenko had caused at the agency. On one side, there was a contingent that had been led by the retired Counterintelligence Chief, James Angleton (though Hart did not identify him by name), and officers of the Soviet Russia Division, most of whom had also retired. These were the men who handled Nosenko from the day in 1962 in Geneva, when he first made contact with the CIA, to the end of his hostile interrogation in 1967, at which time they filed a report assailing his credibility. On the opposite side, there was the faction whose position, based on the Office of Security critique, had prevailed since 1967: Nosenko was a bona fide defector whose story was essentially true. (We would learn that Richard M. Helms, the CIA Director in 1967, was caught in the middle, unable to decide which side to believe.) Hart sought to explain away the discrepancies we had noted between Nosenko's story to the CIA in 1964 and what he had told us in 1978. For one thing, Nosenko had a poor memory — a psychological test in June 1964 showed it to be below normal. Second, his defection had been a traumatic experience: ". . . you cannot expect a man immediately after he has defected [to] . . . behave in a totally reasonable way." Third, he had suffered from a severe drinking problem, which would have affected his powers of recall during the early CIA interrogations. It was Hart's considered opinion that Nosenko had established his credentials by providing valuable information of a sort that would not have been tossed out by the Russians in a disinformation scheme. He had, for example, alerted U.S. authorities to the existence of a surveillance system installed in the U.S. Embassy in Moscow, which led to the discovery of fifty-two microphones. Further, he had identified a KGB penetration agent who had attained a sensitive post in a Western European government, leading to his arrest and conviction for espionage. "There is no reason to believe the Soviets would have given this information away," Hart declared.

Hart described the initial reaction of the CIA officer who was first contacted by Nosenko and who was in charge of the case until 1967. (Hart did not name the officer, referring to him only as the deputy chief of the Soviet Russia Division, or D.C.) On June 11, 1962, Hart testified, the D.C. cabled Washington from Geneva: "Subject has conclusively proved his bona fides. He has provided info of importance and sensitivity. Subject now completely cooperative." Hart said that in 1976 he recorded Angleton's reaction to that message: "Deputy Chief was ordered back to Washington, and we had a big meeting here on Saturday morning. Deputy Chief thought he had the biggest fish of his life. I mean he really did." There was a hitch, however, in that Nosenko was giving information that conflicted with what the CIA was hearing from another Soviet defector. (Hart would only refer to him as Mr. X.) Hart said Mr. X had been diagnosed as a paranoid: "[I]t was one of his contentions that the schism between the Soviet Union and . . . Communist China was simply a KGB . . . ruse. . . . He offered this theory quite seriously, and in some quarters within the agency, it came to be taken quite seriously." (We took "some quarters within the agency" to be Angleton's counterintelligence unit.) Hart contended that by the time Nosenko "came out" in 1964, the Counterintelligence Staff and the Soviet Russia Division, based on allegations by Mr. X, had built a case against him. "[F]rom that point on, the treatment of Mr. Nosenko was never, until 1967, devoted to learning what Nosenko had to say. It . . . was devoted to breaking Nosenko, who was presumed on the basis of supposed evidence given by Mr. X . . . [to be] a dispatched KGB agent sent to mislead the United States."

When Nosenko arrived in the United States in February 1964, Hart testified, he was worried he would be "milked of information" and then discarded, and this compounded his fear that the KGB would try to kidnap or kill him. "He nevertheless remained tractable and cooperative

. . . , although in the succeeding weeks he became more difficult. He had a serious personality crisis, which led to heavy drinking. . . ." Since they had been unable to get a confession from Nosenko under friendly conditions, Hart said, the D.C. and his assistants decided to place him in a more spartan confinement and begin hostile interrogations. The purpose was to put Nosenko at a psychological disadvantage, "to shake his confidence, to make him fearful." The guards at the CIA-controlled house somewhere in the Washington area were ordered not to mistreat him physically, ". . . but . . . they were not to talk to him, they were not to smile at him, they were to treat him very impersonally." Nosenko was kept in a cramped room with one light and little furniture (an original plan to leave it unheated was overruled). He was forced to keep a strict regimen, arising at 6 A.M. and going to bed at 10 P.M., and fed a starvation diet, though his meals were improved when a doctor intervened. He was virtually deprived of distractions, given very little to read and not allowed to listen to music or watch television. (While there was a TV set in the house, it was only for the guards, who were given headsets, so Nosenko could not even hear the broadcasts.) He was kept under constant observation, but the only occasions he would hear someone speak were his interrogations. Hart said the top echelon of the CIA had incorrectly assumed that Nosenko was being interrogated regularly, although he was actually questioned on only 292 days of 1,277 days of incarceration. "The rest of the time . . . he was left entirely unoccupied."

On August 23, 1966, Helms, impatient with the failure of his staff to come to a firm conclusion on Nosenko, ordered that the case be completed within sixty days, causing the interrogators to decide that additional measures must be taken to establish that he was lying. In September they proposed that Nosenko be given a truth drug, sodium amytal, but Helms objected. It was then that they subjected Nosenko to the second of three sets of polygraph tests (the one the Committee's independent experts found to be the most reliable), which determined that Nosenko was not truthful. Hart argued with the statement in our staff report that the series of polygraph tests administered in October 1966 was valid, claiming that our experts had not been aware of certain circumstances that surrounded those tests. "For one thing, the times involved . . . were excessive," he said, claiming Nosenko was kept on the machine for periods of up to seven hours and that during breaks, which lasted for as long as four hours, he was left strapped in the chair, unable to move. What is more, Hart charged, Nosenko was harassed by the polygraph technician, who told him at one point he was a "fanatic," that there was no factual support for his "legend," and his future was "zero."

The deputy chief of the Soviet Russia Division never intended to make a valid assessment of Nosenko's truthfulness, Hart declared, and he quoted a note written by the D.C. that, he said, indicated the real purpose of the polygraph tests: "To gain more insight into points of detail which we could use in fabricating an ostensible Nosenko confession. . . . [I]nsofar as we could make one consistent and believable even to the Soviets, a confession would be useful in any eventual disposal of Nosenko." "Did you use the term 'eventual disposal' of him?" Hart was asked by Congressman Harold Sawyer. "I used the term, 'eventual disposal,' yes sir," Hart replied.

Hart's presentation was a devastating indictment of the CIA's handling of Nosenko. "I would say that the agency failed miserably in its handling of the entire case. . . ," Hart commented, after completing his prepared statement. But he did not succeed in rebutting our staff report, which maintained that Nosenko, at least on the subject of Oswald and the assassination, was a fraud. Congressman Christopher J. Dodd pressed Hart on this point: "[W]hy should this Committee believe anything that Mr. Nosenko has said when . . . you state he was intimidated, not interrogated, for more than three years, . . . that he was . . . a man of a very short memory, that he was drunk or at least heavily drinking during part of the questioning. . . . [W]hy then should we believe any of the statements of Mr. Nosenko, which from point to point contradict each other?" Hart answered that he could not say Nosenko had contradicted himself, *except* on the subject of Oswald. "The important things . . . he has produced . . . which the Agency has been able to check on," he said, "have, by and large, proved out." It was evident that Hart was avoiding the Oswald issue:

Dodd: *I don't recall you once mentioning the name of Lee Harvey Oswald in the hour and 30 minutes that you testified, and I am intrigued as to why, . . . knowing that you are in front of a Committee that is investigating the death of a President, and an essential part of that investigation has to do with the accused assassin.*

Hart: *The answer is a very simple one, Congressman. I retired some years ago from the CIA. About three weeks ago I received a call . . . asking me to . . . be the spokesman before this Committee on the . . . Nosenko case. I said I will be the spokesman on the . . . Nosenko case, but I will not be the spokesman on . . . Nosenko's involvement with Lee Harvey Oswald.*

Dodd: *So, it would be fair for me to conclude that really what the CIA wanted to do was to send someone up here who would not talk about Lee Harvey Oswald.*

Dodd referred Hart to the section of our staff report that covered Nosenko's contradiction on the surveillance of Oswald in the Soviet Union. "Let me express an opinion on Mr. Nosenko's testimony about Lee Harvey Oswald," said Hart. "I, like many others, find Mr. Nosenko's testimony incredible. . . . I, as recently as last week, talked to Mr. Nosenko and tried to get him to admit that there was a possibility that he didn't know everything that was going on. I find it hard to believe that the KGB had so little interest in [Oswald]. . . . There, if I were in the position of deciding whether to use the testimony of Mr. Nosenko . . . , I would not use it." Hart tended to attribute Nosenko's unreliability on Oswald to innocent oversight, pointing out that the KGB, like the CIA, is a compartmentalized organization, and contact could have been made with Oswald without Nosenko knowing about it.

The D.C. had other ideas, which he wished to convey to the Committee. He sent us his analysis of our staff report along with a point-by-point rebuttal of Hart's testimony. He wryly cited the coincidence of the CIA landing a KGB source who "turned out to have participated directly in the Oswald case. Not only once, but on two separate occasions: When Oswald came to Russia in 1959 and again after the assassination. . . ." "How many KGB men could say as much?" he wrote. The D.C. gave the Committee credit for seeing the significance of Nosenko's protests that he was unable to remember what he had told the CIA in 1964. "It shouldn't matter what he'd *said* before"; he argued, "he was supposedly talking of things he'd lived through: the KGB files he'd seen, the officers he'd worked with. If these were real experiences he need only recall them and his reports would, all by themselves, come out more or less the same way each time. . . ." The D.C. was willing to state explicitly the inference that could be drawn from Nosenko's mission. "[I]f Nosenko is a KGB plant, as I am convinced he is," he wrote, "there can be no doubt that Nosenko's recited story about Oswald in the U.S.S.R. is a message from the KGB. That message says, in exaggerated and implausible form, that Oswald had nothing whatever to do with the KGB, [he was] not questioned for his military intelligence, not even screened as a possible CIA plant. Even Mr. Hart finds it incredible and recommends that you disregard it. But his reasons are flawed, and can you afford to disregard it? By sending out such a message, the KGB exposes the fact that it has something to hide. . . . [T]hat something may be the fact that Oswald was an agent of the KGB."

We called the D.C. to testify in executive session on November 16, 1978, as our public hearings had come to a close. He repeated the points of his letter to the Committee and then proceeded to recite what he called "one small case history which illustrates how wrong Nosenko's story is." It was, he told us, "an actual event, which showed

how the real KGB in the real U.S.S.R. reacted to situations.'' (The story
was also told by a former KGB man named Kaarlo Tuomi, and it could
be found in John Barron's book *KGB*.) As it was told in Barron's book,
it concerned a young Finnish couple who illegally crossed the Soviet
border in 1953:

> The couple walked into a militia station and requested Soviet citizenship,
> but the KGB jailed them. Continuous questioning during the next 11
> months indicated only that the couple believed Communist propaganda
> and sincerely sought to enjoy the life it promised. Nevertheless, the KGB
> consigned them to an exile camp for suspects in Korov province. Because
> Tuomi spoke Finnish, the KGB sent him into the camp as a "prisoner"
> with instructions to become friends with the couple. Hardened as he was
> to privation, he was still aghast at what he saw in the camp. Whole families
> subsisted in 5 by 8 wooden stalls or cells in communal barracks. Each
> morning at 6, trucks hauled all the men away to peat bogs where they la-
> bored until dark. Small children, Tuomi observed, regularly died of ordi-
> nary maladies because of inadequate medical care.

"So on the one hand," the D.C. continued, "we have a young ex-
Marine, Lee Harvey Oswald, from the United States; on the other
hand, we have a simple Finnish family. Both say they want to live in
Russia. The Finns are questioned for eleven months by the KGB, then
consigned indefinitely to a hellish camp for suspects. The American is
not even talked to once by the KGB. The Finns' experience fits all we
know about the true Soviet Union from Alexander Solzhenitsyn and
many others. . . . Oswald's experience, as Nosenko tells it, cannot have
happened." (The deputy chief of the Soviet Division, or D.C., was
identified by Robert G. Kaiser of *The Washington Post* as Tennent H.
Bagley. The Soviet defector who supplied information that contradicted
Nosenko was identified by Edward J. Epstein in *Legend* as Anatoli M.
Golitsin.)

The inability of former CIA Director Helms to reconcile the Nosenko
matter left us not at all reassured about the agency's official position.
"This is the issue which remains . . . to this very day," Helms testified,
"that no person familiar with the facts, of whom I am aware, finds Mr.
Nosenko's comments about Lee Harvey Oswald and the KGB to be
credible. That still hangs in the air like an incubus." Helms said that he
did not know how to resolve "this bone in the throat," because he
could not say he believed Nosenko to be a bona fide defector or that we
could rely on what he had said about Oswald. "If Mr. Nosenko turned
out to be a bona fide defector," he said, "if his information were to be
believed, then we could conclude that the KGB and the Soviet Union
had nothing to do with Lee Harvey Oswald in 1963, and therefore had

nothing to do with President Kennedy's murder. If, on the other hand, Mr. Nosenko had been programmed in advance by the KGB to minimize KGB connections with Oswald, if Mr. Nosenko was giving us false information about Oswald's contacts with the KGB from 1959 to 1962, it was fair for us to surmise that there may have been an Oswald-KGB connection in November 1963, more specifically that Oswald was acting as a Soviet agent when he shot President Kennedy.''

Nosenko Analyzed

Warren Commission lawyers Coleman and Slawson, not Helms, in 1964 correctly evaluated the significance of the testimony of Yuri Nosenko. While we found it possible that the assassination was such a compartmentalized KGB operation that no evidence of Oswald's recruitment or control or the mission itself would have shown up in KGB files, we found it unlikely. If Nosenko was telling the truth about Oswald, the Warren Commission, in a rare but not impossible coincidence, had access to a man whose testimony could have gone a long way in negating Soviet involvement in the assassination. On the other hand, if Nosenko was not telling the truth about Oswald, it did not follow that the Soviet Union was the hidden hand in the events in Dallas in 1963. The possible explanations of Nosenko's untruthful testimony about Oswald were, we believed, varied, not a simple "either-or." Nosenko may have been, for example, a bona fide defector, who merely sought to make himself more valuable by pretending to have knowledge about a topic of current interest in 1963. He may not have been a bona fide defector, but one who nevertheless told the truth when he said the KGB was not responsible for the assassination, although he lied about there being no connection between the KGB and Oswald. Why? Because the KGB, from whom Nosenko was taking orders, feared that if any relationship with Oswald (interview without obtaining information, interview obtaining information, recruitment to spy, etc.) were acknowledged, it would inevitably be interpreted in the United States to mean recruitment and assignment to assassinate. Coleman and Slawson, in their original memorandum in which they perceptively analyzed "foreign involvement," recognized the wide range of meanings that the phrase "involvement" might encompass. They also asked the important question when they criticized the popular press in 1963, which was asking if Oswald was an "agent" of some foreign or domestic group. Agent for what? they asked. Not so obvious to a black-and-white press analysis was the important question of the kind of agent Oswald might have been, even if he had been recruited. The KGB, for example, could well have obtained from Oswald what he thought was valuable information about the U-2 spy plane. (The KGB, however, would have known most, if not all, of what Oswald knew, for his information was derived from being a radar operator, and presumably the Soviet government had its own radar operators tracking the U-2.) Having obtained information from Oswald, it could have then merely recruited him to engage in public pro-Soviet (or pro-Cuban) activities in the United States, without intending that he be a spy or something more sinister. Oswald's own character, however, could then have been the driving force behind the assassination. Indeed, he could have proposed it to Moscow, been specifically turned down, and gone ahead on his own. All of this, of course, only explores possibilities: it says nothing about what the evidence shows — either to a likelihood, to a probability, to a preponderance, or beyond a reasonable doubt. The point is that Helms's "either-or" choice does not exhaust a reasonable range of likely possibilities. Coleman's and Slawson's more sophisticated view was the better one.

The CIA officials in charge of evaluating Nosenko apparently did not appreciate these nuances, even if they were aware of them. Nosenko seemingly was treated as an all-or-nothing proposition, bona fide or not. And when the Oswald story was included in the equation (it was never given the central place it warranted), Nosenko was treated as if he had established that either the Soviets were or were not involved in the assassination — nothing in between, nothing else possible. Nevertheless, the most damning criticism that may be made of how the CIA officers mishandled Nosenko goes much deeper. A careful reading of their analytical work shows that Nosenko was largely evaluated apart from his Oswald story. He was not treated as what he was in 1964 — the potentially most important single witness to an important aspect of a crucial issue before the government and the people of the United States. Nosenko was treated merely as another defector from the KGB; he was analyzed as part of the general struggle between the CIA and the KGB; his Oswald information was assigned only a minor role in the assessment of his bona fides and his place in that larger struggle. The CIA response to Nosenko was, in short, a response to the "perceived needs" of the agency and not the "real needs" of the United States government or its people. The agency's quest "to break" Nosenko was not an effort to solve the unanswered questions of the Kennedy assassination, but to prevent the KGB from "putting one over" on the agency. The agency, in short, had its priorities upside down; its expert people had trained themselves out of their common sense.

Any assessment of Nosenko as a witness in the investigation of the Kennedy assassination must begin with the credibility of his story about Oswald, which becomes not just one factor but the linchpin in the assessment of his bona fides. The unanimous judgment of the Committee, after two evenings of carefully hearing him out, was that it "was certain [that] Nosenko [had] lied about Oswald." Because the Committee's mandate was limited, it did not continue on to assess Nosenko's bona fides. Based on the information available to it, the Committee, however, declined to read Nosenko's false testimony as an indication that the Soviet government was involved in the assassination. We agreed with the Committee on the two key points. Too much evidence was inconsistent with that sinister inference to warrant drawing it. As Dean Rusk testified to the Warren Commission, the case for Soviet involvement in the assassination just cannot be made in light of the general evidence available; the specific items in the investigation that raise suspicions did not collectively add up to a likelihood of Soviet involvement. The negative inference from Nosenko's testimony, for example, was not enough by itself. That Oswald saw Kostikov in the Russian Embassy in Mexico City also was not enough — as such officials, to maintain their cover, in fact engage in routine embassy business. Actually, the thrust of the evidence as a whole was the best indication of how the Nosenko affair should have been evaluated. The most coherent single explanation of Nosenko was, in our judgment, the one that interpreted him as having been sent by the KGB, not as a disinformation agent, but to tell the U.S. government and the American people the truth to the ultimate question: Did the Soviet government have a hand in the assassination? (We also satisfied ourselves, contrary to Epstein's assertion in *Legend*, that the bona fides of Nosenko were not inextricably intertwined with those of any other defector, but the details of that process of reasoning are classified.) That the KGB could not bring itself to have Nosenko tell the truth in 1964 about aspects of the Oswald story — principally that the KGB had had contact with Oswald, at least to the degree that it probably debriefed him, for example, on his knowledge about the U-2, or that it subjected him to extensive surveillance — was, for us, a sign of what Chairman Preyer referred to as a defect, not in Nosenko's story, but in the character of the KGB mind. Any important information that Nosenko "gave up" (a disputed point) was a price the KGB would have been willing to pay to establish his bona fides; that his story was not better put together was attributable to the short period of time the KGB had to prepare him for the mission. While Nosenko was not, therefore, a bona fide defector, in our view, his main message was truthful, not a disinformation ploy. It was a matter to be regretted that the officials of the CIA did not have, in their narrow world of intelligence, enough intellectual categories available to them to classify Nosenko as what he most probably was: not bona fide but telling the truth, at least about Oswald.

None of this analysis addresses the barbaric way that Nosenko was treated by the CIA in the effort to break him. The struggle between the CIA and the KGB was not, as the agency apparently believed, a struggle between two intelligence agencies, but a struggle between two views of life, one totalitarian, the other free. President Kennedy himself put it eloquently in his *"Ich bin ein Berliner"* speech:

> There are many people in the world who really don't understand, or say they don't, what is the great issue between the free world and the Communist world. Let them come to Berlin. . . . Freedom has many difficulties and democracy is not perfect, but we have never had to put up a wall to keep our people in. . . .

To adopt Soviet methods in an effort to defeat the Soviets was in our judgment to become like the Soviets to avoid letting them win, a course of action that constituted not the path of victory, but surrender to the Soviet way of life. J. Lee Rankin, a constitutional lawyer with deep faith in our legal system, told us he was "shocked by the way [the CIA] . . . arrive[d] at [its] . . . conclusion[s] and the procedures they apparently went through. . . ." Chairman Preyer spoke for the Committee and all of us associated with it when, at the conclusion of Richard Helms's testimony, he said:

> I think the past two days of testimony have shown the CIA did things fifteen years ago or so which shock us, sometimes shock us profoundly, today.
>
> I heard someone at the luncheon recess conclude from this testimony that America is a lawless society because one of our institutions broke the law some years ago. Well, this is certainly not a lawless society. Russia is a lawless society, where a handful of people control things and where you cannot change things unless a revolution or a war comes along.
>
> I think the past few days' hearings have indicated that we can change things. . . . [I]t is impossible to conceive of a KGB agent, for example, ever admitting that anything they did fifteen years ago was wrong.
>
> The truth about these things, I think, will free up the CIA from past mistakes, and it will free all of us.

8

Castro and the Risk of Retaliation

United States leaders should think that if they are aiding terrorists'
plans to eliminate Cuban leaders, they themselves will not be safe.

Fidel Castro
Associated Press
September 7, 1963

Cuban-American Relations

When a national leader is assassinated, his adversaries are immediate
suspects, so when John F. Kennedy was struck down in Dallas, two
names in particular came to mind: Nikita Khrushchev of the Soviet
Union and Fidel Castro Ruz of Cuba. Then, when the arrest of Lee
Harvey Oswald was followed by word that the alleged assassin had demonstrably paid allegiance to the Communist government of Cuba (his
Fair Play for Cuba Committee activities in New Orleans in August
1963; his attempt to travel to Cuba via Mexico in September 1963), the
notion that Castro had a hand in the President's death became all the
more prevalent. When the Warren Commission concluded in 1964 that
Oswald had acted alone, the suspicions abated, but they were revived
when doubts about that conclusion were given new impetus by findings
of a Senate Select Committee on Intelligence Activities in 1975 and
1976. By developing the details of the CIA-Mafia plots to kill Castro,
the Senate Committee (or Church Committee, for its chairman, Senator Frank Church of Idaho) established that the Cuban president had a
reason to retaliate and seek the death of his American counterpart. The

job before us in 1978 was to evaluate Castro's vindictiveness as a possible factor in the assassination, in light of the CIA-Mafia plots, the existence of which had been withheld from the Warren Commission. There was, in addition, evidence of possible Cuban participation in a plot, which also was not brought to the attention of the Commission (a report, for example, that Oswald was in contact with a Cuban intelligence agent who made a statement shortly after the assassination that could be read as foreknowledge). We began our evaluation by examining the course of Cuban-American relations during Kennedy's incomplete term.

Kennedy set the tone for the Cuban policy of his administration in a State of the Union address on January 30, 1961: "In Latin America, Communist agents seeking to exploit that region's peaceful revolution of hope have established a base on Cuba. . . . Our objection with Cuba is not over the people's drive for a better life. Our objection is to their domination by foreign and domestic tyrannies. . . ." Such domination in the Western Hemisphere, Kennedy vowed, "can never be negotiated." Inevitably, Kennedy administration policy would be rooted in certain commitments of his predecessor, Dwight D. Eisenhower, who along with Vice-President Richard M. Nixon, the 1960 Republican candidate, had been accused by Kennedy during the election campaign of paving the way for the "communization" of Cuba by not recognizing the Cuban revolution for what it was from the outset. Unbeknownst to Kennedy, Eisenhower, in March 1960, had quietly approved a CIA covert action plan that included organizing, training, and logistically supporting Cuban exile troops for the purpose of invading Cuba and overthrowing Castro. By September, a Cuban-exile expeditionary force, Brigade 2506, was in place in Guatemala. Kennedy was informed of the operation after he was elected, and in due course he authorized a landing at the Bay of Pigs, on the southern coast of Las Villas province. It was launched on April 17, 1961, but was soon defeated by Cuban troops said to be commanded by Castro himself. While the President had ordered that no American troops were to set foot on Cuban soil, U.S. sponsorship of the landing was readily apparent, and Kennedy promptly took full responsibility for the aborted invasion. He was hardly contrite, however. On April 20, addressing a meeting of the American Society of Newspaper Editors, he asserted: "Cuba must not be abandoned to the Communists. . . . Should it ever appear that the inter-American doctrine of noninterference merely conceals or excuses a policy of non-action, . . . then I want it clearly understood that this government will not hesitate in meeting its primary obligations . . . to the security of our Nation." Castro declared officially on May Day that Cuba was a socialist nation, and Secretary of State Dean Rusk told the Senate Foreign Relations Subcommittee on Latin American Affairs that if the Castro regime engaged in acts of aggression, the United States would defend itself. On May 17 the House of Representatives passed a resolution declaring Cuba to be "a clear and present danger" to the Western Hemisphere.

The Kennedy administration responded to the Communist challenge in Cuba with economic and social, as well as military, initiatives. It supported the Alliance for Progress, a hemispheric program that was chartered at a meeting of the Organization of American States in Punta del Este, Uruguay, in August 1961. The objectives of the Alliance included: a 2.5 percent annual increase in economic growth; agrarian reform; improved housing conditions; the eradication of illiteracy; fair wages and improved working conditions; and more equitable taxes. Meanwhile, in an effort to isolate Cuba economically, Washington announced in September 1961 that the United States would suspend assistance to any country that offered aid to Cuba.

Cuban-exile commando raids were taking their toll, their most vulnerable targets being the ships of countries such as Great Britain and Spain carrying much-needed manufactured goods to Cuba. Castro was no doubt aware that the CIA was sponsoring the raids, since his agents had infiltrated the Cuban communities of Miami and other U.S. cities. Castro also realized that support for American opposition to his government was building in Latin America, so he extended his ties to the Soviet Union. In January 1962 Russia and Cuba signed a protocol that meant a sizable increase in trade: Soviet oil, metals, chemicals, fertilizers, cotton, and vegetable oil for Cuban sugar, rum, tobacco, and nickel. Meanwhile, Castro hinted that Soviet arms might be on the way, to help him defend against the exile guerrillas.

The Organization of American States met again in Punta del Este in January 1962 to approve sanctions against Castro, voting unanimously for a resolution that stated that Marxism-Leninism and the revolutionary government of Cuba were incompatible with the inter-American system. But when it came to backing up the OAS condemnation by excluding Cuba from the system entirely, the U.S. delegation had to lobby long and hard for the fourteen votes needed to pass the resolution. Tough as the Punta del Este accords appeared to be (they prompted Castro to refer indignantly to the OAS as the "U.S. Ministry of Colonies"), the United States had failed to obtain ratification of more punitive measures — in particular, a trade embargo. But what Washington was unable to do with hemispheric support, it decided to do unilaterally: an embargo was put in effect to deny Cuba American dollars for its tobacco, molasses, and other goods (sugar had already been barred by the suspension of Cuba's quota); and the NATO allies were asked not to trade with Cuba, particularly in strategic materials. The impact of the embargo was evident as early as March 1962, when Castro announced that food and soap would be rationed; shoes and clothing were later added to the list. It was also in March that the United States began to voice concern over the Soviet arms buildup and military aid to Cuba, which, according to a State Department report, had consisted of fifty to seventy-five MIG fighter aircraft and $100 million for the training of Cuban pilots in Czechoslovakia. On July 26, 1962, in a speech marking the ninth anniversary of the revolution, Castro acknowledged and attempted to justify the rising influx of Soviet weaponry by charging that the United States "is set on launching an attack on our country." (That same day the State Department put out a release stating that large quantities of arms, including missiles, and military personnel were arriving in Cuba.) Kennedy replied to Castro's speech by saying he had no intention of invading Cuba — "at this time." In the face of threats from Moscow that a U.S. attack on Cuba or on Soviet ships bound for Cuba would mean war, Kennedy asserted that he would move swiftly against Cuba, if the Soviet military presence threatened U.S. or hemispheric security in any way.

  While Kennedy appeared to be following through on the hard-line Cuba policy he had called for in the campaign, it was not tough enough for some of his critics. Senator Barry Goldwater, an Arizona conservative and the probable Republican candidate for President in 1964, insisted that "the American people will not be satisfied with President Kennedy's reiteration of a 'do-nothing' policy toward Cuba." Former Vice-President Nixon urged "stronger action," perhaps even a naval blockade. On September 20, 1962, the Senate passed a resolution, ". . . to prevent by whatever means . . . necessary, including the use of arms, the Marxist-Leninist regime in Cuba from extending . . . its aggressive or subversive activities to any part of this hemisphere. . . ." The House, on the same day, approved two trade amendments intended to cut off aid to any country whose merchant ships were used to transport arms or other goods to Cuba. Kennedy was not ready to go that far, but he did, in October 1962, reinforce the embargo: foreign shippers engaged in bringing Soviet-bloc arms to Cuba would lose the right to carry cargo owned or financed by the U.S. government.
  The situation became critical on October 22. Kennedy announced that U.S. reconnaissance aircraft had photographed offensive missile sites with a nuclear strike capability under construction in Cuba. He directed that emergency measures be taken: the "quarantine" of all offensive military equipment en route to Cuba; stepped-up surveillance of the military buildup in Cuba; and reinforcement of the U.S. naval base at Guantanamo Bay. Kennedy also vowed full retaliation against the Soviet Union if a nuclear warhead was launched from Cuba; he

called for an immediate meeting of the OAS and an emergency session of the United Nations Security Council; and he appealed to Chairman Khrushchev to halt an action that threatened world peace. In the days that followed, as Castro stood on the sidelines, Kennedy and Khrushchev approached the brink of nuclear war. They reached an understanding, however, and on November 20 the crisis ended. Kennedy announced that the missiles, as well as Ilyushin-28 bombers, were being withdrawn by the Soviets. For its part, the United States made a pledge not to invade Cuba, but this was conditioned on a United Nations inspection to verify that the weapons had been removed. Since Castro did not allow the U.N. inspection, the no-invasion pledge never took force.

In December 1962 the Cuban exile troops taken prisoner at the Bay of Pigs were released, in return for supplies of medicine, and Kennedy welcomed Brigade 2506 at the Orange Bowl in Miami, pledging that its flag would be returned to a free Cuba. There soon were signs, however, that his administration was starting to think twice about its commitment to Castro's overthrow. In February 1963 it withdrew support of Brigade 2506, encouraging its members to join Cuban units that were being established in the U.S. armed forces. At the same time, the State Department denounced guerrilla raids against Castro as capable of doing more harm than good, and the government announced its determination to assure that the raids were not "launched, manned, or equipped from American soil." (While CIA-supported hit-and-run raids continued, they were either launched in defiance of the President or, more likely, with the proviso that he would be officially unaware of them.) In April a group of exiles was arrested in the Bahamas by British authorities on a tip from the U.S. government, and in July the FBI raided a camp in Louisiana where militants had stored a large cache of arms that were to be used against Castro. While Kennedy continued his unilateral effort to isolate Cuba and put economic pressure on the Castro government, he was increasingly frustrated by his inability to obtain the cooperation of U.S. allies in a trade boycott. For example, when Kennedy, in July 1963, appealed directly to the governments of Great Britain, Canada, Spain, and Mexico not to trade with Cuba, it was to no avail. In September Canada announced a wheat deal with Cuba; in November, Spain and Cuba signed a trade pact.

Several times in early 1963 Kennedy detected overtures from Havana that indicated a desire to discuss mutual problems, but he was also hearing from his hard-line critics in Congress. So, the administration echoed its critics while seeking a peaceful solution. In March Secretary of State Rusk said: "Soviet forces in this hemisphere cannot be accepted. . . ." And in April Kennedy went before the American Society of Newspaper

Editors, as he had in 1961, to address the Cuban issue. "Time will see Cuba free again," he said, "and I think that when that happens the record will show that the United States has played a significant role."

Castro, too, was sounding bellicose. In September 1963 he told an Associated Press reporter, Daniel Harker, "United States leaders should think that if they are aiding terrorists' plans to eliminate Cuban leaders, they themselves will not be safe." A threat? Very possibly, but at the same time the Cuban government was proposing that United Nations representatives of the United States and Cuba hold preliminary talks aimed at repairing relations. In response, Kennedy directed that the idea be explored, in what might have been a softening of his stance, though he did not express it openly. On November 18, at a luncheon in Miami Beach attended by many Cuban exiles, Kennedy was as unyielding as ever, referring to Castro and his lieutenants as a "small band of conspirators" who had ". . . stripped the Cuban people of their freedom and handed over the independence and sovereignty of the Cuban nation to forces beyond this hemisphere." Kennedy's assassination ended any chance of an accommodation that both he and Castro apparently were hoping their behind-the-scenes maneuvering would achieve. From what was known publicly, however, Cuba was forever a source of frustration for Kennedy — and defeat.

The Havana Investigation: Part One

Cuban-American relations were no better after the assassination, due to the suspicions that had been aroused, and the hostility affected cooperation between the Castro government and the Warren Commission. W. David Slawson, the assistant counsel assigned to investigate Oswald's trip to Mexico, told us that when he suggested that the Commission attempt to obtain from the Cuban government the originals of documents that Oswald reportedly had filled out in the Cuban Consulate in Mexico City, Chief Justice Warren said no. "He did not want to rely upon any information from a government which was itself one of the principal suspects." (Slawson disobeyed orders and got the State Department to request the information through the Swiss government, later explaining to Warren that he had "misunderstood.") The prevailing antagonism made it impossible for the Commission to take the testimony of Cuban consular officials serving in Mexico at the time of Oswald's visit. Instead, the Commission relied on interviews by Mexican authorities and "confidential sources." We recognized, therefore, that we might be able to go beyond what the Warren Commission could accomplish. For once, the passage of time might work in our favor. We hoped that relations between the United States and Cuba had improved sufficiently since 1964 for us to secure the direct cooperation of the

Cuban government. The time — late 1977 — seemed propitious, since the Carter administration was trying to establish better relations with Cuba, and Castro was apparently receptive. In our investigative plan, therefore, we attached a high priority to the Cuba project. Its purpose was not limited to learning more about Oswald's Mexico City trip, important as that was. We had some specific allegations we wanted the Cuban government to answer, and we also hoped to obtain information about two other groups whose activities in the period leading up to November 1963 were a subject of our investigation — anti-Castro Cuban exiles and members of organized crime. We had prepared a detailed outline of interrogations we wished to conduct in Havana on a trip that we hoped would culminate in an interview with Castro himself. All that remained was to make arrangements with the Cubans.

Our initial intent was to go through Lyle F. Lane, a State Department official who headed the American Interests Section, which was established in Havana in 1977. We soon learned, however, that while the State Department wanted to help, it moved in a manner that would not suit our schedule. We had no time to spare; besides, the kind of questions we had to ask were not exactly diplomatic. We decided, therefore, to act on our own. It happened that as a member of the Congressional Black Caucus, Chairman Stokes had been invited to Cuba in December 1977, so he was able to make preliminary soundings with Rafael Fernandez Duany, the second secretary and vice-consul of the Cuban Interests Section in Washington. As a result, a meeting was set up with Teofilio Acosta Rodriguez, the first secretary and consul of the Cuban Interests Section. We met for lunch at a small Chinese restaurant in Washington on December 5, 1977. It was a frank conversation in which we told Acosta quite bluntly what we hoped to achieve, stressing that the only purpose of our mission was to learn the truth. We also hoped that any trip to Cuba could be accomplished without undue publicity. He seemed somewhat taken aback by our directness, or perhaps he was not used to a congressional committee that wished to avoid publicity, but he promised to take up the matter with his government when he was in Havana that weekend. When Acosta returned to Washington, he told us his government was favorably inclined, but he asked that we prepare a detailed outline of our specific areas of interest and then give his government time to prepare for our visit. Time to prepare meant, we learned, time to run a check on our Committee, its members, and its staff. Eventually, we were informed that the Cuban government had decided to cooperate.

On March 16, 1978, we met in Chairman Stokes's office with Acosta and Ricardo Escartin, also a first secretary and consul of the Cuban Interests Section. They had read our outline, and all was ready for the trip.

It was a "delicate and sensitive" matter, Acosta said, but it was "outstanding" in the relations of Cuban and American people and ought to be resolved. The Cuban government was willing to help, for it too sought "the truth." Acosta said he hoped we would be able to see President Castro, but it would depend on the "personal style" of the Cuban leader. He said he was certain we would be happy with the results of the trip, which was secretly set for the six-day period that began on March 30, 1978.

At 2 P.M. on Thursday, March 30, a red-and-white, twin-engine Piper Aztec took off from Miami for Cuba. On board were Chairman Stokes and Congressman Dodd, representing the Committee (Kennedy Subcommittee Chairman Preyer flew to Havana from Lisbon, arriving at 7 the next morning), and G. Robert Blakey, Gary Cornwell, and Edwin Lopez Soto of the Committee staff. At 3:30 P.M. we arrived at Jose Marti airport, where we were met by Oscar Fernandez Mell, the mayor of Havana; Dr. Armando Torres Santrayll, the Minister of Justice; and Senen Buergo and Ricardo Escartin from the Ministry of Foreign Affairs. In addition, Alfredo Ramirez Otero, a presidential adviser on U.S. relations, and Juanita Vera, a translator, were there. We ate dinner that evening in Old Havana, the guests of Mayor Fernandez. Work began the next morning at 9:30 in a secluded villa outside Havana, where we were joined by a representative of the Ministry of the Interior, Captain Felipe Villa. Meetings were held that Friday and again on Saturday. The sessions were somewhat formal at first, because the Cubans, despite the detailed outline we had supplied, seemed not too sure of our purpose, or that we were on a serious mission. They gave us an opportunity to make it a largely ceremonial visit and to let us spend our time as sightseers. When we declined, and even asked to continue working on Sunday, the ice was broken.

Since the Ministry of the Interior had prepared answers for most of our questions, our work was greatly facilitated. Witnesses had been identified and located; documents, where possible, had been secured. Much time, we were told, had passed since the period we were asking about, and since at that time they were busy "making a revolution," they did not have "mature institutions of government" to document all that we might wish. While we recognized that no government would cooperate without regard for its own interests — and Cuba obviously had interests that conflicted with cooperation — we judged that the Cubans had made an honest effort to assist in most of the areas of our concern, and we were inclined to accept their explanation for an inability to do more for us.

On Friday we reviewed Oswald's 1963 trip to the Cuban Consulate in Mexico City and Jack Ruby's activities on a visit to Havana in 1959. On

Saturday morning the subject was Santo Trafficante, the top organized-crime figure in Havana until he was expelled from Cuba in 1959. Later on Saturday we interviewed Eusebio Azcue Lopez, who was the Cuban consul in Mexico City in 1963, the one with whom Oswald dealt in his unsuccessful effort to get to Cuba. On Saturday evening we had dinner at the Tropicana, a nightclub that in 1959 was also a lavish casino, which was managed by Lewis J. McWillie, Ruby's good friend and his host on the visit to Havana. The Tropicana had been expropriated from owners who were tied to organized crime, and it was now being run by the government. On Sunday we returned to our investigation of Trafficante's activities, focusing on the question: Had he been associated with Ruby? By Monday we had concluded there would have to be a return trip to Cuba; much remained to be done. We would have to postpone, for example, our search for any evidence the Cuban government might provide of involvement in the assassination of anti-Castro groups in the United States. For the time being, we were fully occupied: we were clarifying details of ground already covered; we were investigating the ticklish subject of attacks against Cuba that had been sponsored by intelligence agencies of our government; and we were preparing for our interview with Castro, though we were beginning to wonder whether we would get to see the Cuban president. It was a delicate matter. We were guests in a foreign country, whose leader our government had plotted to assassinate. In addition, we wanted to broach with Castro the possibility that he had retaliated against Kennedy. We knew we were being tested. Castro was monitoring our meetings and judging the Committee's attitude toward Cuba and toward him. We could tell that from the way the Cubans had arranged the trip and structured the meetings, and particularly from the rank of the officials who had been assigned to our visit. Late on Monday afternoon we learned we had passed the test. Castro would see us at 6 P.M. in the Presidential Palace.

We hoped in our meeting with Castro to clear up two especially troubling points. The first had to do with the lengthy (three-hour), supposedly impromptu interview in the Brazilian Embassy on September 7, 1963, with Daniel Harker of the Associated Press. According to Harker, Castro warned that United States leaders would be in danger if they helped in any effort to do away with the leaders of Cuba. "We are prepared to fight them and answer in kind," he said. It was obviously more than an off-the-cuff remark, particularly in view of the CIA-Mafia plots on Castro's life. As Raymond Rocca, a CIA officer who had been assigned to assist the Warren Commission, wrote at the time of the Church Committee investigation: "There can be no question from the facts surrounding the Castro appearance, which had not been expected, and his agreement to the interview, that this event represented a more-than-ordinary attempt to get a message on the record in the United States." The sobering question remained: Did his statements represent a threat that was carried out less than three months later? We had evidence that indicated it did not. We knew, for example, that in the fall of 1963 the tensions between Castro and Kennedy were beginning to ease. The Cuban ambassador to the United Nations, Carlos Lechuga, was in contact with William Attwood of the U.S. Delegation, and better relations seemed to be in the offing. (In fact, by October 31, there was talk, approved by Kennedy, of an American diplomat meeting secretly with Castro in Havana.) It had also become known that Jean Daniel of *L'Express*, a French newspaper, had met with President Kennedy at the White House on October 24. Benjamin C. Bradlee, the *Newsweek* Washington Bureau chief, urged Kennedy to see Daniel, but nothing happened until Kennedy learned Daniel was soon to go to Cuba. "Have him come tomorrow at 5:30," he told Bradlee. In his talk with Daniel, Kennedy was candid and specific about the problems, but he showed a sympathy toward Cuba, aware that on his three-week visit to Havana, Daniel would convey those impressions to Castro. Kennedy then invited Daniel to come and see him when he returned. "Castro's reactions interest me," he said. Daniel spent two days in intense conversation with Castro. At 10 P.M. on November 19, Castro, unannounced, appeared at Daniel's hotel room. He did not leave until 4 in the morning. They carefully went over Daniel's conversation with Kennedy. According to Daniel, Castro said, "I believe Kennedy is sincere." He added, "Personally, I consider him responsible for everything, but I will say this . . . in the last analysis, I'm convinced that anyone else would be worse. . . . You can tell him that I'm willing to declare Goldwater my friend if that will guarantee Kennedy's reelection!" After a long analysis of world tensions, Castro told Daniel, "Since you are going to see Kennedy again, be an emissary of peace, despite everything." Daniel was also with Castro on November 22. It was around 1:30 P.M. Cuban time. They were having lunch in the living room of Castro's summer residence at Varadero Beach. Castro answered the phone, *"Como? Un attentade?"* ("What's that? An attempted assassination?") He told Daniel that Kennedy had been shot in Dallas. *"Herido? Muy gravemente?"* ("Wounded? Very seriously?") He returned to Daniel and repeated three times: *"Es una mala noticia."* ("This is bad news.") Castro then commented, "[A]ll will have to be rethought. I'll tell you one thing; at least Kennedy was an enemy to whom we had become accustomed. You watch and see. . . . I know that they will try to put the blame on us for this thing."

Our second question concerned an allegation that it had been reported to Castro that Lee Harvey Oswald had made a threat against the life of President Kennedy when he was in the Cuban Consulate in

Mexico City. The elements of the report had been pieced together by Daniel Schorr, the television correspondent, in his book *Clearing the Air*. According to Schorr, Comer Clark, a British journalist, interviewed Castro in July 1967. Clark quoted Castro as saying that Oswald had come to the consulate twice, each time for about fifteen minutes. According to Clark, Castro said, "The first time — I was told — he wanted to work for us. He was asked to explain, but he wouldn't. . . . The second time he said he wanted to 'free Cuba from American imperialism.' Then he said something like, 'Somebody ought to shoot that President Kennedy!' Then Oswald said — and this is how it was reported to me — 'Maybe I'll try to do it.' " Schorr went beyond the Clark report and wrote that on June 17, 1964, FBI Director Hoover sent, by special courier, a top-secret letter to Warren Commission General Counsel J. Lee Rankin. It said, ". . . through a confidential source which has provided reliable information in the past, we have been advised of some statements made by Fidel Castro, Cuban Prime Minister, concerning the assassination of President Kennedy." Schorr added that he had learned that the substance of the statements attributed to Castro, which had been deleted in a copy of the Hoover-Rankin letter that was publicly released in 1976, was that "Oswald, on his visit to the consulate, had talked of assassinating President Kennedy." Schorr said that the Cuban ambassador in Mexico City had reported the incident to Havana, but it had not been taken seriously at the time.

It was about 6:30 P.M. April 3, 1978, when we were ushered into the expansive brick- and wood-paneled office and were met by Castro, who was dressed in his customary green army fatigues. In all, we spent more than four hours with Castro, and many topics related and unrelated to the assassination were discussed. Following a few pleasantries (we were offered drinks and fine Cuban cigars), the conversation began in earnest. Castro explained to us his remarks at the Brazilian Embassy:

> We were constantly arresting people trained by the CIA . . . with explosives, with telescopic target rifles . . . . [M]y intention in saying what I said . . . was to warn the government that we [knew] . . . about the . . . plots against our lives. [B]ut I did not mean to threaten by that. I did not mean even that, . . . not in the least, . . . but rather . . . that to set . . . precedents of plotting the assassination of leaders of other countries would be very bad. . . . I did not mean by that that we were going to take measures . . . like a retaliation. . . .

He also expressed his reaction to allegations of his complicity in the assassination:

> Who here could have operated and planned something so delicate as the death of the United States President? That was insane. From the ideologi-

cal point of view, it was a tremendous insanity. [T]hat would have been the most perfect pretext for the United States to invade our country which is what I have tried to prevent for all these years. [T]he death of the leader does not change the system. . . .

We asked Castro about the Oswald threat story. He appeared to read the material from Schorr's book (we knew that he had seen it already since it was in the questions given to Acosta) and replied:

This is absurd. I didn't say that. It has been invented from beginning until the end.

Suggesting that it was implausible that it had happened because if it had, the Cuban government would have reported the threat to the United States, Castro commented:

If [Oswald] . . . would have done something like that, it would have been our moral duty to inform the United States.

We had anticipated what Castro would say about his statements at the Brazilian Embassy. Had his criticism of U.S. leaders in September 1963 stood only in the context of hostility between Cuba and the United States, it might have warranted a sinister interpretation. But when it was also seen in the context of diplomatic overtures at the United Nations, and coupled with sound evidence that both Castro and Kennedy were making moves in the direction of rapprochement, it appeared to be not so much a threat against Kennedy's life as a warning, probably issued in the hope that the American President would call a halt to exile attacks on Cuba. We were surprised, however, by Castro's comment on the Schorr report. We placed little credence in Comer Clark, although, in fairness, we had been unable to talk to him directly, since he had died by the time of our investigation. We knew, however, that he had been a journalist of small reputation, whose published efforts included such titles as "British Girls as Nazi Sex Slaves," "I Was Hitler's Secret Love," and "German Plans to Kidnap the Royal Family." His Castro story was published in *The National Enquirer*, a sensational journal with a reputation for unreliability. On the other hand, we had access, as it was put in the Committee *Report*, to "a highly confidential, but reliable source." The source reported that "Oswald had . . . vowed in the presence of Cuban Consulate officials to assassinate the President." If the confidential source was reliable, Castro had blatantly lied to us, and in such a way that his and his government's credibility were called into question, despite all the cooperation and hospitality that had been extended to us. Ultimately, the Committee decided to believe Castro and not believe Clark or the confidential source. The Committee reasoned:

[B]ased on newspaper reporting alone, the Cuban government might reasonably have believed that the Committee had access to extensive information about conversations in the Cuban Consulate. . . .

The Cuban government permitted two consular officials, Eusebio Azcue and his successor, Alfredo Mirabal, both of whom had had contact with Oswald and who were in a position to have heard the threatening statement, to come to the United States and testify in a public hearing of our Committee. Had the Committee convincingly demonstrated that Azcue and Mirabal were lying, the Cuban government would have been seriously embarrassed. While the Committee did not naively believe that the Cuban government would not lie when it was in its best interest to do so, it did not believe that it would have lightly run the risk of being publicly unmasked as deceitful on the question of Oswald's alleged threat, which might have implied more than a failure to report it. The Committee disagreed, however, with Castro's moral assessment that it would have been his duty to report the threat to the United States. Assuming that Oswald had made the threat, the Committee felt that the Cuban government would have been under no moral obligation to report it to U.S. authorities, since there would have been no reason, when it was made, to regard it seriously. We shared the Committee's judgment on this aspect of its evaluation of Castro's position. Such threats are commonly heard by public officials and properly ignored. Nevertheless, our assessment of Castro's denial of the threat differed from that of the Committee. It was our judgment that the threat probably did occur. While Marina Oswald and others testified that Oswald spoke only highly of President Kennedy, there was evidence that he talked about "shooting the President" at various times in his life. He once made "a threat," for example, against President Eisenhower to a boyhood acquaintance, Palmer McBride. (McBride thought the threat was not "made in jest.") We also learned that Oswald talked, on at least one occasion while he was in the Soviet Union, about "shooting the President." We were told that a friend, Pavel Golovachev, asked Oswald how he would be able to take care of Marina's materialistic demands in the United States. Oswald replied that Golovachev did not understand the United States. "You could always make a lot of money by shooting the President," he was said to have remarked. We also noted the curious similarity between the remarks attributed to the Oswald who visited the Cuban Consulate in Mexico City in September 1963 and those attributed to the Oswald who reportedly visited Silvia Odio, an anti-Castro activist in Dallas in the same month. Given a possible pattern of threatening remarks (although it can hardly be termed extensive), discounting, but not entirely, the Clark report, and noting the previous reliability of the confidential source available to the

Committee, we were inclined to believe that Oswald had uttered the
threat attributed to him in the Cuban Consulate. We were forced to
conclude, therefore, that the Cuban government decided that the risk
of admitting that the threat had occurred, but was not acted upon, was
potentially more damaging than the risk that the deception of its consular officials might be unmasked. (The Cuban government, after all,
could always have explained any evidence used to demonstrate the
truth of the Oswald threat allegation as a CIA fabrication designed to
implicate Cuba in the assassination.) Unlike the Committee, therefore,
we believed that the Cuban government withheld important information. While we believed that the Cuban government generally cooperated with us (the proof of its cooperation lay in the important information that it did provide to us that could be corroborated or authenticated), we also believed that the Cuban government kept a careful eye
fixed on its own best interests. Here, that interest — as the Cubans saw
it — warranted not telling us the truth.

The 1977 CIA Task Force Report

The Church Committee, following its review of the CIA-Mafia plots,
arrived at a judgment that Castro probably had not been aware that the
agency was behind attempts by the underworld to have him assassinated, nor would he have been able to distinguish between the CIA-
Mafia plots and other hostile actions by Cuban exiles. The Church
Committee held, therefore, that the Kennedy assassination was not a
retaliatory act by Castro, at least for the CIA-Mafia plots. As for the
AM/LASH operation, that was quite another matter, in the view of the
Church Committee. While the Mafia plots had been terminated in early
1963, AM/LASH was a high-priority program at the time of the assassination (the Cuban official, code-named AM/LASH, who had of-
fered to attempt a coup, met with senior CIA officials on the morning of
November 22, 1963); and it could have been more easily traced to the
CIA, since the agency was in direct contact with AM/LASH. Still, the
Church Committee could find ". . . no evidence that Fidel Castro or
others in the Cuban government plotted President Kennedy's assassination in retaliation for U.S. operations against Cuba."

In 1977 a CIA task force was designated to evaluate the Church Committee's conclusions and to investigate the critical issues it had raised.
In its report, the task force quite properly took the position that Castro
had ample grounds for retaliation without having been specifically
informed about the CIA-Mafia or the AM/LASH plots, arguing that
those operations were but part of a series of hostile acts taken by the
United States, including an actual invasion. The task force also suggested that the CIA had not been primarily responsible for framing the

Mafia plots. "It is possible," the task force wrote, "that the CIA simply found itself involved in providing additional resources for the independent operations that the syndicate already had underway." As for AM/LASH, the task force expressed the view that the Cuban official who was ready to oust Castro by violent means had no reason to believe he had the backing of the CIA. "Were he a provocateur reporting to Castro, or if he was merely careless and leaked what he knew, he had no factual basis for leaking or reporting any actual CIA plot directed against Castro." As for the failure of the CIA to alert the Warren Commission to the plots against Castro, the CIA took a self-administered light rap on the knuckles with a built-in excuse:

> CIA . . . could have considered in specific terms what most saw in general terms — the possibility of a Soviet or Cuban involvement in the JFK assassination because of the tensions of the time. . . . The Agency should have taken broader initiatives, then, as well. That CIA employees at the time felt — as they obviously did — that the activities about which they knew had no relevance to the Warren Commission inquiry does not take the place of a record of conscious review.

We took a careful look at the 1977 task force report and found little to recommend it. It was particularly disheartening to learn that the CIA had learned so little from the Church Committee's incisive and balanced critique of CIA activities in areas that were crucial to the country's self-respect, not to mention the security of its leaders. Rather than treat the Church Committee's findings with open-minded objectivity, the task force reflected an agency bias: where the findings were favorable to the CIA, it accepted them uncritically; but where investigative oversight was suggested, as in the case of an inadequate post-assassination review of the possible implications of the AM/LASH plot, the task force rejected the Church Committee's conclusions. As for the "broader initiatives" that it said might have been taken in 1963, the task force maintained they would have merely served to head off criticism: "[O]ur findings are essentially negative," the task force wrote. "However, it must be recognized that CIA cannot be as confident of a cold trail in 1977 as it could have been in 1964; this apparent fact will be noted by critics of the Agency. . . ." There was, of course, a chance the task force was right — all that might have been gained from an intense investigation of the various CIA plots against Castro was a public scandal that would not have contributed to an understanding of the President's death. But the 1977 task force did nothing to document its point, and it was a position that rang hollow, especially in light of a conspiracy based on the acoustics evidence developed in our investigation. We were not at all certain that a greater effort by the CIA — in 1964 or in 1977 — would have generated little but scandal, as the task force

implied. And we were disappointed to find that the CIA task force had
nothing to add to what the Church Committee had published about the
plots — the CIA-Mafia plots, in particular. Specifically, there was not a
word about the activities of the plotters in the latter half of 1963, a critical period as far as we were concerned.

The task force observed that a general directive was sent to all CIA
stations overseas: "Tragic death of President Kennedy requires all of us
to look sharp for any unusual intelligence development. Although we
have no reason to expect anything of a particular military nature, all
hands should be on the quick alert for the next few days. . . ." The task
force reasoned the query was necessarily general, for so little information had been assembled at the time it was sent, and it argued that
general guidelines were sufficient, since "relevant information" would
have been reported anyway. But the task force had nothing to say about
what had been done at the various CIA stations to secure such "relevant information." We wondered about the JM/WAVE station in
Miami, for it had been monitoring the activities of most anti-Castro
organizations operating out of bases in the United States. Had the station contacted and debriefed its Cuban sources? Had it sought to determine if its sources had information about Cuban government participation in an assassination plot or about an association of Oswald and
Cuban government agents? Had there been an effort to reconstruct the
activities of Castro agents in the United States in the period leading up
to the assassination? The task force report left the impression that such
efforts were made on the initiative of the stations, but it omitted any
discussion of the results. The 1977 task force report was, in a word, a
self-serving attempt to refute the accusations of the Church Committee, rather than an effort to evaluate the post-assassination CIA investigation or to assess the significance of CIA anti-Castro activities with respect to the President's death. What was called for, we realized, was our
own investigation of the implications of CIA activities that had supposedly had "no relevance" to the work of the Warren Commission.

The CIA position on AM/LASH, as stated in the 1977 task force
report and reaffirmed to us in 1978 by former Director Richard M.
Helms, was that it did not contemplate assassination. (We wondered if
Castro, too, had regarded the plot so benignly.) That was not the
attitude of AM/LASH himself, who envisioned assassination as an essential first step in an overthrow of the Castro government, according to
evidence developed by the Church Committee in 1975 and confirmed
by us. We believed it was the perception of the person in Havana who
was to carry out the act that would have counted so far as Castro was
concerned, not what the CIA might have thought from its perspective
in Langley, Virginia. As far as the question of retaliation was con-

cerned, it was Castro's attitude that would have mattered, not Helms's. We considered the CIA disavowal of the assassination aspect of the AM/LASH operation to be, at best, disingenuous and, at worst, intentionally false.

AM/LASH told his CIA case officer in August 1962 of his interest in assassinating Castro, a Castro lieutenant, and the Soviet ambassador to Cuba, and in sabotaging an oil refinery. The case officer acknowledged that he had told AM/LASH that ". . . schemes like he envisioned certainly had their place, but that a lot of coordination, planning, . . . etc. were . . . prerequisites to . . . the success of such plans." Communications following the meeting with CIA headquarters established that the case officer did not give AM/LASH a "physical elimination mission as [a] requirement," but it was something "he . . . might try . . . on his own initiative." AM/LASH returned to Cuba shortly after the meeting, coming out again in September 1963 to notify the case officer that he had not abandoned his planned coup. On October 21, 1963, the case officer reported that AM/LASH was asking for assurances that Washington would support him if he was able to pull off the coup, and on October 29 Desmond Fitzgerald, the chief of the CIA's Special Affairs Staff, the Cuba covert action group, met with AM/LASH. Saying he was speaking for Attorney General Robert F. Kennedy, Fitzgerald assured AM/LASH of U.S. backing, but he deferred a decision on the Cuban's request for "technical support" in the form of a rifle or some other weapon. (A poison pen, telescopic sight, silencer, and money were actually offered to AM/LASH on November 22, 1963, but, due to the assassination, never delivered.)

We thought it safe to assume that had Castro known about the meetings between the Cuban official and the CIA, he would have learned about the planned coup d'etat and his intended assassination, possibly from AM/LASH himself, who could have been a double agent or else exposed and made to talk. Joseph Langosch, who in 1963 was the chief of counterintelligence for the Special Affairs Staff, told us that it was highly likely that Cuban intelligence had become aware of the dealings of AM/LASH with the CIA. We could not determine with certainty that it had, but we *were* told by the Cuban government on our second trip to Havana, in August 1978, that it believed the traitorous official to be one Rolando Cubela Secades. We were assured, however, that Cubela had not been unmasked until three years after the Kennedy assassination. Was Cubela the plotter? Was his plan to topple Castro not discovered until 1966? The dates of his arrest and trial tended to corroborate what we were told by the Cuban government. We recognized, however, that it was unlikely that Cuban officials would have told us, if, in fact, they had learned of the plot prior to November 22, 1963. That would have lent considerable credibility to the theories of the Church Committee that the assassination might have been in retaliation for the AM/LASH operation. We questioned Cubela, who confirmed the facts and dates of his confession to Cuban authorities and said they had been unaware of his duplicity as of November 22, 1963. We took into account the possible influence of his confinement on his testimony, and even if it was the truth as he knew it, we did not believe that Cubela's testimony was sufficient proof that Castro did not know about the AM/LASH operation as of November 22, 1963.

We agreed with the 1977 task force when it suggested that organized crime was active in Castro assassination attempts independent of any it might have engaged in with the CIA. We noted, however, that the Mafia had good reason to join forces with the CIA: agency sponsorship meant official sanction and logistical support of the plots; and the relationship could be used by organized-crime figures as leverage against prosecution for offenses unrelated to assassination. (As it turned out, a grand jury investigation of one of the Mafia plotters, Sam Giancana, was terminated in 1966 at least in part because the CIA was fearful that his role in the plots against Castro would become public; and John Roselli was fighting deportation and seeking to escape prosecution for illegal gambling, when he began leaking information about the plots in 1967.) We also found circumstantial yet convincing evidence that the Mafia was leading the CIA on; at least after early 1962 its interest in eliminating Castro was not all that sincere. The Soviet domination of Cuba had just about ruled out any hope of regaining the old Havana territory, and there were illicit fortunes to be made in the Bahamas and elsewhere.

We looked into the possibility that the assassination was in retaliation for the CIA-Mafia plots, a notion that was generally rejected by the Church Committee. While we were able to interview several witnesses who had not come to the attention of the Church Committee, and though we had access to the CIA and FBI files on the Mafia plots, we did not have an opportunity, unfortunately, to take fresh testimony from Giancana and Roselli, who were murdered in July 1975 and July 1976, respectively. Roselli was the source of the theory that the President's assassins had originally been members of an anti-Castro hit team that had been caught and forced, through the threat of torture, to turn their guns on Kennedy. The "turnaround" theory first surfaced in January 1967, when a Washington lawyer for Roselli, Edward P. Morgan, approached Drew Pearson and Jack Anderson, the syndicated columnists. Morgan outlined the CIA-Mafia plots, posed the possibility of a Castro-ordered retaliation against President Kennedy, and asked that the information be passed to Chief Justice Earl Warren. Warren in turn called James J. Rowley, the director of the Secret Service, who notified FBI Director Hoover. Morgan told us in 1978 that his source, though he had not revealed it in 1967, was Roselli, who had come to him, complaining of excessive FBI surveillance ever since he had become involved in Castro plots with the CIA. (The FBI had, in fact, kept a close watch on Roselli, who was a target of Attorney General Kennedy's organized-crime drive.) When Morgan's account to Pearson and Anderson appeared in their columns on March 6 and 7, 1967, President Johnson ordered the FBI to investigate, but Hoover, who had decided to do nothing about the allegation, limited the probe to an interview of Morgan. CIA Director Helms, on the other hand, ordered an inspector general's report on the Mafia plots. In 1968 Roselli was sentenced to prison for cheating at cards and for failure to register as an illegal alien, and following his release in 1973, he faced deportation. The CIA contacted the Immigration and Naturalization Service, however, and said a deportation proceeding against Roselli would not be in the best interest of intelligence "sources and methods." The proceeding was still pending at the time of Roselli's death.

We came to two conclusions about the turnaround theory: first, had Castro decided to have Kennedy killed, he had agents who were far more dependable than a hit team sent by the Mafia to assassinate him; second, Roselli's reason for advancing the turnaround idea was apparently to secure immunity from prosecution and deportation, and he was at least partially successful. We did not consider it out of the question that a Mafia hit team was responsible for the assassination, but we did not accept Roselli's assertion that it was ordered to do so by Castro.

A Cuban Defector's Oswald Story

Our investigation turned up evidence of what we believed to be a dereliction of duty on the part of the CIA comparable to its failure to inform the Warren Commission about the Mafia and AM/LASH plots. As in the case of Yuri Nosenko, the KGB defector, a Cuban intelligence officer sought political asylum in the United States in 1963. Like Nosenko, the Cuban defector, whose identity we agreed to protect by referring to him only as A-1, claimed to have information relevant to the Kennedy assassination. Unlike Nosenko, however, A-1's story never was fully shared with the Warren Commission. J. Lee Rankin and Howard P. Willens were notified of A-1's defection and told that he had identified an employee of the Cuban Consulate in Mexico City in 1963, Luisa Calderon, as a likely agent of the DGI, the Cuban Intelligence Directorate. Rankin and Willens were not, however, supplied with the information necessary to evaluate A-1's story.

When we interviewed A-1 in 1978, he not only identified Calderon as a DGI agent, but he told us that in 1963 she might have had a relationship with Oswald that extended beyond her capacity as a secretary in the

Mexico City consulate. A-1, whose "bona fides" the agency did not doubt, told us, as he said he had told the CIA in 1963, the reason for his suspicions. Shortly after the assassination he learned from a DGI officer in Cuba that Calderon had been called home because she had become involved with an American, who A-1 thought might have been Oswald. He had heard, he said, the name of the sender of an intercepted letter to Calderon, which sounded something like "Ower"; and he had learned that, while under DGI surveillance in Mexico City, Calderon had been seen in the company of an American. Her recall to Havana, he understood, was the result of her association with the American. With A-1's story in mind, we looked with renewed interest at a blind memorandum we obtained from the CIA, which told of a reported Calderon conversation on the day of the assassination:

> A reliable source reported that on November 22, 1963, several hours after the assassination of President John F. Kennedy, Luisa Calderon Carralero, a Cuban employee of the Cuban Embassy in Mexico City, and believed to be a member of the Cuban Directorate General of Intelligence [DGI], discussed news of the assassination with an acquaintance. Initially, when asked if she had heard the latest news, Calderon replied, in what appeared to be a joking manner, "Yes, of course, I knew almost before Kennedy."

The CIA suggested to us that the remark attributed to Calderon had been incorrectly translated. In Spanish, it was, "*Si, claro, me entere cusinantes que Kennedy.*" The verb, "*me entere,*" should be read as "I found out" or "I learned," not "I knew." If so, foreknowledge was not implied; Calderon was simply saying she had learned of the assassination at about the time it occurred. This did not explain, however, why the conversation was not reported to the Warren Commission, or why the Commission did not receive A-1's account.

We still were faced with a decision of what to do about the allegation involving Luisa Calderon. When in Cuba, we asked to speak with Calderon but were told she was ill; in response to written interrogatories, she flatly denied foreknowledge of the assassination. In the end, we decided the allegations raised suspicions of the most sinister sort, but they were not enough to warrant an inference of Cuban complicity in the assassination.

Cuban Complicity

The Committee found "persuasive reasons to conclude that the Cuban government was not involved in the Kennedy assassination." They were, first, the apparently real prospects for repairing U.S.-Cuban relations; second, the high risk that the United States would resort to military action if Cuban complicity could be proved; third, the absence of concrete evidence that Castro's agents were conspirators, realizing that the CIA's sources in the exile community and in Cuba would have probably volunteered such evidence, had it existed; and, fourth, the willingness of the Cuban government to cooperate with the Committee. There was a fifth reason that the Committee left unsaid, since it tended to undercut the force of its judgment: the Committee, as a responsible body of government, had an obligation to determine that the Cuban government was not involved in the assassination, if it could not find convincing proof that it was. As individuals, we were under no such restriction. In fact, we did not find the issue of Cuban complicity so clearly resolved, for, at the end of the Committee's investigation, a number of troubling questions remained. We believed that Oswald had, in fact, uttered a threat to murder the President within earshot of consular officials in Mexico City (which meant that, in contrast to the Committee, we did not trust the word of the Cuban government); we were still uneasy about the timing of the unmasking of Cubela and the allegations about Calderon; and we had not settled on the implications of the CIA-Mafia plots (which, we decided, had yet to be evaluated in the context of an organized-crime conspiracy). We could not avoid the judgment, moreover, that the Church Committee was wrong to discount the dangers to President Kennedy that were posed by the anti-Castro activities of the CIA and organized crime, working together. The notion that Castro would not have blamed Kennedy for the plots was, we believed, based on faulty logic: after all, the plots were conceived and carried through their initial stages in the United States. From our review of U.S.-Cuban relations from 1959 on, we had learned that when Castro erred in his assumptions, it was in the direction of attributing more, rather than less, responsibility for attempts to overthrow him to the U.S. government than might have been merited. We also rejected the argument of the CIA to the Church Committee (which accepted it) that the CIA-Mafia plots had no direct relevance to the Kennedy assassination, since they had been terminated in February 1963. It was clear that relationships spawned by the CIA-Mafia association had lingered on. In June 1963, for example, John Roselli had a dinner meeting with William Harvey, who had been chief of Task Force W, the Cuban covert action unit, and the two men stayed in touch at least until 1967, according to CIA files. Roselli was also in contact with the chief of the Operational Support Branch, CIA Office of Security (who was identified by columnist Jack Anderson as James O'Connell) as late as 1971. In any event, how was Castro to know, even if the plots *had* been terminated? Finally, the Church Committee was mistaken, in our view, when it concluded that the AM/LASH operation had more relevance to the assassination than the CIA-Mafia plots. We believed that the reality was the reverse. In terms of the security of American leaders, President Kennedy in particular, the inherent risk of "doing business with . . . gangsters," as Robert Kennedy put it to CIA representatives in May 1962, was far greater than that of encouraging a dissident Cuban official to lead a coup. Dissidents are a fact of life for all leaders. Mafia hit men trained on Presidents are, as Castro put it, a "bad precedent."

While we were able to rule out the "turnaround" theory, the idea that organized crime might *willingly* have joined with Castro in an assassination conspiracy was more difficult to dismiss. By late 1962 and early 1963, while it was still active in the plots, the Mafia had lost much of its incentive to do away with Castro; at the same time, the organized-crime drive at the Justice Department was providing more than sufficient reason to think that the source of trouble lay in Washington, not Havana. We knew Mafia figures to be basically pragmatic businessmen who realign associations, joining forces with ex-enemies when it suits their purpose. Since both the Mafia and Castro were suffering financially at the time — in each case as a result of pressure from the Kennedy administration — they had a mutual motive that made an alliance attractive. It may not have been necessary, in short, for Castro to have ordered the "turnaround." Nevertheless, we rejected this variation of retaliation as well, because all the reasons that militated against Castro's striking at Kennedy by himself could be applied to his doing it in conjunction with gangsters. In addition, the instrumentality in the assassination, Lee Harvey Oswald, a known leftist, pointed squarely at Castro. Had Castro decided to kill Kennedy, he would, we believed, have tried to cover his tracks as best he could.

There was one other theory of Cuban complicity to be considered, one that was raised by Arthur M. Schlesinger, Jr., when he suggested that Castro may not have "exercised complete authority over his own CIA." We had it from Jean Daniel, the French journalist, that Castro was concerned about intelligence agents who might act on their own: "What authority does . . . [Johnson] exercise over the CIA?" Castro asked Daniel the afternoon that Kennedy was assassinated. Could Castro have been in the position of Henry II, whose knights murdered Thomas Becket in 1170? ("Who'll rid me of this meddlesome bishop?") An evaluation of this kind was not one we could readily undertake, so we turned to those more qualified to make an informed judgment and were told it was a remote possibility. The Cuban nation was small; its government was compact and in the hands of loyal comrades of Castro. Unlike Kennedy and the CIA, Castro controlled the DGI, and it would not have acted in the assassination unless ordered to do so by him.

9

Cuban Exiles and the Motive of Revenge

"I hated the United States, . . . Every day it became worse. . . .
I wanted to get a rifle and come and fight against the U.S."

Jose Perez San Roman
Commander, Brigade 2506
(Haynes Johnson, *The Bay of Pigs*)

The Cuban Exile Movement

If it can be said to have a beginning, the anti-Castro Cuban exile movement started in the early morning of New Year's Day 1959 when a DC-4 took off from fog-shrouded Camp Columbia airfield in Havana. Aboard the plane was Fulgencio Batista y Zaldivar, the military dictator of Cuba for the previous six years. When dawn came, the bells tolled in Havana, and 600 miles away, Fidel Castro Ruz began his triumphal march to the capital. Castro arrived in Havana on January 8. Clad in a green fatigue uniform, with three white doves circling above him, he boldly proclaimed, "There is no longer an enemy." It was not true, and Castro knew it. A hard core of Batistianos had fled the country, many long before their leader, and they were already devising counterrevolutionary plots from refuges in the United States and elsewhere. In Cuba itself, dissident movements began to take shape, the result of disillusionment with Castro's soon-evident inclination to embrace Marxism and to ally himself with the Soviet Union in defiance of the United States.

Castro dealt with the opposition he could readily identify in a cruelly

effective way, executing 506 ex-Batista officials in the first three months
of his reign. But in reaction to the violence and the turn to the left, there
were defections within his own ranks. Major Pedro Diaz-Lanz, the chief
of the air force, fled to Miami, charging "Communist influence in the
armed forces and government," and Manuel Urrutia, Castro's handpicked president, was forced to resign when he rejected the support of
Communists. Realizing the need to solidify his position, Castro called a
meeting of province managers of the National Agrarian Reform Institute and announced that he planned to communize Cuba within three
years. The representative from Oriente Province was a young medical
doctor, Manuel Artime. "I realized," he said later, "that I was a democratic infiltrator in a Communist government." Artime returned home
to organize students and others to bear arms against Castro under the
banner of the Movimiento de Recuperacion Revolucionaria, or MRR.
By November 1959 elements of the MRR, the first anti-Castro
organization to spring from the revolution, were active in every Cuban
province. In 1960 Artime joined the anti-Castro cause in Miami, the
exile capital, and was appointed the senior civilian representative of Brigade 2506, which was being trained for an assault on Cuba. It was a
Cuban unit, consisting of Cuban officers and men, but decisions as to
strategy and the timing of an invasion were made in Washington, and
training was conducted by CIA employees with military backgrounds.
Haynes Johnson of *The Washington Post*, who wrote a book, *The Bay of
Pigs*, in collaboration with brigade leaders, found that the exiles had
placed blind faith in their American allies, not only because there was
no other place to turn, but also because the United States was their
friend. Jose (Pepe) Perez San Roman, the brigade commander, told
Johnson: "Most of the Cubans were there because they knew the whole
operation was going to be conducted by the Americans . . . [T]hey did
not trust me or anyone else. They just trusted the Americans."

The defeat at the Bay of Pigs foreshadowed the eventual disintegra-
tion of the Cuban exile movement. Brigade 2506 had been the military
arm of the Frente Revolucionario Democratico (FRD), whose general
coordinator, Antonio de Varona, stepped aside in March 1961 to enable
Jose Miro Cardona, a former prime minister of Cuba, to become president of an expanded and renamed organization, the Cuban Revolutionary Council. The members of the council, who had been sequestered by
the CIA during the landing and who were understandably dejected
(both Varona and Cardona had sons on the beach in Cuba), were taken
to the White House where they heard President Kennedy take personal
blame for the defeat. "We were not charging Mr. Kennedy with
anything, . . ." Varona told us in March 1978. "We knew that he didn't
have any direct knowledge of the problem, and we knew that he was not
in charge of the military effects directly. Nevertheless, President Ken-

nedy, to finish the talks, told us he was the one — the only one respon-sible." On April 24, 1961, the White House issued a public statement, in which Kennedy assumed "sole responsibility" for the U.S. role in the action against Cuba. Mario Lazo, a noted Cuban attorney, vented an anger that was shared by most of the 100,000 Cubans who had fled the revolution: "The Bay of Pigs was wholly self-inflicted in Washington," Lazo wrote in his book, *Dagger in the Heart.* "Kennedy told the truth when he publicly accepted responsibility. . . . The heroism of the beleaguered Cuban Brigade had been rewarded by betrayal, defeat, death for many of them, long and cruel imprisonment for the rest. The mistake of the Cuban fighters," Lazo concluded, "was that they thought too highly of the United States. They believed to the end that it would not let them down. But it did. . . ."

While he publicly took "sole responsibility" for the Bay of Pigs, Ken-nedy was privately as furious with the officials who had mapped the in-vasion as he was determined to reverse the defeat. He dismissed CIA Director Allen W. Dulles and the Deputy Director for Plans, Richard M. Bissell, Jr., and he called on his own close aides, Maxwell Taylor, McGeorge Bundy, Richard N. Goodwin, and Robert F. Kennedy, to take charge of a secret war that was to be waged by several thousand men at a cost of $100 million a year. Day-by-day direction of the effort was entrusted to the CIA. Andrew St. George, a journalist who had covered the revolution from the time it was a guerrilla operation in the Sierra Maestra mountains of eastern Cuba, wrote in *Harper's* in 1973 that within a year of the Bay of Pigs, the CIA had begun "to grow, to branch out, to gather more and more responsibility for the 'Cuban problem.' " The nerve center of anti-Castro activities was the CIA sta-tion situated on a secluded, 1,571-acre tract that was part of the campus of the University of Miami. Code-named JM/WAVE and using an elec-tronics firm, Zenith Technological Services as a front, it was the largest CIA field operation in the world. At the peak of the anti-Castro effort in 1962, JM/WAVE was staffed by three hundred Americans, most of them case officers. Each case officer controlled from four to ten prin-cipal Cuban agents who in turn were in charge of up to thirty regular agents. In addition, JM/WAVE set up fifty-four corporations (boat and gun shops, detective agencies, travel companies) to provide cover em-ployment for the case officers and Cuban agents. As anti-Castro raiding parties embarked by boat regularly from secret CIA bases in the Florida keys with a "green light" from Washington, the Cuban exiles were heartened by the renewed U.S. commitment to their cause.

The resolution of the missile crisis on November 20, 1962, while seen by the world as victory and vindication for Kennedy, was regarded by the exiles as a death knell. The no-invasion pledge that Kennedy gave in return for the removal of the Russian missiles and bombers was termed by Mario Lazo "a soul-shattering blow," and when Kennedy came to Miami on December 29 to greet survivors of Brigade 2506, who had been ransomed from prison in Cuba, an outward display of support masked the bitter resentment of the exiles. On March 31, 1963, acting on a tip from the U.S. State Department, British authorities arrested a group of anti-Castro raiders at a training site in the Bahamas. On April 3, in response to charges from Moscow that the United States was responsible for two commando attacks on Soviet ships anchored in Cuban ports, Washington declared it was "taking every step necessary to ensure that such attacks are not launched, manned or equipped from U.S. territory." On April 5 the Coast Guard announced it was assigning more ships, planes, and men to police the Florida straits; at the same time, the Customs Service and the FBI were cracking down on anti-Castro operations along the coastline. In September the Federal Aviation Administration issued warnings to six American civilian pilots who had been flying sorties over Cuba, and in October the Coast Guard seized four exile ships and arrested twenty-two guerrillas. Kennedy, of course, was damned for his latest "betrayal" by the Cuban exile leaders. (Miro Cardona resigned from the Cuban Revolutionary Council, accusing Kennedy of "breaking promises and agreements.")

On May 1, 1963, U.S. government funding of the Cuban Revolutionary Council was halted, and in June, Antonio Maceo, who had replaced Miro Cardona as president, was forced to step down in the wake of a reported landing in Cuba of 3,000 commandos that turned out to be a hoax. Antonio de Varona again assumed the CRC leadership, but by the summer of 1963 the Cuban exiles no longer posed a threat to Castro.

Our investigation of the possible participation of the Cuban exiles in the Kennedy assassination was based on a judgment that they had the motive (Kennedy's "betrayal" of their cause), the means (the guerrilla warfare training they had received from the CIA), and the opportunity (Kennedy's exposure in cities like Miami, Tampa, and Dallas) to kill the President. We initiated our investigation by identifying the most frustrated and violent anti-Castro groups and their leaders from among the more than 100 exile organizations in the United States in November 1963. We recognized that if the assassination had been the work of a small, unaffiliated group, it would probably escape our net, as it had escaped the attention of the FBI and the Warren Commission in 1964. We could not, however, investigate every organization, so we concentrated on the principal action groups, those whose leaders actually carried out infiltration missions into Cuba and who planned and sometimes attempted the assassination of Castro. Our investigative theory was not entirely original, since it was proposed in 1964 by Warren Commission Assistant Counsel William T. Coleman, Jr., and W. David Slawson, who wrote in an internal memorandum:

> The evidence here could lead to an anti-Castro involvement in the assassination on some sort of basis as this: Oswald could have become known to the Cubans as being strongly pro-Castro. He made no secret of his sympathies, and so the anti-Castro Cubans must have realized that the law-enforcement authorities were also aware of Oswald's feelings and that, therefore, if he got into trouble, the public would also learn of them. . . . Second, someone in the anti-Castro organization might have been keen enough to sense that Oswald had a penchant for violence. . . . On these facts, it's possible that some sort of deception was used to encourage Oswald to kill the President when he came to Dallas. . . . The motive of this would, of course, be the expectation that . . . Oswald would be caught . . . . [T]he law enforcement authorities and the public would then blame the assassination on the Castro government, and the call for its forceful overthrow would be irresistible.

As it turned out, there was substantial support for our investigative theory in the evidence. Indeed, we were to learn that there had been reports of active threats against Kennedy by anti-Castro Cubans around the time of the assassination that had neither been pursued by the FBI nor reported to the Warren Commission. In addition, there were reports that anti-Castro Cubans had met with Lee Harvey Oswald, but the Warren Commission had either chosen not to believe the meetings had occurred or had dismissed them as insignificant.

Oswald's Contacts with Exiles

Lee Harvey Oswald returned to New Orleans, the city of his birth, on April 25, 1963, having lived in Fort Worth and Dallas since his return from the Soviet Union the previous June. He spent the first two weeks job hunting, staying with the Murrets, Lillian and Charles, or "Dutz," as he was called, the sister and brother-in-law of Marguerite, Oswald's mother. When he was hired by the William B. Reily Company, a coffee distributor, as a maintenance man, Oswald sent for his wife Marina and their baby daughter, and they moved into an apartment at 4907 Magazine Street. In May Oswald wrote to Vincent T. Lee, national director of the Fair Play for Cuba Committee, saying he wished to establish an FPCC chapter in New Orleans.

Oswald lost his job in July and was unable to find another, so there was some mystery about his activities for the balance of his stay in New Orleans (he left about September 25, but even that date was not precisely determined). The FBI did learn that on August 5 he approached

Carlos Bringuier, a Cuban exile leader, at a clothing store Bringuier managed, the Casa Roca, and applied for membership in the Cuban Student Directorate. Oswald told Bringuier he had been in the Marine Corps, he had been trained in guerrilla warfare, and he was willing to train Cubans to fight Castro. "Even more, he told me that he was willing to go himself to fight against Castro," Bringuier told the Warren Commission. But Bringuier turned Oswald down, suspecting he was an infiltrator, either for Castro or the FBI. The next day Oswald returned to Bringuier's store and dropped off a copy of his Marine Corps training manual. On August 9 Bringuier was returning to his store from lunch when an anti-Castro associate, Celso Hernandez, alerted him to a demonstration on Canal Street, in which a young American was parading with a "Viva Fidel" sign and passing out pro-Castro literature. Along with Hernandez and another activist, Miguel Cruz, Bringuier went to confront the Castro partisan, who turned out to be Oswald. The Cubans began shouting that he was a Communist and a traitor, and following a scuffle, they all were arrested. Oswald spent the night in jail, and at a hearing on August 12 he pled guilty to disturbing the peace and paid a $10 fine. The Cubans were not charged.

Other anti-Castro Cubans came in contact with Oswald in the aftermath of the fight. Frank Bartes, the Cuban Revolutionary Council's New Orleans delegate, appeared with Bringuier at the arraignment the next day and got into a shouting match with Oswald and the news media because he believed the Cubans were not getting their share of attention. Carlos Quiroga was sent by Bringuier to see what he could find out by visiting Oswald at home, and Quiroga reported that Oswald had a Russian wife and spoke Russian himself. Quiroga also said that Oswald had offered him a Fair Play for Cuba Committee membership application, though he did not seem intent on enlisting members. Bringuier had another confrontation with Oswald on August 21, in a debate that had been arranged by a reporter for a New Orleans radio station. A tape that had been stored at Cuban Student Directorate headquarters in Miami was, on the afternoon of November 22, 1963, seized upon by Cuban exiles as proof that the President's assassin was a Castro agent. We were reminded again of the Coleman-Slawson memorandum.

While the unexplained overtures to Bringuier had a sinister implication (the most logical explanation was that Oswald was attempting to infiltrate the anti-Castro forces), a report that Oswald met in Dallas in September 1963 with a young Cuban exile woman was far more disturbing, for there was in the report an explicit reference to the assassination of the President. Silvia Odio, 26, was a member of the Junta Revolucionaria Cubana, or JURE. (Her uncle, Agustin Guitart, was a prominent Cuban exile in New Orleans, at whose home Antonio de Varona of

Miami, general coordinator of the Cuban Revolutionary Council, stayed when he was in New Orleans on November 15, 1963, for a CRC rally.) Odio, however, did not like to advertise her activism, since her parents, Amador and Sarah Odio, had been imprisoned in Cuba. (Members of Cuba's aristocracy, the elder Odios had been in the forefront of opposition to a succession of tyrants who had ruled Cuba. Twice under Batista they were forced into exile, and they had provided trucks that kept Castro supplied with weapons and ammunition when he was fighting in the mountains. When they decided that Castro had betrayed the revolution, they were among the founders, along with Manolo Ray, who later became the head of JURE, of an aggressive anti-Castro organization, the Movimiento Revolucionario de Pueblo, or MRP. When Reynaldo Gonzales, the national coordinator of MRP, who had engaged in a plot to assassinate Castro, was caught hiding out at the Odio's country estate, Amador and Sarah Odio were jailed.)

Silvia Odio told the FBI and the Warren Commission that on September 25 or 26, three men came to her home in Dallas to ask for help in preparing a JURE fund-raising letter. (Odio did not volunteer her story. A friend who had learned of the incident informed the FBI.) Odio said that two of the men who had come to her apartment, the two who looked like "Latins," had given their war names, "Leopoldo" and "Angelo." She said the third man, an American, was introduced to her as "Leon Oswald," and he fit the description of Lee Harvey Oswald. According to Odio's account to the FBI in 1963 and to us in 1978, the three men told her they had come from New Orleans and were about to leave on a trip. (September 25 was, in fact, the day the Warren Commission fixed for Oswald's departure from New Orleans for Mexico City via Houston.) Odio said she was frightened and did not permit the men to enter her apartment, although they used the correct code names for her mother and father and seemed familiar with her family background. They stayed only briefly, but the next day Leopoldo telephoned her to explain he was bringing the American into the exile underground, "because he is great; he is kind of *loco.*" He had served in the Marine Corps and was an excellent shot, said Leopoldo, who then quoted Oswald: "[Cubans] don't have any guts. . . . President Kennedy should have been assassinated after the Bay of Pigs, and some Cubans should have done that, because he was the one that was holding the freedom of Cuba. . . ." Odio claimed that upon seeing television news footage of Lee Harvey Oswald after the assassination, she was convinced he was the "Leon Oswald" who had come to her apartment. The only other witness to the visit, Silvia Odio's sister, Annie, supported her story.

In the summer of 1964 the FBI was pressed by the Warren Commission to dig more deeply into the Odio incident, although Commission

General Counsel J. Lee Rankin, in a letter to FBI Director J. Edgar Hoover on July 24, diluted the urgency of the matter by stating: "[T]he Commission already possesses firm evidence that Lee Harvey Oswald was on a bus traveling from Houston, Texas, to Mexico City, Mexico, on virtually the entire day of September 26." Assistant Counsel Wesley J. Liebeler, who had taken Odio's testimony, disagreed: "There really is no evidence at all that [Oswald] left Houston on that bus," he said in a memo to Howard P. Willens. Liebeler argued that a proposed Commission conclusion that there was "persuasive" evidence that Oswald was not in Dallas at the time Odio gave for the visit to her apartment was "too strong." "There are problems," Liebeler wrote. "Odio may well be right. The Commission will look bad if it turns out she is." On August 23 Rankin again wrote to Hoover. This time, his tone was urgent: "It is a matter of some importance to the Commission that Mrs. Odio's allegation either be proved or disproved." The FBI investigation was not completed, however, by the time the Commission's report was published on September 24, and even when an FBI report was sent to Rankin on November 9, it was inconclusive. The bureau did try to alleviate some of the "problems." It had produced an interview of Loran Eugene Hall, who claimed he was in Dallas in September 1963, accompanied by Lawrence Howard and William Seymour, and it was they who had visited Odio. Even though Howard and Seymour, when interviewed a week after Hall, denied ever having met Odio, and despite a subsequent retraction by Hall, the Commission relied on the partially complete (it so noted) FBI investigation to support its final conclusion: "Lee Harvey Oswald was not at Mrs. Odio's apartment in September 1963."

Not satisfied with that finding, we took a fresh look at Odio's story. We interviewed Hall, Howard, and Seymour and determined they could not have been the three visitors. We took depositions from Silvia Odio, members of her family, and a psychiatrist she was seeing in 1963, Dr. Burton Einspruch of Dallas. (Realizing that the mere fact she was under a psychiatrist's care might cast doubt on her account, we were careful to determine that Odio's emotional troubles would not have affected her powers of perception or her veracity.) We also interviewed Odio and Einspruch together, by means of a telephone conference call, and the doctor confirmed that she had told him about the visit shortly after it occurred and well before the President's assassination. Further, we secured photographs of scores of pro-Castro and anti-Castro Cubans (none of whom Odio recognized), and we asked the CIA to do a computer survey of individuals who might have used names like Leopoldo, Angelo, or Leon. The screening produced the names of three Cuban DGI agents who could have been in Dallas, but when photos of them were shown to Odio, she did not recognize them. We also interviewed Amador Odio and several members of JURE, including Manolo Ray, to no avail. No one could recall a JURE member who had used either "Leopoldo" or "Angelo" as a war name.

Based on all this evidence, we believed Silvia and Annie Odio: three men, who identified themselves as members of an anti-Castro organization, did visit their apartment in Dallas about two months prior to the Kennedy assassination; and one of them, who was either Lee Harvey Oswald or his look-alike, was introduced to them as Leon Oswald. Rather than dismiss the visit, as the Warren Commission had, we considered it a significant, if mysterious, association of Oswald (or someone posing as Oswald) with two individuals who were engaged in anti-Castro activities, or acting as if they were.

Oswald in New Orleans

The New Orleans address Oswald stamped on some of his "Fair Play for Cuba" leaflets was 544 Camp Street, and we, as the FBI and the Warren Commission had in 1964, wondered why. The Warren Commission did determine that from October 1961 to February 1962, while Sergio Arcacha Smith was its New Orleans delegate, the Cuban Revolutionary Council had occupied an office at 544 Camp Street; but it did not draw a sinister inference from that, since Oswald did not arrive in the city until April 1963. Moreover, Sam Newman, the owner of the three-story building whose address was 544 Camp Street, swore to the FBI and Secret Service that he had not rented an office to Lee Harvey Oswald. We sought to learn more about the address by investigating the other occupants of the building during the period in question. We learned from Newman that there were two tenants at the address in the summer of 1963, both labor unions: the Amalgamated Association of Street Electric Railway and Motor Coach Employees of America and the Hotel, Motel, and Restaurant Workers. We also learned that 544 Camp Street was not the only address for the Newman Building, since there was also an entrance at 531 Lafayette Street. The only tenant listed at 531 Lafayette in the summer of 1963 was the private detective agency of W. Guy Banister, a former FBI agent (Special Agent-in-Charge, Chicago) and a fervent anti-Communist who was deeply involved in the anti-Castro crusade.

Born in rural Louisiana in 1901, Banister was with the FBI for twenty years, retiring in 1954 to become assistant police superintendent in New Orleans, with a specific assignment to investigate corruption in the department. His determination to extend the cleanup to elected officials was not well received by powerful politicians, however. (There were also reports that he shot a man during Mardi Gras festivities.) So Banister quit public service and opened a detective agency, Guy Banister Associates. For the rest of his life (Banister died in the summer of 1964), he was preoccupied with the issue of a Communist Cuba: he ran background checks on Cubans, who had applied to join the Cuban Revolutionary Council; he advised exile military leaders on guerrilla tactics; he helped obtain arms for shipment to Cuba; and he formed, in 1961, Friends of Democratic Cuba, to lend financial support to the Cuban Revolutionary Council, whose chief New Orleans delegate was Banister's close friend, Sergio Arcacha Smith. (Banister introduced Arcacha to Sam Newman, which led to the CRC's leasing an office at 544 Camp Street.) Banister was also closely associated with G. Wray Gill, an attorney for Mafia leader Carlos Marcello, and David W. Ferrie, who performed investigative services for both Banister and Gill, in return for their aid in a dispute with his employer, Eastern Airlines. Another Banister associate was Jack Martin, who, on November 23, 1963, telephoned the office of New Orleans District Attorney Jim Garrison and said Ferrie was a longtime colleague and tutor of Lee Harvey Oswald. (Martin claimed to us that he had, on at least one occasion during the summer of 1963, seen Oswald with Ferrie in Banister's office.) Martin and Ferrie had once been friendly, but there had been a falling out over their respective roles in a fraudulent ecclesiastical order, The Holy Apostolic Catholic Church of North America, and this antipathy, along with Martin's reputation as an alcoholic, tended to cast doubt on his claims about Ferrie.

Banister, also a heavy drinker, had a violent temper, and Martin was a victim of it in the early evening of November 22, 1963, after they had returned to Banister's office from a neighborhood bar. Delphine Roberts, Banister's secretary, recalled the incident for us. Martin came in first, she said, and walked to a filing cabinet. When Banister entered, he looked at Martin and accused him of stealing files, then pulled out a pistol and struck Martin on the head several times, causing him to bleed. Martin's version of the incident was more elaborate: "What are you going to do — kill me, like you all did Kennedy?" he said he had demanded of Banister in the heat of the argument.

It was difficult to evaluate the significance of this circumstantial evidence bearing on Oswald's summer in New Orleans, yet we recognized we were getting indications of an Oswald connection with anti-Castro activists, who had the motive and means to plot the assassination. Additionally, not all of the evidence was circumstantial. There was, for example, a news photo of Oswald, as he was passing out "Fair Play for Cuba" literature on August 16, 1963, in front of the International Trade Mart in New Orleans, assisted by a Latin-looking young man, quite likely a Cuban, who has never been identified. While we were no more successful than the Warren Commission in learning who the man was, we realized, in light of undeniable evidence of a second gunman in Dealey Plaza, that his association with Oswald in a political activity may well have had sinister significance. Was he pro-Castro or anti-Castro? Was he apparently one, but in fact the other? We knew that after Oswald's approach to Carlos Bringuier and the confrontation over "Fair Play for Cuba" leaflets, the Cuban Student Directorate had decided to infiltrate Oswald's FPCC organization. Was he an "infiltrator"? Referring to the Coleman-Slawson hypothesis again, we asked ourselves: Did the Trade Mart photograph represent valid evidence that in August 1963, in New Orleans, an Oswald association had been established that would lead ultimately to the events in November in Dallas?

In light of the photograph, we reviewed the other evidence. Martin's allegation that Oswald had visited Banister's office was hardly persuasive by itself, and it was not substantially bolstered by Delphine Roberts, who said she saw Oswald "on several occasions," since her demeanor as a witness did not lead us to place much credence in her testimony. Ross Banister, an official of the Louisiana State Police, offered the explanation that Oswald had used the 544 Camp Street address to embarrass his brother, but that would not explain the reports that copies of the leaflet in question had been found in Banister's files after he died. The reports were never substantiated. The blunt truth was that we had failed to document a Banister-Oswald connection, despite the evidence that it might have existed. But there was an established association between Banister and David Ferrie, and that was very interesting, because we were able to link Ferrie not only with Oswald, but with Carlos Marcello.

David Ferrie: 1918-1967

David W. Ferrie was born in Cleveland in 1918, the son of an Irish Catholic police captain. Ferrrie's early life was, by all available accounts, quite normal, in stark contrast to what it was to become. There was one indication of a personality problem when he abandoned the priesthood, dropping out of a seminary due to "emotional instability," but he was considered a brilliant student and earned a bachelor of arts degree in philosophy from Baldwin-Wallace College in 1941. Ferrie studied medicine well into his adult life, receiving a "doctorate" in psychology from an unaccredited college in Italy when he was nearly forty. An excellent pilot, he was by then employed by Eastern Airlines and based in New Orleans, where he was also the commander of a Civil Air Patrol unit.

By the early 1960s, Ferrie's world had begun to shatter. His physical appearance, marred by the loss of all his hair as a result of a rare disease, was made all the more bizarre by a homemade mohair wig and pasted-on eyebrows. He was an aggressive homosexual with a penchant for teenagers, leading to complaints by parents, which brought about his forced resignation from the CAP. On August 8, 1961, he was arrested for contributing to the delinquency of a juvenile, and on August 11 he was arrested again, for a crime against nature with a fifteen-year-old and indecent behavior with three other boys. On August 26 Eastern Airlines suspended Ferrie indefinitely.

While avidly anti-Communist, Ferrie was critical of every American President from Roosevelt to Kennedy. This was in keeping with his character — opinionated, resentful of authority — and it reflected his belief that the respective administrations in Washington had sold out to communism. He had been particularly upset over the failure of the United States to support a successful invasion of Cuba at the Bay of Pigs, so much so that, as he was addressing the Military Order of World Wars in July 1961, he was asked to step down when the vehemence of his criticism of President Kennedy became excessive. Following his 1963 arrest by Garrison's men in connection with the assassination, Ferrie admitted to the FBI that he had criticized Kennedy over the Bay of Pigs and had observed that anyone could hide in the bushes and shoot the President, but he denied that he had seriously stated that Kennedy should be killed. His fervent opposition to Castro had led Ferrie to join Sergio Arcacha Smith in the Cuban counterrevolution: he obtained rifles and mortars to arm exile invaders; he taught Cubans how to fly and reportedly flew secret missions to Cuba; and, according to a Border Patrol report, he tried to buy a C-47 for the purpose of shipping arms out of New Orleans. There was even an indication that Ferrie participated in the Bay of Pigs landing: after his request for extended leave in the spring of 1961 was denied, he took a vacation — from April 16, the day before the invasion, until April 30. We made a careful check to see if there was a Ferrie-CIA connection before, during, or subsequent to the unsuccessful invasion of Cuba, and there was none to be found.

In the proceedings on his suspension as an Eastern Airlines pilot, Ferrie got legal and investigative assistance from G. Wray Gill and W. Guy Banister. In return, Ferrie assisted Gill in defending Carlos Marcello against federal charges of obstructing justice, a charge that was based on a fraudulent birth certificate held by Marcello, and illegal entry into the country. For Banister, Ferrie analyzed autopsy reports, among other chores. Ferrie had filed a grievance against Eastern, and in February 1963 he went with Gill to Miami to appear before an appeal board. When the airline ruled against him, Ferrie filed another grievance, which led to a series of hearings in July and August. Eastern presented its case: Ferrie's original application for employment contained deliberate omissions and inaccuracies; he had misrepresented himself as a medical doctor; he was guilty of moral turpitude. Banister, a character witness, could not explain to the board's satisfaction a number of Ferrie's actions, including his public denunciations of President Kennedy over the Bay of Pigs. In September Ferrie was notified that his discharge was final.

Although he held no regular job after being fired by Eastern, Ferrie managed to support himself up to the time of his death in 1967 as a freelance pilot and, apparently, as an agent of Marcello. Marcello himself, an FBI report indicated, may have been involved in anti-Castro activities, offering Arcacha and the Cuban Revolutionary Council financial support in return for concessions, including gambling, in Cuba after Castro's overthrow. There was some evidence indicating that Ferrie was Marcello's agent in the transfer of funds. According to Carlos Quiroga, an exile activist (the one who was sent by Carlos Bringuier to check out Oswald), Ferrie often provided Arcacha with funds. "Ferrie lent [Arcacha] money when he needed it for his family," Quiroga told the FBI. "He had $100 bills around all the time. . . ."

In the fall of 1963 Ferrie, according to his own statements to the FBI following his arrest on November 25, was fully occupied with Marcello's federal case, which entailed trips to Guatemala from October 11 to 18 and from October 30 to November 1. He spent the weekends of November 9–11 and November 16–17 at Marcello's estate outside New Orleans, Churchill Farms, where Ferrie allegedly helped map trial strategy. He was in federal court on November 22, where he witnessed Marcello's acquittal, and that night he drove with two young friends to Houston, then to Galveston on Saturday, and back to New Orleans on Sunday. From Houston, according to telephone records of the Alamotel, Ferrie or one of his companions telephoned two New Orleans radio stations and the Town and Country Motel, which was owned by Marcello and used by him as a headquarters. On Monday, November 25, aware that he was wanted in connection with the assassination, Ferrie turned himself in at the office of New Orleans District Attorney Jim Garrison, who released him a short time later.

In early 1969 Clay L. Shaw, the only person charged in the belated Garrison investigation of the Kennedy assassination, was acquitted. The case against him was flimsy, and the testimony of the "star witness," Perry Raymond Russo, had been blatantly concocted. All Garrison had was a circumstantial case of association: between Shaw and Oswald, almost none, once Russo's story had fallen apart; and between Shaw and Ferrie, only an indirect link (a close friend of Ferrie, going back to his youth in Cleveland, had been Shaw's next-door neighbor).

But even if there had been encounters, evidence of another element of a conspiracy, an intent to commit a crime, was absent. We came to believe, however, that Garrison might have been on the right track, at least up until Ferrie's untimely death on February 22, 1967, for evidence of an association between Ferrie and Oswald, presented at the Shaw trial, was found by the Committee to be credible. Here we had an Oswald association as significant as the one indicated by the Trade Mart photograph — possibly more so, since the identity of the associate was known, and he, in turn, was associated with an organized-crime leader.

The evidence we found persuasive was the testimony of six residents of Clinton, Louisiana, the county seat of East Feliciana Parish, some 130 miles from New Orleans. They included a state representative, a deputy sheriff, and a registrar of voters. During the summer of 1963 Clinton was targeted by the Congress of Racial Equality in a voting rights drive, and it was during demonstrations in late August or early September that Oswald came to town, accompanied by two older men, one of whom was Ferrie. While the other might have been Shaw, that was not so clearly established. Oswald first appeared in nearby Jackson, seeking employment at East Louisiana State Hospital. Advised that a job would depend on his becoming a voter in the county, Oswald went to Clinton to register, though there was no record that he was successful. In addition to physical descriptions that identified the man as Oswald, other observations of the Clinton witnesses substantiated the accuracy of their account: he identified himself, for example, as "Oswald" and produced Marine Corps discharge papers as credentials. The question of the credibility of the Clinton witnesses was squarely put to the members of the Committee who listened carefully to their testimony in executive session: it was their considered opinion that the witnesses were "honest folks," telling the truth as they knew it.

Allegation of a Mafia-Exile Plot

Right after the assassination the Chicago Field Office of the Secret Service heard from an informant about a meeting that had occurred on November 21, 1963, at which a Cuban exile, an outspoken critic of President Kennedy named Homer Echevarria, reported he was ready to proceed with an illegal arms purchase; that he had "plenty of money" and would make the deal "as soon as we take care of Kennedy." The Secret Service checked further on Echevarria and found that he was an associate of Juan Francisco Blanco-Fernandez, military director of the Cuban Student Directorate (DRE), a particularly militant group of anti-Castro activists. (The New Orleans DRE chapter was run by Carlos Bringuier, whose run-in with Lee Harvey Oswald in August 1963 made headlines.) Echevarria's arms purchase, according to Secret Service reports, was being financed via Paulino Sierra Martinez by "hoodlum elements" that were "not restricted to Chicago." The Secret Service was inclined to proceed with an investigation, but the FBI, which on November 29 was designated by President Johnson as the primary investigative agency in the assassination, took the position that the Cubans who had been named probably were not involved in illegal acts. At first the Secret Service decided to go ahead anyway, based on its understanding that Johnson's order meant primary, not exclusive, investigative responsibility. But when the FBI objected, the Secret Service turned the files over to the bureau, and the case was closed.

Even though the trail was cold in 1978, we were able to learn that Homer Echevarria was one of the many Cuban exiles who had come to despise Kennedy as much as he did Castro. We also learned that the anti-Castro group to which Echevarria belonged, the 30th of November, was hardly one that should have been termed by the FBI in 1963 not apt "to be involved in illegal acts." As for Paulino Sierra, a background check stimulated our interest in a Cuban exile-Mafia connection that just might have had a bearing on the assassination.

When Sierra came to Miami in May 1963 from Chicago, where he practiced law, the exile movement was in disarray: the United States had just stopped funding the Cuban Revolutionary Council; U.S. law enforcement agencies were cracking down on guerrilla activities; and factions within the exile community were politically polarized — in some cases, as much at odds with each other as they were with Castro. Sierra proposed a solution that offered financial backing of an invasion of Cuba in return for unity. To many of the Cubans in Miami, Sierra was either crazy or supremely naive. He was virtually unknown (his only mark of public prominence was that he had formed a Cuban lawyers association in Chicago), yet he was proposing to bring unity to a complex of organizations that was splintered, not only by politics, but also by the clashing personalities of the various exile leaders. However, Sierra had an impressive manner to match his ambitious plan. He was tall, dapper, fluent in Spanish, English, Italian, and French, and he had served as an assistant to officials of the Batista regime. After he left Havana in 1960, he lived for a time in Miami, working as a judo instructor and as a translator; then, in 1962, he moved to Chicago where he was admitted to the Illinois bar and employed as an assistant to William Browder, the general counsel of the Union Tank Car Company. Sierra told the exile leaders that he spoke for a group of American businessmen in Chicago who wanted to join forces with them to overthrow Castro, with or without the approval of the U.S. government. If the Cubans would put away their political differences and unite, Sierra proposed, his backers would finance an invasion to the tune of about $30 million. Further, Sierra said, even though it was to be an independent operation, high-ranking U.S. Army and Navy officers were willing to help procure arms and establish training bases in a Latin American country. Acceptance of Sierra's scheme was not across-the-board, but by July he had put together a coalition of the more conservative exile groups, which were led by former Batistianos like himself. Sierra named his amalgam the Junta de Gobierno de Cuba en el Excilo and appointed himself secretary general.

Where was the money to come from? Sierra was saying publicly that it was being donated by U.S. corporations whose assets in Cuba had been expropriated. But while he was in the habit of dropping the names of major corporations such as U.S. Steel, Standard Oil, and United Fruit, the only company he would positively identify was Union Tank Car, and it appeared to be a conduit, not an actual source of funding. (Interviewed by the FBI in October 1963, Browder, the Union Tank Car lawyer, acknowledged that it was he who controlled the Junta's money, but he would not say where he or Sierra had obtained it or how much had been spent, except that it was a "considerable" amount.) According to several sources, the real benefactors were members of the underworld, whose gambling interests in Cuba had indeed been expropriated by Castro. "Gamblers Pop Out of Exile Grab Bag," *The Miami News* headlined on May 19, 1963, and while the paper did not reveal the source of the story, it was either Sierra himself or a mysterious American named William Trull, who had accompanied Sierra to a meeting with Cuban exile leaders. Sierra and Trull had parted ways by the time they were interviewed by the FBI, and they differed on key points. Sierra said that Trull had approached him on a joint Cuba venture, implying he represented Texas oil interests, but Sierra wanted nothing to do with Trull because his financial backing was "impure." Trull, who described himself as an ex-entertainer from Dallas, claimed that Sierra had telephoned him in March 1963 and had asked for help in explaining his unification plan to Cuban exiles and had sent him a ticket for a flight to Miami. Trull said he believed the reason Sierra had picked him was that in his professional career he had performed before Cuban audiences. The plan, as Trull said Sierra had explained it to him, had the backing of "gambling figures" in Las Vegas and Cleveland. They had offered to put up $14 million in return for 50 percent of Cuban gambling if Castro was successfully ousted. Trull said Sierra told him that he intended to establish a provisional government with a former Cuban prime minister, Carlos Prio Socarras, as president and himself as vice-president.

There were other indications that organized-crime figures were behind the Sierra plan: first, a participant in the initial meetings in Miami was George Franci, who was believed by authorities to have been active in gambling in pre-Castro Havana; second, on a trip to Nicaragua in July, Sierra reportedly declared to other Cubans that he represented American gamblers; and, third, a Cuban associate of Sierra in Chicago, an attorney named Cesar Blanco, reported that he and Sierra had been approached by gamblers from the West. Sierra reportedly mentioned that he had been offered $10 million if he would guarantee the Cuban casino business.

The Chicago Field Office of the FBI closed its file on Sierra in June 1963, having decided he was a con artist, but the CIA kept tabs on him right up to the time of the assassination. (A CIA memo on Sierra's far-ranging activities was dated November 20, 1963.) The FBI Miami Field Office picked up information on him from time to time through its contacts among anti-Castro activists, in particular a group of soldiers of fortune, many of them Americans, that went by the name of INTERPEN (International Penetration Forces), and whose leader was Gerry Patrick Hemming, a flamboyant ex-Marine with a craving for publicity. As the FBI in Miami learned, Sierra was keeping busy, and by October 1963 he had run up an $11,000 expense account, which was paid by Union Tank Car. In July he and the vice-secretary general of the Junta, Felipe Rivero, toured Nicaragua and Colombia in search of a training site; they then went to New York, Chicago, St. Louis, and Washington to meet with backers. Sierra was also assembling an arsenal. In August he contracted with Rich Lauchli, a well-known supplier of weapons to right-wing causes, for small arms, and in October he ordered a two-man submarine to be shipped from California. At about the same time, he went on a shopping spree in Detroit, buying $6,000 to $7,000 worth of weapons to be shipped to Miami. Sierra was also in touch with some of the most intrepid and determined exile fighters: Eloy Gutierrez Menoyo, whose Second Front of the Escambray was planning a major action in Oriente Province from a base in the Dominican Republic; Tony Cuesta of Commandos L, who later was wounded and captured on a mission to Cuba; and Antonio Veciana, the leader of Alpha 66, probably the most active of all the guerrilla organizations. (Veciana planned the attempted assassination of Castro that resulted in the imprisonment of Silvia Odio's parents.) Ultimately, Sierra was the victim of the dissension he had sought to overcome, as members of the Junta resigned in protest to his leadership, or lack of it. In November he was summoned to Chicago, dressed down by Browder and, in effect, fired, although he was able to hang on for another two months, which was as long as the Junta continued to exist. It struck the author of the November 20 CIA memo as curious that Sierra had for so long managed to hold a position in the exile hierarchy: "Perhaps his mysterious backers are providing him with sufficient funds to keep the pot boiling. . . ."

While we were able to document in detail Sierra's activities and his apparent connection, or that of his backers, to organized crime, the relevance to the assassination remained undetermined. We did, however, find some pieces of the puzzle that matched some of those we had discovered in our investigation of the reported visit of Lee Harvey Oswald to the home of Silvia Odio in Dallas in September 1963. We learned, for example, that more attention might have been paid in 1964 to a statement by a Catholic priest, Walter J. McChann. McChann, a close friend of Silvia Odio, told the Secret Service that Odio had in fact identified one of the Latins who had accompanied Leon Oswald as "Eugenio" Cisneros. In our Sierra investigation, we learned that Cisneros's true first name was Rogelio, and "Eugenio" was his war name. In 1964 Cisneros acknowledged to the Secret Service that he had been in Dallas during the summer of 1963, though he said it was in June, and he was there alone. In addition, he said that he had contacted Silvia Odio for the purpose of being placed in contact with a Uruguayan named John Martin, an arms dealer. He denied seeing Odio in September or knowing anyone named Leopoldo or Leon. Cisneros was, we learned, a prominent member of JURE, the anti-Castro organization to which Odio belonged. According to a CIA memorandum dated June 29, 1964, Manolo Ray, the leader of JURE, was ordered to move his operations out of the United States, because Cisneros had illegally purchased $50,000 worth of arms from a manufacturer in California.

There was also a connection between Sierra and Loran Hall, Lawrence Howard, and William Seymour, the three anti-Castro activists who, according to Hall in an FBI interview, were the ones who paid the visit to Odio, though all three of them subsequently denied it. Hall, Howard, and Seymour belonged to INTERPEN, the soldier-of-fortune group that the Miami FBI office used for information on Sierra. The INTERPEN connection to Sierra, at least one of them, was a Cuban, Manuel Aguilar, in whose garage Sierra stored the two-man submarine he ordered from California. In September 1963 Hall and Howard drove from Los Angeles, heading for Miami with a trailer-load of arms, but they were forced to leave the trailer in Dallas for lack of a hiding place in Florida. In October Hall and Seymour, back in Dallas to retrieve the trailer, were arrested for possession of drugs; but with the help of an influential financial supporter, they were released. They took the arms back to Miami, but the mission for which they were intended, Hall told us, was aborted in late October when he, Howard, Seymour, and some Cubans were arrested by customs officials as they were driving to their embarkation point south of Miami. No charges were filed, but their arms and equipment were confiscated, so they returned to Miami, frustrated, and in early November, headed west. All three swore they were at their respective homes — Hall and Howard in California, Seymour in Arizona — on November 22, 1963.

We believed Silvia Odio's account of the Oswald visit, while the FBI and the Warren Commission dismissed it. We did not know what to decide about the allegation of a Mafia plot originating in Chicago, because the failure of the FBI to follow it up prevented us from compiling enough information to come to a conclusion. From our assembling of the background information on Sierra, however, we could not escape a disturbing question: If organized crime was putting as much money and effort into anti-Castro activities as was indicated, what were its members willing to do about Kennedy, who, by 1963, had become a far greater anathema to them than Castro?

Other Allegations of Oswald-Cuban Exile Ties

Following the assassination, other reports of specific connections between Lee Harvey Oswald and the anti-Castro Cubans began to circulate, though many of them had to be rejected for lack of substantiation. Over the years, however, some of the reports gained momentum, if not credence, to a degree that we could not ignore them. We proceeded to run out the various leads, and the result was a bit ironic. While we were ready to believe that Oswald's mysterious Latin associations — as demonstrated, for example by the visit to Silvia Odio — were significant, our assessment of the claims of exile leaders who actually claimed encounters with Oswald was negative. After careful analysis, we decided not to credit a claim made originally in 1976 by Antonio Veciana, the commander of Alpha 66, of having been introduced to Oswald in Dallas in August or September 1963 by his CIA case officer, a man Veciana identified as Maurice Bishop. We also rejected the story of Marita Lorenz, who told us she had driven from Miami to Dallas on November 15, 1963, with Oswald and several anti-Castro activists, including Gerry Patrick Hemming, Orlando Bosch, a terrorist (who was charged in the 1975 bombing of a Cubana Airlines plane, which took seventy-three lives), Pedro Diaz-Lanz, the former Cuban Air Force chief, and Frank Sturgis, who was arrested in the Watergate break-in in 1972. All four men denied Lorenz's charge emphatically, and we could find no evidence to refute them. Lorenz, who claimed to have been Fidel Castro's mistress as well as the instrument of an attempt by the CIA to poison Castro (possibly as part of the CIA-Mafia plots), did not help her credibility by telling us that when she arrived in Dallas with

Oswald and the anti-Castro activists, they were contacted at their motel by Jack Ruby.

The Havana Investigation: Part Two

On our second trip to Cuba, from August 25 to August 29, 1978, our party consisted of Chairman Preyer, Chief Counsel Blakey, and Edwin Lopez. Our purpose this time was, in large part, to find out what light the Cubans might be able to shed on complicity by anti-Castro Cubans in the assassination. We knew for a fact that the Cuban intelligence service (DGI) had made inroads into the anti-Castro community in the United States, and its sources had produced information that might have a bearing on the death of the President. Up to the time of our investigation there had been no appropriate way for the Cubans to communicate this information, if it existed, to the American people. The Cuban government could not be expected to have made it available to a U.S. government agency, the FBI or the CIA, and if it had simply made the information public, the Cubans no doubt figured (rightly, in our view) that it would be rejected as propaganda. For years Cuba had been seeking information about plots against its own leaders. While we could hardly expect that the Castro government would have used its intelligence apparatus to detect plots against an American President, it was not unreasonable to suppose that if there had been a conspiracy by any of the major exile groups to assassinate President Kennedy, the Cuban DGI would have learned about it. Moreover, the Cuban exiles were not the Mafia; they were not bound by an *omerta*, a code of silence. If, in fact, the exiles had plotted the assassination, and more than a handful of activists were involved, it might well have been revealed — to wives, girl friends, compatriots. There was no reason, in addition, for the Cubans to withhold the information, if they had it. We even expected they might manufacture it.

On Sunday, August 28, we were at the International Hotel in Varadero Beach to interview a vacationing Cuban diplomat. On a break, we walked along the beach with Felipe Villa, our escort from the Ministry of Interior. We passed a V-20, a 20-foot, V-hulled CIA assault boat, which had been captured and turned into a pleasure craft. We were in a relaxed mood, but seeing the V-20 occasioned a discussion of U.S.-Cuban relations. Eventually, we came to what turned out to be a frank analysis by Villa of the possibility that anti-Castro Cubans had played a part in the assassination. Villa candidly acknowledged that his government had extensive reliable sources in the exile community in the United States. If they had provided trustworthy evidence of exile involvement in Kennedy's death, Villa assured us, his government would have gladly turned it over to us. There just was no such evidence, he said. He was cautious, but he noted that there might be significance in the inability of his government to implicate the anti-Castro organizations in the President's death.

Oswald and New Orleans

New Orleans, the home of Lee Harvey Oswald from April to September 1963, is a southern seaport with a climate well suited to the Cuban taste. The size of its exile community in the early 1960s was second only to Miami's "Little Havana." In August 1960, just three months after the Democratic Revolutionary Front was founded in Miami, Sergio Arcacha Smith was sent by Antonio de Varona to form a New Orleans chapter of the FRD, which at the time of the Bay of Pigs invasion, in April 1961, became the Cuban Revolutionary Council. Arcacha remained the chief CRC delegate in New Orleans until January 1962, at which time he was fired for not being able to gain the confidence of the New Orleans Cuban community. There was a quick succession of CRC delegates after Arcacha: Luis Rabel held the job until October 1962, when business pressures forced him to step aside in favor of Frank Bartes, the former president of Consolidated Railroads of Cuba, who ran the chapter until the CRC was dissolved in 1964. We interviewed Arcacha, Rabel, and Bartes, and each denied having had any dealings with Oswald. They said that the CRC chapter had been primarily engaged in fund-raising, leading us to believe that the more combative activities were left to the student affiliate of the chapter, the New Orleans branch of the Cuban Student Directorate. Oswald's contact with the chief DRE delegate in New Orleans, Carlos Bringuier, had been well documented, and Bringuier maintained that what he told the FBI and the Warren Commission was the extent of it. We could not say, however, that the testimony of Arcacha, Rabel, Bartes, Bringuier, and others in New Orleans, in light of what we *had* learned about Oswald in the summer of 1963, left us with a feeling that we knew all there was to know.

As we wound up the New Orleans phase of the investigation, what we did know — what had survived the passage of time and had not been contaminated by the Garrison investigation — was that significant Oswald connections had been established: with anti-Castro activists and, at least through David Ferrie, with organized crime. Neither of these connections had been adequately taken into account by the FBI or the Warren Commission. We also knew that Oswald, as he was departing New Orleans in September, had probably gone with two of his Cuban associates to the home of Silvia Odio in Dallas. We were, candidly, at a loss to find a fully satisfactory explanation for the contradictions of Oswald's anti-Castro and pro-Castro activities (as he passed out leaflets in front of the New Orleans Trade Mart, he was obviously acting in support of Castro, although we were unable to determine the loyalties of his unidentified Latin associate). The Coleman-Slawson deception hypothesis — anti-Castroites posing as Castro supporters for Oswald's benefit — was as logical as any we could reach. As for the organized-crime aspect of Oswald's associations in New Orleans, where it had been overlooked by the FBI and the Warren Commission, it had been studiously avoided by District Attorney Garrison, for reasons we believed had become apparent. If Ferrie was to have a place in history, as Garrison predicted he would at the time of his death, it would be, in our judgment, because he was a connection between Oswald and the Marcello organization.

10

Organized Crime in Perspective

If we do not on a national scale attack organized criminals, . . .
they will destroy us.

Robert F. Kennedy
The Enemy Within

Organized Crime

We concluded from our investigation that organized crime had a hand in the assassination of President Kennedy. We had come to the investigation predisposed to conclude that organized crime figures would not have taken the considerable risk entailed in plotting the assassination of the President. The reasoning process that led us to change our minds only becomes explicable when the myth and folklore are put aside. With the true nature of organized crime, as opposed to the public perception of it, rightly understood, we believed, that fateful day in Dallas would, as it did for us, finally appear in sharp focus.

Al Capone summed up the ambivalent public attitude toward organized crime at the peak of his career: "[T]hey call Capone a bootlegger. . . . What's Al done? He's supplied a legitimate demand. . . . Some call it racketeering. I call it a business." Capone successfully cloaked his true self in the image of a folk hero, and many failed to consider the ultimate source of his power: his willingness to commit cold-blooded murder. Often the violence has been rationalized, as it was, for example, in the title of Dean Jennings's 1967 popular biography of another gangster, the late Benjamin "Bugsy" Siegel, *We Only Kill Each Other.* And too few eyebrows were raised when a fashionable New York hostess, Marta Orbach, invited a Mafia killer, Joseph Gallo, to regular Sunday brunch, where people like Neil Simon, the playwright, made small talk, that is, until Gallo was gunned down on April 7, 1971, as he celebrated his forty-third birthday in Umberto's Clam House on Mulberry Street in Manhattan. Four months later, a short, stocky man walked into a bar in Manhattan, took a sip of water, set the glass down, pulled out two pistols, and fired nine bullets at a group of four kosher meat dealers, killing two and seriously wounding the others. The Jewish businessmen had just taken the place at the bar of four members of the Mafia family of Joseph Colombo, and the gunman apparently was out to avenge the killing of Gallo, who had been at odds with Colombo. There has never been necessary limitation on the violence of organized crime. It can affect anyone.

"When I use a word," Lewis Carroll's Humpty Dumpty said, "it means what I choose it to mean — neither more nor less." As in Humpty Dumpty's language, the term, "organized crime," can mean whatever the speaker chooses. It can be used to refer to crimes committed — bootlegging, gambling, prostitution, and so on, or it can refer to the criminal groups themselves. A distinction is sometimes drawn between an organized crime "enterprise," which engages in providing illicit goods or services, and an organized crime "syndicate," which regulates relations among individual "enterprises" — allocating territory, settling personal disputes, offering protection from rival groups and against prosecution. Syndicates, too, have been of different types. They have been defined as metropolitan, regional, national, or international in scope, and they have been limited to one field of endeavor — narcotics, for example. Often, but not always, "organized crime" is used to refer to a particular national syndicate known as the Mafia or, more simply, the mob. The organization is called by its own members, however, by a variety of names. In Chicago, it is "The Outfit"; in Buffalo, "The Arm"; in New York City, "La Cosa Nostra." Only the public continues to call it the Mafia or the mob. The degree to which terms like Cosa Nostra or Mafia conjure up stereotypes of Italian-American gangsters is unfortunate. As Joseph Valachi, the mob informer, put it, "I'm not talking about Italians, I'm talking about criminals."

The National Awakening

A national effort to understand and combat organized crime may be best dated from the Conference on Organized Crime that was called by Attorney General J. Howard McGrath in 1950. Law enforcement officials from all over the nation met in Washington in February of that year, to consider the growing nationwide scope of organized crime, particularly professional gambling. De Lesseps S. Morrison, the mayor of New Orleans, spoke for the majority:

> We do not have the whole picture — but each of us present — and hundreds of other[s] . . . [have] seen small segments of this national scene of organized . . . crime. These pieces fit together in a pattern of mounting evidence concerning several highly organized . . . syndicates whose wealth, power, scope of operations, and influence have recently grown to . . . alarming proportions.

Morrison's view of the nationwide character of organized crime was echoed by Will Wilson, the District Attorney from Dallas, who cited as evidence slot machines and punchboards that had come to his city from Chicago. Wilson added that the syndicate's monopoly on gambling in his area was maintained "by dealing in killing, killing of the most reckless kind." (He told of the effort to kill a policeman by wiring a bomb to his car, but it killed the policeman's wife instead. Later, the policeman himself was wounded, but not killed, as he left his home. The gang finally finished the job by shooting him through a hospital window.) The majority view at the conference, however, was not universally shared. The U.S. attorney from Chicago, Otto Kerner, dissented. "There was," Kerner said, "no organized gambling in the city of Chicago. . . ." He then told the conference that he "did not know that the Capone syndicate exist[ed]. I have read about it in the newspapers. I have never received any evidence of it."

The 1950 conference was an important step toward the development of a national awareness of organized crime, and a number of its participants subsequently made significant contributions in the effort to control it. Price Daniel, the attorney general of Texas in 1950, for example, became a U.S. senator, whose efforts led in 1956 to tough narcotics laws, which were to result in the convictions of several important syndicate leaders. Otto Kerner, on the other hand, though he went on to become governor of Illinois in 1960 and a U.S. circuit court judge in 1968, was convicted on February 19, 1973, of accepting $150,000 in bribes from horse-racing interests. And J. Vincent Keogh, the U.S. attorney from Brooklyn and later a New York Supreme Court justice, was convicted in 1962 with Anthony Corallo, a New York underworld figure, of improperly attempting to influence a bankruptcy petition. (The brother of J. Vincent Keogh, Eugene, had been a close friend of John F. Kennedy and one of the "five people who were most helpful to the President in the [1960] election," according to Robert F. Kennedy.) The 1950 Conference on Organized Crime considered a number of recommendations, the most important of which was for a Senate investigation of organized crime, though its adoption was blocked by Attorney General McGrath. Nevertheless, a resolution authorizing a Select Senate Committee to probe organized crime was then pending in the Senate under the sponsorship of Senator Estes Kefauver of Tennessee.

Concerned about what he had learned from a 1948 study by a crime commission appointed by California Governor Earl Warren, Senator Kefauver had introduced Senate Resolution 202 on January 5, 1950. It called for a sweeping examination of organized crime in the United States. Swift passage of the resolution, however, was not assured. Democrats feared that too much light would be shed on alliances of gangsters and big-city political machines that their party dominated; Republicans expected a whitewash. "As I look back on the struggle to get the Committee," Senator Kefauver later observed, "I sometimes wonder that we were ever able to bring it into existence." In fact, it took a tie-breaking vote by Vice-President Alben Barkley to bring the Senate Special Committee to Investigate Organized Crime in Interstate Commerce — the Kefauver Committee — into existence. Kefauver's concern was not with crime in general, but organized crime. He wanted answers to certain basic questions: Did a nationwide crime syndicate exist? If so, where did its sources of power lie? To what degree had it purchased the cooperation of local governments? He was permitted to move ahead in an independent fashion, according to Theodore Wilson, the historian, "not because he was trusted, but because few people in either party believed that his investigation would receive much attention." They could not have been more wrong. The nation paid careful attention, and Kefauver almost became President.

Hearings were held from May 10, 1950 until May 1, 1951. Kefauver himself traveled 52,380 miles and presided over ninety-two days of hearings. In all, the Committee heard more than 800 witnesses in Miami, Kansas City, St. Louis, Philadelphia, Chicago, Tampa, Cleveland, Detroit, New Orleans, Las Vegas, San Francisco, Los Angeles, Saratoga, New York, and New York City. The New York City hearings were televised live and seen by an estimated 30 million people. On the eve of the opening day of the probe, Attorney General McGrath declared that the Justice Department had no persuasive evidence that a "national crime syndicate" existed. Kefauver supplied that evidence.

The principal interest of the Kefauver Committee was professional gambling, particularly casino gambling, which was found to be operating throughout the country. Bookmaking was equally widespread, as were illegal slot machines and punchboards. The Kefauver Committee made only a cursory examination of the narcotics traffic (it found it to be a "highly organized crime"), but it made a pioneer study of the infiltration of legitimate business. It found the ". . . use of unscrupulous and unethical business practices, extortion, bombing, and other forms of violence" being used by racketeers in legitimate enterprises; and it found "evidence of hoodlum infiltration in approximately 50 areas of business," ranging from A to T, "advertising" to "transportation."

The Kefauver Committee visited Chicago on three separate occasions. Quite contrary to Otto Kerner's view, it found that the rackets were thriving. The committee estimated the play in policy (a form of illegal lottery) for the previous five years at $150 million. Chicago was also found to be the source of slot machines and punchboards used throughout the United States; and it was the base of the racingnews service that was essential for offtrack betting by bookmakers. Most disturbing, however, was the open and bipartisan alliance that existed in Chicago between crime and politics. Roland V. Libonati, a Democratic state senator, and James J. Adducci, a Republican state senator, both from Chicago's West Side, were identified as leaders of a bloc of legislators that associated with racketeers and fought to defeat reform legislation. The committee's final report quoted John Roselli, a Chicago hoodlum at the time:

> [T]he wire service, the handbooks, the slot machines, and the other rackets which have thrived in the city of Chicago cannot operate without local corruption; if the handbooks are open, the conclusion is inescapable that the police are being paid off.

And Senator Kefauver wrote in his book, *Crime in America:*

> If we had gone no farther than Chicago in our quest for evidence of . . . the link between organized crime and politics, we could have written a complete report-in-miniature of the picture of nationwide criminal and political corruption.

The Kefauver Committee traced the rise to power in Chicago of Alphonse Capone from an obscure, scar-faced, twenty-five-year-old bodyguard of Johnny Torrio, his mentor, in 1924, to the absolute master of Chicago crime by 1929 — brothel keeper, bootlegger, and gambler. Capone was convicted in 1931 for tax evasion, and his reign ended, although he left behind an organization that would be run for years by the men around him: Jake Guzik, his business adviser, Frank

Nitti, Felice DeLucia, Anthony Accardo, Murray Humphries, and the Fischetti brothers, Joseph and Rocco, Capone's cousins.

As described by Francis X. Busch in *Enemies of the State*, a raid was conducted on the Strip, a gambling house in Cicero, just outside Chicago, following the brutal murder, apparently by Capone gunmen, of Assistant State Attorney William H. McSwiggin on April 26, 1926. What the raid uncovered led to Capone's downfall at the hands of the U.S. government.

In March 1929, after he met with a group of citizens and was told the situation in Chicago, President Herbert C. Hoover ordered all federal agencies to concentrate on Capone. A two-pronged strategy was devised: Frank J. Wilson headed up a special unit of the Internal Revenue Service that directed its attention to Capone's tax returns; Eliot Ness was in charge of a special unit of the Prohibition Bureau, which investigated Capone's beer empire. (Of the two, Ness's job was the more dangerous. Only wiretap coverage of Capone's headquarters enabled Ness to avoid being ambushed by Capone's gunmen.) As a result of the raid on the Strip, a dusty cashbook was found, and it was possible, through a bank deposit slip, to identify Lou Schumway, a Capone bookkeeper. Further bank-record examinations led to Fred Reis, another Capone employee. Both men eventually were persuaded to cooperate with the government and were kept in hiding until the trial began. Based on their testimony, Capone was charged with failing to file income tax returns in 1924, 1928, and 1929 and with tax evasion for the years 1925 through 1929. (He was also indicted for a violation of the Prohibition law, though never tried.) The government's tax case largely consisted of proof of specific items of income not reported and Capone's lavish life-style. The principal defense argument presented by Capone's lawyer, Albert Fink, was that the prosecution would not have been brought but for the name of the defendant. United States Attorney George E. Q. Johnson responded to Fink's charge:

> They say we prosecute because of the name. . . . Consider the thousands of little men and women who earn only a little more than $1,500 a year and pay their taxes. Is it public clamor to demand taxes due in time of national financial stress and treasury deficit from a man who buys two-hundred-and-fifty-dollar diamond belt buckles and twenty-seven-dollar shirts?
>
> There is no denying the public interest, but I am not asking you to think of this man as Alphonse Capone. Future generations will not remember this case because of the name Alphonse Capone, but because it will establish whether or not a man can go so far beyond the law as to be able to escape the law.

Johnson's comment about the public awareness of future generations did not prove accurate, but his argument was persuasive. On October 17, 1931, the case was submitted to the jury, which deliberated for eight hours. Capone was found not guilty on failure to file a tax return in 1924, but guilty on five of the remaining counts against him. On October 24 Capone was sentenced to two consecutive five-year terms and fined a total of $50,000. After two years in the federal penitentiary in Atlanta, he was transferred to Alcatraz in San Francisco, where he remained until 1939. At the time of his release he was a desperately sick man, suffering from paresis, the deterioration of mind and body stemming from untreated syphilis.

While the tax conviction ended Capone's lawless career, the public was deprived of a full appreciation of the character of the man when he was not tried for his other crimes. Capone was born on January 17, 1899, in Brooklyn, New York, of immigrant parents who had come from Naples in 1883. His death came forty-eight years later. One of his most infamous acts was the St. Valentine's Day Massacre in 1929, in which seven men were machine-gunned. Capone was also the personal author of an unrecorded number of other murders, including the baseball bat bludgeoning of three enemies at a dinner in their honor in May 1929. (They were Giuseppe Giunta, Albert Anselmi, and John Scalise, three officers of the Unione Siciliana, a legitimate fraternal organization when it was founded in 1895, but which had been taken over and made into a front for the Mafia.) No witnesses were ever found to testify against Capone in a murder trial. Until the federal government stepped in with its tax case, he was above the law.

According to the Kefauver Committee, Capone's power passed first to Frank Nitti, who committed suicide in 1943 while under indictment in a highly publicized motion picture industry extortion prosecution; then to Felice DeLucia; and then to Anthony Accardo, an old Capone bodyguard, who was thought by police to have been one of the planners of the St. Valentine's Day Massacre. The faces changed, but the nature of the syndicate did not. Its response to the Kefauver hearings was typical, as evidenced by the murder of two important witnesses before they could testify: William Drury, a former police captain, and Marvin J. Bas, an attorney. Kefauver commented on the evidence developed in Chicago:

[O]rganized crime and political corruption go hand in hand. . . . There [can] . . . be no big-time organized crime without a firm and profitable alliance between those who run the rackets and those in political control.

The Kefauver Committee visited New Orleans and called it "one of

America's largest concentrations of gambling houses.'' Among the most elaborate was the Beverly Club, which was owned by Phil Kastel, Frank Costello, and Jake Lansky, all of New York, and Carlos Marcello, whom the Kefauver Committee identified as the local Mafia leader. The slot machine racket had been imported to New Orleans in the mid-1930s by Costello, who, when he was threatened with banishment from New York City by Mayor-elect Fiorello La Guardia, made a deal with Huey P. Long, then a U.S. senator. After De Lesseps Morrison was elected mayor of New Orleans in 1946, the Costello operation was moved to the neighboring parishes, but illegal pinball machines still flourished in the city, apparently with the aid of corruption. (The Kefauver Committee found there was an alliance between gangsters and corrupt "sheriffs, marshals and other law enforcement officials.")

The Kefauver Committee prepared a profile of the man it identified as the organized crime leader in New Orleans. Carlos Marcello was born on February 6, 1910, in Tunisia, of Sicilian parents who immigrated to New Orleans later that year. (His real name was Calogero Minacore, but it was subsequently changed to Marcella and later masculinized to Marcello.) Marcello was, the Committee found, active in all phases of the rackets in the New Orleans area. He operated casinos, horse-betting parlors, and slot machines; he was also involved in the narcotics traffic. In addition, he had invested heavily in legitimate businesses, including bars, restaurants, and food-processing companies. Marcello's nationwide criminal contacts included Costello, Joseph Civello of Dallas, Sam Yaras of Chicago, and Mickey Cohen of Los Angeles. Marcello's New Orleans organization was also found by the Kefauver Committee to have supplied the weapon for a Mafia murder in Tampa, Florida, where Santo Trafficante, Sr., had been the "reputed Mafia leader . . . for more than twenty years."

As the Kefauver Committee traveled from city to city, it seemed as if "Kefauver had accomplished . . . his aim," as Theodore Wilson noted, "of conducting a fair, nonpartisan inquiry . . . [bringing] the staggering dimension of organized crime before the American people." Understandably, there was opposition to the probe. Senator Pat McCarran of Nevada, for example, was outraged by the Kefauver Committee's report on the dominance of organized crime in Las Vegas. But there was little the opposition could do, as attention turned to the hearings in New York City, which opened on March 12, 1951. The New York hearings personalized the alliance of crime and politics by focusing on two men — Frank Costello and William O'Dwyer.

Costello was born Francesco Castiglia on January 26, 1891, in Lauropoli, a hill town in Italy's southernmost province, Calabria. When he was four, he was brought to New York City by his parents, where they traded rural squalor for urban poverty. Yet by the time of the Kefauver Committee's hearings, Costello was hardly a man of the slums: his apartment was in a fashionable West Side neighborhood of New York City; his summer home was in Sands Point, on Long Island; and he traveled regularly each year to Florida, New Orleans, and Hot Springs, Arkansas. He presented himself as a legitimate businessman, with interests in real estate and oil, but the Kefauver Committee saw him differently: he was a bootlegger, who had moved into the legitimate liquor industry; he was the owner of illegal casinos and operator of slot machines; and he was a bookmaker. The criminal syndicate he had headed included such big-name criminals as Meyer Lansky, Joe Adonis, Willie Moretti, Abner Zwillman, Vito Genovese, and Joseph Profaci; he was associated with Joseph Lanza, Charles Luciano, and Carlos Marcello, all reputed hoodlums. The Kefauver Committee presented evidence that in 1942, at least, Costello had exercised political dominance over Tammany Hall, the New York City political organization. The evidence on Costello was unusually reliable, since it had been obtained from wiretaps by Manhattan District Attorney Frank Hogan, which, the Committee observed, "gave a vivid picture of Frank Costello as a political boss and an underworld emperor."

William O'Dwyer was a policeman from 1917 to 1924, when he left the force to practice law. He was elected to a judgeship in 1938 and, in 1940, as district attorney of Kings County, which gave him jurisdiction over the borough of Brooklyn. As D.A., he conducted an important investigation of more than twenty gangland murders that had been committed in one year. With the help of one of the hired killers, Abe Reles, O'Dwyer's office identified an organization, popularly known as Murder Inc., which was headed by Albert Anastasia and staffed by Italian and Jewish gunmen. Murder Inc. was responsible for numerous killings in New York and elsewhere, but on November 12, 1941, before an indictment could be returned against Anastasia, Reles plunged to his death from the bedroom of his suite on the sixth floor of Coney Island's Half Moon Hotel, even though he was under police protection. According to the Kefauver Committee, it was doubtful that O'Dwyer ever intended to seek an indictment of Anastasia, who continued to maintain a "stranglehold" on the Brooklyn waterfront through control of a local of the International Longshoremen's Association. The Murder Inc. investigation was, the Kefauver Committee found, riddled with "glaring deficiencies." Nevertheless, O'Dwyer was able to turn it to political advantage, and in 1945 he was elected mayor of New York. Yet, the

Committee concluded about O'Dwyer, who was United States Ambassador to Mexico at the time of the hearings:

> A single pattern of conduct emerges from . . . [his] official activities in regard to the gambling and waterfront rackets, murders, and police corruption, from his days as district attorney through his term as mayor. No matter what the motivation of his choice, action or inaction, it often seemed to result favorably for men suspected of being high up in the rackets.

As a case study of the nationwide operations of organized crime, the Kefauver Committee examined the wire service, which provided bookmakers with up-to-the-minute racing news that was essential to any betting operation. The first wire service, Nationwide News Service, was founded in the 1920s by Moses L. "Moe" Annenberg, whose principal associate was James M. Ragen. In the face of a monopoly investigation and an income tax inquiry, however, Annenberg divested himself of his interest in 1939, and the company was transformed into Continental Press Service. By 1946, its management having changed more than once, Continental was in Ragen's hands, but that was when trouble began. Mickey Cohen and Joseph Sica, acting on behalf of West Coast Mafia leader Jack Dragna, tried to muscle into the company, and a Chicago firm controlled by Anthony Accardo and the Capone syndicate, R & H Publishing, began to give Continental competition. On June 24, 1946, Ragen was shotgunned in typical gangland style. He died three months later. Four witnesses identified Lenny Patrick, Dave Yaras, and William Block as the gunmen, but after one witness was murdered, two recanted, and another fled, the indictment was dropped. Continental quietly passed into the control of the Capone syndicate. Carlos Marcello was named its New Orleans distributor, and Jack Dragna was awarded a $50,000 "service contract." Bookies everywhere had to deal with the national syndicate's front operation, and either had to pay a premium or go out of business.

Senator Kefauver was particularly interested in the structure of organized crime, and his committee concluded at the completion of its hearings:

> Organized crime today is far different from what it was many years ago. New types of criminal gangs have emerged during Prohibition. Organized crime in the last thirty years has taken on new characteristics. Criminal groups today are multi-purpose in character, engaging in any racket wherever there is money to be made. The Mafia . . . has an important part in binding together into a loose association the . . . major criminal . . . gangs and individual hoodlums throughout the country. The domination

of the Mafia is based fundamentally on "muscle" and "murder." [It] . . .
will ruthlessly eliminate anyone who stands in the way of its success. . . .

Beyond its clear delineation of organized crime, the accomplishments
of the Kefauver Committee were hard to measure. With the exception
of the Johnson Act, which regulated the interstate shipment of gambling devices, its legislative proposals were not acted upon until they
were embodied in the Kennedy administration's legislative program,
which was passed by Congress in 1961. Some scholars were even critical
of its work. William Moore, in *The Kefauver Committee and the Politics
of Crime*, argued that Kefauver launched the probe for political gain and
that the thesis of the existence of a national crime syndicate was
erroneous. If there was agreement on anything, it was generally conceded that the Kefauver Committee was successful in arousing the consciousness of the public and stirring its sensitivity to organized crime.
Nevertheless, professional politicians — urban bosses, vengeful congressmen, white southerners, and a resentful outgoing President —
denied Kefauver the presidential nomination in 1952. (Kefauver did secure the vice-presidential nomination in 1956, following a down-to-the-
wire roll-call contest with the junior senator from Massachusetts, John
F. Kennedy.) But in 1956, as it had in 1952, the election went to the Republicans. That Senator Kefauver came close to being elected President
was in large part due to the crime fighter image his hearings had established for him.

The Apalachin Meeting

The upstate New York area known as the Southern Tier is not
renowned for the hospitality of its autumn weather. It rains a lot — a
cold, wet, depressing, raw rain. And November 14, 1957, was a typical
fall day in Apalachin, a small town near Binghamton in Broome County.
For some time Sergeant Edgar D. Crosswell of the New York State Police had been keeping an eye on the 130-acre estate of Joseph Barbara,
Sr., on McFall Road, a dirt road that ran from old Route 17 to
Apalachin Creek. Crosswell knew that Barbara, who owned a Canada
Dry distributorship, had been mixed up in bootlegging, was associated
with gamblers, and was a suspect in several gangland slayings. On
November 13 Crosswell and a fellow trooper noticed suspicious out-of-
state cars at the Parkway Motel in Vestal, which is near Apalachin.
Crosswell alerted the Alcohol and Tobacco Tax Division of the U.S.
Treasury Department, and the following day, Crosswell, his partner,
and two ATT agents drove to the Barbara estate, arriving there about
12:40 P.M. They drove into a parking area, planning to take the license
numbers of the few parked cars they expected to find. Instead, there

were as many as ten cars in the lot and another twenty to twenty-five over near a barn. As the officers backed out of the parking area, eight to ten men came from behind the garage. They were, Crosswell said, "sharply dressed" in "dark clothing," like "men in the rackets wear"; they looked like "hoodlums." As the officers left, Mrs. Barbara looked out the window and said, within earshot of Crosswell, "There's the state troopers."

The officers decided to set up a check point on old Route 17 near its junction with McFall Road. From this vantage point, they could see the gathering begin to break up about 1:20 P.M. The first car, with five persons in it, was stopped at 1:25 P.M. The driver was Russell Bufalino of Pittston, Pennsylvania, whom Crosswell recognized as having been arrested for receiving stolen property. A passenger was Vito Genovese of New Jersey, who, Crosswell knew, had "an extensive criminal background." Crosswell asked Genovese: "What are you doing in this area?" "I don't think I have to answer your question, do I?" Genovese replied. "No," Crosswell answered. The car was permitted to pass on. By 2:30 twenty-five persons were counted at the check point, while others were stopped in the woods or along other roads. In all, fifty-nine men were identified as having been at the Barbara residence. From New York City, they included Joseph Bonanno, Joseph Magliocco, Carlo Gambino, Carmine Lombardozzi, Joseph Profaci, and John Bonventre; from Niagara Falls, Anthony Magaddino; from New Jersey, in addition to Genovese, Gerardo Catena, Joseph Ida, and Frank Majuri; from California, Frank DeSimone; from Texas, Joseph Civello; and from Tampa, Florida, and Havana, Cuba, Santo Trafficante, Jr.

The Apalachin roundup put organized crime back in the public eye. There were no less than 133 examinations of the Apalachin attendees by federal grand juries, the FBI, and other law enforcement agencies. What was the meeting about? Like Genovese, most said nothing, while some claimed they were merely there to visit "a sick friend." That was Russell Bufalino's story. DeSimone said he had come east to see an eye doctor, and Bufalino had invited him and Civello, his cousin, to a party. Civello, on the other hand, told Dallas Police Chief Carl F. Hanson that "Russ," a man he did not know but had met in New York City, had invited him to a barbecue and a crap game. Not one would admit it was more than pure coincidence that so many mobsters had gathered together at one time. The government did not believe it was a chance event for a number of reasons, not the least of which was the order Barbara had placed on November 5, 1957, with Armour and Company of Binghamton for 207 pounds of steak, 20 pounds of veal cutlets, and 15 pounds of luncheon meat.

In due course, a federal grand jury indicted twenty-seven of the attendees for conspiracy to obstruct justice and perjury. The trial lasted eight weeks, and on January 13, 1960, a verdict of guilty was entered by the Honorable Irving R. Kaufman, U.S. district judge for Manhattan. (One of the eighty-four witnesses who testified at the trial was Robert F. Kennedy, the former chief counsel of a U.S. Senate committee that had conducted its own investigation of the Apalachin meeting. Joseph Profaci had sought, as part of his defense, to show that he did not speak English well. Kennedy testified that he had spoken with Profaci before and after he testified before the Senate committee. Profaci "spoke . . . in perfect English — perfect English, broken perfect English, but he understood what I was saying to him and I understood what he was saying to me, . . ." Kennedy testified.) The guilty verdict was not upheld on appeal, however. The evidence of conspiracy, the appellate court held, was insufficient. Noting that there were "suspicions . . . that [the Apalachin meeting] was . . . of underworld overlords and their vassals, commonly credited with being members of the Mafia," the Court observed that it was "surely a matter of public concern that more [was] not known of" the purposes of the meeting, but its judgment had to rest on the evidence, and it was lacking, "if not on the question of falsity itself, at least on the question of agreement to tell false stories."

The Court's judgment epitomized an attitude that was a source of great frustration for law enforcement officials. Apalachin had occurred, and common sense told all but the agenda of the meeting. Yet, even with the power to grant immunity, the government could not break the wall of silence or prevent perjury from being committed. Several attendees even spent months in jail for civil contempt for not talking or for giving evasive testimony when they did talk. The significance of Apalachin lay in the circumstantial evidence that the participants had come together for sinister purposes, though the exact nature of those purposes could not be ascertained. Much of what the public learned about the meeting was the result of the efforts of the Senate Select Committee on Improper Activities in the Labor or Management Field — called the McClellan Committee after its chairman, John L. McClellan of Arkansas. The chief counsel of the McClellan Committee, the working-level leader, was Robert F. Kennedy.

Robert F. Kennedy and the McClellan Committee

In November and December 1956 Robert Kennedy, a Senate committee counsel, made a trip to the West Coast, visiting Los Angeles, Portland, and Seattle. Kennedy had been taking a preliminary look at labor racketeering, and stopping in Chicago on his way back to Washington, he made a critical determination: Dave Beck was a crook. The implications were disturbing, for Beck was the president of one of the nation's largest unions, the International Brotherhood of Teamsters. If Kennedy was right, there was justification for a full Senate investigation. But what committee should undertake it? After much discussion among the Senate leadership, the decision was made to create a select committee, with Senator McClellan as chairman. The membership included Senator John F. Kennedy of Massachusetts. "Bobby wanted me on that committee," John Kennedy said later, "in order to keep it more balanced." Otherwise, it would have been too conservative, too antilabor. The McClellan Committee was created by a unanimous vote of the Senate on January 30, 1957. In its first major investigation, it found that Dave Beck had abused his trust by receiving more than $32,000 in kickbacks, and he had helped himself to more than $370,000 in union funds. Beck was convicted in state court and imprisoned for larceny in 1957, and he was found guilty of tax evasion in federal court in 1959. As a power in the labor movement, he was through (he went free in May 1975, having obtained a full pardon from President Gerald R. Ford). But Beck's downfall was the occasion for the rise to the presidency of the union of a labor leader who was, if anything, even more corrupt — James Riddle Hoffa.

Born on February 14, 1913, in Brazil, Indiana, Hoffa lost his father, a coal miner, when he was seven. His mother had to go to work to support him and his two sisters. In 1924 she moved to Detroit, where she was employed on an auto assembly line. In 1932 Hoffa, while working on the loading platform at the Kroger Food Company, started a work stoppage and founded a union, Local 19341, which was affiliated with the American Federation of Labor. In 1936 it was merged into Teamsters Local 299, which was to be Hoffa's power base for nearly forty years.

Hoffa's association with racketeers began on a romantic note. As a young labor organizer, he had an affair with an attractive woman named Sylvia Pigano. (Pigano later moved to Kansas City, where she married Sam Scaradino, who was involved in the rackets. When Scaradino changed his name to Frank O'Brien, Pigano's son took the name of his stepfather and became Charles O'Brien. After Frank O'Brien died, Pigano had an affair with Frank Coppola, her son's godfather. Coppola, who lived in Kansas City and Detroit, was a major narcotics smuggler and an associate of Charles Luciano, Phil Kastel, and Carlos Marcello.) It was through Pigano that Hoffa met Santo Perrone and Angelo Meli, both of whom were Mafia leaders in Detroit. Hoffa's friendship with Perrone and Meli led to the success of the first Teamsters citywide strike, in April 1937, for he was able to get the mob to stay neutral. It also was the beginning of an alliance that contributed mightily to Hoffa's rise to the Teamsters presidency in September 1957 in an election the McClellan Committee said had been "rigged."

Following its investigation of Beck, the McClellan Committee turned to Hoffa. It was the beginning of what Hoffa termed the "Kennedy vendetta." "We were like flint and steel," Hoffa said. "Every time we came to grips the sparks flew." The McClellan Committee's investigation considered Hoffa's rapid ascent to leadership, his centralization of power, his questionable business transactions with trucking companies, and his associations with a number of organized crime figures, including John Dioguardi and Anthony Corallo of New York, and Paul Dorfman of Chicago. Hoffa's relationship with Dioguardi and Corallo typified the subversion of the labor movement by the underworld. Dioguardi was described by the McClellan Committee as a "three-time convicted labor racketeer and the suspected instigator of the [acid] blinding of columnist Victor Riesel," who had been writing a newspaper expose on corruption in the labor movement. (The case against Dioguardi for the Riesel assault was dismissed when the actual assailant was found dead and the other witnesses refused to testify.) Dioguardi, identified in subsequent investigations as a member of the Thomas Lucchese family of La Cosa Nostra in New York, obtained control of a local of the Allied Industrial Workers of America in 1950 with the help of Paul Dorfman. Dorfman was described by the McClellan Committee as "an associate of Chicago mobsters and the head of a local of the Waste Material Handlers Union" in Chicago. As Dioguardi's influence grew, he enlisted the assistance of Corallo, a "long-term kingpin in the New York narcotics and labor rackets," according to the McClellan Committee. (Subsequent investigation identified him as a *caporegime* in the Lucchese family.) Dioguardi and Corallo brought into the industrial workers union forty individuals who had been arrested 178 times and convicted seventy-seven times for such crimes as theft, narcotics, extortion, bookmaking, assault, robbery, burglary, forgery, and murder. The union hardly represented its members. Instead, it worked closely with employers to legitimize the misery of thousands of black and Puerto Rican employees, who were forced to tolerate low wages, high initiation fees and dues, no welfare benefits, no seniority, and sub-standard working conditions.

In July 1957, before the McClellan Committee held hearings on the Dioguardi-Corallo local, Hoffa was tried and acquitted for attempting to bribe a committee lawyer, John Cye Cheasty. Despite FBI films of the passing of information and an arrest of Hoffa right after the money was exchanged, Hoffa won acquittal from a jury of eight blacks and four whites with a variety of tactics. They included the appearance of Joe Louis, the former heavyweight champion, who came into court and publicly embraced Hoffa. According to Robert Kennedy, however, there were three chief reasons Hoffa won the case: he hired an able defense attorney, Edward Bennett Williams; he was a forceful witness in his own behalf; and the government's case was poorly prepared. Following his acquittal, Hoffa testified before the McClellan Committee; he avoided pleading the Fifth Amendment, claiming a poor memory instead. Kennedy, using a lawful phone tap secured from the office of Manhattan District Attorney Frank Hogan, conducted a devastating cross-examination, bringing out the close ties between Hoffa and Dioguardi; and Hoffa left the Committee hearing a wounded, but not disabled man. The McClellan Committee held further hearings on Hoffa in 1958, confirming and adding sordid detail. Nevertheless, unlike Beck, Hoffa's contest with the committee did not result in his unseating. The Kennedy-Hoffa confrontation was blunt and acrimonious, but the score would not be settled until after November 22, 1963.

Following the meeting of underworld leaders at Apalachin on November 14, 1957, the McClellan Committee turned its attention to organized crime — its structure and membership. In June and July 1958 there were hearings on the background of the Apalachin attendees, which was summarized in the committee's final report. Of the 59 men who had been identified as in attendance, 50 had arrest records, 35 had convictions, and 23 had spent time in jail or prison. The committee broke the statistics down further: 18 of the men had either been arrested or questioned in connection with murder investigations; 15 had been arrested or convicted for narcotics; 30 had been arrested or convicted for gambling; and 23 had been arrested or convicted for the illegal use of firearms. As to their legitimate business activities, 9 were or had been in coin-operated machine businesses; 16 were involved in garment manufacturing or trucking; 10 owned grocery stores or markets; 17 owned taverns or restaurants; 11 were in the olive oil-cheese importing or exporting business; 9 were in the construction business. The McClellan Committee did not credit the participants' story that the meeting had been a chance event, citing the extensive telephone communications among the attendees that preceded it. The conclusion of the Committee was reflected in remarks of Chairman McClellan during the hearings, which were quoted in the Committee's final report:

> There exists in America today what appears to be a close-knit, clandestine, criminal syndicate. This group has made fortunes in the illegal liquor traffic during Prohibition, and later in narcotics, vice and gambling. These illicit profits [are today invested in] . . . legitimate business. . . . [T]he criminal syndicate . . . is not . . . localized . . . but national in scope.

A measure of the wealth that the syndicate members and their associates had amassed was set out in Robert F. Kennedy's book, *The Enemy Within*, published after the hearings. Kennedy described the life-style of a well-known West Coast mobster:

> Our investigation and hearings show[ed] that Mickey Cohen spent $275 for his silk lounging pajamas, $25,000 for a specially built bulletproof car and at one time had 300 different suits, 1,500 pairs of socks and 60 pairs of $60 shoes.

(A movie script of *The Enemy Within* was prepared by Budd Schulberg, author of *On the Waterfront*, an exceptional 1954 film about union corruption. But when Columbia Pictures was advised through William Bufalino, an attorney for Hoffa, that Twentieth Century-Fox had wisely decided not to produce the film out of fear that Teamster drivers would refuse to deliver the print to theaters, Columbia also decided to abandon the project. *The Enemy Within* was never made into a movie.) In separate remarks attached to the McClellan Committee report, Senator Kennedy noted that in "the modern criminal underworld we face a nationwide highly organized and highly effective internal enemy." He called for new approaches to "racketeer control."

The Kennedy Organized Crime Program

On January 20, 1961, at noon, John Fitzgerald Kennedy was sworn in by Chief Justice Earl Warren as the 35th President of the United States. The contrast between the outgoing and the incoming Presidents was striking. One, a product of the rural Midwest; the other, a native of the urban Northeast. There were differences in age — seventy and forty-three; religion — Protestant and Catholic; and philosophy of life and politics — conservative and liberal. Dwight D. Eisenhower seemed to represent an ending, John F. Kennedy a beginning; yet Eisenhower had served eight years; Kennedy would be President but a thousand days.

As President-elect, Kennedy had talked with his brother at their home in Hyannisport, Massachusetts, a conversation that was reconstructed by Arthur M. Schlesinger, Jr., in *Robert Kennedy and His Times*. Was he interested in becoming Attorney General? Robert Kennedy said, "No." He had, he said, "been chasing bad men for three years," and he didn't want to spend the rest of his life doing that. In the end, the President told him he needed him. The younger brother had no choice.

Robert F. Kennedy had a number of priorities as Attorney General. He was concerned about the disadvantages of the poor in the administration of justice and about civil rights programs, but most of all he was concerned about organized crime. In his first interview as Attorney General, Kennedy told Peter Maas, a magazine writer, that organized crime was his number-one concern. At his first press conference, he announced that his organized-crime drive had the President's backing. "Don't tell me what I can't do," he would say to the ever-negative staff attorneys at the Department of Justice. "Tell me what I can do." Before Robert Kennedy, recalled Henry Petersen, a career attorney in the Organized Crime and Racketeering Section of the Criminal Division, "people would ask you to define [organized crime] . . . . Robert Kennedy came in and said, 'Don't define it, do something about it.' " Nevertheless, the obstacles were formidable. As late as January 1962 J. Edgar Hoover was on record as saying, "No single individual or coalition of racketeers dominates organized crime across the nation." Some of the other twenty-six federal investigative agencies may have been more receptive to the idea that a national crime syndicate existed — the Bureau of Narcotics, in particular — but none of them was especially excited about cooperating and sharing information, or working under the leadership of Justice Department attorneys. Robert Kennedy may not have changed attitudes, but he did change the quality of performance with impressive results.

Hoover said the FBI did not have adequate legal jurisdiction to investigate organized crime. Kennedy fought for and secured the passage of new criminal statutes dealing with interstate racketeering, legislation that had originally been proposed by the Kefauver Committee, but had been ignored by Congress. He tried hard, too, but failed to get legislation authorizing court-order wiretapping. The number of attorneys in the Organized Crime and Racketeering Section was increased from seventeen to sixty-three between 1960 and 1964. Criminal intelligence from the various investigative agencies was pooled. Targets were selected for concentrated attention: the list started out at forty, including Mickey Cohen and John Roselli on the West Coast; Anthony Accardo and Sam Giancana in the Midwest; Carlos Marcello and Santo Traffi-cante, Jr., in the South; and numerous Apalachin attendees in the Northeast. By 1964 the list had grown to 2,300 top mob figures and their associates, and the Organized Crime and Racketeering Section had 175,000 cards in its master file of information on racketeers and their associates.

Kennedy's way of using the Internal Revenue Service in the Treasury Department illustrated the impact of his personality as well as his power, in his own right and as the President's brother. Mortimer M. Caplin, who had taught Robert Kennedy at the University of Virginia Law School, was appointed Commissioner of Internal Revenue, but first Kennedy made sure that Caplin supported vigorous enforcement of taxes of mob figures. Kennedy knew that he would be, as Arthur Schlesinger wrote, "criticized on the grounds that tax laws are there to raise money for the government and should not be used to punish the underworld." Assistant Attorney General Ramsey Clark believed, for example, that even if you applied "tax criteria," it was not "okay to *select* organized crime cases. . . ." But that was precisely Kennedy's point. Should mob figures, because they were mob figures, be free to evade taxes? Moreover, Kennedy could argue that revenue raising *was* a result of the organized-crime program, for while he was Attorney General, the IRS civilly assessed top racketeers a quarter of a billion dollars beyond the amount paid when they had filed their returns. In 1961, for example, Carlos Marcello of New Orleans had federal tax liens of $835,396 filed against him. In 1962 Santo Trafficante, Jr., of Tampa was the subject of a $200,000 federal tax lien. Attorney General Kennedy addressed a group of IRS agents on the importance of the tax program:

> The reason that this [program] has received such top priority . . . is not that [Secretary of the Treasury] Mr. Dillon is interested in it . . . but the fact that the President himself is personally interested. . . . [He] served on the McClellan Committee for three years and became personally interested. . . . [Y]our work is of great importance.

Kennedy did more than make speeches. He saw to it, for example, that regional IRS directors who did not support the program were transferred. The results were concrete. IRS man-days of participation in organized-crime investigations rose from 8,836 in 1960 to 96,182 in 1963. (In 1967 the President's Commission on Law Enforcement and the Administration of Justice found that 60 percent of all organized-crime prosecutions brought between 1961 and 1965 turned out to have originated in tax investigations.)

In addition to developing legislation and bringing civil actions, Kennedy sought to focus public attention on organized crime. He spoke widely and freely gave interviews. He also worked closely with his old boss, Senator McClellan, in presenting a comprehensive set of hearings, beginning on September 25, 1963, on the nationwide structure of the Mafia, or La Cosa Nostra, as it was known by its members. The hearings featured the testimony of Joseph Valachi, the first member of La Cosa Nostra ever to testify willingly in public about the nature of the organization. The lead-off witness was Attorney General Kennedy, who commented on the structure of organized crime:

> Because of intelligence gathered from Joseph Valachi and from informants — we know that Cosa Nostra is run by a commission [of nine to 12

men], and that the leaders of Cosa Nostra in most cities are responsible to
the commission.

He described his organized-crime program:

> Syndicate leaders and their associates have been identified and all are now
> under intensive investigation. A number of major racketeering figures
> have been convicted and many more cases are in the indictment or inves-
> tigative stage.

> It is an organization. It is [the] Mafia. It is the Cosa Nostra. There are
> other names for it, but it all refers to the same organization.

He noted the difficulty in solving organized-crime murders:

> [T]he members of the commission, the top members, or even their chief
> lieutenants, have insulated themselves from the crime itself. . . . If they
> want to have somebody knocked off, for instance, the top man will speak
> to somebody who will speak to somebody else who will speak to some-
> body else and order it. The man who actually does the gun work . . . does
> not know who ordered it. To trace that back is virtually impossible.

Finally, Kennedy discussed the tendency of organized-crime figures
to move out of gambling and narcotics into legitimate business and
unions, but he added:

> I don't want anybody to misunderstand the fact that they are also doing
> the same things that they were doing during the days of Al Capone.
> Because there have been large numbers of very brutal murders which
> have been committed by those in organized crime just over a period of the
> last two years. Certainly not a week goes by that somewhere in the United
> States an individual is not killed or murdered in some kind of gangland
> battle or a witness is not garroted and killed.

The Attorney General was followed by law enforcement officials from
all over the country, who advised the Committee on the structure of
organized crime in their respective areas. In addition, from federal and
local intelligence reports, the Committee was able to identify the
organized-crime families, their bosses, underbosses, *consiglieri*,
caporegime, and their members. For his part, Valachi added a personal
knowledge of the history of organized crime in New York, where he had
for years been a member of the Vito Genovese family.

The overall statistics of the Kennedy organized-crime program were
impressive. In 1960 Organized Crime and Racketeering Section attorneys spent 61 days in court, 660 days in the field, and 100 days before a

grand jury; in 1963 they spent 1,081 days in court, 6,177 days in the field, and 1,353 days before a grand jury. The number of indicted individuals rose from 121 in 1961 to 615 in 1963; convictions, which always lag two to three years behind indictments, rose from 73 in 1961 to 288 in 1963. In all, 116 individuals who, according to subsequent investigations, were members of La Cosa Nostra, were included in the Justice Department's racketeering indictments between 1960 and 1964. Among them were such top syndicate figures as Anthony Accardo (tax evasion) in Chicago, Anthony Provenzano (extortion) in New Jersey, Alfred Sica (tax evasion) in California, Carlos Marcello (conspiracy) in New Orleans, Carmine Lombardozzi (tax evasion) in New York, Angelo Bruno (extortion) in Philadelphia, Anthony Giacalone (tax evasion) in Detroit, and Joseph Glimco (unlawful payments) in Chicago. In addition, Mickey Cohen, a major West Coast underworld figure, though not a member of La Cosa Nostra, was convicted of tax evasion. Robert M. Morgenthau, the U.S. Attorney for the Southern District of New York, who was later elected District Attorney in Manhattan, told of the impact of the Kennedy organized-crime program when he was interviewed by Victor S. Navasky, who was doing research for his book, *Kennedy Justice*:

> It really wasn't until Robert F. Kennedy became Attorney General that an organized program was developed. . . . It's kind of like a good football team. You know, they can lose a few of the top players, and they can fill those spots with substitutes, but when it reaches a point where there are no substitutes available . . . I think . . . . that's what . . . happened . . . [to] organized crime.

Robert Kennedy was holding a two-day organized-crime meeting in his office in late November 1963. Robert Morgenthau was there. The last subject to be discussed before lunch on November 22 was Sam Giancana and political corruption in Chicago. Thomas McBride, an Organized Crime and Racketeering Section attorney who later joined the special prosecution force in the Watergate case, recalled the day for Navasky:

> About forty of us were at the long round-up meeting on assassination day. [Kennedy] never met the section again, and we had met regularly for two and a half years. The round-up meetings didn't accomplish that much, but they were valuable . . . . [T]hey kept the level of steam up. They proved that this was a serious business.

After the President's assassination, the steam went out of the organized-crime program. Whatever was intended, the mob proved to be the principal beneficiary of Dallas. It started with little things: no longer did the FBI send a car to pick up the attorney general when he traveled around the country, for example. The statistics told the story. By 1966 the number of attorneys in the Organized Crime and Racketeering Section was down to 48; days in court fell to 606; days in the field, to 3,480; days before the grand jury, to 373. IRS participation was down to 74,938 man-days in 1966; by 1968, it was only 42,120.

Joseph Valachi in Perspective

For a brief time, the Kennedy crime program was sustained by its own momentum. The McClellan Committee, in July and August 1964, resumed hearings that had been suspended in October 1963, and its principal interest was syndicate activity in narcotics. In a three-part final report dated March 4, 1965, the committee set out its basic findings about the national syndicate, drawing in particular on what it had learned from the testimony of Joseph Valachi, which it credited as trustworthy. In the Annual Report of the Attorney General for 1963, Robert Kennedy had termed Valachi's testimony a significant intelligence breakthrough, which had enabled the Justice Department "to prove conclusively" the existence of the nationwide organization known as Cosa Nostra. Nevertheless, not everyone agreed. Arthur Schlesinger, in *A Thousand Days*, apparently reflected his own feelings in 1965 when he observed that "[c]riminologists . . . were skeptical of the sanction the Department [of Justice] gave to the notion of a centrally organized and all-pervasive Mafia. . . ." On the other hand, Ralph Salerno, a retired New York City police official widely regarded as one of the two or three leading authorities on organized crime, wrote in *The Crime Confederation*:

> The Valachi confessions are ranked next to Apalachin as the greatest single [intelligence] blow ever delivered to organized crime in the United States. This evaluation came from the lips of those most affected by it: members of the criminal network whose comments were overheard through bug and wiretap.

> Many of the incidents Valachi described had . . . been known to the police, but . . . [Valachi] was able to fill in the gaps and connect one incident to another . . . . [Valachi] . . . drew a schematic picture of the organization, described it and told how it worked. The police, for example, had long realized that certain underworld figures were often seen with each other, but they did not realize that these were formal, not casual, associations, relationships of rank in a system governed by rules and regulations. The pattern that Valachi furnished made it possible for police intelligence men to begin to see the dimensions of syndicated crime and stop looking at it as a series of unconnected cases.

Valachi had agreed to testify against other members of organized crime only after Vito Genovese had marked him for death, thinking he was an informer. One of the most protected prisoners in the history of the federal prison system, Valachi died of natural causes at LaTuna Federal Penitentiary, El Paso, Texas, on April 3, 1971.

The Investigation of James R. Hoffa

Just as James R. Hoffa's stewardship of the Teamsters Union was the subject of enduring interest at the McClellan Committee when Robert F. Kennedy was its chief counsel, Hoffa was high on the list of targets of the Department of Justice program against corruption in the labor movement after Kennedy became Attorney General. In 1958 Attorney General William P. Rogers had established a special group on organized crime to look into the Apalachin meeting. Attorney General Kennedy followed that precedent in designating a special group in the Labor Rights Unit of the Organized Crime and Racketeering Section to look into the Teamsters Union. Headed by Walter Sheridan, a former investigator for the McClellan Committee, it was charged by Kennedy, as Schlesinger noted, "to take a fresh look at the findings of the McClellan Committee and to probe generally into the field of labor racketeering, particularly into the activities of Hoffa and the Teamsters." The group came to be known as the "Get Hoffa Squad," and it was effective: 201 Teamster officials and their associates indicted, and 126 of them convicted. But the most important prosecutions were the three brought against Hoffa himself. They have been chronicled in *The Fall and Rise of Jimmy Hoffa* by Walter Sheridan.

On May 18, 1962, Hoffa was indicted under the Taft-Hartley Act in Nashville, Tennessee, for receiving a million dollars in illegal payments through a trucking company, the Test Fleet Corporation, which had been set up in his wife's name. His trial ended with a hung jury on December 23, 1962, but the judge, William E. Miller, ordered the convening of a grand jury to investigate charges of jury tampering. Judge Miller commented:

The right of a defendant in a criminal case to be tried by a jury of his peers is one of the most sacred of our constitutional guarantees. The system of trial by jury, however, becomes nothing more than a mockery if unscrupulous persons are allowed to subvert it by improper and unlawful means.

The grand jury investigation resulted in Hoffa and five others being indicted in Nashville on May 9, 1963. Hoffa was also indicted, along with seven others, in Chicago on June 4, 1963, for obtaining by fraud $20 million in loans from the Teamsters Central States Pension Fund, from which, it was charged, they had diverted one million dollars for their own benefit.

On November 7, 1963, Sheridan learned that an effort was being made by a Hoffa attorney, Z. T. "Tommy" Osborn, Jr., to tamper with the jury in the jury tampering trial. (Osborn was a prominent Tennessee lawyer. He was the leading candidate for president of the Nashville Bar Association, and he had successfully argued *Baker* v. *Carr*, the Tennessee reapportionment case, before the U.S. Supreme Court.) Eventually, Osborn was indicted and tried for endeavoring to obstruct justice. He was found guilty and sentenced to three and a half years in prison, a conviction that was upheld by the Supreme Court in 1966. It was later learned that in January 1964 Osborn received $127,500 of a diverted Teamsters pension fund loan, but it was not enough to repair the damage to a promising career. Osborn was paroled in April 1969, apparently after congressional intervention. On February 2, 1970, he committed suicide.

The assassination of the President occurred in the midst of the legal proceedings against Hoffa who, upon learning that the flag at Teamster headquarters in Washington was at half-mast, flew into a rage. On Sunday, November 24, Hoffa was in Nashville, where, in a television interview, he commented, "Bobby Kennedy is just another lawyer now."

Hoffa's jury tampering trial, which had been shifted to Chattanooga, got underway on January 20, 1964, before Judge Frank W. Wilson. Six weeks later Hoffa was found guilty, principally on the basis of the testimony of Edward Grady Partin, the secretary-treasurer of Teamster Local 5 in Baton Rouge, Louisiana. Partin had been part of Hoffa's retinue during the Nashville trial, but he had decided to cooperate with the government in September 1962. (At that time Partin told Justice Department lawyers about a June 1962 conversation in Washington in which Hoffa had talked about assassinating Robert Kennedy. "He's got to go," Hoffa had said. An FBI lie detector test indicated Partin was telling the truth.) Partin agreed to tell Sheridan what he knew about Hoffa's effort to influence the jury in the Nashville trial, and his incriminating testimony survived five days of grueling cross-examination. It was on the basis of Partin's account that the jury verdict ultimately rested. Judge Wilson sentenced Hoffa to eight years in prison on March 12, 1964, and the Supreme Court upheld the conviction in 1966.

Hoffa's Chicago trial for fraud in connection with the pension funds got underway on April 27, 1964. After thirteen weeks he was found guilty and sentenced, on August 17, 1964, to serve five years in addition to his jury tampering term. (Eight days later Robert Kennedy, having resigned as attorney general, announced his candidacy for the U.S. Senate from New York. He was elected in November.)

Hoffa did not go to jail until March 1967, when all his appeals had been exhausted. It had been a contest of wills of two determined, bitterly opposed men. Hoffa would contend he had been framed, but juries and the judicial system had decided otherwise. There was more to Hoffa's battle to stay out of prison than showed in the court records. According to Sheridan, the Chicago underworld had a plan to fix Judge Miller in Nashville, but no one had the courage to offer the bribe. There was also a threat, which was ignored, against the brother of Supreme Court Justice William J. Brennan in connection with Hoffa's appeal. And there were various other desperate efforts, all of which failed: allegations of government wiretapping and an offer of $100,000 to J. Edgar Hoover if he would testify they were true; and accusations (later discredited) that the judge and jury in Chattanooga had been supplied prostitutes by U.S. marshals. A U.S. senator who had enjoyed Teamster support, Edward Long of Missouri (he had once received well over $100,000 in questionable fees from one of Hoffa's attorneys), was behind an effort to undercut the organized-crime program and embarrass Attorney General Kennedy, and Congressman Roland V. Libonati of Chicago demanded (but failed to get) an investigation by the House Judiciary Committee of the Hoffa prosecutions. Finally, agents of Carlos Marcello — his lawyer, G. Wray Gill, and an associate, Pete Rotella — sought to help Hoffa by securing fraudulent exculpating tape recordings, and a million-dollar fund was made available to Marcello by union and underworld supporters of Hoffa, to be used to free the Teamster leader.

Hoffa received an executive grant of clemency from President Richard M. Nixon on December 23, 1971. The clemency was granted without the customary consultation with the judge who passed sentence, and in defiance of the U.S. Parole Board, which on three occasions in the preceding two years had unanimously rejected Hoffa's requests for release. The Parole Board's decisions had in part been based on advice from Henry Petersen, a Justice Department attorney and an organized-crime expert, who warned that Hoffa was tied to the underworld. There were ugly rumors about the clemency grant. *The New York Times* termed it a "pivotal element in the strong love affair between the [Nixon] administration and the . . . union," implying it was related to the 1972 election. The terms of his release, however, forbade Hoffa from engaging in direct or indirect management of a labor organization. Much as the union wanted Hoffa out of prison, it seemed the mob did not want him in a position of union leadership. The parole restriction had been bought, according to one rumor, with a $500,000 contribution to the Nixon reelection campaign, engineered by Anthony Provenzano, a Teamster leader in New Jersey and, according to the McClellan Committee, a *caporegime* in the Genovese family of La Cosa Nostra. Once out of prison, Hoffa filed suit to declare the restriction null and void, and he began to make his move to regain the Teamsters presidency. He was sounding like a reformer, and one ironic promise he made, if elected in 1976, was to end Teamster relations with the mob. On July 30, 1975, Hoffa left home to go to a meeting and did not return. Though it never could be tested by the judicial process, there was an account of what happened to him — the principal participants and their rationale — that appeared in two books published during our investigation: *The Teamsters*, by Steven Brill, and *The Hoffa Wars*, by Dan E. Moldea. Although the authors differ on certain details, their investigations, taken together, showed how the mob worked to eliminate someone who stood in their way.

The Death of James R. Hoffa

At about 1:15 P.M. on July 30, 1975, Hoffa left his Detroit home on Robson Drive to go to the Red Fox Restaurant in suburban Bloomfield. There he was to meet, he apparently thought, with Anthony Provenzano and Anthony Giacalone; Giacalone, according to the McClellan Committee, was a *caporegime* in the Detroit La Cosa Nostra family. Hoffa arrived at the Red Fox about 2:00 P.M. Neither Provenzano nor Giacalone was there (they would both subsequently establish their whereabouts elsewhere as concrete alibis). Hoffa was evidently picked up between 2:45 and 2:50 P.M. by Charles O'Brien, the son of Hoffa's one-time girl friend, Sylvia Pigano. Hoffa trusted O'Brien, even though he had taken the side of Frank Fitzsimmons, Hoffa's handpicked successor as Teamster president, who wanted to retain power. At least two other men were in the car, one of whom was Salvatore Briguglio, who served as business agent for Teamster Local 560, Provenzano's power base. According to Brill, Hoffa was probably knocked unconscious, which would explain why hair particles and traces of blood were found in the back seat of the maroon Mercury that O'Brien had borrowed from Giacalone's son, Joey. O'Brien also had close ties to Giacalone, whom he called Uncle Tony. (O'Brien's mother, Sylvia, who died in 1970, had been Giacalone's girl friend. She also had been a close friend of Hoffa's wife, Josephine, and it was rumored that the two women were double-dating Giacalone and Anthony Cimini, another Mafia leader in the Detroit area, in the early 1960s. Hoffa was only able to break up his wife's affair, according to the reports, by appealing to Joseph Zerilli, the Cosa Nostra boss in Detroit.) There were conflicting reports as to where Hoffa was actually killed. It could have been at a house where O'Brien was staying (but unbeknownst to the people who lived there). There were also contradictions as to how Hoffa's body was disposed of. One informant report suggested that it was stuffed into a 55-gallon drum and shipped to a New Jersey dump. It was also suggested that the facilities (shredder, compactor, and incinerator) of Central Sanitation Services in Hamtramck, Michigan, were used. According to FBI informants, Central Sanitation Services, which was owned by Rafael Quasarano and Peter Vitale, two Detroit La Cosa Nostra members, had been used to dispose of at least ten other bodies of Mafia murder victims. Finally, there was disagreement over how much O'Brien knew or what his role was: "I never did anything to hurt Jimmy Hoffa," was how O'Brien himself answered the question. (Moldea maintained that O'Brien did not know of Hoffa's fate in advance, and the hit men were not with him in the car. By this account, Hoffa was driven to O'Brien's temporary residence four minutes from the Red Fox. "Waiting calmly at the house," Moldea wrote, "were Salvatore and Gabriel Briguglio and Thomas Andretta, who were flown in on a private plane." Moldea believed Hoffa was shot, and his body was disposed of in a junk car compactor. "Hoffa is now a goddamn hub cap," he quoted a source as having told him.)

In *The Teamsters*, Brill, relying largely on circumstantial evidence, traced Hoffa's murder to Russell Bufalino of Pittston, Pennsylvania, a Mafia family leader and an Apalachin attendee in 1957. (In addition to Bufalino, we believed that the most likely mob leader responsible was Joseph Zerilli, since neither Provenzano nor Giacalone had the stature to order a hit on Hoffa in the Zerilli territory.) The balance of evidentiary factors, however, tipped suspicion to Bufalino. Bufalino had long been associated with both Provenzano and Giacalone; he had been in telephone contact with Quasarano and Vitale in the months that preceded Hoffa's disappearance; and he was close to his cousin, William Bufalino, a former Hoffa attorney who showed up to represent *all* of the suspects and their alibi witnesses in a grand jury probe of Hoffa's disappearance. Finally, Frank Sheeran, the president of Teamster Local 326 in Delaware, who shepherded the alibi witnesses before the grand jury, had been involved with Russell Bufalino in a "labor leasing" scheme to circumvent wage provisions of the National Master Freight Agreement, which would have been in jeopardy if Hoffa had returned to power.

Despite the abundance of circumstantial evidence, there did not seem to be, as of the time of our investigation, much hope of obtaining

indictments in the Hoffa disappearance. (Salvatore Briguglio, a principal suspect, was himself gunned down in New York City on March 24,
1978.)

We believed that Hoffa's disappearance and presumed murder deserved to be placed in a broader context than concern that he might
have put an end to a labor-leasing scheme, the motive Brill tended to
emphasize. As union president — and to some extent after he went to
prison — Hoffa represented the mob's access to an important source of
wealth: the Teamsters Central States Pension Fund. It seemed emi-
nently logical to us that Hoffa's death was related to his determination
to regain control of the fund. (It was reported in September 1980 that a
federal grand jury was investigating the possibility that Hoffa was murdered because he stood in the way of a Teamsters pension fund loan to
organized crime figures in New Jersey.)

That Hoffa had been the underworld's "connection" to the fund was
indicated by FBI electronic surveillance conducted between 1961 and
1964 at the Home Juice Company of Detroit, a soft-drink distributorship that was owned by Anthony Giacalone and his brother Vito. According to Vito Giacalone, Mike Polizzi, a Detroit mob figure, had remarked that "he would have never gotten his loan of $630,000 without
Jimmy." Several factors contributed to Hoffa's influence over the fund,
a joint employer-union trusteeship for the employees which was established in January 1955. The union had de facto control over investment
decisions, as the employers did not want to antagonize Hoffa. In addition, the decision was made to invest the fund's assets directly and not
to turn their management over to professionals. Hoffa was, therefore,
the controlling figure in the making of loans, and he was responsible for
a general preference for real estate loans, as, for example, one in 1959
for $3.6 million to build the Cabana Motel in Dallas.

Hoffa's chief adviser on pension loans was Allen Dorfman, the step-
son of Paul Dorfman, through whom Hoffa had established and maintained his Chicago mob connections. (Paul Dorfman was one of the five
or six closest associates of Anthony Accardo of the Capone organization.) According to Brill, when Hoffa went to prison in 1967 he told
Fitzsimmons that Allen "speaks for me on all pension fund questions."
Dorfman, like Hoffa, had been successful in beating a number of criminal prosecutions. He was found not guilty in Hoffa's Chattanooga jury
tampering prosecution in 1964; he was also found not guilty in 1974 of
embezzlement and mail fraud in connection with a fund loan of $1 mil-
lion. Charged with him in the 1974 prosecution were Anthony Spilotro
and Felix Alderisio, both Chicago mob figures, and Irwin Weiner, a
Chicago bail bondsman long suspected of organized-crime ties. (On

September 27, 1974, a witness in the embezzlement and mail fraud case was shotgunned to death in front of his wife and two-year-old son.) Dorfman's one guilty verdict came in 1972 — for conspiracy to take a $55,000 kickback for arranging a $1.5 million loan.

Most pension funds tend to follow a conservative policy, investing primarily in government bonds and having less than 2 percent of their assets in real estate. Yet, by 1963, the Central States Pension Fund, with accumulated assets of $213 million, had 63 percent of its investments in real estate and only 3 percent in government bonds; the rest was held in bank accounts and corporate bonds. Fund loans included in 1959 and 1960 several made to Morris "Moe" Dalitz, a gambler and former bootlegger from Cleveland, whom Hoffa had known in Detroit and through whom a payoff had been allegedly arranged to settle a Teamster laundry strike in 1949. Dalitz obtained the loans to build Sunrise Hospital in Las Vegas, as well as to finance the Stardust Hotel and Country Club, the Fremont Hotel, and the Desert Inn, all also in Las Vegas. (According to FBI evidence, the Stardust, Fremont, and Desert Inn casinos were taken to the tune of $100,000-a-month in the early 1960s by a skim operation for the benefit of organized-crime figures, including Sam Giancana of Chicago, John Scalish of Cleveland, and Meyer Lansky of Miami.) Pension fund records also showed that from 1965 to 1972 $20.4 million was lent to another Las Vegas hotel and casino, Caesars Palace, the ostensible owner of which was Jay Sarno, who was actually, according to the FBI, a front for organized-crime interests in the Midwest and New England. (Skimming was suspected at Caesars Palace but not documented by the FBI.) In 1971, on Dorfman's recommendation, pension fund assets were put into the Circus Circus Hotel and Casino, also in Las Vegas. Loans of $15.5 million and $2 million were approved, the total figure finally reaching $26 million. Jay Sarno was again the paper owner, while the real party in interest, according to the FBI, was Anthony Spilotro, described by the Illinois Crime Investigation Commission as "one of the most dangerous gang terrorists in the Chicago area." (Skimming was also suspected by the FBI at the Circus Circus.) Finally, in 1974 the fund approved a $62.7 million loan to the Argent Corporation, owned by Allen R. Glick, to purchase the Stardust and the Fremont. Glick, in turn, put Frank Rosenthal in charge of his gambling operations. Rosenthal, who was an associate of Spilotro, and who was convicted in the 1960s of bribing a college basketball player, proceeded to organize a sophisticated scheme to defraud the casinos and the state of Nevada of at least $20 million in eighteen months, the largest known skim operation up until that time.

In *The Teamsters* Brill estimated that if all of the organized-crime-connected loans since 1957 were added up, they would amount to $600 million of the approximately $1.2 billion that had been loaned by the Central States Pension Fund. Brill added that at least $100 million had been lost in undercharged interest, and there had been another $285 million in defaults. Indeed, the mismanagement of the fund was so blatant that it ceased making loans in 1974, and in 1979, under Labor Department pressure, the trustees resigned and the Central States Pension Fund was put into the hands of the Equitable Life Assurance Society and Victor Palmiere & Company. Real estate investments dramatically declined from 70 percent to about 35 percent by 1979, and the cash return went up to more than 9 percent from roughly 4 percent. Nevertheless, Jim Drinkhall of *The Wall Street Journal*, an expert on the fund, reported in November 1979 that a move seemed to be under way to get rid of the new manager and go back to the old system.

If Hoffa's demise were to be put in the larger context of control over the fund, where we believed it belonged, Bufalino would not have the stature to order it on his own, particularly since it occurred in Detroit. It would have been a matter for the organized-crime commission to pass on, once the top figures of the underworld, including Zerilli, had decided they had too much at stake to permit Hoffa to return to the Teamsters presidency. It would have been decided that, as Hoffa said of Robert Kennedy, "He's got to go."

The FBI Electronic Surveillance Program

As a result of the priority the Kennedy administration placed on organized-crime control, a vast amount of information was developed. There was, for example, a witness-protection program that induced several underworld insiders to follow Valachi's lead and trade firsthand information for a promise of security. Second, the stepped-up emphasis on prosecution produced hearing and trial transcripts that could be perused for leads and insights. But the single most important source of organized-crime information was the transcripts and summaries of conversations of underworld figures that were obtained in the course of a comprehensive program of electronic surveillance conducted by the FBI between 1959 and 1965. As Hoover himself acknowledged in 1967, the bureau would never have learned what it did "about the Cosa Nostra without electronic surveillance." The intelligence gathered by the FBI was termed "significant" by the President's Commission on Law Enforcement and Administration of Justice, which, in its report in 1967, also noted that only the FBI had been able "to document fully the national scope" of organized crime. The existence of the electronic surveillance, or ELSUR, program was a carefully kept secret in 1964, and the intelligence product was not made available to the Warren Commission. But it was obtained and carefully analyzed during our investigation. As the Committee observed in its *Report*:

[T]he FBI had comprehensive electronic coverage of the major underworld figures, particularly those who comprised the commission. The Committee had access to and analyzed the product of this electronic coverage; it reviewed literally thousands of pages of electronic surveillance logs that revealed the innermost workings of organized crime in the United States. The Committee saw in stark terms a record of murder, violence, bribery, corruption and an untold variety of other crimes. Uniquely among congressional committees, and in contrast to the Warren Commission, the Committee became familiar with the nature and scope of organized crime in the years before and after the Kennedy assassination, using as its evidence the words of the participants themselves.

The investigations that followed the criminal conclave at Apalachin on November 14, 1957, served to point out how little was known by law enforcement about organized crime in the United States. As Robert Kennedy recalled, "The FBI didn't know anything, really, about [the Apalachin attendees]. . . . [T]hat was rather a shock to me." Apalachin, however, marked the beginning of a broad effort to catch up. By 1959 the FBI in Chicago had installed the first of a series of electronic devices, which would reveal so much about the underworld until the program was terminated by President Johnson in July 1965.

Two special agents in Chicago, Ralph Hill and William Roemer, were especially imaginative and enterprising. They had learned that mob figures regularly met in a second-floor tailor shop on North Michigan Avenue owned by one of them, Gus Alex. After getting clearance from Washington and suffering through a series of frustrating Sunday morning failures, Hill and Roemer gained entry to the tailor shop. Electronic surveillance equipment of the day was relatively unsophisticated: the microphone, installed behind a radiator, was of World War II vintage, as big as a Coke bottle. The technician who installed it was competent but clumsy, and while stringing wires in a crawl space between the tailor shop and a restaurant below, he fell and almost collapsed the ceiling. But in the end, the equipment worked. As William Brashler wrote in *The Don*, a biography of Sam Giancana, the Chicago Mafia leader:

[The agents] heard from the hoods' own lips who had the power and how it was distributed, who put the fix in and where it was put, what decisions were made and who was affected, who had the solutions. They heard stories, anecdotes, family problems, even a history of mob decisions as told with relish by Murray Humphreys [the mob's senior fixer]. . . . [It] was to be the biggest, most reliable source of information on the Chicago syndicate anywhere at anytime.

The surveillance program was accelerated after Attorney General Kennedy, in July 1961, criticized the quality of FBI intelligence. Devices were installed elsewhere in Chicago and throughout the country, as the effort was directed at the major organized-crime figures: Stefano Magaddino, the chairman of the commission and family boss in Buffalo, at Memorial Chapel, a funeral home he owned in Niagara Falls; Sam Giancana, a commission member as well as the family boss in Chicago, at the Armory Lounge in Forest Park, Illinois; Angelo Bruno, a commission member and family boss in Philadelphia, at his Penn Jersey Vending Company in Philadelphia; and Raymond Patriarca, a commission member and family boss in New England, at National Cigarette Service, a vending-machine company he owned in Providence, Rhode Island. Other important Mafia members put under surveillance included Sam DeCavalcante, a family boss in New Jersey, at the Kenworth Corporation, a plumbing company he operated in Kenilworth; Angelo DeCarlo, a *caporegime* in the Genovese family, at The Barn, a restaurant in Mountainside, New Jersey; and Michael Clemente, a member of the Genovese family, at the Prisco Travel Bureau in New York City. Some of the surveillance was aimed not so much at individual criminals as at areas of operation. For example, certain Las Vegas casinos, including the Stardust, Fremont, and Desert Inn, were bugged, and a device was placed in the office of the First Ward Democratic organization in Chicago, the base of operations of politicians who had traditional ties to the Chicago syndicate. In all, the FBI had in operation at any given time from 75 to 100 "bugs" planted in most metropolitan areas, and many were in operation for substantial periods. On August 24, 1964, Courtney Evans, Associate FBI Director for the Special Investigative Division, could say with confidence to Alan Belmont, Associate Director for the General Investigative Division:

> We are probably in the unique position of better understanding Giancana's reaction [to an incident involving Joseph Bonanno, a commission member in disfavor] than [are other family bosses]. . . . Our recent expansion in development of intelligence on the existence and activity of La Cosa Nostra [into the smaller states] . . . tends to confirm that there is no adequate substitute for [electronic surveillance] . . . for the development of accurate information. . . .

Charles Luciano: 1896–1962

That there was in existence a national structure of organized crime prior to Prohibition may be doubted. There was substantial evidence, however, that there were various independent Mafia groups in major American cities. In 1903 Nicola Gentile, finding little opportunity in his native village of Siciliana, Sicily, came to the United States as a youth of nineteen. After a career in organized crime, he returned to Sicily in 1937, having been charged with a narcotics violation in New Orleans, where he jumped bail. In the 1950s he began writing a long, rambling memoir entitled *Vita di Campmafia*, which was published in Rome in 1963. Gentile wrote:

> [T]he Honored Society, or Mafia, as it is commonly called, . . . finds its reasons for existence in force and in terror. It . . . was brought to America in the sections of the country where Sicilians, Calabrians and Neapolitans lived . . . In the city of New York and Brooklyn alone there were five . . . *borgatas* or families. . . .

A national syndicate was formed in the years immediately before Gentile's return to Sicily. The eyewitness accounts of Gentile and Joseph Valachi were independently substantiated by the reminiscences of other insiders — picked up on FBI bugs.

Giuseppe Masseria ruled a Mafia family in New York City in the 1920s that numbered among its members three of the most familiar names in the infamous history of organized crime: Charles Luciano, Vito Genovese, and Frank Costello. One reason that these men were to become synonymous with crime itself was the part they played in a conflict between Masseria and Salvatore Maranzano. Maranzano arrived in New York in 1927, and promptly founded a Mafia family to rival Masseria's. The feud was called the Castellammorese war, since Maranzano and many of his followers were natives of the Sicilian town of Castellammore del Golfo, and other Mafia groups, from Chicago as well as New York, were drawn into it. Allied with Masseria were a family headed by Steve Ferrigno, a boss from the Bronx (Ferrigno would later be succeeded by the Mangano brothers, Philip and Vincent, then by Umberto [Albert] Anastasia, then by Carlo Gambino), and Al Capone's organization in Chicago. Maranzano commanded the loyalty of a Mafia family headed by Joseph Profaci, a boss from Brooklyn (Profaci would be succeeded by Joseph Magliocco, then by Joseph Colombo), and the Joseph Aiello family in Chicago.

Valachi remembered how the war went. Masseria had ordered the murder of another Mafia boss, Gaetano Reina, who was killed on February 26, 1930, because he had resisted Masseria's efforts to move in on his ice-distribution racket. Masseria forced the Reina family to accept as its boss Joseph Pinzolo, who in turn was killed on September 9, 1930. Valachi was inducted into the old Reina family when Pinzolo was its boss, and Maranzano himself presided over the induction ritual. Joseph Bonanno, who was to succeed Maranzano as boss, was Valachi's godfather, or *compare.* Valachi's first assignment was to watch Ferrigno. He recalled for Peter Maas, author of *The Valachi Papers:*

> Now I'm in the apartment on Pelham Parkway. It's on the second floor. It's over a court, and on the other side of the court is the entrance to the apartment of Ferrigno . . . . One of the guys who stayed on and off in my apartment is Joe Profaci, and he explains a lot of the history of what has been going on. He tells me how Maranzano and Gagliano have put up $150,000 each for the war against . . . [Masseria]. Besides that he says we got $5,000 a week coming in from Steve Magaddino in Buffalo and $5,000 from Joe Aiello in Chicago. . . . Then one day he comes in with a sad face and says, "We're out that money from Chicago. Capone got Aiello."

Ferrigno was killed on November 5, 1930, as he left his apartment at 759 Pelham Parkway South in the Bronx, but the Castellammorese war would not end until one or the other, Masseria or Maranzano, was eliminated — an ideal situation for a treacherous underling like Charles Luciano.

Salvatore Lucania (Charles Luciano) was born on November 11, 1896, at Lercara Friddi in the province of Palermo, Sicily, the son of Antonio and Rosa Lucania, who brought him to the United States in 1905. They settled on the Lower East Side of Manhattan. Luciano left school before completing the fifth grade. He went to work in a hat factory but quit after two years. "If I had to be a crumb," he said, "I would rather be dead." (Luciano later explained to a probation officer that a "crumb" was someone who worked, saved, laid his money aside, and indulged in no extravagance.) At eighteen, Luciano was charged with unlawful possession of narcotics (heroin). He was convicted and served six months of an indefinite term. He was arrested again in 1921 for carrying a loaded revolver; in 1923, for heroin; in 1926, for carrying loaded weapons; and in 1928, for armed robbery. During this time, Luciano was forming criminal associations that were not limited to Sicilians and Italians. They included Meyer Lansky, who became a lifelong friend, Arnold Rothstein, John T. Nolan (Legs Diamond), Arthur Flegenheimer (Dutch Schultz), and Benjamin (Bugsy) Siegel.

On October 18, 1929, Luciano was kidnapped, beaten, and left for dead, suspended from a beam in an abandoned warehouse on Staten Island. *The New York Times* reported:

> Charles (Lucky) Luciania [*sic*], associate of the late Arnold Rothstein, the notorious Diamond brothers, and the late Thomas (Paddy) Walsh, awoke at 2 A.M. yesterday . . . and thought he was dreaming.

Part of the Luciano legend was that this incident gave rise to the nickname, "Lucky," the falseness of which the *Times* account exposed by indicating that the nickname predated Luciano's narrow escape. In reality, the nickname was no more than a corruption of Luciano.

By 1931 Luciano was a ranking lieutenant of Masseria, but the Castellammorese war was not going well (Maranzano had accomplished at least 60 successful ambushes), so Luciano decided to end it his own way. He arranged a "peace" meeting to be held on April 15, 1931, at the Nuovo Villa Tammaro Restaurant on Coney Island. At least three other Masseria men, including Vito Genovese, who was loyal to Luciano, were there. After a leisurely meal, everyone but Luciano and Masseria left the restaurant, according to the reconstruction by police and crime reporters. Luciano suggested cards while they waited for Maranzano. They played until about 3:30 P.M., at which time Luciano got up, he told the police, "to go to the washroom." While he was gone, three men, identified by the underworld grapevine as Benjamin Siegel, Albert Anastasia, and Joe Adonis, entered the restaurant and fired some 20 shots, six of which hit Masseria in the back and head. He never had a chance to turn around.

According to Nicola Gentile, a friend of Maranzano, Vincent Troia, was called to Luciano's apartment that night. "Don Vicenzo," Luciano said, "tell your *compare* Maranzano that we have killed Masseria — not to serve him but for our own personal reasons. . . . Tell him that within 24 hours he must give us an affirmative answer for a meeting. . . ."

Luciano got his affirmative answer. The war had ended, but for Luciano it was just the beginning.

Toward the end of April 1931 Maranzano held a five-day celebration at a big hall on Washington Avenue in the Bronx. Valachi, who was there, remembered:

Mr. Maranzano called a meeting. . . . [T]he place was packed. There was at least four or five hundred of us jammed in. . . . [I]n the new set up he was going to be the *capo di tutti capi*, meaning the boss of all bosses. He said that from here on we were going to be divided up into new families. Each family would have a boss and an underboss. Beneath them there would be lieutenants or *capiregime*. To us regular members, which were soldiers, he said, "You will each be assigned to a lieutenant. When you learn who he is, you will meet all the other men in your crew."

According to Valachi, Maranzano discussed other rules. No longer would there be war — Sicilians, Neapolitans, and Calabrians would forget their differences. The organization would come first, chain of command would be respected, death was decreed for talking, hearings would be held to decide disputes and so on. It was also at this meeting

that Maranzano announced the family structure that was still in existence in 1963. The organization Maranzano had formed in 1927 was divided into two families, one under Joseph Profaci, the other under
Joseph Bonanno. Gaetano Gagliano headed another family, with
Thomas Lucchese as underboss, and Charles Luciano headed the old
Masseria family, with Vito Genovese as underboss. Control of the fifth
family was awarded to Philip and Vincent Mangano.

In *The Valachi Papers*, Peter Maas recounted how the FBI first
learned the name, "Cosa Nostra," from Valachi. On September 8,
1962, certain that Valachi had not begun to tell all he knew, Special FBI
Agent James P. Flynn, an expert in interrogation, suddenly said, "Joe,
let's stop fooling around. You know I'm here because the attorney
general wants this information. I want to talk about the organization by
name, rank, and serial number. What's the name? Is it Mafia?"

"No," Valachi said. "It's not Mafia. That's the expression the outsider uses."

"Is it of Italian origin?"

"What do you mean?"

"We know a lot more than you think," Flynn said. "Now I'll give
you the first part. You give me the rest. It's Cosa ————."

Valachi went pale. For almost a minute he said nothing. Then he
rasped hoarsely, "Cosa Nostra! So you know about it."

Flynn's advantage over Valachi was the result of intelligence obtained by the FBI electronic surveillance program. In the assassination
investigation we analyzed the transcripts of the wiretaps that confirmed
the authenticity of the name, La Cosa Nostra. We also discovered how
much more the bureau had learned about the structure of the Mafia.
FBI File 92-6054, which contained the basic intelligence collected on
the national syndicate of organized crime, was originally entitled "The
Criminal Commission." In September 1959 the bug in Gus Alex's tailor
shop in Chicago had picked up a conversation between Sam Giancana
and Anthony Accardo in which a "commission" was discussed. Giancana reviewed its membership, in addition to himself: Raymond Patriarca of Providence, Stefano Magaddino of Buffalo, Joseph Zerilli of
Detroit, Joseph Ida of Philadelphia, Sebastian John LaRocca of Pittsburgh, and Joseph Profaci, Vito Genovese, Thomas Lucchese, and
Joseph Bonanno, all of New York City. As the ELSUR program was expanded under the Kennedy administration, the FBI developed a more
sophisticated awareness of the Mafia. We were actually able to trace in
the file a thought process by which agents deduced the meaning of
different words. For example, agents listening to a conversation in Philadelphia on February 11, 1962, thought they were overhearing La
Causa Nostra, and the file was renamed accordingly on January 16,

1963. On July 1, however, the semiannual summary of the status of the intelligence program listed several variations of the name, including La Cosa Nostra, La Causa Nostra, and Onorata Societa. Finally, on August 12, 1963, Courtney Evans, the associate director for the Special Investigative Division, wrote to Alan Belmont, his counterpart in the General Investigative Division:

> Information on La Cosa Nostra [was] first received from a live informant in September 1961 in New York as La Causa Nostra, meaning Our Cause. Within months there was corroboration from other sources, including members, who also gave La Causa Nostra.
>
> There appeared to be some disagreement as to translation. Finally, Bureau translators opted for Our Thing. The sources who had used Causa, did not speak Italian well.

Maranzano established himself in a luxurious apartment behind the Hotel Commodore, next to Grand Central Station in Manhattan, and he set up a business front, the Eagle Building Corporation, a real estate company located at 230 Park Avenue. But Maranzano, it seemed, was not content to win. Less than five months after Masseria's murder, he told Valachi to come by his house at 2706 Avenue J in Brooklyn. Valachi arrived about 5 P.M. He later testified:

> Mr. Maranzano got right to the point. He said, "I can't get along with these two guys [Luciano and Genovese] and we got to get rid of them before we can control anything."
>
> Then Mr. Maranzano tells me that he is having one last meeting the next day at two o'clock with Charley Lucky and Vito.

It was Maranzano's last meeting, but it was not with Luciano and Genovese, whom he planned to have killed as they left his office. On September 10, 1931, at 3:50 P.M., Maranzano was shot four times and stabbed six times by four unidentified men who came to his office posing as police officers. Valachi was later told that the killers were Meyer Lansky's men (one of whom, Red Devine, confirmed the story to Valachi), acting on Luciano's behalf. They had wanted to cut Maranzano's throat, Valachi was told, but he resisted and had to be shot.

The Maranzano murder was not an isolated event. According to many sources, Luciano had been planning a purge of old-line Mafia leaders across the country, although Humbert S. Nelli, author of *The Business of Crime*, suggested the murders were largely restricted to New York. There was no record of just how many men died, but Thomas E. Dewey, who later was to prosecute Luciano, represented the general view when he estimated it at "some 40."

Maranzano had held his celebration in New York City, while Luciano held his in Chicago, but that was not the only difference. Instead of proclaiming himself "boss of all bosses," Luciano established a commission of bosses, and he organized the old families of the Mafia into a national syndicate of crime. According to Gentile, the commission consisted of Luciano, Profaci, Bonanno, Gagliano, and Vincent Mangano of New York, Capone of Chicago, and Frank Milano of Cleveland.

Luciano had come a long way from being left for dead on Staten Island in 1929. He moved into the Waldorf Towers in New York City, registering under the name of Charles Ross. He was impeccably groomed, a man-about-town who enjoyed high living. There was, however, serious business to attend to. For example, political alliances had to be cemented. At the 1932 Democratic National Convention in Chicago, at which Franklin D. Roosevelt was nominated, a number of interesting figures were on hand. Joseph P. Kennedy, the successful financier, was widely credited with convincing William Randolph Hearst, the publisher, he should swing California's crucial 44 votes to Roosevelt. James J. Hines, the powerful political boss from the west side of Manhattan, was also there, accompanied by Frank Costello. They stayed together at the Drake Hotel where, several floors down, Luciano himself was ensconced in the entourage of Albert C. Marinelli, the Tammany Hall leader. Meyer Lansky also was at the Democratic Convention.

Luciano was also busy bolstering alliances within his own organization and sorting out territorial arrangements. J. Richard (Dixie) Davis, a corrupt lawyer who represented Dutch Schultz, described the new order of the underworld in a series of articles for *Collier's* in 1939. Davis wondered at the skill with which the underworld had been "drawn into cooperation on a national scale" by Luciano.

In *The Mobs and the Mafia*, Hank Messick suggested that Luciano's "system of alliances," which Davis described, constituted a national syndicate of which the Mafia was only a part. According to Messick, the Mafia leaders involved in the syndicate, called the "combination," were "more as partners . . . than as leaders of a separate entity." Messick wrote that the Mafia figures referred to this national syndicate as the *combineesh* (*sic*). He also claimed that as Luciano was about to go to prison in 1936, he issued an order to his Mafia subordinates: "Cooperate with Meyer," meaning Meyer Lansky, who then became *the* leader of the syndicate. First of all, we questioned whether Luciano possessed the power to transfer his authority to Lansky or anyone else. Second, if Angelo DeCarlo, a *caporegime* in the Genovese family, could be believed, Messick was mistaken. On October 17, 1961, DeCarlo was reminiscing about "the good old days" with several other members of the Genovese family, as the FBI was listening:

"In the good old days, they did it the right way," said one man.

"You bet your life," DeCarlo agreed. "Today they've talked about like everybody knows. You never read nothing in the paper about [La Cosa Nostra] years ago. Today we got an Americanized mob, a Polack mob, a Jew mob, an Irish mob — they all know about this thing."

"They had Jew mobs then," another observed.

"I mean they didn't know about it — maybe Meyer knew about it, but the rest of the mob didn't," said DeCarlo. "Today they all know. *** The newspapers know! *** [T]hey know how you get started, how you take the oath and everything. Look at the kid they made the boss over [in Philadelphia]. Angelo Bruno. He's only in this thing about five years, six years. And he's the boss."

"It's always been that way," another man said.

"But not as bad," DeCarlo corrected. "Before it was more relationship. All the bosses — it was through relations — cousins. That's the way this thing was supposed to start. All relations. That's the way it started in Italy. We were with the *combanesche.* . . ."

"Combination, what combination?" a man asked.

"Combanesche!" DeCarlo replied. "We were with the *combanesche.* . . . Vito [Genovese] was a *combanesche.* . . . Vito got in, I think he told me . . . in 1923."

A year later, in another conversation, DeCarlo was heard to say: "The *combanesche* and the Mafia is the same [thing]. When they had it all by themselves, nobody knew . . . who the hell they were. And then they started letting Americanized guys in. . . . "

Luciano made skillful use of an awesome squad of assassins called "Murder Inc.," a name that was given to it in 1940 by a New York journalist, Harry Feeney. Composed mostly of Jewish killers, Murder Inc. was organized in 1927 by Louis "Lepke" Buchalter, who was electrocuted in 1944. The services of Murder Inc. were not for hire. They were performed on retainer, and the Mafia was the exclusive client. The principal advantage of Murder Inc. was that it separated the party with the motive for the murder from the party that carried it out. Luciano, for example, would issue a contract to Joe Adonis, who would pass it on to Albert Anastasia, the Mafia's contact with Murder Inc. As Burton B. Turkus, the district attorney who prosecuted the leaders of Murder Inc., observed: " [A]ssassinations were ordered, contracted and

performed . . . to sustain rackets." Turkus made another point about
organized-crime investigations, which was as pertinent in 1963 as it was
in 1940. "[T]here is," he said, "only one way organized crime can be
cracked. Unless someone on the inside talks, you can investigate forever and get nowhere."

Luciano, who had contracted gonorrhea seven times and syphilis
once, did not relish his role as a pimp. "I don't like the racket," he confided to one of his madams, Florence "Cokey Flo" Brown. "There's
not enough in it for the risk we take." Nevertheless, he ran 200 houses
with 1,000 girls, which amounted to an annual gross of $12 million from
organized prostitution. The girls who worked for him had their complaints too. When Luciano was finally brought to trial, testimony indicated that many of them had been kidnapped, hooked on heroin,
repeatedly raped, and forced into prostitution. As one said, "They
worked us six days a week, the syndicate did. They worked us like dogs,
and then they kicked us out." At first not wanting to get into an investigation of prostitution, Thomas E. Dewey, a special New York County
prosecutor, saw a chance to make an airtight case against Luciano.
Three telephones were tapped from January 11 to February 1, 1936,
and from the information obtained, over 100 arrests were made. Sens-
ing there was safety in numbers, the prostitutes began to talk. On April
1, 1936, Luciano was indicted on 90 counts of compulsory prostitution.
He was arrested in Hot Springs, Arkansas, and returned to New York to
stand trial. Dewey's opening statement to a special blue-ribbon jury
summarized the prosecution's case:

> The vice industry, since Luciano took over, is highly organized and oper-
> ates with businesslike precision. It will be proved that . . . Luciano sat way
> up at the top, in his apartment at the Waldorf, as the czar of organized
> crime in this city. . . . We will show you his function as the man whose
> word, whose suggestion, whose very statement, "Do this," was suffi-
> cient. . . .

In all, 68 witnesses testified, including 40 prostitutes, 12 bookers,
pimps, and madams. The high point of the trial was Dewey's cross-examination of Luciano, who while denying any connection with prostitution, could not explain the source of an income that enabled him to live
like a millionaire. Faced with his tax returns for 1929 to 1935, which
showed that he had not declared more than $22,500 for any one year,
Luciano was reduced to stammering, "I don't remember." Dewey also
pointedly questioned Luciano about his long-distance phone calls to
reputed organized-crime figures, as the case he presented went beyond
the prostitution charges. Convict Luciano, Dewey told the jury, or "say

to the world and the public that the base gangster can go free." The jury returned its guilty verdict on June 7, 1936. Justice Phillip J. McCook passed sentence on June 18:

> Charles Luciana [*sic*], an intelligent, courageous and discriminating jury has found you guilty.... You [are] ... responsible ... for every foul and cruel deed, with accompanying elements of extortion performed [by your] band. [There appears] no excuse for your conduct, nor hope for your rehabilitation. ...

The court imposed a sentence of 30 to 50 years imprisonment on a stunned, thirty-eight-year-old Luciano. Dr. L. E. Kienholz, the psychiatrist at Sing Sing Prison who examined Luciano after his conviction, did not disagree with the need for Luciano's incarceration. He found him to be "a dangerous individual . . . [who] should not be given too much freedom."

(Luciano was not the only prominent underworld figure to feel the heat of Dewey's determination. Dutch Schultz, by strong-arm tactics and a political fix he had secured with James J. Hines, had seized control of the numbers racket in Harlem. From June 10 to October 29, 1936, Dewey had a tap on a phone in Hines's office, from which he learned enough about the role of J. Richard Davis, Schultz's lawyer, and his link to Hines, to persuade Davis to testify against Hines, who was convicted and sent to prison.)

Luciano was sent first to Sing Sing and then to Clinton State Prison at Dannemora, in upstate New York, where he became Inmate 92168 and went to work in the laundry. He did not come to public attention again until January 3, 1946, when Dewey, by then governor of New York, forwarded an executive clemency message to the state legislature, as required by the state constitution. The message recited Luciano's conviction, sentence, and prison record and noted that Luciano was "deportable to Italy." The next to last paragraph of the message would have farreaching repercussions:

> Upon the entry of the United States into [World War II], Luciano's aid was sought by the Armed Services in inducing others to provide information concerning possible enemy attack. It appears that he cooperated in such effort, although the actual value of the information procured is not clear.

Luciano's alleged government service during World War II broke into print in February 1947. Walter Winchell, the columnist, wrote that the Mafia leader, who had been deported to Italy the year before, was going to be awarded the Congressional Medal of Honor. The Army and Navy each formally denied that Luciano had made any contribution to the war effort, as did the Office of Strategic Services, the precursor of the Central Intelligence Agency. The military services reiterated their denials to the Kefauver Committee in 1951, but the rumors would not be quieted. Then, in 1971, Meyer Lansky told his version of the story in an interview with the press in Israel. (Lansky, who was under indictment on charges related to skimming the profits of a Las Vegas casino, was fighting to remain in Israel and avoid standing trial.) Lansky was quoted as saying:

> When Italy entered the Second World War there was a feeling that some Italians are not patriotic enough. The Intelligence Branch of the American Navy was afraid that those Italians working on the docks or Italian fishermen using their boats, might collaborate with the enemy. . . . Mr. Hogan [the New York prosecutor who succeeded Dewey] called the lawyer [for] . . . Luciano . . . to [s]ee if he might be helpful. [Frank Costello and I] made a white lie and we decided that we will tell . . . [Luciano] that if he will be helpful . . . it might help him to get . . . out . . . . [He] sent some words to his men . . . . [He] was much respected in the labor unions. . . .

We found good reason to believe Lansky, despite the official denials. Dewey had ordered the New York Commission on Investigation to conduct an inquiry into Luciano's release from prison, which was kept confidential, in order to secure the cooperation of the Navy. In 1977, after Dewey's death, his estate released the relevant papers, which were summarized by Rodney Campbell in *The Luciano Project.* It was a thorough investigation: from January 28 to September 17, 1954, 57 witnesses — Navy officers, state officials, racketeers — filled 2,883 pages of testimony transcript. In addition, the commission had access to wiretap records from District Attorney Frank Hogan's office. (Hogan had kept the operation under surveillance, leery of what appeared to him to be the Navy's naive readiness to work with racketeers.) The wiretaps confirmed that the Navy *had* enlisted the cooperation of the Mafia in much the way Lansky outlined it to the press in Israel. Fearful of sabotage and espionage along New York's sprawling waterfront and advised by Joseph Lanza, a Mafia member who ruled the Fulton Fish Market work force, that there was but one man who could "snap the whip in the entire underworld," the Navy decided to seek Luciano's help. Luciano agreed, through his organized-crime network, to gather intelligence and maintain control of the docks. He also assisted in making contact with Mafia figures overseas, in anticipation of the invasion of Sicily. Commander Paul A. Alfieri, who landed in Sicily, was asked by the commission if his contacts there were members of the Mafia. He replied, "Well, they would never admit such, but from my investigative experience in New York City, I knew that they were."

As best the New York Commission on Investigation could determine, the Mafia figures were motivated purely by patriotism — there was no *quid pro quo*, no preferential treatment granted in return (in sharp contrast to the CIA-Mafia Cuban operation in the early 1960s). Lanza, for example, who was under indictment for extortion when he agreed to cooperate, was prosecuted by Hogan, convicted, and sent to prison. As for Luciano, the U.S. government did all it could to keep him confined, once he had been deported. It used its good offices with the postwar Italian government, which barred Luciano from Rome, Milan, and the island of Sicily; and it thwarted a move by Luciano to establish a base of operations in Cuba, advising President Ramon Grau San Martin that all shipments of medicine would be embargoed as long as Luciano remained in Cuba.

Luciano settled in Naples, taking a modest but comfortable apartment at 464 Via Tosso. While it was widely believed that he lived in luxury until his death (of an apparent heart attack at the Capodichono Airport near Naples on January 26, 1962) another version of his exile seemed closer to the truth. Angelo DeCarlo and several friends recounted it for the FBI in October 1962:

"Now wait a minute," someone said, "I happen to know that . . . [Luciano] didn't need for nothing."

"Not in the last couple of years, but you don't know before that," DeCarlo said.

"Vito [Genovese] is the man that made it so he didn't need for nothing. Vito got it for him."

"That's right," someone said.

"But that was only the last four or five years," DeCarlo said.

"Vito is the type that looks after people," someone added. "He had to check to see what it was all about. He found out . . . [Luciano] owed grocery bills, butcher bills, everything . . . ."

"When he left to go over, . . . [t]hey cut him off and gave him ten thousand dollars," DeCarlo said. "Then after that he got on the pad for two a month; after that, just before he died, he was getting three."

"It was . . . [Luciano] that straightened everything out, and it was . . . [Luciano] that got everybody together," came another comment.

"This thing would never have turned out the way it is today if it wasn't for . . . [Luciano]."

"Charlie and Vito," someone said.

Vito Genovese: 1897–1969

Vito Genovese was born in Rosiglino, near Naples, on November 27, 1897, and came to the United States with his parents at the age of fifteen, settling in the New York borough of Queens, where his father established a small contracting business. He soon became too much for his family to handle (his first arrest, at age twenty, was for carrying a gun, for which he spent sixty days in jail), so he was sent to live with relatives on Mulberry Street in the heart of Little Italy on Manhattan's Lower East Side. There he met Luciano and a number of other young toughs who would become lifelong criminal associates. In their younger days, Luciano and Genovese practiced a method of theft that involved heaving a rock through the show window of a jewelry store, then speeding away with as much loot as they could carry. Gradually, Genovese moved out of petty crime into the rackets. He was involved with Luciano in prostitution, and he had a piece of the Italian lottery. By the middle of the 1920s, he was a rising figure in organized crime.

According to Valachi, Genovese was a man of brutal tendencies — more Florentine than Neapolitan. "If you went to Vito," he said, "and told him about some guy who was doing wrong, he would have this guy killed, and then he would have you killed for telling on the guy." Genovese's penchant for violence was not limited to the rackets. After his first wife died, apparently of natural causes, his eye turned to Anna Petillo, a fourth cousin, twelve years younger than he. There was only one obstacle to his desire — her husband, Gerard Vernotico. New York police records show that Vernotico, 29, was found dead at 12:12 P.M. on March 16, 1932, garroted along with Antonio Lonzo, who, it seemed, was a witness to Vernotico's slaying. According to Valachi, Genovese had ordered Vernotico killed. Genovese and Anna Petillo were married twelve days later.

Not all of Genovese's plans worked so smoothly. Two years after his marriage to Anna he set up a rigged card game and swindle, out of which he made about $150,000. Ferdinand Boccia, who had lined up the victim, pressed Genovese for his share. Instead of paying off, Genovese hired Ernest Rupolo and William Gallo to kill Boccia. (Rupolo was also supposed to kill Gallo after they had taken care of Boccia.) According to Valachi, Genovese actually had Boccia murdered by other killers, but Rupolo attempted, on September 9, 1934, to kill Gallo, who, in turn, identified Rupolo as his assailant. Rupolo was tried, convicted, and sentenced to nine to twenty years for the Gallo assault. Eventually, the investigation of the Boccia murder led to Genovese, and he was indicted. Seeing no alternative, Genovese fled to Italy in 1937.

During eight years of self-imposed exile, Genovese lived well. He and Anna had traveled to Italy in 1933 on a delayed wedding trip, and they had taken with them a letter of introduction to Achille Pisani, the secretary of the Fascist Party, enabling Genovese to make contacts in the government. According to Valachi, when Genovese returned to Italy in 1937, he took $750,000, which was supplemented from time to time by Anna, who would come to Italy to visit her husband with his share of racket profits in $50,000, $60,000, and $100,000 increments. Apparently Genovese used some of the money to ingratiate himself with the regime. According to Anna, he contributed $250,000 to the construction of a Fascist Party headquarters in Nola. Mussolini himself expressed gratitude by conferring on Genovese the title, *Commendatore de Re*, a civilian honor. (There was also evidence that Genovese arranged to have Carmine Galante murder Carlo Tresca, the editor of an anti-Fascist publication in New York, *Il Martello*, on January 11, 1943.)

The authorities in New York resumed their interest in the Boccia murder in 1944 when Rupolo, who had been released on parole, got mixed up in another shooting. In an effort to avoid going back to prison, Rupolo told the Brooklyn police that Genovese had been responsible for the Boccia murder. Rupolo named Peter LaTempa, a cigar store salesman, as a witness who could verify his story (corroboration is a prerequisite for conviction under New York law). Based on the testimony of Rupolo and LaTempa, a new indictment against Genovese and three others was returned.

As the surrender of Italy in World War II became imminent, Genovese shifted his allegiance and signed on as an interpreter for the Allied Military Government at Nola. He could not resist the temptation to revert to his old calling, however, and he was arrested on August 27, 1944, by Orange C. Dickey, a special military intelligence agent, for running a black market syndicate. While Genovese was in Dickey's custody, he offered him a $250,000 bribe, which Dickey refused. Then, when Dickey learned from a routine check with the FBI of the outstanding murder indictment in Brooklyn, he made arrangements to bring Genovese back to the United States to stand trial. Genovese pressed his demands. "Now, look, you are young," he told Dickey, who was twenty-four. "[T]here are things you don't understand. . . . Take the money . . . ." When Dickey again refused, Genovese turned ugly. Dickey would, Genovese warned, regret his actions. Subsequently, Genovese's attitude changed and he said to Dickey, "You are doing me the biggest favor anyone has ever done to me. You are taking me home.'' Genovese had a reason for feeling relieved. He knew that LaTempa was being held in protective custody at the Raymond Street jail in Brooklyn. LaTempa suffered from gallstones, and on January 15, 1945, he took a prescription for pain. The city toxicologist reported he had been given a dosage of poison potent enough ''to kill eight horses.'' Genovese was returned to the United States on June 1, 1945, but without LaTempa's corroborating testimony, he could not be convicted of the Boccia slaying, and he was released from custody in the summer of 1946.

Rupolo, who was released from prison in 1949, was apparently ''forgiven'' for testifying against Genovese, since he had done his jail time on the Gallo assault in silence. But on August 27, 1964, his tightly bound corpse broke loose from concrete weights and surfaced in Jamacia Bay. His murder was apparently unrelated to his testimony against Genovese. He had had a run-in with members of the Profaci family, who were tried for his killing, but acquitted.

In November 1946 Luciano made a surprise appearance in Havana, from where he placed calls to New York, Chicago, Detroit, and New Orleans to announce an important meeting. All the top underworld figures came: Genovese, Costello, Anastasia, Accardo, Marcello, Lansky. Luciano had hoped to establish himself in Cuba, but when that proved not feasible, his trip to Havana became the occasion for him to pass the power to Genovese. The succession did not come to the attention of authorities until 1949, when Costello, who had been acting boss of the Luciano family while Genovese was in Italy and in prison, hosted a dinner at the Copacabana in Manhattan. John F. Shanley, Deputy Chief Inspector of the New York Police Department, told the McClellan Committee:

> Vito was met at the door by Costello, and he was ushered in and he sat at the best place, and this spread through the city in no time, that Vito had emerged.

But Genovese was not satisfied. According to Valachi, he was angry that others had been allowed ''to sew up everything'' while he was in Italy. Genovese had decided to take action against a number of his associates, including Costello. First, however, he had a domestic problem to settle.

When Genovese got out of jail, he and Anna bought a $75,000 mansion in Atlantic Highlands, New Jersey, on which, Anna said, he spent $350,000 for renovations and furnishings. Their marriage was hardly ideal, however. According to Anna, Genovese was involved with other women, and he beat her to the point that she feared for her life. In December 1952 Anna filed for divorce, and her testimony at the hearing caused a sensation. It also provided an unusual insight into the lifestyle of an American gangster, whose fortune the Bureau of Narcotics would estimate in 1960 to be $30 million. According to Anna, Genovese took in $20,000 to $30,000 a week from the Italian lottery. "I know, ..." she said, "because I myself ran [it] . . . ." Their home, she added, "had 24-carat gold and platinum dishes." The silverware was "the best money could buy." Their personal wardrobes were equally impressive, considering 1952 prices — a $4,500 mink coat, $250 suits, and $60 shoes. Genovese also had funds in hiding — at least $500,000 in one safe-deposit box in Switzerland. Yet between 1952 and 1956, he declared only between $7,000 and $15,000 in taxable annual income. Though he denied his wealth, the court ordered him to pay $300-a-week alimony and $1,500 court costs.

Valachi recalled the divorce proceedings: "Nobody could understand why Vito didn't do anything about her." Apparently, Genovese still had affection for Anna. "[W]hen we . . . were in [the federal prison at] Atlanta, . . . he would sometimes talk about her, and I would see the tears rolling down his cheeks," Valachi said. "I couldn't believe it." One of Anna's associates was not so fortunate. On June 19, 1953, when she was about to be called before a New Jersey grand jury, Steven Franse, her partner in the 82 Club, in Greenwich Village, was found strangled. It was, Valachi indicated, a warning to Anna to keep quiet, and she took the hint. She told the grand jury that she knew nothing, and if she ever did, she had forgotten it.

Frank Costello was having his own problems. He had been convicted of contempt of Congress as a result of his conduct as a witness before the Kefauver Committee. His appeals exhausted, he started serving an eighteen-month term on August 22, 1952, but with time off for good behavior, he was released on October 29, 1953. In April 1954 Costello was back in court on an income tax evasion charge. Internal Revenue agents had carefully compared his expenditures with his declared income and found a $51,095 discrepancy over a four-year period. The verdict was never in doubt, and after extensive appeals, Costello went back to prison on May 14, 1956. But he hired a new lawyer, Edward Bennett Williams, who entered another appeal and got him out on bail after he had served only eleven months of his five-year term. Costello returned to his normal routine: mornings holding court at the Waldorf-Astoria; afternoons at the Biltmore steam room; and evenings dining out.

On May 2, 1957, Costello ate dinner at the fashionable Manhattan restaurant L'Aiglon and returned to his apartment in the Majestic,

115 Central Park West, at about 11 P.M. As he entered the foyer, a fat man in a dark suit, his hat pulled down, shuffled by. Then his hand came out of his pocket, holding a gun. "This is for you, Frank," he yelled, firing one shot point blank at Costello's head before he fled. Wounded, but not seriously, Costello was rushed to Roosevelt Hospital. As he lay in bed, New York detectives inventoried the contents of his pockets. They found $3,200 in cash and a cryptic note: "Gross Casino Win as of 4-27-57 — $651,284." District Attorney Frank Hogan's office, with the help of the Nevada Gaming Control Board and Aaron Kohn of the New Orleans Metropolitan Crime Commission, determined that the figure matched the house take at the new Tropicana Hotel in Las Vegas. Apparently Costello had a hidden interest in a Nevada casino, despite the supposedly strict oversight by the state of the ownership of its gambling establishments. Costello declined to explain the note, nor was he helpful as to the identity of his would-be assassin. "I didn't see nuthin'," he said. "I haven't an enemy in the world." His assailant was, however, identified from a description the doorman provided as Vincent Gigante, a soldier in the Genovese family. (Valachi later confirmed that Gigante had been given the contract on Costello by Genovese.) Nevertheless, Costello testified at Gigante's trial that he had never seen the man before, and Gigante was acquitted. Costello took the hint, however, and let it be known that he was retiring from the rackets.

The final ruling on his tax case was handed down in October 1958; it went against Costello, and he was returned to prison and not released until June 1961. When an effort was then made to deport him, a spokesman for the Italian government aptly observed:

> Italy should not be expected to carry the burden of a man who was born in Italy, lived here only a short time, and then spent most of his life in the United States. It's not blood that makes a man a criminal; it's society, and we definitely do not want to pay for such men.

The Supreme Court intervened in February 1961, and Costello was not deported.

On February 7, 1973, Costello suffered a mild heart attack in his Manhattan apartment and was hospitalized. He apparently thought he would recover, for he sent word through a friend that he would let Peter Maas, the writer, prepare his biography. At 7:30 A.M. on February 18, however, he suffered a fatal coronary. There was no evidence that he had not kept his promise to retire.

As explanation for the assault to the rest of the underworld, Genovese let it be known that Costello had been talking to the government, a rationale that Albert Anastasia, for one, did not accept. No one was safe, Anastasia argued, if Genovese could order Costello's execution without the prior approval of the national commission. Anastasia's fears were well-founded. At about 10:15 on the morning of October 25, 1957, accompanied by two bodyguards, Anastasia strolled into the barbershop of the Park-Sheraton Hotel at Seventh Avenue and 56th Street in Manhattan. He seated himself in chair number four, loosened his tie, and closed his eyes for the last time. As his barber, Joseph Bocchino, covered his face with a hot towel, the bodyguards disappeared, and two other men walked in from the hotel lobby. They strode up behind chair number four and fired .32 and .38 caliber bullets into Anastasia's head and body, literally blasting him out of the chair.

Several independent sources claimed to have inside information about the Anastasia murder. Sidney Slater, who operated a B-girl bar on East 55th Street for Joseph "Crazy Joe" Gallo, a New York gang leader, told District Attorney Frank Hogan's office that, shortly after it occurred, the murder became a running topic of conversation for Gallo and four of his henchmen. "From now on, Sidney," Slater quoted Gallo as having said, "you can just call the five of us the barbershop quintet." Vincent Teresa, a soldier in the Mafia family of Raymond Patriarca of Providence, told a biographer that while Gallo set up the murder, having received the contract from Anthony Strollo, Genovese's underboss, the actual killers were imported from Patriarca's family. According to Teresa, both Carlo Gambino, Anastasia's underboss, and Carmine Lombardozzi, an Anastasia soldier, had taken part in the plot. A slightly different version was provided by Peter Diapoulos, one of Gallo's bodyguards. He said that the contract came through Joseph Profaci to the Gallos (Joseph Gallo and his brothers), and they were "made," that is formally accepted into La Cosa Nostra, as a result of the Anastasia murder. Finally, according to Valachi, the murder was the result of a Genovese-Gambino conspiracy for the sake of power.

None of the accounts was fundamentally inconsistent with the others, and all were in agreement that Genovese was ultimately responsible for Anastasia's death. It was evident, however, that they all reflected only a superficial view of a complex event. Valachi's account, in particular, had to be seen as incomplete and distorted by his anti-Genovese bias. To be sure, Genovese's motivation could have been read as a simple thirst for power, but the involvement of other major figures — Patriarca and, it turned out, Santo Trafficante, Jr. — indicated that the murder of Anastasia had the support of others within the organization and was rooted in reasons that went beyond the personal ambitions of Genovese and Gambino. Those reasons would have to be explained, it turned out, because Genovese would be called on to justify

the killing of Anastasia. Anastasia's complaint, after all, was more pertinent than ever: no one was safe unless Genovese was required to follow
the rules. According to Robert Kennedy, when he testified before the
McClellan Committee in September 1963, the principal purpose of the
Apalachin meeting in November 1957 was to permit Genovese to explain to the other leaders of La Cosa Nostra the assault on Costello and
the murder of Anastasia.

Genovese had wanted to hold the meeting in Chicago, Valachi told
the McClellan Committee: "Stephen Magaddino talked him into going
to Apalachin. Vito never stopped beefing about it." Genovese's case
against Anastasia could not be based merely on "personal ambition";
there had to be reasons that would command general support within La
Cosa Nostra. According to Valachi, Anastasia was killed because he had
been selling Mafia memberships to unfit applicants for up to $40,000,
but this hardly seemed sufficient to warrant an unauthorized execution
of a family boss. Far more significant, it appeared, was Anastasia's
attempt to move in on gambling operations in Cuba, which belonged, in
large measure, to Santo Trafficante. In fact, there reportedly was a
showdown meeting between Anastasia and Trafficante in Anastasia's
suite at the Warwick Hotel on October 24, 1957. Trafficante, who was
registered in the hotel as "B. Hill," checked out an hour or two after
Anastasia was gunned down the next morning in the barbershop of the
Park-Sheraton, only a few blocks away from the Warwick. Anastasia
should have realized that there was too much at stake in Havana for it to
be given up without a fight.

Havana Gambling

In 1957 there were two ways to reach Havana from the United States —
by auto and by airplane. By auto, the traveler first felt the Cuban climate
at Key West, a bad translation, say the Cubans, of *Cayo Hueso*, which
means "bone key." There, while still on U.S. soil, a Cuban customs inspector would go thoroughly over the car. "There is a revolution in
Cuba," he would say. "No guns! No ammunition! No explosives!"
Then, the car was carefully driven aboard a ferry for the trip to Havana.
The flight time to Havana was less than five hours from New York, and
from Miami it was only about an hour. By sea, the first glimpse of Cuba
was the 350-year-old *Castillo de Los Tres Reyes del Morro*, or Morro Cas-
tle, imposing from where it stood on a point to the left of the narrow
entrance to Havana harbor. By air, the traveler's first close-up view was
Rancho Boyeros International Airport, later renamed for Jose Marti,
the hero of the revolution against Spain.

Cuba was conquered in 1511 by Diego Velasquez, and it remained in

Spanish hands — commercially exploited, and inefficiently, corruptly, and repressively administered — until December 10, 1898, when Spain "relinquished" the island to the United States, which held it in trust for its inhabitants. Largely supported by the Cuban population, American military rule lasted from November 5, 1900 to February 21, 1901. After that, American dominance was assured by the Platt Amendment to the Cuban Constitution of 1901. Until it was abrogated in 1934, the Platt Amendment legitimized intervention by the United States to keep order or maintain independence. Intervention first occurred during an insurrection against the newly established government on September 29, 1906, and U.S. troops remained in the country until April 1, 1909. Between 1909 and 1925 the United States intervened twice again and threatened to on several other occasions. On May 20, 1925, General Gerardo Machado y Morales was elected president and became Cuba's first full-fledged dictator. In the face of a general strike in 1933, Machado fled the country. He was succeeded by a number of presidents, but they were usually made and unmade by Fulgencio Batista, a sergeant who gained control of the Army at the time of Machado's downfall. In 1940 Batista, then a colonel, was himself elected president, and he served until 1944, when he was defeated by Ramon Grau San Martin, who was followed by Carlos Prio Socarras in 1948. Batista moved to Daytona Beach, Florida, in 1944 but returned to Cuba to become a senator. Realizing he would not be elected in an upcoming presidential election, Batista simply took power in a bloodless coup on March 10, 1952. Three years later, on February 25, 1955, he was elected to a full four-year term, though he would not last it out. Batista was overthrown by Fidel Castro on New Year's Day 1959.

By 1937 Meyer Lansky had, according to Hank Messick, acquired the gambling concession in the Hotel Nacional. But then came World War II, as Messick noted in *The Silent Syndicate*, quoting Lansky: "We stopped when the war broke out because after that there weren't any boats, . . . [a]nd at that time you didn't have enough planes." Lansky added, "You can't live from the Cuban people themselves." When Batista returned to power in 1952, Lansky and his kind were quick to follow. On June 29, 1962, Angelo DeCarlo wistfully remembered for an FBI bug how it had been under Batista: "[T]he mob had a piece of every joint down there. There wasn't one joint they didn't have a piece of." Knowing the value of legalized gambling to a government willing to exploit it, Batista had changed the Cuban laws to attract the gambling industry and create for himself a lucrative source of illicit income. In 1955 casino gambling was permitted in any nightclub or hotel worth $1 million or more. The Cuban government agreed to match investment money or find Cuban organizations that would. The license fee would cost only $25,000 plus 20 percent of the profits. (The word in the underworld was that the licenses in reality cost $250,000 under the table to Batista and his friends.) Import duties that ran as high as 70 percent were waived on building materials, and pit bosses, stickmen, and dealers were made eligible for two-year instead of six-month visas. New casino hotel complexes sprang up. Lansky built the Hotel Havana Riviera for $14 million, at least $6 million of which was provided by government-controlled banks; and the Cellini brothers, Dino and Eddie, organized-crime figures from Ohio, ran the casino. The 30-story Havana-Hilton cost $24 million, most of which came from the pension and welfare funds of the Cuban Cooks and Bartender Union. In addition, old casinos were taken over by organized-crime figures. For example, Jake Lansky managed the gambling at the Hotel Nacional, whose principal owners were his brother Meyer and three syndicate gamblers from Cleveland — Morris Dalitz, Sam Tucker, and Thomas J. McGinty. But the undisputed Mafia gambling boss in Havana was Santo Trafficante, Jr. He owned substantial interests in the Sans Souci, a nightclub and casino where fellow racketeer John Roselli had a management role; the Hotel Capri, in which Charles Tourine of the Genovese family also had a share; the stately Hotel Commodoro; and the brand-new Havana-Hilton. The Tropicana, where the lavish casino was as much a tourist attraction as the extravagant nightclub review, was managed by associates of Trafficante, Martin and Pedro Fox, for Batista's brother-in-law, Roberto Fernandez y Miranda, who also had a monopoly on the slot machines throughout Cuba.

In terms of criminal activity, there was more to the casino operations in Havana than bribery for the purpose of obtaining licenses. The exact dimensions of the skim, the theft of casino profits to avoid taxes, was not documented, but it was at least implied by one incident. In September 1958 Jake Lansky arrived in Miami, where Customs thoroughly searched him, a departure from its usual routine, and found $200,000 in cash and $50,000 in checks. Lansky said the money was for deposit in the Bank of Miami, an explanation that was appropriate enough for the checks. But for the $200,000 in cash, as Hank Messick noted in *The Silent Syndicate*, the usual procedure was for it to flow the other way to replenish the supply at the casino, since patrons wanted to be paid off in dollars, not pesos. The inference was inescapable: the $200,000 represented skim.

In a report issued for 1958, which put Cuba's tourism revenues at $60 million, the Cuban National Council of Economy noted that while 27,000 Cubans were employed in gambling, another 11,500 lived on prostitution. Havana, in short, was a full-service vice capital, owned and operated by the mob.

Santo Trafficante: 1914–

Santo Trafficante, Jr., born in Tampa, Florida, on November 14, 1914, was the namesake of a Mafia leader who had come from Sicily in 1904 and was described by the Kefauver Committee as "a reputed leader in Tampa for more than twenty years." When Santo Trafficante, Sr., died in 1954, Santo, Jr., one of six sons, succeeded to the leadership of the Tampa organized-crime family, whose principal activities were narcotics trafficking and gambling — both casino gambling and *bolita*, a Cuban version of policy. He had been well schooled. He had run the *bolita* for his father and had extended his own interests to Havana, where he acquired the Sans Souci from Gabriel Mannarino, an underworld figure from Pittsburgh. Trafficante's status in organized crime was clearly recognized on June 4, 1955, at the marriage of Joseph Profaci's daughter, Carmella, to Anthony Tocco, the son of William Tocco, a Mafia leader in Detroit. The reception at the Hotel Commodore in Manhattan gave law enforcement agents an opportunity to observe the deference paid him.

Although he was a family boss, Trafficante had cloaked his interests well. The Tampa police told the McClellan Committee in October 1963 that they knew of "no legitimate businesses owned or controlled by [him]. His house, automobile, and all his other possessions," they said, "[were] held in the name of others." They did, however, identify a Trafficante money courier, Louis Coticchia, who had served as a gambling casino pit boss in Havana and Las Vegas. His arrest record included rape in Cleveland in 1938, grand larceny in Baltimore in 1942, and a securities violation in Dallas in 1961. The Tampa police also described for the McClellan Committee the record of gangland violence in Tampa since 1928. Of the twenty-three known slayings, only one had resulted in a conviction. At the time of the McClellan Committee hearings, Trafficante's wife of twenty-five years, Josephine, told a *Tampa Tribune* reporter that the testimony about organized crime in Tampa was "trash." Pressed on related matters, however, she conceded that her husband had "made quite a bit of money while he was in Havana." Allegedly retired, Trafficante himself, who divided his time between a large comfortable home in Tampa and a more modest concrete block bungalow in Miami, was unavailable for comment.

The Federal Narcotics Program

Another item on the agenda at Apalachin, apparently, was the question of La Cosa Nostra involvement in the narcotics traffic. According to Valachi, Frank Costello, during the Luciano-Genovese interregnum, flatly forbade it, but at Apalachin, or shortly thereafter, the ban was moderated. Members would be prohibited from direct involvement in narcotics, although financing and importation were permissible. In other words, dealing was to be "franchised" to non-Mafia criminal groups — blacks, Puerto Ricans, and so on. During the period between the Costello edict in 1948 and the Apalachin meeting in 1957, Congress passed legislation to control the narcotics problem. The Boggs Act of 1951, sponsored by Representative Hale Boggs of Louisiana, provided for mandatory penalties after a first conviction. The Boggs-Daniel Act of 1956, sponsored by Boggs and Senator Price Daniel of Texas, provided for stiff mandatory penalties for all narcotics convictions. Enforcement of this legislation caused the mob deep concern, but, as Valachi noted, narcotics trafficking was too lucrative to be curbed by the self-policing of the underworld. Bureau of Narcotics Commissioner Henry L. Giordano told the McClellan Committee in July 1964 that since 1956 the bureau had developed 20 major conspiracy cases against 206 prominent organized-crime offenders, principally through the use of informants turned by the threat of the penalties called for in the Boggs-Daniel Act. Nineteen percent of the Genovese family, 40 percent of the Lucchese family, and 20 percent of the Gambino family had been convicted of narcotics violations.

Vito Genovese himself was among those convicted. His 1959 narcotics prosecution resulted from the routine arrest and conviction of Nelson Silva Cantellops, a Puerto Rican dealer in upper Manhattan, for a drug sale to an undercover officer. Faced with a possible life term, Cantellops agreed to testify against sixteen coconspirators, Genovese among them, who stood trial for the importation, sale, and delivery of narcotics. The trial lasted three months in Manhattan federal court, with Cantellops, though a minor figure in the ring, the principal witness against Genovese. He was on the stand for nineteen grueling days, during which Judge Alexander Bick had to order from the courtroom hecklers who made threatening gestures at Cantellops. (The Judge could do nothing about the midnight calls to the witness's wife: "We'll get Cantellops. We'll get you 'n' the kids too.") Despite the harassment and guided by the careful questioning of Assistant U.S. Attorney Arthur H. Christy, Cantellops identified Genovese as the man who had directed the ring's activities. The jury believed Cantellops, and Genovese was sentenced to twenty years. He challenged his conviction, securing the services of Edward Bennett Williams, but it was affirmed. Having been transferred from the federal prison at Leavenworth, Kansas, Genovese died at the Medical Center for Federal Prisons at Springfield, Missouri, of a heart ailment on February 14, 1969. As for Cantellops, he was slain in a barroom brawl in 1965.

The National Structure of Organized Crime

Within days of the Apalachin meeting, the FBI established what it termed its Top Hoodlum Program, in which selected field offices around the country were required to collect intelligence on the attendees. Under the Kennedys, the effort was expanded, with particular emphasis on electronic surveillance. On June 29, 1962, the FBI sent to the Department of Justice a summary report entitled, "The Criminal Commission," which documented the structure of the national syndicate of organized crime. From there on, the report was updated every six months.

The FBI identified the *commissione* or commission, established by Luciano in the 1930s, as the highest ruling body of La Cosa Nostra, which was composed exclusively of individuals of Italian birth or extraction. The powers of the commission — its authority, for example, to overrule individual family bosses — was discussed within earshot of the FBI on September 21, 1964, by Sam DeCavalcante of New Jersey and Joseph Zicarelli, a member of the Bonanno family. (Zicarelli's background illustrated the wide range of activities in which mob members could participate. He was known to be a gunrunner who had been in contact with Rafael Trujillo, the dictator of the Dominican Republic, and President Marcos Perez Jimenez of Venezuela. National security electronic surveillance by the FBI established that, in 1952, Zicarelli was responsible for the murder of Andres Requena, an anti-Trujillo exile, in New York City. He also had reportedly arranged the kidnapping of Jesus de Galindez, another anti-Trujillo activist, who disappeared in Manhattan on March 12, 1956. Zicarelli also was closely associated, according to a report in *Life* in August 1968, with Cornelius E. Gallagher, a U.S. congressman from New Jersey, who was convicted in 1972 of evading $78,000 in income taxes.) The DeCavalcante-Zicarelli conversation was typical of the intelligence obtained by the FBI electronic surveillance program on the internal politics of La Cosa Nostra:

DeCavalcante: *The commission was formed by people — all bosses — who have given the commission the right to supersede any boss. Joe [Bonanno] knows that! He made the rules! . . . [H]e tried to move in California. The commission chased him out of California. . . . They were trying to take over DeSimone's [Los Angeles] outfit.*

DeCavalcante explained to Zicarelli the commission's power over Bonanno by citing precedent:

The commission went in there and took the family over. When [Joseph] Profaci died (June 5, 1962), Joe Magliocco [Profaci's underboss] took over as boss. They threw him right out! "Who the hell are you to take over a *borgata*?". . . . And Signor Bonanno knows this. When we had trouble in our outfit, they came right in. "You people belong to the commission until this is straightened out." They done the same thing in Pittsburgh. They made the boss John . . . uh. . . .

Zicarelli:	*LaRocca.*
DeCavalcante:	*LaRocca . . . step down.*
Zicarelli:	*He's no more boss?*
DeCavalcante:	*[I]t's all straightened out now. But Joe Bonanno was in on that deal. They made LaRocca take orders from the commission until everything was straightened out.*

In 1963 the membership of the commission included Gerardo Catena (the underboss who took over for Vito Genovese when he went to prison), Thomas Lucchese, Carlo Gambino, and Joseph Bonanno of New York City, as well as Sam Giancana of Chicago, Joseph Zerilli of Detroit, Stefano Magaddino of Buffalo, and Angelo Bruno of Philadelphia. The members of the commission were called *rappresentanti,* or bosses. The bosses settled disputes between members in an *arguimendo,* or sit-down. Angelo Bruno reviewed the practice for Sam DeCavalcante on February 11, 1962:

Bruno:	*Sam, look, Sam. Let's say this thing [a disputed gambling debt] goes to* arguimendo, *which I don't want it to go.*
DeCavalcante:	*I don't either.*
Bruno:	*I don't want it to go, you understand. If it goes to* arguimendo, *I have to represent [the alleged debtor] whether I want to or not. . . . Now if we go to their* arguimendo, *you understand, and your* rappresentanti *[DeCavalcante was not a boss in 1963] is there and I'm there and let's say a few other* rappresentanti *are there. . . .*

An individual group was called a family, a *borgata,* or *brugad.* A boss of a family was also called a *capo.* Under him was an underboss, or *sottocapo,* the second in command, and available for consultation to any member was a *consiglieri* or *consulieri,* a counselor, who was usually an elder of the family. Families were divided into subgroups, or *regime,* which were headed by *caporegime,* also called *capodecine,* or captains. The terminology was illustrated by two overheard DeCavalcante conversations. On August 31, 1964, DeCavalcante was talking with Joseph Sferra, a *caporegime* in the DeCavalcante family and a business agent of Local 394 of the Laborers International Union, Elizabeth, New Jersey:

DeCavalcante: *It's about Joe Bonanno's* borgata. *The commission don't like the way he's comporting himself.*
Sferra: *The way he's conducting himself, you mean?*
DeCavalcante: *Well, he made his son* consiglieri — *and it's been reported, the son, that he don't show up [when the commission asked to see him].*

On June 4, 1965, DeCavalcante told Louis Larasso, another *caporegime*, that he was removing Sferra "from everything."

Larasso: *Are you taking him off* caporegime, *too?*
DeCavalcante: *Yeah.*

A *capodecine* was literally the head of ten, which apparently was the number originally intended for each subgroup. Individual members of each subgroup were known as *soldati*, or soldiers, or buttonmen. Sam DeCavalcante, Anthony Boiardo, and Angelo DeCarlo enlightened the FBI even more in a conversation sometime in the early 1960s:

Boiardo: *My father said you must be made (inducted into La Cosa Nostra) 25 years ago.*
DeCavalcante: *No. Twenty years. About the same time as you. . . .*
DeCarlo: *Around 1945.*
Boiardo: *You were made with the "Blade" [Charles Tourine], weren't you?*
DeCavalcante: *No. . . . [I] was made before the "Blade." Two or three years before the "Blade." . . . Jerry [Catena] . . . was made six months before me. . . . When they made me, they made me in Italian. They all spoke in Italian.*

The membership of La Cosa Nostra in 1963 was estimated to be between 4,000 and 5,000, with 50 percent of it based in the New York metropolitan area. In all, there were thought to be twenty-four families. In New York City, there were five families: Genovese (600 members); Lucchese (150 members); Gambino (1,000 members); Bonanno (400 members); and Profaci (200 members). In other cities, just one family reigned: Philadelphia, Bruno (200 members); Chicago, Giancana (300 members); Buffalo, Magaddino (300 members); Detroit, Zerilli (250 members); Newark, DeCavalcante (40 members); Milwaukee, Balistrieri (50 members); San Jose, Cerrito (30 members); Kansas City, Civella (75 members); Denver, Colletti (40 members); San Francisco, Lanza (12 members); Pittsburgh, LaRocca (50 members); Los Angeles, DeSimone (75 members); New Orleans, Marcello (50 members); New England, Patriarca (150 members); Cleveland, Scalish (150 members); St. Louis, Giordano (35 members); Scranton, Bufalino (50 members); Tampa, Trafficante (75 members); and Dallas, Civello (25 members).

The various families were not equal in wealth, power, or status. Some were small and more or less ineffective. Others were largely satellites of more important families, as in the case of the Milwaukee family, which was dominated by the Chicago family. On the other hand, some families had a measure of independence from the commission, as Joseph Colombo, who had taken over the Profaci family, explained to some of his members on December 4, 1968. New Orleans was, he said, the first Cosa Nostra family in the United States; it was set up by members from Sicily. As such, it had special privileges. It did not have to submit to the commission on various matters, including membership approval.

In 1963 it was quite apparent that the national structure forged by Luciano in 1931 had produced leadership stability, and with stability, the amassing of wealth and power. New York, with its five families and violent struggle for control, was the exception, not the rule. In Cleveland, leadership easily passed from Frank Milano, who retired to Mexico, to John Scalish, as the Mayfield Road Mob was merged into La Cosa Nostra. In Philadelphia, power was transferred smoothly from Joseph Ida to Angelo Bruno. The pattern of power consolidation with a minimum of bloodletting was perhaps best illustrated by the Zerilli family in Detroit. Joseph Zerilli and William Tocco, his brother-in-law, both of whose families were from the Terrasini province of Sicily, formed an alliance with Joseph Profaci, which was cemented by the marriages of Profaci's daughters to Zerilli's son, Anthony, and Tocco's son, also named Anthony. In the 1920s Zerilli's group, known as the East Side Gang, was involved in a variety of legal and illegal activities, including bootlegging. A Jewish group, the Purple Gang, operated in the northwestern part of Detroit, at first preying on shopkeepers (hence they were tainted, or "purple"), but subsequently turning to labor racketeering and then to rumrunning. By the end of 1930 the Purple Gang had been run out of town, and since Zerilli was able to consolidate his power over the various Sicilian and Italian factions, a state of relative peace was achieved. The effect of the peace was demonstrated statistically in 1963 to the McClellan Committee: from 1917 to 1930, there were 135 gangland slayings in Detroit, while from 1931 to 1962, there were only 38.

Organized Crime and Kennedy (before Dallas)

During the course of our investigation, we reviewed literally thousands of pages of electronic surveillance summaries based on the bugging of organized-crime figures in an effort to find evidence that the national syndicate or any of its members had engaged in a plot to assassinate the

President. During the years of the Kennedy administration, organized-crime figures who for years had been secure in their positions of wealth and power, were finding themselves investigated, indicted, and convicted as they never had been before. They voiced many complaints, some quite threatening, against law enforcement officers, FBI agents in particular. Occasionally, J. Edgar Hoover himself was the target of a mobster's wrath. The real anger, however — as demonstrated by the most vituperative language to be picked up on the bugs — was reserved for the Kennedys, especially Attorney General Robert F. Kennedy.

On February 9, 1962, Angelo Bruno and William Weisberg, a Bruno associate, discussed the Kennedys in a lengthy conversation that reflected frustration and bitterness, but also caution on the part of the Mafia leadership:

Weisberg: *See what Kennedy done. With Kennedy, a guy should take a knife, like one of them other guys, and stab and kill the f____r, . . . Somebody should kill the f____r, I mean it. This is true. Honest to God. It's about time to go. But I tell you something. I hope I get a week's notice. I'll kill. Right in the . . . White House. Somebody's got to get rid of this f____r.*

Bruno, however, counseled caution:

Bruno: *Look, Willie, do you see there was a king, do you understand. And he found out that everybody was saying that he was a bad king. This is an old Italian story. So, there was an old wise woman about 140 years old. So, he figured, let me go talk to the old wise woman. She knows everything. So he went to the old wise woman. So he says to her, I came here because I want your opinion. He says, do you think I'm a bad king? She says, no, I think you are a good king. He says, well, how come everybody says I'm a bad king? She says, because they are stupid. They don't know. He says, well how come, why do you say I'm a good king? Well, she says, I knew your great-grand-father. He was a bad king. I knew your grandfather. He was worse. I knew your father. He was worse than them. You, you are worse than all of them, but your son, if you die, your son is going to be worse than you. So it's better to be with you. So Brownell [former Attorney General Herbert Brownell] was bad. He was no f____g good. He was this and that.*

Weisberg: *Do you know what this man is going to do? He ain't going to leave nobody alone.*

Bruno: *I know he ain't. But you see, everybody in there was bad. The other guy was good because the other guy was worse. Do you understand? Brownell came. He was no good. He was worse than the guy before.*

Weisberg: *Not like this one.*

Bruno: *Not like this one. This one is worse. Right? If something hap-*
      pens to this guy. . . .

Weisberg: *Let me tell you something. The FBI always hated the IRS.*
      Always. The IRS never checked with the Treasury men. They
      went separate ways. They wouldn't give each other informa-
      tion. They wanted the credit themselves. He made it with local
      authorities. He made it ring-around-the-rosy, pal.

Bruno: *Oh yeah. This guy is an accountant, see. So, now, he had to do*
      something worse. So what? He started to think, what can I do
      more than the other guy? The other guy made an antiracke-
      teering law, gambling laws, he did this and he did that. What
      can I do? He says, I know what I can do. Anybody that has a
      record that is police property, when he gets pinched, no bail.
      [Bruno then compares the Italian process of not allowing
      bail and incarcerating individuals until proven innocent.]

Weisberg: *It's still America, though.*

Bruno: *So, it's still America. They are trying to pass a federal law that*
      you can't take the fifth [amendment]. When they grant you
      immunity you can't take the fifth.

Weisberg: *They are not going to pass that law.*

Bruno: *But they might.*

Slowly, however, the attitude of caution changed. On May 2, 1962, Michael Clemente, a *caporegime* in the Genovese family, was heard to say:

> Bob Kennedy won't stop today until he puts us all in jail all over the country. Until the commission meets and puts its foot down, things will be at a standstill.

As evidence of the mounting pressure, there was an unheard-of development — an outbreak of hostility between the Mafia and the FBI. On April 3, 1963, Carmelo Lombardozzi, the father of Carmine Lombardozzi, a *caporegime* in the family of Carlo Gambino, was buried from Immaculate Heart of Mary Church in Brooklyn. Law enforcement officers covered the wake and requiem mass for intelligence purposes. As the funeral cortege entered the church, several young men from among the mourners assaulted Special FBI Agent John P. Foley, who had a camera. Foley was badly beaten, and his service revolver was stolen. The assault caused deep concern at the FBI. On April 30, 1963, Associate Director Courtney Evans wrote to Associate Director Alan Belmont that, in his opinion, general permission to retaliate against law enforcement officers, although it had been requested, had not yet been given by the organized-crime leadership. He noted, however, that Sam Giancana was watching the reaction to the Foley incident and "would be guided accordingly. . . ." As for FBI agents at the street level, they initiated a series of interviews designed, apparently, to intimidate members of the Gambino organization, and there was evidence that on at least one occasion a Lombardozzi associate was beaten up and dumped in an ash can. In May 1963 two of Gambino's men, Michael Scandifia and Peter Ferrara, were overheard by a bug that had been installed under order from the New York County Court. FBI agents had intimated to Ferrara that they would interview his daughter, a Catholic nun, unless appropriate amends were made for the Foley assault:

Scandifia: *[In] other words they are telling you they don't want to embarrass you. In other words, they won't go to the convent. Well, I would say right now they are giving you the zing. You want us to go to the convent? You want us to embarrass you? Well then, see that the right thing is done.*
Ferrara: *Yeah.*

Of far greater significance was the reaction of various family bosses to physical retaliation taken by FBI agents. On May 20, 1963, Angelo Bruno discussed the incident with several men at his Penn Jersey Vending Company in Philadelphia. He quoted one FBI agent as having asked a confederate of Carmine Lombardozzi:

Did you change the laws in your family, that you could hit FBI men, punch and kick them? Well, this is the test, that if you change the laws and now you are going to hit FBI men, every time we pick up one of your people we are going to break their head for them.

Bruno then related what happened to one of Lombardozzi's men:

They almost killed him, the FBI. They don't do that, you know. But they picked up one of his fellows, and they crippled him. They said, "This is an example. Now the next time anybody lays a hand on an FBI man, . . ."

On June 6, 1963, Stefano Magaddino discussed the incident with several of his men at his funeral home in Niagara Falls:

Here, we . . . are situated with this administration. . . . [W]e got from the President down — against us. . . . [B]ut we got to resist. Today. You see this table? (Magaddino could be heard hitting the table) You have to do something material. . . . They beat up Carmine plenty. When his father died. . . . When they beat up that FBI. . . . So after the beating . . . [the FBI] said to him, "We are even now. If you others continue to do the same thing again, we will change our methods with you people!"

On October 31, 1963, Magaddino had a conversation with his son,

Peter, who said the President "should drop dead," adding, ". . . [T]hey should kill the whole family — the mother and father too!"

On June 22, 1962, Joseph Valachi, a prisoner in the U.S. penitentiary in Atlanta, seized a two-foot length of iron pipe, rushed a fellow inmate, John Saupp, and beat him to death. Valachi, it turned out, had mistaken the man he had killed for Joseph DiPalermo, who, Valachi believed had been ordered by Vito Genovese, who was also an inmate, to kill him. The incident precipitated Valachi's break with La Cosa Nostra and his public testimony on the structure of organized crime. Valachi's decision to cooperate was not made public at the time, but it was not long before members of the Mafia were discussing it. On April 23, 1963, for example, Angelo DeCarlo had a discussion with a man named Barney:

Barney:	*[T]he thing they talk about today. Somebody must talk because they could never know these things. They know who's boss, underboss, the commission, the caporegimis. They talk like* amici nostra *(friends of ours). . . . And you can't do nothing about it.*
DeCarlo:	*And, oh, the other guy. In New York. What's his name? That was in the can with Vito.*
Barney:	*Joe Cago [Valachi's nickname].*
DeCarlo:	*I hear he's talking like a bastard. . . . He must have known something about this thing?*
Barney:	*He knows about things from thirty-five years ago.*

Once Valachi began to testify, the anger mounted. On September 28, 1963, Magaddino said, "Vito should have killed Valachi." On October 10 he added, "He talks too much. He's gonna get himself killed for that." The reactions of organized-crime figures were not limited to expressions of anger against Valachi or Robert Kennedy. Mafia members in New York developed a strategy to discredit Valachi's testimony by suggesting he was insane, citing a history of mental illness in his family. Efforts were also made to plant other unfavorable stories with members of the press. On March 2, 1964, FBI Director Hoover got right to the point in a phone call to Senator McClellan. The hearings, said Hoover, "shook . . . [the mob] up."

Carlos Marcello: 1910–

Carlos Marcello, the Cosa Nostra boss in New Orleans, was familiar with congressional investigations. He had been a witness before the Kefauver Committee in 1951, as well as the McClellan Committee in 1959, when its investigation of labor racketeering was directed by Chief Counsel Robert F. Kennedy. Marcello beat a contempt charge that grew out of his Kefauver Committee appearance; his claim of possible self-incrimination was not challenged in court by the McClellan Committee. Undoubtedly, Marcello had learned to live with the adverse publicity generated by such investigations. The advent of the Kennedy administration in 1961, however, threatened much more.

Marcello was erroneously identified by the Kefauver Committee as the head of organized crime in New Orleans. In fact, the leader in New Orleans in 1951 was Sam Carolla, who had, in 1922, succeeded Charles Montranga. (Montranga was a survivor of a mass lynching in 1891, which followed the Mafia murder of Police Chief David C. Hennessey.) Carolla, an eight-year-old Sicilian immigrant in 1904, was, at twenty-two, one of Montranga's key lieutenants. With the coming of Prohibition in 1919, Carolla turned to rumrunning, but in 1923 he was convicted in federal court of alcohol theft and sentenced to two years in prison. Returning to New Orleans in 1925, he proceeded over the next five years to consolidate his power, personally shotgunning, in 1930, William Bailey, his chief rival for control of the illicit liquor traffic. In 1931 Carolla and Frank Tedaro, one of his *capiregime,* were tried and convicted for wounding a federal agent, Cecil Moore, in a gun fight. Sentenced to two years, Carolla entered prison in 1932. Meanwhile, Frank Costello, with the blessing of Senator Huey P. Long, was moving his slot machines to Louisiana, as Mayor-elect Fiorello La Guardia had vowed to have them removed from New York City. Carolla supported the enterprise *in absentia* and donated the services of a young soldier, who had himself just been released from Angola state prison after serving four years for "masterminding" a grocery store robbery. At twenty-two, Carlos Marcello was beginning his climb to the top.

The year 1947 was a significant one for both Carolla and Marcello. It was the year that they, along with Costello and Meyer Lansky, expanded Louisiana gambling to include a racetrack wire service and several plush casinos, as well as more slot machines. It was also the year the government succeeded in deporting Carolla to Sicily, despite efforts by a Louisiana congressman, James Morrison, to have private immigration bills passed to grant him citizenship. Although Carolla returned illegally to the United States on two occasions (he died in New Orleans in 1972), his power passed to Marcello.

By 1963 Carlos Marcello was one of the wealthiest men in Louisiana. His ventures, according to the New Orleans Metropolitan Crime Commission, were grossing many millions annually: $500 million from illegal gambling; $100 million from illegal activities in over 1,500 syndicate-connected bars; $8 million from professional burglaries and holdups; $6 million from prostitution; and $400 million from diverse "legitimate investments" in the fields of transportation, finance, housing, and service. Marcello claimed he only earned "a salary of about $1,600 a month" as a tomato salesman, although he did acknowledge making certain "land investments." In 1967, however, *Life* estimated Marcello's personal worth to be $40 million. He owned motels, a juke box and vending-machine company, a sightseeing bus line, and a 6,500-acre, $22 million estate, Churchill Farms, just outside New Orleans in Jefferson Parish. Much of what Marcello owned, however, he concealed by putting the property in the names of close relatives. His son Joseph owned The Town and Country Motel; his brother Peter held a striptease joint, the Sho-Bar, on Bourbon Street in the French Quarter. (It was typical of Marcello to act through others to avoid trouble with the authorities, as he did by sending another brother, Joseph, the family underboss, to the Apalachin meeting in 1957.) Eventually, Marcello was less successful in escaping attention. He was a target in an FBI investigation of efforts to skim $1 million from Teamster insurance premiums. The investigation, made public in February 1980, was codenamed BRILAB, for bribery and labor. Undercover agents reportedly got Marcello to admit his Mafia membership in secretly recorded conversations, but he pointedly refused to discuss the Kennedy assassination.

As with Sam Carolla, there was a long-standing deportation order against Marcello starting with proceedings that were brought against him following his appearance before the Kefauver Committee. Born in Tunisia of Sicilian parents and brought to the United States before he was a year old, Marcello held no passport except a Guatemalan one, which he obtained in 1956 by paying a bribe, perhaps as much as $100,000, to Antonio Valladares, the law partner of Guatemala's prime minister. Other bribes, including $25,000-a-year to a high-ranking official of the Italian court, had prevented a final deportation order (the receiving country must agree before the order can be issued). Nevertheless, as the Kennedys came to power, Marcello was running out of maneuvering room. On December 28, 1960, *The New Orleans States-Item* reported a promise by Robert F. Kennedy, then Attorney General-designate, to expedite Marcello's deportation. How Marcello was reaching out for help was the topic of a conversation between Angelo Bruno and a group of friends, including Russell Bufalino, on July 17, 1962, which the FBI overheard. Bruno said that Marcello, whom he referred to as the New Orleans "representando officiale," had contacted Santo Trafficante in Florida and Sam Giancana in Chicago in an effort to secure the assistance of Frank Sinatra, who was friendly with "the President's father." In Bruno's opinion, however, the contact had only made matters worse.

Organized Crime in Perspective* 243*

On March 3, 1961, Joseph Swing, the director of the Immigration and Naturalization Service, advised the FBI in a memorandum that "the Attorney General had been emphasizing . . . the importance of taking prompt action to deport . . . Marcello . . . [whose] final order . . . [had] been entered . . . but . . . [was] being held in strictest confidence." Marcello did not learn of the order until April 4, 1961, when he came to the INS office in New Orleans for his regular quarterly appointment as an alien. He was arrested, handcuffed, and, sirens blaring, taken to Moisant International Airport, where a United States Border Patrol aircraft was waiting, its engines warmed up. Marcello later said, "You would have thought it was the President coming in instead of me going out." Marcello was flown 1,200 miles to Guatemala City and dumped there, without luggage and with little cash. He quickly regained his composure, however, and soon was installed in a plush suite at the Biltmore Hotel, as his brothers flew in cash and clothes. But when his presence in Guatemala caused a political uproar, President Miguel Ydigoras Fuentes ordered him expelled. Marcello and a lawyer who had come to help him, Michael Maroun of Shreveport, Louisiana, were unceremoniously flown to an out-of-the-way village in the jungle of El Salvador, where they were left stranded. Salvadorian soldiers jailed and interrogated the two men for five days, then put them on a bus and took them twenty miles into the mountains, where they were again left to fend for themselves. Eight hours and seventeen miles later they reached a village. They were hardly prepared for the mountain hike, as they were dressed in silk shantung suits and alligator shoes. (A portly five-foot-two, Marcello fainted three times.) In the village, they hired *muchachos* to lead them to an airport, but fearful that their guides had robbery and murder in mind, they took the first opportunity to flee back into the jungle. During a downhill scramble, Marcello fell and broke two ribs. Eventually, they found their way to a small coastal town, and from there they flew by commercial airline to Miami, where Marcello illegally reentered the United States. (That was the way Marcello returned, according to his statement to us in 1978. We learned from a wiretap, however, that he was flown back in a Dominican Republic Air Force plane.) On June 2, 1961, Marcello's lawyers acknowledged that he had returned to the United States, that he was in hiding, but that he could be produced in court if necessary.

On April 5, 1961, Attorney General Kennedy publicly acknowledged that Marcello had been summarily flown out of the country. Kennedy took responsibility for Marcello's ouster, contending it "was in strict accordance with the law." Kennedy was further quoted as saying he was "very happy Carlos Marcello . . . was no longer with us," but he added that if he had been on the scene and personally handling the matter, he "would have used different steps." In fact, while he knew that the deportation was going to take place, Kennedy was not aware beforehand of the manner of the deportation, since it had been the responsibility of Director Swing. (The INS procedures were upheld in subsequent legal proceedings.) Responsibility aside, Marcello was deeply offended. In response to our subpoena, he appeared in executive session before the Committee on January 11, 1978. Generally, his answers were in curt monosyllables, but when the subject of his deportation came up, the atmosphere in the hearing chamber turned tense. Marcello showed fire in his eyes and resentment in the tone of his voice, as he animatedly told us: "[T]wo marshals put the handcuffs on me and they told me that I was being kidnapped and being brought to Guatemala, . . . and in thirty minutes . . . I was in the plane. . . . They dumped me off in Guatemala. . . . They just snatched me, and that is it, actually kidnapped me!" Marcello explicitly fixed the responsibility for his deportation: "[Kennedy] said . . . he would see that I be deported just as soon as he got in office. Well, he got in office January 20, . . . and April the 4th he deported me."

Marcello's troubles with the Kennedy administration were only beginning with his forced march through Central America. On April 10, 1961, the Internal Revenue Service filed a $835,396 tax lien against him and his wife. On June 8, 1961, six days after his attorneys announced Marcello had returned, a federal grand jury in New Orleans indicted him for illegal entry. Four months later Attorney General Kennedy himself announced that the federal grand jury in New Orleans had indicted Marcello for conspiracy to defraud the United States in connection with his false Guatemalan birth certificate. Marcello, meanwhile, had sued to have a 1938 drug conviction set aside (he was accused at the time of being a member of "the biggest marijuana ring in New Orleans history"). On October 31, 1962, his suit was rejected, thus rendering his chances of remaining a U.S. resident all the more tenuous, since he needed to have the conviction voided to block another deportation.

Marcello's anger could have constituted a motive for the assassination. There was a witness, moreover, who said the New Orleans Mafia leader had been quite specific about the manner and method of his revenge. Edward Becker, a former Las Vegas promoter who had lived on the fringe of the underworld, told of a meeting in September 1962 at Churchill Farms at which Marcello became enraged at the mention of Robert Kennedy's name. "Don't worry about that little Bobby son-of-a-bitch," Becker reported Marcello said. "He's going to be taken care of." Then he muttered a Sicilian curse: "*Livarsi na petra di la scarpa.*" ("Take the stone out of my shoe.") Becker said Marcello had even devised a plan: he would use a "nut" to do the job, someone who could be manipulated, for it was important that his own people not be identified as the assassins. Marcello then offered a metaphor. The President was the dog, the Attorney General Kennedy was its tail. If you cut off the tail, the dog will keep biting; but if you chop off the head, the dog will die, tail and all.

In 1967 the FBI learned of the Becker allegation from Ed Reid, a former editor of the *Las Vegas Sun* and author of the then soon-to-be-published book, *The Grim Reapers*. Bureau files indicated that Becker had said that Marcello had threatened President Kennedy. An FBI memorandum stated:

> Marcello was alleged to have said that in order to get Bobby Kennedy they would have to get the President, and they could not kill Bobby because the President would use the Army and the Marines to get them. The result of killing the President would cause Bobby to lose his power as Attorney General because of the new President.

FBI Director Hoover told the Warren Commission in 1964 that the President's assassination would "continue in an open classification for all time" and that "any information . . . from any source . . . [would be] thoroughly investigated. . . . " Nevertheless, our investigation of the Becker allegation, as well as the FBI's handling of it, showed that the bureau made no real effort to verify it. Rather than interview Becker, the bureau tried to discredit him as an unreliable source, and Reid was urged to drop the account from his book. (He refused.) The FBI even got the date of the alleged meeting wrong, listing it in the report as September 1963, although Becker told us he had been precise about it having occurred in September 1962, and Reid backed him up.

In our effort to evaluate the story, we found that Becker, a former public relations man for the Riviera Hotel in Las Vegas, had been involved in shady transactions with Max Field, a criminal associate of Joseph Sica, a prominent mob figure in Los Angeles. Such an association, we believed, helped explain Becker's presence at a meeting with Marcello. Next, we talked to Julian Blodgett, a former FBI agent and chief investigator in the Los Angeles district attorney's office who, as a private investigator in 1962, had employed Becker on occasion. Blodgett conceded that Becker was "a controversial guy," but he believed his account of the meeting with Marcello. We were able to obtain substantial corroboration for Becker's presence in the New Orleans area in September 1962, and we learned that he had said he went to Churchill Farms with a longtime friend, Carl Roppolo of Shreveport, to discuss a promotional scheme with Marcello. According to FBI information, the Marcello and Roppolo families "were quite close at one time as they came from the 'old country' at approximately the same time and lived as neighbors in New Orleans." And Aaron Kohn of the New Orleans Metropolitan Crime Commission told us that Roppolo's mother Lillian "was considered to be something of a courier for Marcello." Finally, Reid told us he believed Becker's account, since he had obtained trustworthy information from him on other occasions.

We questioned Marcello about the alleged threat when he appeared in executive session on January 11, 1978. "Positively not," he replied. The meeting never occurred. He "never said anything like that."

We learned in our investigation of another statement with threatening overtones that was allegedly made by a major organized-crime figure in September 1962. Jose Aleman, a prominent member of the Cuban exile community in Miami, was quoted in *The Washington Post* in 1976 as having stated that Santo Trafficante, Jr., told him in a private conversation that President Kennedy was "going to be hit." In March 1977 Aleman confirmed the allegation to us, saying that he had believed Trafficante was serious and that a plot was afoot at the time. But when Aleman appeared in public session in 1978, he changed his story in a dramatic fashion. Indicating that he feared for his life, he requested the protection of U.S. marshals while he was in Washington. Then, he testified that he had understood Trafficante to mean that the President was going to be "hit by a lot of votes" in the 1964 election. Trafficante appeared before the Committee after Aleman, and he categorically denied making the statement. But he did acknowledge knowing Aleman and meeting with him to discuss pension fund loans at about the time Aleman claimed he had heard him make the threat. In contrast to the Becker allegation, we were skeptical of Aleman's story. He had not reported the threat to the FBI in 1963, or so his bureau contacts told us. (Aleman insisted he had.) We were struck, however, by the parallel time of the alleged Marcello threat and Trafficante's alleged statement that he knew a plot was in the works.

On November 4, 1963, Marcello went on trial in New Orleans on criminal charges in connection with his false Guatemalan birth certificate. He was acquitted on November 22, 1963. News of President Kennedy's assassination reached the courtroom only shortly before the verdict was returned. On October 6, 1964, Marcello was indicted for jury bribing in connection with the November 1963 verdict. The indictment also charged obstruction of justice, in that Marcello had plotted the murder of the principal witness against him, Carl I. Noll. Marcello was subsequently acquitted of the bribery charge (despite the testimony of one juror, Rudolph Heifler, that he had accepted $1,000 to vote not guilty), and the obstruction of justice charge was dropped when Noll refused to testify against Marcello.

Sam Giancana: 1908–1975

On October 10, 1963, Sam Giancana, the family boss in Chicago, was overheard by the FBI in conversation with Charles English, an associate, at the Armory Lounge in Forest Park, Illinois. Valachi could not, they thought, hurt the Chicago organization, but he was doing great harm to the New York members. Like Marcello, however, Giancana was by no means free of pressure from the Kennedy administration. In fact, he was one of the principal targets of the organized-crime drive because of his leadership position in Chicago, which he had attained over a long period by dint of an aggressive nature and a willingness to resort to raw violence.

It was 1905 when Antonino Giangana, twenty-four, arrived at Polk Street Station in Chicago without his nineteen-year-old wife, Antonia, whom he called Lena. She was not to come to the United States until the end of 1906. Giangana had been a street peddler in the Sicilian town of Castelvetrano; he would be a street peddler in Chicago. In Sicily, there had been poverty, but at least the air was clean and the sun bright and warm. Chicago was dirty with soot and smoke, the sky was gray, and it was often cold, damp, and windy. The area of tenements into which the new immigrants crowded was ultimately called Little Italy or Little Sicily, though sometimes Little Hell, the Valley, or the Patch. Antonio and Lena at first lived at 223 South Aberdeen, an area west of Chicago's Loop, which in 1906 was heavily Irish. At that time few Italians lived west of Halsted Street; they were concentrated between Taylor to the south and Mather to the north. On May 24, 1908, Lena gave birth to her first son, who was named Salvatore. Shortly thereafter the family moved to 1127 West Van Buren Street. This was also an Irish area at the time, but it would become an Italian neighborhood as it expanded northward from Taylor, the main street of the Patch. By 1925 Salvatore, then known as "Sam" or "Mooney," Giancana, lived at 1422 West Taylor Street and was a member of a street gang called the "42's." Like Valachi in New York, Giancana took pride in his ability as a "wheelman." His first arrest and conviction came in September 1925 — for auto theft. Before he was twenty, he had been arrested in three murder investigations, one of which was for the slaying of an eyewitness to a robbery, another was for the killing of Octavius Granady, a black who sought election as a committeeman in the largely Italian 20th Ward. By 1963 Giancana had been arrested sixty times, and he had served time for auto theft, burglary, and moonshining.

In November 1928 Giancana was arrested for an attempted burglary of a clothing store. Caught red-handed, he pleaded guilty and was sentenced to one to five years in the state penitentiary at Joliet. He was released on Christmas Eve 1932, at which time he came to the attention of Felice DeLucia, who worked at the Bella Napoli Cafe, which was the base of operations of Joseph Esposito, one of Chicago's most notorious beer runners. DeLucia, who was better known as Paul "The Waiter" Ricca, had also worked for the Genna brothers (Sam, Angelo, Peter, Anthony, and James), all vicious killers and bootleggers who were allied with Al Capone, and finally for Capone himself. DeLucia took over as the head of the syndicate, succeeding Frank Nitti in 1943. When Giancana became DeLucia's chauffeur, he was on his way to underworld prominence.

Giancana's career was momentarily interrupted in May 1939 when he was sentenced to a four-year term in the federal prison at Leavenworth, Kansas, for moonshining. He had been caught in a barn in Elgin, Illinois, with 8,800 gallons of mash, 1,000 gallons of alcohol, and 1,000 gallons of uncolored spirits. Giancana had been in Leavenworth for only two months when he was transferred to the federal facility at Terre Haute, Indiana. There he was tested for intelligence, scoring 74 verbal and 93 nonverbal. It was also there he went to school — not to learn a legitimate trade, but to be introduced to the world of policy. His teacher was Edward Jones, a black racketeer who had run the game in Chicago before he was sentenced to twenty-two months for income tax evasion. For Giancana, it spelled opportunity — not "nickel and dime," but involving a cash flow of thousands of dollars. By the time he was released from prison, in December 1942, he had learned his lessons well.

With a criminal record and a family (he had married in 1933 and by 1942 had two children, Antoinette and Bonita Lucille), Giancana had little to fear when he registered for the draft. (His interviewer wrote on Giancana's 4-F exemption form that "he was a constitutional psychopath with an inadequate personality manifested by strong antisocial trends.") He was free to return to his old pursuits, but his mentor, DeLucia, was himself in prison in 1944, having been convicted of extortion in the famous motion picture industry case.

Prohibition had come to an end, and the Chicago syndicate was looking for new fields of endeavor. Labor racketeering was one likely prospect. Just as Paul Dorfman had taken over the Scrap Iron and Junk Handlers Union in 1939, the Capone mob had moved in on the International Alliance of Theatrical Stage Employees. Willie Bioff, a small-time thief and extortionist, had developed a relationship with George E.

Browne, the business agent of Local 2 of IATSE. With the backing of the Capone organization, Browne was installed as president of the union in a rigged election in 1934. Two years later Bioff told Nicholas M. Schenck, the president of Loews and the industry's representative to the union, that the price for labor peace would be $2 million. The Hollywood giants, such companies as Twentieth Century-Fox, RKO, Warner Brothers, MGM, and Loews, thought it over and decided to pay. The extortion scheme was uncovered, however, when Joseph M. Schenck, chairman of the board of Twentieth Century-Fox, was prosecuted for income tax evasion. Schenck testified against Bioff and Browne who, in turn, implicated Chicago Mafia figures Frank Nitti, Nick Circella, Louis Compagna, John Roselli, and DeLucia.

The extortion trial was held in New York. Even though violence was used to intimidate witnesses, including any of those charged who might have been thinking about cooperating with the government (on February 2, 1943, Circella's girl friend, Estelle Carey, was tied to a chair in her apartment, doused with gasoline, and set afire), the defendants were found guilty of extortion on December 31, 1943, and sentenced to ten years at Leavenworth (all but Nitti, who had committed suicide). In spite of recommendations against early release by both the prosecutor and the judge, they all were paroled on August 13, 1947, having served the bare one-third minimum of their sentences. Murray Humphreys, a Chicago mob figure, took credit for masterminding the release, as he indicated in an overheard conversation on October 16, 1964. Attorney General Tom Clark had been, he said, "100 percent for doing favors," but after the parole scandal broke, "you couldn't get through for nothing." Humphreys elaborated on the fix: "The guy [Maury Hughes] who went to him [Attorney General Clark] was an ex-law partner [from Dallas], and then the scandal broke." The Kefauver Committee called the granting of parole to the motion picture industry extortionists "a shocking abuse of power," and *The Chicago Tribune* found Clark "unfit" when he was nominated for the Supreme Court in 1952.

Shortly after he got out of prison in 1942, Giancana turned to Edward Jones, the policy racketeer, for a bankroll, which supplemented his income from various illicit enterprises, including the counterfeiting of gas- and food-rationing stamps. (One indication of his improved financial status was that Giancana was able to move out of the Patch to the fashionable Chicago suburb of Oak Park.) In May 1946 Giancana showed his gratitude to Jones by engineering his abduction on a Chicago street. Five days later Jones was left unharmed, standing on the corner of 62nd and Loomis streets, adhesive tape covering his eyes and cotton stuffed in his ears. There was talk of high ransom, but it apparently did not involve money. As Jones retired to Mexico, Giancana made himself a partner in the policy racket, and he proceeded to lead the syndicate's takeover of the major policy operations in Chicago's Black Belt. It was part of a general effort to consolidate syndicate control of all gambling in Chicago — the horse rooms, racetrack wire service, casinos, and policy wheel. But success had its price, as more than a dozen syndicate members died during a period of bombings, kidnappings, and ambushes. As for Giancana, his rising status was symbolized by his new job as Anthony Accardo's chauffeur. Accardo, a one-time Capone gunman, succeeded to the leadership of the Chicago syndicate when Felice DeLucia went to prison for extortion in 1944. But Accardo, too, had legal troubles. He was indicted for tax evasion in 1960, and although his conviction was reversed on appeal, he chose to retire. His successor was Sam Giancana.

The popular images of organized-crime figures often reduce them to their most common characteristic — a bent for violence; they are made to appear animal-like and little more. Nothing could be further from the truth. Like many underworld figures, Giancana had about him, for all of his viciousness and his renowned temper, "a beguiling, lilting charm," as William Brashler put it in *The Don*. He was, Brashler observed, "able to envelop those around him into a coven of understanding, and speak with them as one who understood and cared, be it about affairs mundane or treacherous." Giancana was particularly appealing to women. He had been more or less faithful to his wife, Angeline, before her death in April 1954, but from then on he was ever on the make, pursuing waitresses, secretaries, dancers, hat-check girls, and the wives of associates. All he asked was that the woman have a pretty face and nice figure. But it was different with Phyllis McGuire, the youngest and prettiest of the McGuire Sisters, a popular singing trio. They met in Las Vegas.

The Chicago syndicate got interested in Las Vegas in the late 1950s, and both Giancana and Accardo acquired hidden interests in a number of casinos (hidden because criminals were banned from casino ownership by Nevada law). Giancana had a piece of the Desert Inn and the Stardust, both nominally owned by Morris Dalitz, and it was at the Desert Inn, sometime in 1960, that he first met Phyllis McGuire. She was having a good time at the gaming tables but had run up a debt of over $100,000. Giancana said he would take care of her markers, which he did by telling Dalitz to "eat it." In 1961 Phyllis leased the Green Gables Ranch, four miles outside of Las Vegas, and Giancana made it his Nevada headquarters. His relationship with McGuire, however, was attracting attention, which became a sore point with him. In July 1961, according to Brashler, Giancana and McGuire were flying from Phoenix to New York. On a stopover in Chicago, Giancana was angered when a team of FBI agents tried to question McGuire.

"Whataya wanna know?" he said. "I'll tell ya, I'll tell ya anything ya wanna know."

"Okay," one agent said. "Tell us what you do for a living."

"Easy," Giancana said. "I own Chicago. I own Miami. I own Las Vegas."

When McGuire did not immediately return from the FBI interview, Giancana became more angry.

"F___k you," he said. "F___k your boss, too. F___k your boss's boss." Then he exploded. "I'll get you for this. You lit a fire tonight that will never go out. You'll rue the day. I'll get you."

As time went on, Giancana's troubles stemming from the publicity over his relationship with McGuire, got more serious. In 1963 Frank Sinatra, a close friend of Giancana, owned 50 percent of the Cal-Neva Lodge, a resort and casino on the Nevada side of Lake Tahoe. Giancana often bragged that, through Sinatra, he owned a share of the Cal-Neva, and Sinatra seemingly confirmed this by hiring Paul D'Amato, a New Jersey gangster, whose role appeared to be to protect Giancana's interests. Giancana and McGuire were frequent guests at the Cal-Neva, but visits on two successive weekends in July 1963 stirred up enough publicity to attract the attention of the Nevada State Gaming Commission. Called to account for Giancana's share of ownership, Sinatra was defiant at first, but he could see no alternative to divesting himself of his $3 million interest in the Cal-Neva, as well as his $350,000 share in the Sands in Las Vegas. (In 1962 Sinatra, along with Dean Martin and Sammy Davis, Jr., made a special appearance at the Villa Venice, a Giancana nightclub near Chicago. The FBI wanted to know why, and Sinatra claimed it was a favor for a friend, Leo Olsen, Giancana's front man at the Villa Venice. But Davis was more candid. "I got one eye," he told an FBI agent, "and that one eye sees a lot of things that my brain tells me I shouldn't talk about. Because my brain says that if I do, my one eye might not be seeing anything after a while.")

Jet air travel, a booming economy, and its growing reputation as an entertainment capital made Las Vegas in the 1960s a rich source of illicit profits. Publicly reported gaming income increased from $216.3 million in 1961 to $295.4 million by 1964. But both the FBI bugging program and IRS physical surveillance revealed that substantial sums were not being reported to the gaming authorities. In March 1962, for example, $200,000 was skimmed from the Desert Inn alone, while in January 1963 a total of $280,000 was skimmed from the Fremont,

Sands, Flamingo, and Horseshoe. The minimum estimated illegal take from 1960 to 1964 was $10 million a year. The skim money was couriered out of the country to the International Credit Bank in Geneva or to the Bank of World Commerce in Nassau, or it was distributed directly to mob leaders in the United States. A hidden share of a casino was priced in the underworld market at $52,500, and the dividend hovered around $1,000 to $1,500 a month — an annual return of about 25 percent. As Angelo DeCarlo put it when the FBI bug was on: "You get a thousand a month for a point, and sometimes you get fifteen hundred." "You got to win a hundred thousand," someone broke in. "Steal a hundred thousand, not win it," DeCarlo corrected. "You don't get nothing out of the winnings. The only thing you get is a piece of what they steal."

The government was threatening the investment, however, with the attorney general's organized-crime program: FBI strength in Nevada was tripled; the IRS opened a 40-agent office in Las Vegas. It was potentially the worst financial disaster for the mob since Castro closed the Havana casinos in 1959. In March 1962 DeCarlo voiced a general concern when he said, "There's a lot of money invested in Las Vegas, a lotta people got money. If anything goes wrong. . . . "

Organized Crime and Political Power

The reason the Kennedys were so resented by the Mafia was that they had renounced a century-old alliance between gangster and politician that had, in Chicago particularly, been an imperative for survival. As Robert Kennedy said, in a discussion of crime with reporters for *The Chicago Daily News* three months after his brother's assassination, "So much is tied to politics."

Popular imagination notwithstanding, organized crime in Chicago did not originate with Prohibition. The city was founded in 1837 and within a decade came to be reputed as a center of vice and corruption. After the famous 1871 fire the saloons and brothels were clustered on Dearborn Street, near 22nd, in an area known as the South Side Levee. Politically, it was the First Ward, which also consisted of the commercial district, or The Loop; and at the turn of the century the ward bosses were Michael "Hinky Dink" Kenna and John "Bathhouse" Coughlin. Their power was immense, for there was little distinction between the Kenna-Coughlin political machine and the forces that controlled liquor, gambling, and prostitution. It was from these roots that the Capone organization grew. James "Big Jim" Colosimo, the first Chicago crime boss, was a pimp and a restaurateur. His headquarters, Colosimo's Cafe, was at 212 South Wabash. It was only under his successor, John

Torrio, Capone's immediate predecessor who had been a Colosimo bodyguard, that the organization got into the illicit beer-and-liquor traffic.

Torrio's headquarters was The Four Deuces, which was located in a building at 2222 South Wabash Avenue. It was a four-story monument to liquor, chance, and illicit sex. Capone's base was the Lexington Hotel on South Michigan, where he occupied the entire fourth floor, most of the third floor, and parts of the rest of the building. It was no coincidence that both Torrio and Capone located their operations in the First Ward, where Kenna and Coughlin collected votes and tribute from every racket and vice operation. By the time of their deaths (Coughlin in 1938, Kenna in 1946) they had, however, become mere figureheads for Jake Guzik, the Capone syndicate overlord of the First Ward. (Gus Alex succeeded Guzik on Guzik's death in 1956.) In 1947 the First Ward was merged with the 20th, from which it had been separated by the south branch of the Chicago River and which contained the neighborhood known as the Patch. Politicians from the redistricted ward and adjacent hoodlum-dominated jurisdictions came to be known as the West Side Bloc, the character of which was typified by the political career of one of its notorious members, Roland V. Libonati.

First elected to the state legislature in 1931, Libonati was photographed the following spring with Capone and Jack "Machine Gun" McGurn at a Chicago Cubs baseball game. In later years Libonati said of his relationship with Capone: "He treated me with respect, . . . and I never did anything not to merit his respect." As for Felice DeLucia and Anthony Accardo, Libonati said they were "charitable" and "patriotic" fellows. For twenty-two years in the legislature (six as a Republican representative, sixteen as a Democratic senator), Libonati was unswervingly loyal to his hoodlum friends, as the Kefauver Committee noted. In 1957 he was rewarded with the nomination to Congress from the Seventh District of Illinois, and he won with 89 percent of the votes. How he got those votes was alluded to in a conversation he had with two associates on October 23, 1962, which was overheard by the FBI. Libonati said he did not even know the name of his opponent in the upcoming election. He then remarked: "Last time, you guys built me up to 98,000 votes, and the other guy to 23,000."

Libonati had been appointed to the Judiciary Committee of the House, which had jurisdiction over anticrime legislation sought by the Kennedy administration, and in that same conversation on October 23, 1962, he took credit where credit was due. "I killed six of [Kennedy's] bills, that wiretap bill, the intimidating informers bill. . . ."

In January 1963, however, Giancana ordered Libonati to step down "for reasons of poor health," although Ovid Demaris, the author of

Captive City, had a different explanation. He wrote that Giancana acted because Mayor Richard J. Daley had been informed by Attorney General Kennedy that if Libonati returned to Congress, Kennedy "would personally see to it that he went to jail." Libonati's successor was Frank Annunzio, a former First Ward committeeman and a partner of two syndicate figures in an insurance business. When Annunzio ran for Congress in 1964, he said he thought that Americans of Italian ancestry had been unfairly linked with crime syndicate hoodlums. "I feel our image has been treated unfairly," he added. The FBI, in a report not then made public, commented in 1964: "Annunzio will follow [the] dictate[s] of [the] mob." (Annunzio, who did not support the creation of our Committee in 1976, was an influential member of the House Administration Committee, which controlled our budget.)

One of Libonati's last acts in Congress was the introduction of legislation that would have made it a crime for federal agents to keep gangsters under surveillance. At the time he told a Chicago television newscaster: "Yes, I know Giancana. [M]y bill would cover him."

FBI agents who had kept Giancana under periodic surveillance since he was named a principal target of the attorney general's organized-crime program in 1961, decided in the late spring of 1963 to change tactics. On their own, although with approval from Washington, the agents decided to institute "lockstep" physical surveillance — a twenty-four-hour tail, no matter where he was or who he was with. As Brashler wrote in *The Don*:

> With his temper and his volatile moodiness, they saw a chance to disrupt the man's routine, his private affairs, his very equilibrium, to such an extent that . . . it would cause him to make mistakes.

The lockstep surveillance was more effective than expected. Giancana became isolated; it was no longer possible for him to conduct "meets." Other organized-crime figures shunned him. (The surveillance apparently aborted a plan by Giancana, approved by the commission over the objections of a Florida mob figure, Charles Tourine, to take over the gambling casinos in the Dominican Republic. Because of the FBI surveillance, the final meeting with Dominican Republic officials could not be held.) As Charles English, a Giancana associate put it: "The guy . . . [had] trouble even having a date."

At first Giancana tried to elude the agents, displaying all of his old skills as a wheelman. Once he raced through a car-wash, as attendants who knew him stepped aside and cheered, "Go, Mo, Go!" But the agents were on the other side waiting for him. He was followed on the golf course, crowded by agents who were better golfers and who occasionally drove into his foursome, or held off and snickered while Giancana — flustered — four-putted. Desperate, Giancana decided to take an unprecedented step. With the help of his son-in-law, Anthony Tisci, a lawyer on Libonati's congressional staff, he sought to enjoin the agents' conduct as a violation of his civil rights. He hired a private detective, who made surveillance films of the FBI. ("Take this side [of me]," an agent taunted. "This is my best side. Then I'll take a picture of you and put a nice number under it.") Giancana also adopted the routine of a legitimate businessman, even going to church one Sunday. (An assistant pastor at St. Bernardine's told a newspaper reporter that Giancana's last visit had been three years earlier, on the occasion of his daughter's graduation.) On June 27 Giancana filed suit in federal court, claiming he had been "harassed, . . . humiliated, . . . [and] embarrassed. . . ." His attorney described the decision to put Giancana under surveillance as "the work of some New Frontier lawyer who forgot his lessons in constitutional law." The court at first refused to act, but then did set a date for a hearing in July. Giancana himself was the star witness, narrating a five-minute color movie of the FBI. "Those four guys are playing right behind us," he said, referring to a golf course sequence. "One of these fellas is Roemer." Giancana identified William Roemer as an FBI agent he said he met "at O'Hare Airport nine months ago." The Department of Justice, in its defense, took the position that the court had no power to supervise a surveillance. Consequently, no evidence was presented, nor was Giancana cross-examined by the government. When Martin W. Johnson, the special agent-in-charge of the Chicago FBI office, was called to testify, he refused to answer thirteen specific questions on the direct order of Attorney General Kennedy. The court refused to sign an order submitted by Giancana's lawyers, which would have, one government official noted, "prevented virtually any investigation . . . by any police . . . agency." But to the deep chagrin of the Department of Justice and the FBI, the court entered a limited order and held Johnson in contempt for failure to testify, fining him $500. The court's order provided that the FBI could not have more than one car parked within a block of Giancana's home; only one car could be used to follow him; and there had to be at least one foursome between Giancana and the agents when they followed him on the golf course. The government, at the direction of Attorney General Kennedy, appealed. On July 26, 1963, the Circuit Court of Appeals stayed the injunction, pending full appeal. The court observed:

> [The FBI agents] are a part of the executive department, . . . and they are not subject to supervision or direction by courts as to how they shall perform the duties imposed by law upon them.

The stay was made permanent on June 30, 1964, although Johnson's contempt citation was affirmed. Giancana lost more than he won by going to court, since the publicity generated by the suit turned his home into a tourist attraction. "I never saw anything like last night," said Norma Boerema, who lived across the alley from him. "There were 150 to 200 cars . . . circling around. . . ." Other mob figures were heard to grumble that Giancana had lost his effectiveness.

Organized Crime and Kennedy (after Dallas)

When word of the Kennedy assassination came, Sam Giancana was at the Armory Lounge in Chicago with Keely Smith, the professional singer and a longtime friend, and Charles English, an associate. Robert Kennedy would "not have the power he previously had," Giancana accurately observed. Three days later, Giancana and English were again within range of an FBI device as they watched a television replay of the President's funeral. English started to sing, "When the caissons go rolling along, . . ." and he observed that Lee Harvey Oswald was supposed to have been "an anarchist" and "a Marxist Communist." "He was a marksman who knew how to shoot," Giancana replied, adding that, with Oswald dead, the government would not be able to know if he had "other contacts or what."

On November 26, 1963, at Stefano Magaddino's funeral home in Niagara Falls, there also was a conversation about the President's death. Magaddino voiced the opinion that Jack Ruby would not be convicted. His son, Peter, a *caporegime*, believed that Ruby "would be released on a plea of insanity." Frederico Randaccio, the family underboss, proposed that congratulations were in order, and everyone laughed until the old man interrupted. The public around them would be "watching for their reaction," he cautioned, and it was not wise to "speak in this fashion." Then he offered a sober judgment: Robert Kennedy had invited his brother's assassination, he said, because "he pressed too many issues." Three days later there was more talk about the assassination. Stefano Magaddino appraised the murder of Oswald by Ruby. It had been "arranged in order to cover up things," he said, which, if publicized, "might have led to civil war." This was his own opinion, Magaddino said, but he again cautioned his men to be careful: "You can be assured that the police spies will be watching carefully to see what we . . . think and say about this."

On February 2, 1964, Angelo Bruno was on the phone with an unidentified associate, who said, "It is too bad his brother Bobby was not in that car too." And on August 13 Russell Bufalino was overheard. "The Kennedys are responsible for all my trouble," he said. "They killed the good one. They should have killed the other little guy."

While our examination of the FBI surveillance logs for eleven months before and eight months after the assassination revealed the structure of organized crime in detail, at the same time indicating how much the Kennedys were hated by a powerful group of vicious men, we found no direct evidence of a plot to kill the President. There was no discussion before the event of specific trips by the President, much less of the Dallas visit, nor was there any discussion of contacting Oswald. No conversation revealed that an effort had been made to obtain permission to kill the President or that such permission had been granted by the organized-crime commission. Because the electronic coverage of commission members was so thorough, we came to believe that it was unlikely that the commission was involved in the assassination. Too many of its other plans to engage in criminal endeavors, including murder, were overheard to suppose that it could have carried out the assassination without the FBI picking up some trace of it.

Our examination of the FBI surveillance program, however, went beyond the national commission. We hoped that we would be able to identify individual organized-crime figures who might have been responsible for the assassination, or, else be able to say that it was unlikely that any were involved. Ultimately, we were unable to make such a determination, for the electronic surveillance was not comprehensive. It did not cover at all adequately the major criminal groups and individuals in Texas, Louisiana, and Florida. Nor was the absence of electronic surveillance made up for by strategically placed informants or vigorous traditional investigations. FBI headquarters was well aware of these deficiencies. On October 14, 1959, J. Edgar Hoover wrote the New Orleans office to urge the use of "unusual investigative techniques" (a euphemism for electronic surveillance), noting that other offices had been successful in their use at "locations where hoodlums meet." Yet by February 15, 1963, it was still necessary to call for a "special effort" by the New Orleans office. Agents had tried twice to bug Carlos Marcello, but they had not been successful. (Incredibly, the FBI case agent assigned to Marcello in 1963, Regis Kennedy, told us in 1978 that he believed that Marcello, from 1959 to 1963, was a legitimate businessman and not involved in organized crime. According to Aaron M. Kohn, who during the period in question was the managing director of the New Orleans Metropolitan Crime Commission, Kennedy's attitude toward organized crime was negative, which we took to mean jaded. Patrick Collins, his successor as the Marcello case agent, told us Kennedy was bored by the routine reports he was required to file on Marcello.) Al Staffeld, an FBI inspector in Washington, who in 1963 was second in command of the organized-crime intelligence program, acknowledged to us in 1978, "[W]ith Marcello, you've got the one big exception in our work back then." The FBI had, Staffeld said, "nothing

in electronic surveillance on Marcello and his guys." Marcello was not
the only exception, we learned. Santo Trafficante was under electronic
surveillance on only four occasions in 1963, each time in a restaurant.
While he was heard to attack the Kennedy administration's organized-
crime program and bitterly complain about the pressure ("I know when
I'm beat"), these snippets of conversation could not, we believed, justify broad conclusions either way. Here, too, Staffeld conceded to us:
"[W]e were never really able to penetrate . . . [Trafficante] very clearly.
Certainly nothing like we were able to do in Chicago and New York."
Finally, crime-condition reports, which were not based on electronic
surveillance or good informant coverage, generally reflected negative
conclusions. One filed for Dallas on March 1, 1962, read: "No evidence
of illegal activity by Joseph Francis Civello." Civello was the head of
the Mafia family in Dallas, and he was closely allied with Marcello.
(Marcello told us in 1979 that he had known Civello "for some twenty
years.")

The preassassination deficiencies of the FBI intelligence in Texas,
Louisiana, and Florida were not remedied by the Warren Commission
in 1964. The Warren Commission's field investigation of Ruby, for example, did not get underway until March, and its senior staff attorneys
began to leave the Commission in June. Important information was
withheld from the Commission: the CIA-Mafia plots, for example, and
even the existence of the organized-crime surveillance program. Nor
did the FBI make up for its earlier shortcomings. As the Church Committee concluded in 1975: "Rather than addressing . . . all possibilities
of conspiracy, the FBI investigation focused narrowly on Lee Harvey
Oswald." Hoover himself made the major decisions, and while he did
pursue certain conspiracy leads, his attitude was reflected in a telephone
conversation with President Johnson on November 24, 1963, just
hours after Oswald had been shot by Ruby. "The thing I am most concerned about, . . ." said Hoover, "is having something issued so we can
convince the public that Oswald is the . . . assassin." Two days later
Hoover received a memorandum from a subordinate that stated: "[W]e
must recognize that a matter of this magnitude cannot be fully investigated in a week's time." Hoover scrawled on the bottom of a page:
"Just how long do you estimate it will take. It seems to me we have the
basic facts now." As our Committee concluded in 1978, the FBI's conspiracy investigation was "seriously flawed." In fact, it was so flawed
that had a conspiracy existed, the Committee commented, "[the] investigation was in all likelihood insufficient to have uncovered . . .
[it]." In the absence of direct evidence that specific organized-crime
figures were involved, or that their involvement was unlikely, we proceeded to examine each possibility in light of what we knew about the

general character of those figures and their confrontation with the Kennedy administration. The first step in that process was to see if either Jack Ruby or Lee Harvey Oswald, or both, had any connections with organized crime. For if they had such ties, an organized-crime conspiracy in the assassination would move from the realm of possibility to the realm of likelihood.

The Kennedy brothers at the Democratic convention in Los Angeles, July 1960. In the Greek sense of tragedy, a perripteia, a reversal of fortune, befell the president on November 22, 1963, in Dallas. But an anagnorisis, a recognition of the reason why, was for the younger brother to bear until he too was murdered. Convinced of Oswald's guilt, Robert Kennedy voiced suspicions of a larger plot.

2

November 24, 1963 — the Kennedy family and the new president, Lyndon B. Johnson, descend the steps of the Capitol in Washington, where the slain president lay in state. The stoic widow, Jacqueline, has her children, Caroline and John, Jr., by the hand, followed by Robert Kennedy and his sisters, Patricia (with daughter Sydney) and Jean, and their husbands, Peter Lawford and Stephen Smith. Then, President and Mrs. Johnson.

November 25, 1963 — the cortege, with its riderless horse a symbol of a fallen leader, crosses Memorial Bridge on its way to Arlington National Cemetery. As a nation mourned, there was reason to wonder if indeed there was meaning in the death of a man whose life had been full of purpose. Or was it simply a senseless event? "The innocent suffer," Robert Kennedy later wrote on a note pad. "How can that be possible and God be just?"

4

While being transferred to the custody of the Dallas sheriff, the accused assassin was gunned down. Oswald's killer, Jack Ruby, claimed it was a spontaneous act, but this was at odds with evidence that he was stalking Oswald shortly after his arrest. Ruby's murder conviction was reversed; he died before standing trial a second time.

5

Ruby, a strip-joint operator, owned the Carousel in Dallas. He had come from Chicago at a time (1947) when the syndicate had been attempting to control racketeering in Dallas. A sheriff-elect, who was offered a bribe if he would cooperate, said Ruby was in on the scheme (as the manager of a "front"). Ruby denied it, but his ties to organized crime were evident.

6

Jack Ruby, master of cere-
monies. As a strip-club operator, Ruby was a dealer of vice,
although he stuck to the custom,
if not the letter, of the law.
Clubs like the Carousel had, by
the 1960s, replaced illegal
houses of prostitution, offering
sex on the side with b-girls,
whose union was dominated by
the mob.

A Ruby idol was Mickey Cohen,
the West Coast gangster (seen
here with stripper Candy Barr, a
mutual friend). Ruby and Cohen shared a youthful admiration for the notorious Al Capone. In Chicago, in the 1920s,
Ruby worked as an errand-boy
for Capone, and it is fair to infer
he regarded him as a role
model.

7

8

Acoustics expert Mark Weiss points to the grassy knoll as he testifies to the Committee about his finding of four shots: the first two from the Texas School Book Depository; a third from the grassy knoll; and a fourth, the fatal shot, from the Book Depository. Probability of the third: ninety-five percent plus, a number that "would not go away."

The Warren Commission, from left: Ford, Boggs, Russell, Warren, Cooper, McCloy, Dulles, and Rankin, chief counsel. While right about Oswald, they were wrong about conspiracy. In hindsight, it must be said many bad decisions were made, in particular the failure to look further into the character of Jack Ruby and his organized-crime connections.

9

At the moment of the fatal shot (above), the picket fence from where the third shot was fired is seen from across Elm Street. The motorcycle officer, Bobby W. Hargis, thought he heard shots from both the book depository and a railroad overpass ahead. Seconds earlier (below left) a movie camera recorded the motorcade as it turned from Main onto Houston (first frame of the sequence) and from Houston onto Elm. A radio on motorcycle 352, ridden by Officer H. B. McLain, transmitted during the shooting, due to a stuck microphone switch. The last frame of the sequence shows McLain heading north on Houston at about the time of the first shot. S. M. Holland, a railroadman, said he saw smoke curl from the trees on the grassy knoll, and the Newman family fell to the ground at the sound of firing, as Mr. Newman said, "from the garden behind me."

14

Seated between his brother, a Massachusetts senator, and Chairman John L. McClellan, Chief Counsel Robert F. Kennedy conducts a hearing on the Teamsters in August 1957. The investigation initially was directed at corrupt union practices, but following the Apalachin meeting in November, it was focused on the structure of organized-crime.

The first Senate inquiry into organized crime was a cross-country sweep in 1951–52 by the Kefauver Committee. The hearings, with a televised climax in New York (below), exposed the Mafia's domination of the rackets and its techniques of murder and bribery. Senator Kefauver, in 1956, won the vice-presidential nomination from Senator Kennedy.

15

16

Teamster President James R. Hoffa was a target of the McClellan Committee, and while his organized crime ties were shown in hearings, he was not successfully prosecuted. But the Kennedy Administration pressed the case, and in March 1964 he was sentenced to eight years for jury tampering. Pardoned in 1971, Hoffa was killed by the mob in 1975.

The first member of La Cosa Nostra to talk publicly was Joseph Valachi, who testified before the McClellan Committee in October and November 1963. Valachi had been a member of the Mafia family of Vito Genovese (below right), a ruthless leader whose practice of engineering mob assassinations was the chief reason for the meeting at Apalachin.

7

18

While federal investigations of organized crime were not pushed until the 1950s, local prosecutors, in rare but noteworthy instances, were dogging the mob as early as the 1930s. The most vigorous "gangbuster" was Thomas E. Dewey, shown here being sworn in as a special New York State prosecutor by Supreme Court Justice Philip J. McCook. Tapped telephones led to the arrest of over 100 prostitutes, who gave Dewey the evidence to indict Charles "Lucky" Luciano for compulsory prostitution. It happened at a time Luciano (shown being brought to appear before Judge McCook for sentencing) had reached the peak of his criminal career, having established a national commission of Mafia leaders. Luciano got 30 to 50 years, but in 1946 he was released and deported.

19

Even though Luciano confided to Florence "Cokey Flo" Brown, one of his madams (below), that he would gladly get out of prostitution, he ran 200 houses with 1,000 girls, a $12 million-a-year operation. The girls said they had been coerced by rapings and heroin.

21

20

22

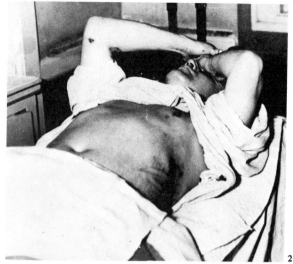

23

24

Dewey also set his sights on Arthur "Dutch Schultz" Flegenheimer (seated upper left), a bootlegger and Harlem numbers racketeer. Flegenheimer responded by issuing a contract on Dewey to Albert Anastasia, but when Luciano found out, he ordered the assassination of Flegenheimer instead. Flegenheimer was shot down, along with three henchmen, in a Newark tavern, and he died after lingering briefly in a hospital (above). Another victim of mob justice, Benjamin Siegel (left), was accused of stealing Las Vegas investment funds, which were deposited in a Swiss bank by his paramour, Virginia Hill (below). Siegel's murder was ordered at a meeting in Havana, which Luciano presided over in December 1946, and carried out on June 20, 1947, in the living room of Hill's mansion in California.

5

26

271

27

28

In 1946 the power passed from Luciano to Vito Genovese, who maintained it with vengeful brutality. On May 2, 1957, Frank Costello (left) narrowly survived an attack by a hired gunman. If Genovese was permitted to act unilaterally, complained Albert Anastasia (right), then no one was safe.

Anastasia spoke prophetic words. On October 25, 1957, in the barbershop of a New York hotel, he was blasted out of his chair by two masked gunmen. According to accounts by insiders, the Anastasia contract was awarded to Joseph Gallo by Genovese and another New York Mafia leader, Carlo Gambino.

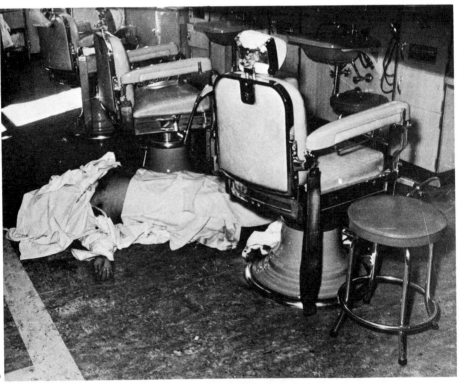

29

30

To fulfill the Anastasia contract, Gallo (above) employed a typical gangland method: a public hit with no attempt to conceal its nature. But in 1971, in the shooting of Mafia figure Joseph Colombo, Gallo employed a different technique. He saw to it that the hit was made by an outsider, Jerome Johnson (below). When Johnson, who was himself slain at the scene, was identified as a psychotic misfit, suspicion that it had been a mob hit was diverted. Authorities theorized that Gallo had been able to manipulate Johnson through a group of black hoodlums, whom he had met while in prison. Joseph Gallo was shot and killed by five Colombo men in April 1972.

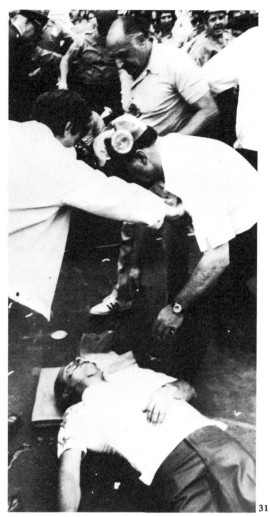

31

Joseph Colombo was shot on June 28, 1971, at the second annual rally of the Italian-American Civil Rights League, which Colombo had organized. (He considered the term "Mafia" discriminatory.) Johnson, wearing press identification and carrying cameras, approached the speakers' stand and shot Colombo five times in the head. Colombo survived five hours of brain surgery but was comatose until his death seven years later.

32

273

33

The Committee went to Havana to inquire about Castro complicity in the assassination, as well as the possible involvement of anti-Castro exiles and organized crime. At a meeting with Castro on April 2, 1978, Congressmen Preyer and Stokes are seated to the left of the Cuban president; Chief Counsel Blakey and Deputy Gary Cornwell, at right.

Havana gambling was a prized province of organized crime in the days of Batista, which was the likely reason for the murder of Albert Anastasia. On the day before he died Anastasia met with Santo Trafficante (left), the Mafia boss in Cuba. The pioneer of Havana gambling, however, was Meyer Lansky (right), an old associate of Lucky Luciano. A 1959 trip to Havana by Jack Ruby was related to Trafficante's troubles with Castro.

34

35

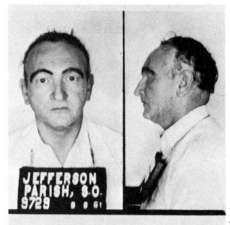

In New Orleans in the summer of 1963 Oswald drew attention by handing out pro-Castro leaflets (top left), but the identity of the man behind him was never learned. It is known that he had purchased his Mannlicher-Carcano, with which he posed before moving to New Orleans (left); and he was associated with David W. Ferrie (top right). Ferrie, who had known Oswald as a teenage air cadet and who was seen with Oswald in 1963 by reliable witnesses, worked as an investigator for Carlos Marcello, the Mafia leader in New Orleans (bottom left). In 1966 New Orleans District Attorney Jim Garrison launched an investigation of the assassination and named Ferrie, but not Marcello, as a suspect in a conspiracy. In 1967 the FBI reported that Garrison, on a visit to Las Vegas (bottom right), got a $5,000 gambling credit from a Marcello associate.

On February 7, 1960, Kennedy, then a senator but a candidate for president, was introduced by Frank Sinatra to Judith Campbell (right), and a two-year romance began. While Campbell was "dating" the President, she was in regular contact with Chicago Mafia boss Sam Giancana.

41

Sinatra was the leader of the Rat Pack, a funloving bunch of celebrities that also included actor Peter Lawford, Kennedy's brother-in-law at the time, and entertainer Sammy Davis, Jr. Gangsters like John Roselli, the Chicago mob's man on the West Coast, also ran with the Pack.

Kennedy met Campbell at the Sands in Las Vegas, whose hidden owners included underworld figures. Subsequent meetings were arranged in New York, Los Angeles, Chicago, Palm Beach, and Washington. White House telephone logs showed some seventy calls to or from Campbell during the period.

42

43

276

44

Kennedy (with Sinatra at a fund-raising dinner in Los Angeles on the eve of the 1960 Democratic convention) no doubt regarded his liaison with Campbell as harmless. He was not corrupt, as his energetic anti-organized crime program proved. But in the view of the mob, his acceptance of sexual favors made him vulnerable to retaliation.

Giancana (with girl friend Phyllis McGuire in a London nightclub) and Roselli were murdered, Giancana in 1975, Roselli in 1976. Giancana's daughter blamed the "people responsible for killing the Kennedys."

45

46

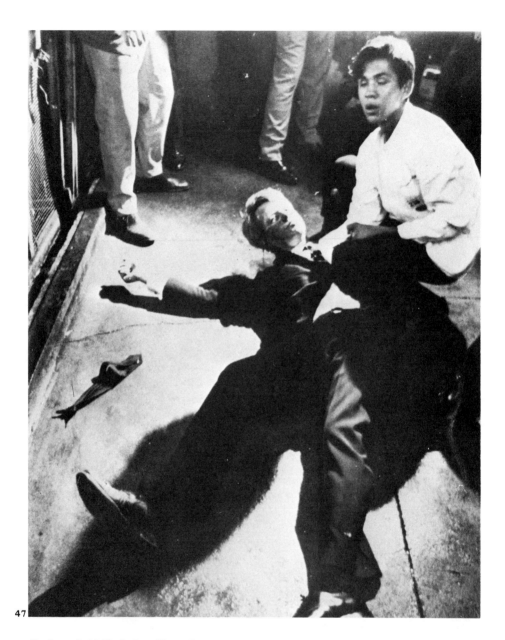

47

On June 4, 1968, Robert Kennedy was campaigning for the presidency in Los Angeles. His prospects were bright. President Johnson had announced he would not stand for reelection, and Kennedy had, that day, won the all-important California primary, as well as one in South Dakota. Kennedy was leaving the Hotel Ambassador ballroom, where he had thanked supporters, when he was struck down by a shot to the back of the head.

11

Jack Ruby: His Role Reconsidered

"I am not a gangster."

Jack Ruby
Warren Commission
Hearings, Volume V

Warren Commission Analysis

Lee Harvey Oswald was fatally shot by Jack Ruby at 11:21 A.M. on Sunday, November 24, 1963, less than forty-eight hours after President Kennedy was assassinated. As the Warren Commission observed: "[A]lmost immediately speculation arose that Ruby had acted on behalf of members of a conspiracy who had planned the killing of President Kennedy and wanted to silence Oswald." In our investigation, therefore, we recognized that the implications of the murder of Oswald were crucial to an understanding of the assassination of the President. We were able to reduce the credible alternatives to just a few. Oswald was one of two or more conspirators, which we knew to be the case, and he was killed by Ruby, also a conspirator in the assassination of the President, because other conspirators wanted Oswald silenced. A second possibility was that Ruby was not a conspirator in the assassination, but he was brought in after the fact, still to silence Oswald. Third, even though Oswald was a participant in a plot, Ruby acted alone, as he explained, out of personal anger and grief and because he wanted to save Mrs. Kennedy the agony of testifying at Oswald's trial, or, as his lawyer contended, because he was suffering from mental illness. If Ruby did act alone, for whatever reason, his killing of Oswald did not cast light on the nature of the conspiracy that brought about the President's death. If, on the other hand, it could be shown that Ruby was associated with parties who had the motive to kill the President, especially if they were parties also associated with Oswald, we would have a strong indication of the nature of the assassination conspiracy.

The Warren Commission examined Ruby's conduct and his contacts from November 21 to 24, 1963, to determine if they reflected a conspiratorial relationship with Oswald, and it found no evidence that Ruby and Oswald were even acquainted. The Commission also investigated possible Ruby associations that might have obviated the need for direct contact with Oswald. It found no Ruby ties to Cubans, either pro- or anti-Castro, and it determined he was not linked to "illegal activities with members of the organized underworld," despite some disturbing circumstantial evidence: his early life on the West Side of Chicago; rumors about why he moved to Dallas in 1947; and the nature of his work as the proprietor of a nightclub that featured striptease dancers. The Commission noted that Ruby "disclaimed that he was associated with organized-criminal activities," and it did not find reason to reject his testimony. The evidence, the Commission found, "fell short" of demonstrating that Ruby "was significantly affiliated with organized crime"; he was at worst "familiar, if not friendly," with some criminal elements, but he was not a "participant in organized-criminal activity." The Commission investigation, in short, "yielded no evidence that Ruby conspired with anyone in planning or executing the killing of Lee Harvey Oswald," and it accepted as true Ruby's explanation that his shooting of Oswald stemmed from "genuine shock and grief" and a strong affection for President Kennedy and his family.

In our evaluation, we directed our attention to Ruby's cultural background, his immediate family and associates, and his career in Chicago and Dallas, with particular emphasis on his relationship with organized crime. Ultimately, our conclusions differed from those of the Warren Commission.

The Cultural Matrix

Jane Addams, in *Twenty Years at Hull House*, wrote a vivid description of the area of Jewish settlement in Chicago that by 1910 had come to be called the West Side Ghetto. It was two miles wide and three miles long; it was hemmed in on all sides by acres of railroad tracks and a wide fringe of factories, warehouses, and commercial establishments; and it was one of the most densely populated districts in the city — 50,000 people per square mile. The settlement was centered around the market that was located where Halsted Street was crossed by Maxwell; Hull House itself stood on the corner of Halsted and Polk, ten blocks to the north.

While the outward characteristics of the West Side Ghetto could be easily sketched, its cultural significance was more subtle. It represented a transition to the New World of the essential elements of Old World ways. Centered around a closely knit family, that spoke its own language, Yiddish, a crowded market, and an Orthodox synagogue, life for the older generation changed little. But for the young, life was not the same. In the schools and on the streets they would experience a different world. Even in the ghetto there were street gangs, and they were known to engage in warfare with gangs from the adjacent areas. As time passed, the Jewish families underwent a process of acculturation, the effect of which was for them to abandon both the physical location and the cultural mindset of the West Side Ghetto.

As it was portrayed in 1928 in Louis Wirth's classic study, *The Ghetto*, the near West Side was the home of the first-generation immigrant. Lawndale, which lay to the west, was predominantly the area of second settlement. While the physical move was seldom more than three blocks, far greater distances were symbolically traversed in the relocation. In contrast to the tenements of the ghetto, Lawndale was a quiet residential zone of lower-middle-class standards. It was *Deutschland*, and its people were *Deitchuks*, because they affected German ways. They were not so particular about kosher food; they did not go to the synagogue quite so often; they patronized the central downtown district, or The Loop; and they did not speak Yiddish, except perhaps at home. (It was only a short step from the world of the *Deitchuks* to the world of the *Goyim*, the gentiles.) While most of the youth groups of Lawndale took the form of basement clubs, a tentacle of gangland influence was extended into residential areas along Roosevelt Road. Several notorious Jewish gangs — bootleggers and rumrunners, for the most part — hung out in the restaurants, poolrooms, and gambling dens. Families tended to disintegrate under the stress of contradictions that arose over behavior patterns brought home by the children, who absorbed the culture of the street from running with gangs. A gang was formed when boys, not finding a society adequate to their needs, created one of their own; and it tended, as its members grew older, to drift into habitual delinquency and crime. Games of chance turned into gambling; malicious mischief became robbery; roughhouse begot violence. Adolescence is an age of hero worship, wrote Frederic Thrasher in a seminal study of street gangs in Chicago, *The Gang*. Beginning as a truant, he becomes, as Thrasher noted: "a minor delinquent, a hoodlum, a reckless young sport, . . . an occasional criminal, and finally, if

nothing intervenes, he develops into a seasoned gangster or a professional criminal.''

What the boy learns from the gang are personal habits, familiarity
with the techniques of crime, and a marshaling of attitudes that facili-
tates delinquency of a more serious type. Gangs of boys and criminal
groups of younger and older adults merge by imperceptible gradations.
The corrupt character of the world around him plays a crucial role in
forming the character of the boy. Successful criminals and their corrupt
influence undermine moral restraints. The West Side Ghetto was the
physical and cultural world to which Jack Ruby's parents came soon
after the turn of the century, and it was the world of crime and corruption into which Jack Ruby was born.

Jack Ruby: 1911–1967

Joseph Rubenstein, Jack Ruby's father, was born in 1871 in Sokolov, a
small town near Warsaw, Poland, then under the rule of Czarist Russia.
In 1893 he joined the Russian artillery, and in 1901 his marriage to Fannie Turek Rutkowski was arranged by a professional matchmaker, a
shadchen. After serving in China, Korea, and Siberia — detesting these
places and Army life generally — Rubenstein deserted and found his
way to England and Canada, entering the United States in 1903 and settling in Chicago in 1904. He worked at carpentry in Chicago fairly
steadily until the beginning of the Depression in 1928, but he was largely unemployed thereafter.

Ruby's mother, who was born in Warsaw around 1875, followed her
husband to the United States, accompanied by two children, Hyman
and Ann, in 1904 or 1905. At home she spoke mostly Yiddish, and her
children remembered the home as kosher — "change of dishes and all
that." She was, according to her daughter Marion, "selfish, jealous, and
disagreeable," and her life with Joseph Rubenstein was a constant battle. Eventually (around the spring of 1921), Ruby's parents separated,
and Fannie's mental health suffered. In July 1937 she was committed to
Elgin State Hospital, where her case was diagnosed as deteriorating
paranoia. She died of heart failure complicated by pneumonia in 1944.
Joseph Rubenstein died in 1958.

Jack Ruby was born in 1911, probably on March 25. He was the fifth
of eight surviving children, all but two of whom were born in Chicago:
Marion in 1906, Eva in 1909, Sam in 1912, Earl in 1915, and Eileen in
1917. When Jack was born, the Rubensteins resided near 14th and
Newberry streets, four blocks south and one block west of the market at
Maxwell and Halsted streets. In 1916 they moved to 1232 Morgan
Street. Earl Ruby described the neighborhood as the "ghetto [area] . . .

of the Maxwell Street district of Chicago . . . where they . . . [had] pushcarts. . . ." Eva Ruby described it as "below the middle class, but yet it wasn't the poorest class." Jack Ruby himself termed it "the real tough part of Chicago." The family lived near the Italian section of the West Side, and there were frequent ethnic fights. Earl Ruby remembered: "We lived a half block from Roosevelt Road, and on the other side . . . was . . . Dago Town. . . ." Jack, he said, used to meet his sisters at the bus stop and walk them home to protect them.

At eleven, Ruby was referred to the Institute for Juvenile Research by the Jewish Social Service Bureau as "incorrigible at home" and for truancy. The institute recommended that he be placed in a new environment, one that would stimulate his interest and keep him off the street. On July 10, 1923, after a dependency hearing in Juvenile Court, Jack, as well as Sam, Earl, and Eileen, were placed in foster homes, where they remained for four or five years. Nevertheless, Ruby continued to run with street gangs; in fact, he went one step further. Barney Ross, a boyhood friend of Ruby who went on to become the welterweight boxing champion, recalled that he and Ruby met Al Capone at the Kit Howard Gymnasium in 1926 and that Capone had used them to deliver envelopes to downtown Chicago. (It might be fair to infer that Ruby found in Capone a role model. Mickey Cohen, the West Coast hoodlum, told a biographer that Capone had been an influence in *his* early life in Chicago.) At 16, having completed the fifth grade, Ruby quit school and took to the streets full time. Questioned by the FBI, a number of those who knew Ruby then tried to paint a picture of a well-behaved, even-tempered youth. In truth, he was quarrelsome and easily moved to violence — a "street brawler," as Art Petacque, a crime reporter for *The Chicago Sun-Times* and a Ruby acquaintance, told the FBI in 1964. Ruby was, in fact, a member of a group of young toughs who hung out at the Lawndale poolroom on Roosevelt Road and at Davey Miller's Restaurant and Health Club at 12th Street and Kedzie Avenue.

We learned that there was a distinct likelihood that Ruby had actually been a member of the Dave Miller gang, although the evidence, beyond association, was not conclusive. Petacque said he was a member, while Earl Ruby would only acknowledge that Ruby hung around Miller's restaurant. (Whatever, Ruby had in Miller another role model.) John Landisco, in a study of organized crime for the Illinois Crime Survey in 1929, described the Miller brothers — Dave, Hirschel, Max, and Harry — as deeply involved in "vice, gambling, booze, politics, and gang warfare. . . ." Hirschel Miller and Samuel "Nails" Morton were tried and acquitted (on grounds of self-defense) in the murder on August 23, 1920, of two police officers in the Beaux Arts Club, a "black and tan" cabaret at 2702 South State Street. Dave Miller was a rival of Dion

O'Bannion, an opponent of Al Capone in the Chicago "beer wars." O'Bannion personally shot, but did not kill, Dave and Max Miller on January 20, 1924, in front of the LaSalle Theater, and O'Bannion was himself killed in his flower shop by Capone gunmen eight months later. Hirschel Miller was a founder of the Chicago Hand Laundry Owners Association, a racketeer group, and Max Miller was tried once for murder but found not guilty. At the very least, Ruby was among Miller-led street fighters who tried to break up meetings of the German-American Bund in the 1930s. Earl Ruby noted: "Jack was always one to go and see if he could help break [Nazi Bund meetings] . . . up."

During the 1964 investigation Ruby's relatives and friends attempted to minimize his criminal associations and acts of violence during the early Chicago years. (His sister Eva went so far as to claim that she "knew more racketeers" than Jack did.) But their testimony, when weighed against the other evidence, rang hollow. While Ruby was away from Chicago from 1933 to 1937 (he was in San Francisco, where he sold gambling tip sheets and newspaper subscriptions), his youth, we concluded, was spent as a brawler and a street hustler who earned his living in any way possible, most often by scalping tickets to athletic events. As his older brother Hyman told the Warren Commission, "Jack never cared for no steady jobs." Some early acquaintances told the FBI in 1964 that he "seemed to be always well-off financially" and that "friends often wondered where he obtained his income." (Others said he was often broke.) There was also persuasive evidence that Ruby was a strong-arm man, a "goon," for a racket-ridden union in Chicago.

From 1937 to 1940 Ruby was connected with Local 20467 of the Scrap Iron and Junk Handlers Union, which was, according to an AFL-CIO report, "largely a shakedown operation." The report was written in 1956, as the AFL-CIO was acting to place the local in trusteeship because of mob domination. The president of the local in 1956, Paul "Red" Dorfman, had taken it over from John Martin in 1939. On December 8, 1939, Martin, who had underworld ties, shot and killed Leon Cooke, the founder and financial secretary of the local, in a dispute over funds. Martin was acquitted on grounds of self-defense. Ruby, who was hired as an organizer, denied to the Warren Commission (without being asked) that he was a member of a "goon squad," but there was evidence he was just that. The FBI learned of one incident in which Ruby pulled a gun in an argument that grew out of an organizing drive at the Lissner Paper Grading Company in Chicago. One of his fellow organizers, moreover, was Carlos Fontana, a West Side hoodlum. Ruby told the Warren Commission that he quit the union when it was taken over by a "notorious organization." While it was true that he left when Dorfman became president, it was also true that he worked for Martin, whose mob credentials were as solid as Dorfman's.

In 1941–1942 Ruby was part owner of the Spartan Novelty Company, a manufacturer of small cedar chests that contained candy and punchboards, games of chance; and in 1942–1943 he "worked out of" the Globe Auto Glass Company. During this time, according to his draft card, he was also employed by Universal Sales Company. We could not firmly establish how Ruby was occupied, but there was evidence that he was associated with Ben Zuckerman, also known as "Zuckie the Bookie." Zuckerman was the gambling kingpin of the 24th Ward on Chicago's West Side, the political base of some of the city's most powerful and corrupt bosses, including Jacob M. Arvey, who called Zuckerman his "very good friend." (Ruby's older brother Hyman was active in Arvey's organization.) In May 1943 Ruby was drafted and inducted into the U.S. Army Air Forces. When he was discharged in February 1946, he went to work for his brother Earl, whose Earl Products Company, like Spartan Novelty, produced cedar chests and punchboards. Ruby left Earl Products in 1947 to move to Dallas.

The Move to Dallas

On November 24, 1963, Jack Wilner, a crime reporter for *The Chicago Daily News*, told the FBI he had heard that Jack Ruby had played a role in an effort by the mob in 1946 to take over the rackets in the Dallas area. It involved, according to Wilner's "syndicate sources," the attempted bribery of a newly elected sheriff, Steve Guthrie. On December 7, 1963, the FBI interviewed Guthrie, who said that shortly after he won the Democratic primary in July 1946, he was contacted on a Dallas golf course by a man named Paul Roland Jones, who asked if he would like to make "some big money." Dallas at the time was wide open — gambling and prostitution were thriving, and Jones said he represented the Chicago syndicate, which was planning to gain control of them. Ruby's name came up several times in the "negotiations," Guthrie said, for he had been designated to open a "fabulous" club, which was to be a front for syndicate gambling operations. With the help of the Texas Rangers, Guthrie recorded a number of his conversations with Jones and other mobsters from Chicago. The FBI reviewed transcripts of the recordings (two out of twenty-two original recordings were missing in 1963), and it could find no discussion of Ruby. The Warren Commission took testimony from other law enforcement officials, who did not remember hearing Ruby named in the conversations, and from Jones, who said he had not mentioned Ruby. The Commission decided, therefore, that Guthrie was mistaken.

We closely reexamined the attempted bribery of Sheriff Guthrie in 1946. We confirmed that Jones had offered the bribe, and we learned he had introduced Guthrie to Pat Manno, a West Side Chicago policy operator and close associate of Anthony Accardo. We also learned from George Butler, a retired Dallas police lieutenant, some of the substance of the Jones-Guthrie talks. "Wilson . . . [was] . . . already in the bag," Jones said, according to Butler (Will Wilson had just won the Democratic primary for District Attorney), and Eddie Vogel (termed by the California Crime Commission in 1949 as "near the top of the slot machine racket [and] a member of the Capone syndicate") had "put up $168,000 to elect [Beauford] Jester for governor and Guthrie for sheriff." Finally, Butler told us, he was introduced to Dominic Joseph "Butch" Blasi, a Chicago hoodlum, though he was told that Blasi was Murray Humphreys, the principal fixer of the Chicago syndicate. Arrests were eventually made, and at Christmastime 1946 Jones and others (but not Blasi) were indicted. They were convicted in early 1947 of attempted bribery. Jones was sentenced to three years, though he was released on bail pending appeal.

We determined that Wilner's lead was not entirely without foundation, for Ruby had close ties to individuals involved in the bribery attempt. He arrived in Dallas about June 1947 to assist his sister Eva in opening and running the Singapore Club, a night spot that evidently was frequented by Jones and his co-defendants, who were out on bail. But George Butler was certain that Ruby had had no part in the takeover effort. "Ruby didn't amount to anything," Butler said, "but he was trying to get in with them." Jones himself acknowledged to the FBI in 1964 that he had represented "syndicate" interests in jukeboxs and slot machines in Dallas in the 1940s, and he named some of the mob figures he worked with at the time: Sam Yaras, Nick DeJohn, Joseph and Rocco Fischetti, and Eddie Vogel. He also admitted he had met Ruby at the Congress Hotel in Chicago. (We learned from the U.S. Bureau of Narcotics that Ruby had, for a period in 1946–1947, kept a regular room, number 6–142, at the Congress Hotel.) Jones said he was in Chicago in 1946 (hotel records indicated it was in 1947) for a meeting with Paul Labriola and James Weinberg, "to discuss the slot machine and policy business." (Labriola and Weinberg were garroted, and their bodies were found stuffed in the trunk of a car in 1954.) Jones said that while he was in the hotel lobby one day, he was introduced to Ruby by Labriola and Weinberg, who, they said, was "O.K." When Ruby learned Jones was from Dallas, he asked him about Weldon Duncan, a chiropractor who was going with his sister Eva. Jones said he told Ruby that Duncan had a "bad reputation." Ruby said he was going to Dallas to straighten his sister out, and he asked Jones for help. Labriola and

Weinberg, according to Jones's statement to the FBI in 1964, "repeated that Ruby was all right and urged . . . [him] to help. . . ." Jones said that he did help Ruby when he got to Dallas, while there was no concrete evidence, any more than there had been from the earlier investigations of the FBI and Warren Commission, that Ruby was actually involved in the attempt by the Chicago syndicate to take control of gambling and prostitution in Dallas, our investigation did determine what probably happened.

On November 24, 1963, from an informant, the FBI heard another account of why Ruby left Chicago in 1947, one the Warren Commission did not mention, if it was aware of it. A man named Zuckerman, the informant said, a gambler friend of Ruby, had been shot and killed in the mid-1940s for not giving Leonard Patrick a cut of his bookmaking proceeds. Subsequently, Ruby was told by Patrick to leave town because he was operating a handbook without permission. Patrick reportedly warned Ruby that if he did not leave town, "he would get what Zuckerman got." In the 1964 investigation the FBI questioned Patrick, who denied the story. Ruby's brothers Hyman and Earl and his sister Eva all acknowledged that Leonard Patrick had been a neighborhood acquaintance, but each insisted he was neither a friend nor a business associate of their brother. Eva elaborated to the Warren Commission. She had known racketeers, "gambling men," she called them, who "ran districts in Chicago." She also recalled some who "in the early forties . . . were, as you say, bumped off. . . ." Eva's denial that Ruby knew these individuals was hard to accept in light of what we learned.

We probed the informant's tip more deeply than the record indicated the FBI or the Warren Commission had, finding out as much as we could about Leonard Patrick's career in the Chicago rackets. He had been convicted of bank robbery in 1933 and had gone on to build a reputation as one of the most notorious hoodlums on Chicago's West Side. By the late 1940s it was not possible, according to FBI informants, to operate in the Roosevelt Road area unless you had an "O.K." from Lenny Patrick. In 1946 the FBI was told that Patrick and Dave Yaras, who were described as "torpedos" for the syndicate, had, on January 14, 1944, taken part in the killing of Ben Zuckerman. Patrick and Yaras were also prime suspects in the shotgunning, on June 24, 1946, of James M. Ragen, the owner of Continental Press Service, whose death three months later gave the Chicago syndicate control of the only nationwide racetrack wire service. Moreover, Patrick was said by an FBI informant to have taken part in the kidnapping of Edward Jones, a policy racketeer whose abduction was engineered by Sam Giancana as part of the syndicate's move to take over the policy racket in Chicago. In 1955 Patrick was reported by *The Chicago Tribune* to be one of Giancana's two top lieutenants; and in 1963, the FBI was told, he was in charge of gambling operations in Lawndale. Patrick and Yaras were linked by an informant to the killing, on February 13, 1963, of City Alderman Benjamin F. Lewis.

While we believed that Patrick may well have been responsible for the murder of Zuckerman and knew, as well, of Ruby's reported ties to "Zuckie the Bookie," we also were aware that Ruby was in the Army in 1944 and did not move to Dallas until 1947, so his departure from Chicago did not appear to be an immediate result of Zuckerman's murder. On the other hand, Ruby told people in Dallas, who in turn told the FBI in 1963, he had been "exiled" from Chicago, and James H. Dolan, one of Ruby's Dallas associates, told us in 1977 it was a "common story" that "Ruby had been run out of Chicago by the mob." (Dolan had more than a common reason to know, since he himself had an extensive criminal background.) Another friend of Ruby, Lawrence V. Meyers, told us in 1978 that Ruby had once confided to him he had been a "runner for somebody in the numbers racket" in Chicago.

When the FBI interviewed Patrick on November 28, 1963, he acknowledged having known Ruby as "a neighborhood chum," but he insisted Ruby had never run a "book," and he denied that he forced Ruby to leave Chicago. "No matter how much you investigate, you'll never learn nothing, as he never had nothing to do with nothing," was how Patrick put it. He was not much more helpful when we took his deposition in 1978. He said Ruby had lived "in the next block from me" and that they "used to hang around on the West Side." He acknowledged he had heard that Ruby had organized-crime connections when he was with the scrap union, but he was certain Ruby had not been involved in bookmaking. Patrick maintained he knew nothing about Zuckerman's death, and he repeated his denial that he had ordered Ruby to leave Chicago.

The Warren Commission, while conceding that Patrick was a witness of questionable dependability, relied on his statements to the FBI in 1963 in finding that Ruby had no organized-crime connections and in concluding that there was "no evidence" he had ever "participated in organized-criminal activity." From our review of the FBI investigation, as well as our own, we saw no reason to accept the Commission's position. We found it a distinct possibility that Ruby had been associated with Zuckerman in gambling and was told to leave Chicago by syndicate figures, who used the Zuckerman murder to add force to the expulsion.

The Strip Club Operator

Prostitution is a sordid aspect of American history. Open bawdy houses

were a common sight in metropolitan centers in the late nineteenth
century, in Chicago particularly, where they were a staple of the economy. The turn of the century saw nationwide development of a white
slave trade, as newly arrived immigrants not only created a market for
prostitution, but they also provided the human material of the trade. In
Chicago, regular barracks were maintained for "breaking" new girls by
means of repeated rape and narcotics. Once their spirits were shattered,
the girls were sold at auction, the better-looking ones going to the plush
houses, the rest relegated to the cribs and dance halls. The enactment of
the Mann Act in 1910 put a stop to the national trade of human flesh,
and reform movements at the state and local level signaled the extinc-
tion of the brothel, the cheap dance hall, and the workingman's stand-
up saloon. But there soon was a substitute for the sin palaces of the past.
It was the strip joint and sit-down bar — less blatant perhaps, but a
direct descendant, and organized crime's control of the traffic in alcohol
and sex continued. Control that had been clearly visible came to be
exercised by more subtle means, often through racket-dominated
unions, of which none was more corrupt than the American Guild of
Variety Artists, or AGVA.

In June 1963 the Senate Permanent Subcommittee on Investigations,
whose chairman was John L. McClellan of Arkansas, published a report
that reviewed the nature and scope of strip joints, particularly as they involved corrupt unions and organized crime. Daniel P. Sullivan, the
operating director of the Crime Commission of Greater Miami,
described for the McClellan Committee the typical strip club as a "pool
of illegitimacy" and "the modern aspect of the vice and prostitution
racket." In other testimony the clubs, in contrast to what they appeared
to be, were exposed for what they were. They were purportedly legitimate show business establishments operated under a state liquor license; they advertised in the newspapers; they had their shows
reviewed by the amusement editor; they had a contract with a union,
typically AGVA. Yet there was ample evidence that they were the scene
of abuses that would not have been tolerated by police in the old-
fashioned brothels: bills were padded; drinks were substituted (cheap
wine for champagne); patrons were robbed. Strip clubs were, in a word,
"clip-joints," where obscenity and lewdness were common. Sex was in-
discriminately offered by "B-girls," who made improper advances by
hand motions and conversation, and oral sex was sold in dark booths.
There were other illicit practices: police and liquor control agents were
corrupted; union contracts were flaunted; and there was a circuit re-
miniscent of the routes of white slave traffic. As Ovid Demaris vividly
pictured it in *Captive City*, a study of organized crime and corruption in

Chicago, girls were passed from club to club in New York, Miami, Houston, Dallas, Phoenix, Las Vegas, Denver, and Seattle.

The McClellan Committee attributed a major role in the exploitation of the women who worked in strip joints to AGVA, which was, in 1963, a union of actors, singers, dancers, and other types of entertainers. While there were national officers of AGVA who served without compensation, day-to-day business was managed by a salaried national administrative secretary and the staffs of salaried professionals in the branch offices. The membership of AGVA in 1963 was 13,000, and it ranged from celebrities like Bob Hope, Bing Crosby, and Dinah Shore to the unfortunate young women who had been lured into the "exotic" dancing trade. There was another striking aspect of AGVA in 1963: many of the branch offices — at times, even the national headquarters — were under the control of organized crime. For example, Jack Irving, the manager of the Chicago branch of AGVA from 1940 until he was named national administrative secretary in 1953 (a job he held until 1955), was tightly tied to the Chicago syndicate. The national administrative secretary in 1963, Jackie Bright, acknowledged to the McClellan Committee that Irving's "claim to fame was his handling of the Chicago office," but at the same time he "was doing business with the mob. . . ." The McClellan Committee noted that AGVA branches were, by and large, content to collect initiation fees, dues, and welfare contributions, exerting little enforcement of withholding taxes, since they would reveal not only the legal income of the women, but also what they were making (and sharing with the owners) from "B-drinking" and prostitution. (Tax records were virtually nonexistent, since most clubs were operated on a cash basis.) Finally, AGVA failed, according to the McClellan Committee, to perform the basic function of a labor organization: national headquarters and the local branches were little more than fiefdoms of the salaried managers, whose tenure was based on corruption and who cared little about the interests of the members. "The conclusion [was] inescapable," the McClellan Committee wrote, "that . . . the union officials' prime objective has been [to be] . . . nothing more than a dues collecting agency."

From the time he arrived in Dallas in 1947 until he murdered Oswald in 1963, Jack Ruby was a strip club operator. Ruby did two things when he first got to Dallas: he assisted his sister Eva on a criminal charge (a $2,700 swindle) that was pending against her but was eventually dropped; and he helped her run the Singapore Club, a dance hall she had purchased. Then, when Eva moved to California a short time later, he took over full-time management of the Singapore, changing its name to the Silver Spur, which he continued to run until he sold it in 1955. In

1953 he bought an interest in the Vegas Club, which was housed in a cheap one-story masonry building in an outlying semicommercial district of Dallas. Ruby's partner in the Vegas, Joe Bonds, also known as Joe Lecurto, was typical of Ruby's business associates.

In 1948 Bonds, who like Ruby, had come from Chicago, and Ralph Paul, a Ruby financial backer later on, bought the Blue Bonnet Bar. Seth Kantor, the author of *Who Was Jack Ruby?,* described the Blue Bonnet as "a notorious downtown hangout for criminals, on the first floor of a fleabag hotel." The Bonds-Ruby partnership was turbulent. For example, the FBI was told in 1963 of an incident in which Ruby chased Bonds with a pistol, firing it but not hitting him. When Bonds went to prison (he was convicted in 1954 of white slavery and of sodomy with a fifteen-year-old girl), Ruby continued to run the Vegas Club and still owned it in November 1963, though it was being run by his sister Eva, who had returned from California in 1959. In an FBI report dated August 11, 1953, Vincent Lee, the AGVA representative in Dallas, was quoted as saying Jack Ruby and Joe Bonds always carried pistols and "ran with" James Robert Todd. Todd, we found, had an arrest record for burglary, transporting explosives, and murder. We were unable to develop more on Ruby's relationshp with Todd, who in 1978 would tell us only that he and Ruby had a "passing acquaintanceship." Todd also acknowledged he had been a "casual acquaintance" of Joseph Civello and Sam and Joseph Campisi, prominent organized-crime figures in Dallas.

In 1959 Ruby entered into a partnership with Joe Slater to establish the Sovereign Club at 1312½ Commerce Street, a "private club," meaning that under Texas law it could sell hard liquor by the bottle to "members." But it did not succeed. Ruby's temperament was not suited to catering to the demands of a higher-class clientele, and Slater, whose experience had been running a club that attracted homosexuals, withdrew his investment. Ruby turned to Bonds's former partner, Ralph Paul, who put up the money Ruby needed on the condition that the name be changed to the Carousel and that the club be converted into a strip joint. Ruby's management of the club was hardly the model of civility. As the Warren Commission observed, he tended "to dominate his employees, frequently resorted to violence in dealing with them, publicly embarrassed them, sometimes attempted to cheat them of their pay, and delayed paying their salaries." As Ruby's underworld friend Paul Roland Jones put it, the Carousel was a "real clip joint." Thomas Palmer, the AGVA representative in Dallas in November 1963, told the Warren Commission that the McClellan Committee investigation had made the union "quite sensitive to certain practices," and he had been collecting affidavits to show that Ruby was violating union rules with respect to B-drinking, welfare fund payments, and the treatment of his employees. A more dramatic statement was made by one of the girls herself, who was hired by Ruby when she was 17. She was quoted by Gary Cartwright in *The Texas Monthly*:

> Jack would tell us to come on to the customers, promise them anything — of course he didn't mean for us to deliver, but sometimes we did on our own time. The price for a bottle of cheap champagne (the label covered with a bar towel) was anywhere from fifty to seventy-five dollars. We'd sit with the customer as long as the bottle lasted, drinking out of what we called spit glasses — frosted glasses of ice water. We worked for tips or whatever we could steal.

Many of Ruby's girls came from Chicago, as the FBI was told in 1963 by Irving "Buzzy" Rifkin, manager of Le Bistro, a nightclub on the Near North Side, which was controlled at the time by Noss Prio. Prio was identified by Joseph Valachi as one of the seven "top-power" hoodlums in Chicago.

In keeping with his street-brawling days in Chicago, Ruby was his own bouncer, and on some fifteen occasions he beat with his fists, blackjacked, or pistol-whipped unruly patrons of his clubs. Ruby's violence was not restricted to his work as a bouncer, for often he would beat people who were not his customers. The Warren Commission found that a typical Ruby victim was "drunk, female, or otherwise incapable of successfully resisting Ruby's attack." Ruby "was often malicious," the Commission noted, and he was frequently in trouble with the law. He was arrested eight times in fourteen years for a variety of offenses that included disturbing the peace, carrying a concealed weapon, and assault. Nevertheless, his most severe penalty was forfeiture of a $35 bond.

Paul Roland Jones told the FBI in 1964 that "very probably Ruby . . . had to make some kind of payoff to operate the 'strip shows' at his nightclubs," otherwise he would not have been able to put on such "raw shows." Concrete proof of payoffs was not turned up by the Warren Commission, or by us, but there was ample evidence that Ruby gave policemen favors in the form of reduced prices, as well as free soft drinks and coffee. We thought it likely, given the corrupt nature of his operation, that outright bribes were paid, noting the testimony of Joe Bonds to the FBI in 1963. Ruby, said Bonds, made "women available to [police] officers. . . ."

Ruby in Havana

Although the Warren Commission conceded there was "some uncertainty" about a trip Ruby took to Cuba in 1959, it found nothing "sinister" about it. Ruby told the Commission in 1964 that he made an "eight-day" visit to Havana "in August 1959," to visit Lewis J. McWillie, a friend whom he said he "idolized." Ruby further described McWillie as a "key man" at the Tropicana, a Havana nightclub and casino. On December 21, 1963, Ruby told the FBI that he had not gone to Cuba "since or before" the August 1959 trip. The FBI also talked to McWillie in 1963, and he backed up Ruby's story of a one-week Cuban "vacation."

The evidence — even that available to the Warren Commission — hardly supported the Commission's conclusions. In fact, the carefully worded final report did not reflect the attitude of the staff lawyers responsible for the Ruby aspect of the investigation. In memorandums dated March 19 and April 1, 1964, Leon D. Hubert, Jr., and Burt W. Griffin tried to convince the Commission it had "substantial evidence" that there was more to Ruby's Cuban connection than he was admitting. On March 19 Hubert and Griffin wrote: "The number and length of Ruby's stays in Cuba are not entirely clear. Ruby admits having been in Cuba only once: in 1959 for about 10 days. However, records of the Immigration and Naturalization Service show that Ruby flew to Havana from Miami on the night of September 12, 1959, and returned to New Orleans on September 13, 1959. Ruby has not explained this trip, unless it is the trip to which Ruby admits." Commission General Counsel J. Lee Rankin and Howard P. Willens, a principal assistant, were, however, opposed to an extensive investigation of Ruby's trip to Cuba. "These Cuban pursuits represented some kind of bottomless pit," Willens told us in 1977, adding, ". . . our investigation had to be wrapped up." The Hubert-Griffin memorandums did result in additional investigation by the FBI, but it was limited largely to reinterviewing witnesses. The outstanding questions were not resolved, such as one posed by Seth Kantor in *Who Was Jack Ruby?* In light of the "turnaround" trip to Havana on September 12 and 13, Kantor wondered if Ruby might not have been serving as a "courier." Other questions were raised about organized-crime connections Ruby might have had in Cuba. Was he, it was fair to ask in view of his friendship with McWillie, associated with syndicate gambling figures such as Santo Trafficante, Jr., the Mafia leader in Havana? Interestingly, it was during the period of Ruby's 1959 visit (or visits) to Cuba that Trafficante, who had been imprisoned by the Castro government, was released and ordered out of the country.

In our investigation we established beyond reasonable doubt that Ruby lied repeatedly and willfully to the FBI and the Warren Commission about the number of trips he made to Cuba and their duration. It was, we concluded, an obvious effort to conceal the truth. It was clear, for example, that the trips were not social jaunts; their purpose, we were persuaded, was to courier something, probably money, into or out of Cuba. We were not able to establish quite so positively the nature of Ruby's association with Trafficante, although the evidence indicated strongly that an association existed and that Ruby's trip was related to Trafficante's detention and release. We came to believe that Ruby's trips to Cuba were, in fact, organized-crime activities.

When Fidel Castro took control of Cuba on January 1, 1959, he was hailed as a champion of the people, a leader of a free and democratic Cuba; but to the gambling interests the success of his revolution was bad news. Both McWillie and Trafficante told us how their fortunes turned sour. McWillie said he arrived one morning at the Tropicana, where he managed the casino: "[T]hey stuck a gun in my stomach," he said, "and I gave them the keys and turned around and walked off." "[I]t was a bad time to be around there," said Trafficante, claiming that Castro's men raided his apartment and tore up his furniture. "They used to come and get me at nighttime," he continued, "[and] take me out to the woods, trying to [get me] to tell where I had my money . . . until finally I went into hiding." Castro at first closed the casinos down, but several months later he ordered them reopened to reduce unemployment. As Trafficante put it: "You either had to open up or . . . go to jail."

We were only able to infer from circumstantial evidence the relevance of Ruby's trips to Cuba to Castro's gradual prohibition of gambling and the detention of Trafficante and other organized-crime figures. Nevertheless, what we could tell from the picture that was beginning to appear — like a nearly complete jigsaw puzzle — was quite enlightening. The pieces of the puzzle had been shaped from a variety of sources. We had Ruby's statements to the FBI and Warren Commission, for what they were worth. We had the testimony of other witnesses: McWillie, Trafficante, a former gunrunner named Robert McKeown, and the Cuban prison official who ran the detention camp where Trafficante was held. We also had background information on the people involved — law enforcement files and other materials. But most important, we had the documentation of Ruby's activities: airline records, Cuban government tourist cards, a record of Ruby's contacts with an FBI agent in Dallas, and the access records of Ruby's safe-deposit box in a Dallas bank.

In his interview with the FBI on December 21, 1963, Ruby said that "at a time when Cuba was popular" he had read of a man in the

Houston area who had run guns to Castro. Ruby said he telephoned the man, whose name he did not recall, to propose selling jeeps to the Castro government, but nothing came of it. FBI agents in Houston located Robert McKeown, who had been convicted of conspiracy to smuggle arms to Cuba in October 1958. McKeown said that about a week after Castro came to power he got a call from a "Rubenstein," who wanted to get "three individuals out of Cuba who were being held there by Castro." The man said, according to McKeown, that there would be a payment for their release — "$5,000 for each person." The caller added that "a person in Las Vegas . . . would put up the money." McKeown told the FBI he had indicated an interest, but he had demanded $5,000 up front. The caller said he would check with his Las Vegas contact, and that was the last McKeown heard from him. About three weeks later an individual McKeown identified for the FBI as Jack Ruby came to discuss with him the possible sale of jeeps to Castro, although, according to McKeown, nothing came of that proposition either. We interviewed McKeown in 1976, and he furnished us with a newspaper clipping about himself dated January 3, 1959. "Gunrunner Hails Castro Victory," the headline read. McKeown reasoned, and we agreed, that this article had led Ruby to him.

We were unable to determine the identity of the three Las Vegas individuals whose release from a Cuban prison McKeown was supposedly asked to secure. Lewis McWillie had not been detained, so he would not have been one of them. The Cuban government identified for us some of the organized-crime figures involved in the casinos, in addition to Trafficante, who had been picked up and placed in an "immigration camp." They included Guiseppe de George, Charles Tourine, Jr., Jake Lansky, Lucien Rivard, Dino Cellini, and Henry Saavedra. Adequate records were not kept, however, so we were unable to determine the exact periods of detention for each one of them, though it was known that Trafficante was detained from June 6 to August 18, 1959. Trafficante and the others were kept at Trescornia, a minimum-security camp outside Havana.

Charles W. Flynn, a special agent of the FBI, reported that he was contacted on March 11, 1959, by Jack Ruby, who said he wished to assist the FBI by supplying criminal information on a confidential basis. Flynn opened a "potential criminal informant" file, or PCI, on Ruby, and he met with him eight times between April and October 1959, which covered the period of Ruby's trips to Cuba. On November 6, 1959, however, Flynn closed Ruby's PCI file, because Ruby had not been particularly helpful. (Ruby's PCI relationship with the FBI, which did not become public until 1975, occasioned speculation with sinister overtones that were not, it turned out, justified.) We carefully reviewed Ruby's PCI file, and, on November 16, 1977, we questioned Flynn, who was unable to shed any light on why Ruby had contacted him in the first place. Ruby could, of course, have contacted the FBI with no ulterior motive, and it could have been wholly unrelated to his Cuban activities, which, incidentally, he never discussed with Flynn. We believed, however, that Ruby's behavior was consistent with the pattern of seasoned offenders, who often cultivate a relationship with a law enforcement agency during a period when they are engaging in a criminal activity in the hope that, if they are caught, they can use the relationship to secure immunity from prosecution. We were, of course, unable to establish Ruby's reasoning with certainty, but we did establish from the Ruby-Flynn contacts fixed points in time of Ruby's presence in Dallas, which, along with the safe-deposit box records, added to our understanding of Ruby's activities in the late summer of 1959.

On April 27, 1959, Ruby rented safe-deposit box 488 at the Mercantile State Bank in Dallas, and from then until March 1961, according to the signature cards, he used the box ten times, six of which were between May and October 1959. (When the box was opened by court order on December 3, 1963, it was empty. Further, there was no record of another safe-deposit box in Ruby's name during the period he lived in Dallas.) While Ruby was not questioned by the FBI or the Warren Commission about his safe-deposit box, we found it reasonable to infer its rental was in some way connected to his activities in Cuba.

Ruby entered the box on May 7, 1959, and soon thereafter, though the date cannot be fixed with certainty, he gave to Elaine Mynier, a mutual friend of Ruby and McWillie, who was on her way to Cuba, a note and asked her to give it to McWillie. As Mynier explained to the FBI, it was a "short written message in code consisting of letters and numbers that included the word 'arriving.' " She also said that Ruby directed her to tell McWillie that "Sparky from Chicago is coming." When he was questioned by the FBI in 1963, McWillie said he knew Elaine Mynier and that she had visited Cuba, but he denied that she had delivered a message to him. He said there was no need to use Mynier as a courier, since Ruby could have telephoned him. (McWillie told us in 1978, however, there was "no way" he could call Ruby, ". . . because every call was monitored in Havana. . . .") We asked McWillie if Ruby had made an effort to help organized-crime figures who had been detained, and he answered that to his knowledge Ruby took no action on their behalf. Neither the Warren Commission nor the FBI questioned Ruby about the message transmitted via Elaine Mynier or about the possibility that Ruby assisted Trafficante and the other detainees.

From May 22 to July 20, 1959, Ruby used the safe-deposit box six times. In July or August, according to Seth Kantor, Ruby had dinner at a restaurant at Love Field in Dallas with Pedro and Martin Fox, the owners of record of the Tropicana, a Havana nightclub and casino. (Drug Enforcement Administration files indicated that the Fox brothers were involved in the drug traffic as well as gambling.) Ruby, in fact, volunteered to the Warren Commission that he had had dinner with the Foxes at a time when they were still living in Cuba, explaining they had come to Dallas "to collect a debt." (McWillie told us that the Fox brothers stayed in Cuba for a while after Castro took over, then fled to Miami. Trafficante told us that while he was in Trescornia, the Foxes were trying "their best to get me out.") Ruby also told the Warren Commission that a Dallas attorney, David McCord, was at the dinner. McCord ackowledged to us on September 28, 1978, that he had attended the dinner, but the name of the brothers was Guadano, not Fox. (McCord might not have been the most reliable witness. According to Kantor, he abandoned his law practice rather than face disbarment for a shady securities transaction. The only other party to the dinner, another lawyer, Alfred E. McLane, was killed in an automobile accident in 1963. The Fox brothers had also died by the time of our investigation, but we did learn that after they moved to Miami from Havana, they ran *bolita* for Trafficante.) Though the dinner remained a mystery, it logically could have been related to the plight of the imprisoned gamblers. As Trafficante told us, the Foxes were trying "their best to get me out."

On August 8, 1959, Ruby flew to Cuba from New Orleans, listing the Capri Hotel Casino as his destination on his Cuban tourist card. (We authenticated his signature on the card.) On August 21 Ruby entered his safe-deposit box in Dallas; on August 31 he met with FBI Agent Flynn; and on September 4 he entered his bank box again. According to his Cuban tourist card, however, he did not leave Cuba until September 11, 1959. In 1963 three American tourists from Chicago told the FBI they had seen Ruby in Havana around Labor Day 1959, from September 5 to 7. They said Ruby had engaged them in conversation at the Tropicana, told them he was also from Chicago, and that he ran a nightclub in Dallas. That Ruby was in Cuba over the Labor Day weekend was corroborated by a postcard, dated September 8, that he sent to a girl friend in Dallas, Alice Nichols. He wrote that he was staying at the Fosca Building, which was consistent with his testimony to the FBI and Warren Commission and with a deposition we took from McWillie in 1978. Cuban tourist records also indicated that Ruby entered the country on September 12 and left again on September 13; U.S. immigration records showed that Ruby flew to Havana from Miami on the 12th and returned to New Orleans on the 13th.

From what were at first separate fragments of evidence, we were able to piece the puzzle together. Ruby evidently returned to Dallas after first going to Cuba on August 8 (though, for some reason, Cuban Immigration did not record his departure). He used his safe-deposit box on August 21 and September 4, and he met with FBI Agent Flynn on August 31. Sometime before the Labor Day weekend (though, again, Cuban Immigration did not record it), Ruby returned to Havana. He flew to Miami on September 11, returned to Havana on September 12, and reentered the United States again on September 13, at New Orleans. (Ruby's turnaround trip was corroborated by Meyer Panitz, a friend of both Ruby and McWillie, in a statement to the FBI in 1964. Panitz, a bookmaker, said that in the summer of 1959 he got a phone call from McWillie saying that Ruby was in Miami, and Panitz recalled actually seeing Ruby in Miami on two occasions, presumably on September 11 or 12.) The trip to Cuba that Ruby and McWillie were willing to acknowledge was, we were forced to assume, the eight-day "jaunt" from September 4 to 12, leaving two trips unexplained, the earlier one in August and the "turnaround" on September 11 to 13.

We were left with no alternative to the conclusion that Ruby lied about the time and duration of his trips to Cuba, so it was also likely that he lied about their purpose. The purpose, which surely was not social, as Ruby claimed, was what interested us the most.

Ruby told the FBI in 1963 that while in Cuba he remained in Havana "except to go to a small area on one occasion with one of the Fox brothers," thus establishing that he was in contact with the Foxes in Cuba. McWillie told us in 1978 that Ruby was at the Tropicana "every night that he was in Havana" and that he "introduced" him to Pedro and Martin Fox. While McWillie, therefore, confirmed a contact between Ruby and the proprietors of the Tropicana, his claim to have introduced them was inconsistent with the report that Ruby already knew the Fox brothers and had met them for dinner in July or August in Dallas. McWillie's account also contradicted a statement by Ruby to the Warren Commission in 1964. To explain why he was detained momentarily by Cuban customs officials on his trip to Havana, he said he was carrying a photograph of the Fox brothers that had been taken at the Vegas Club when they were in Dallas. According to Ruby, McWillie had known of the incident, for he told Ruby later that Cuban customs had "never [done] this to anyone before." We had to conclude, therefore, that either Ruby had lied to the Warren Commission, which we found unlikely, or that McWillie had lied to us when he said he "introduced'' them. It could not have been an honest mistake on McWillie's part, and we doubted he had introduced Ruby to the Fox brothers, not realizing they were already acquainted. McWillie knew Ruby too well: the "whole time he was [in Cuba] he was running around with me except when he went to bed,'' McWillie testified.

We asked McWillie if he knew that Trafficante was under detention in 1959 and if he had gone to the prison camp to visit him. Yes, McWillie acknowledged, he had known of Trafficante's detention; and he had gone to the camp, but it was to see another inmate. McWillie would only concede that Trafficante "could have been there" at the time of his visit. Further, he emphatically denied that Ruby had known Trafficante. McWillie also told us he knew nothing about Ruby's travels on September 11 to 13 from Havana to Miami to Havana to New Orleans, and he assured us that he would have known about the turnaround trip had it occurred. It was evident to us that an understanding of Ruby's activities in Cuba depended in large measure on an evaluation of McWillie.

Lewis J. McWillie was born May 4, 1908, in Kansas City, Missouri. He resided in Dallas from 1940 to 1958, and he acknowledged to us in a deposition in 1978 that he was acquainted with Joseph Civello and Sam and Joseph Campisi, who were important organized-crime figures in Dallas. He also knew Sam Yaras, who had "slot machines" in Dallas, as McWillie put it. In 1941 and 1942 McWillie worked at the Blue Bonnet Hotel; then at the Top of the Hill Terrace, an illegal gambling club in Arlington, Texas; and he ran the Four Deuces, also an illegal gambling house, in Fort Worth. In September 1958 he moved to Cuba to manage the casino at the Tropicana for the Fox brothers. (Another of McWillie's duties for the Foxes in 1958 and 1959, according to his 1978 deposition, was to take money to Miami and deposit it in the Pan American Bank, an interesting admission in light of Ruby's turnaround trip to Miami.) After the Tropicana was closed by the Cuban government, McWillie moved to the Capri Hotel where, from May 1960 to January 2, 1961, he was the pit boss in the casino. (McWillie claimed to the FBI in 1964 and to us in 1978 that he did not know the identity of the owners of the Capri at the time, one of whom, according to a variety of FBI organized-crime sources, was Trafficante. We could only conclude that McWillie had reason to conceal his relationship with Trafficante.) In 1961 McWillie went to work as a pit boss at the Cal-Neva Lodge in Lake Tahoe, Nevada, where Sam Giancana had a substantial hidden interest, and he later worked at the Horsehoe Inn in Reno, which was run by Benny Binion, a Dallas racketeer who moved to Nevada at the time the Chicago mob was trying to take over in Dallas. (There was one last item about McWillie that we learned from his testimony and from

Ruby's, though there were details in the two versions that could not be reconciled: on one occasion and perhaps two, while McWillie was in either Cuba or Nevada, he used Ruby to obtain guns for him.)

Having reviewed McWillie's background, we realized we could attach little credence to what he had to say, and there was yet another reason not to believe McWillie's account of the Ruby trip to Cuba. He told the FBI in 1964 there had been no "ulterior motive" for the trip; he had simply decided that Ruby had been "working hard" and "needed a rest." He bought the tickets in Havana, he said, because they were cheaper there. When we talked to McWillie in 1977 and deposed him in 1978, his explanation had changed. The Fox brothers were looking for new business, he said, and Ruby knew Tony Zoppi, an amusements columnist for a Dallas newspaper. The idea was for Ruby and Zoppi both to come to Havana, so Zoppi could write a column that would promote gambling in Cuba. The Fox brothers paid for the airline tickets, said McWillie, who produced a letter from Zoppi to corroborate his new explanation for Ruby's trip. He said he had simply forgotten to tell the FBI about Zoppi. When we talked to Zoppi, he affirmed that a trip to Cuba had been planned, but he did not go. He went instead to Las Vegas to cover an appearance at the Sands of Frank Sinatra, Sammy Davis, Jr., Joey Bishop, Dean Martin, and Peter Lawford. When we produced records showing that those entertainers had appeared at the Sands, not in September 1959, but from January 20 to February 16, 1960, Zoppi admitted that he must not have been involved in Ruby's trip to Cuba after all.

There was other evidence that portrayed perhaps more accurately the true purpose of Ruby's mission to Cuba. On November 28, 1963, the State Department received a cable from London:

> On 26 November 1963, a British Journalist named John Wilson, and also known as Wilson-Hudson, gave information to the American Embassy in London which indicated that an "American gangster-type named Ruby" visited Cuba around 1959. Wilson himself was working in Cuba at that time and was jailed by Castro before he was deported.
>
> In prison in Cuba, Wilson says he met an American gangster-gambler named Santos who could not return to the U.S.A. . . . Instead he preferred to live in relative luxury in a Cuban prison. While Santos was in prison, Wilson says, Santos was visited frequently by an American gangster-type named Ruby.

Several days later, the CIA received information that Wilson-Hudson was a "psychopath" and decided not to investigate his allegation; nor was it forwarded to the Warren Commission. We interviewed Jose Verdacia Verdacia, the warden of the Trescornia prison camp, who said there had in fact been "an English journalist" in the camp, who had been "deported from Argentina." He could not remember his name, though he did recall that his term at the camp had coincided with Trafficante's. Trafficante himself told us in 1978 he had a "vague" recollection of "some guy" at the camp who fit the description of Wilson-Hudson, "a little bit of a screwball." Trafficante said he could not "recall" a visit by Ruby, though he "might have" seen McWillie while he was at Trescornia.

The most convincing evidence that Ruby and McWillie did go to Trescornia in August or September 1959 to meet with Trafficante, however, was the rather transparent attempt that McWillie and Trafficante each made to avoid any indication that such a meeting occurred. Trafficante's testimony was especially revealing for what he tried to hide. He knew McWillie. "I seen him around Havana a lot," Trafficante told us, but he denied having any "personal business dealings" with him. While readily admitting to an ownership interest in three Havana casinos, the Sans Souci, the Deauville, and the Commodoro, Trafficante denied that he had owned a stake in either the Tropicana or the Capri, the two places where McWillie worked. That he had owned an interest in at least the Capri was a matter of FBI record.

We came to believe that the efforts by Trafficante and McWillie to avoid revealing that they had been associated, as well as Trafficante's attempt to separate himself from Ruby, told us they had something more to conceal (apart from what might be inferred with respect to the Kennedy assassination). This was indicated by the circumstances of Trafficante's release. While Trafficante denied that he paid money to get out of Trescornia, there was evidence that he did. The Cuban official who was responsible for his deportation was Manuel Pinero Losada, the commander of the Moncada Barracks from January to June 1959 and a member of the Directorate of Intelligence of the Army General Staff. According to the Cuban government, Pinero interviewed Trafficante shortly after his release and gave him twenty-four hours to leave the country. When we were in Cuba, the government complied with most of our requests, but when we asked to interview Pinero, who then was Chief of the America Department of the Cuban Communist Party, the answer was no, he was not available. We also asked why Ruby's tourist cards had been retained, since most such records were routinely destroyed. The government's answer was they had been preserved because of Ruby's role in the Kennedy assassination as the murderer of Oswald. We considered this an unlikely explanation, since the assassination occurred over four years after Ruby's trip to Cuba. We were led to infer that the tourist cards had been held because Ruby was the subject of an earlier investigation, one unrelated to the assassination, which also served to explain Ruby's troubles with Cuban customs in 1959. We reasoned that this investigation might have had to do with Trafficante's detention, which got us back to Pinero. Was Pinero not permitted to talk to us because he was suspected of having taken a bribe to release Trafficante? If he was responsible for Trafficante's release, we believed it quite likely he had taken the bribe, whether he was suspected of it or not.

Finally, our belief that there was something to hide in the Ruby-McWillie relationship was borne out by a remark Ruby made to Wally Weston, a comedian who had worked in his nightclub. It was after Ruby had been convicted of murdering Oswald, and they were talking in Ruby's jail cell. "Wally, they're going to find out about Cuba," Ruby said. "They're going to find out about the guns, find out about New Orleans, find out about everything."

The picture that was being formed by the pieces of the puzzle was coming into focus: Ruby's trips to Cuba were an important, if minor, part of an organized-crime operation, which may have had to do with Trafficante's detention. It was a conclusion radically at odds with the view of Ruby in 1964, since the Warren Commission found nothing "sinister" in his travels and determined he was not part of the "organized underworld." Had the Commission found otherwise, it is doubtful that its conclusion that Ruby was a lone gunman would have received such wide acceptance. Our conclusion about Ruby in Cuba did not necessarily mean organized crime had a hand in the events in Dallas in 1963, but it did shift the balance in the careful process of weighing the evidence.

Ruby's Telephone Contacts

A specific recommendation that Leon Hubert and Burt Griffin made to the Warren Commission for the Ruby phase of the investigation was that an extensive inspection of telephone toll records be made. After prolonged discussion, however, it was decided to limit the scope of the project to tracing Ruby's communications with associates and the communications of Ruby's associates with one another, to see if there were indications of conspiratorial contacts. (None was developed.) The limited approach was adopted, we were told by Howard Willens, so as not to "impose burdens on private parties . . . not justified by the possible results to be obtained." Willens did concede, however, that if a significant pattern of phone calls was developed in our investigation, the failure of the Commission to undertake a more comprehensive effort would be "an important conclusion" for us to reach.

We did not have, as did the Warren Commission, access to all records, since some had been routinely destroyed. No longer available, as an important example, were records of Ruby's associates (we were particularly interested in his underworld associates) talking among themselves. We could trace Ruby's calls to them, but it was not possible to learn if the calls from Ruby were preceded or followed by calls among organized-crime figures. We wanted to know specifically if a call from Ruby had precipitated a series of calls from person to person. (We recognized there was little likelihood that the assassination was plotted over the telephone, but it might have been possible to see meetings being set up or other indicative activity, such as that which occurred prior to the underworld meeting at Apalachin, New York, in November 1957.)

We were interested in calls that were made over the entire summer and fall of 1963, which again was a departure from the Warren Commission approach. The Commission apparently believed that press speculation about the President's trip did not begin until September 13, 1963, but we had found a story in *The Dallas Times Herald* on April 24, 1963, that quoted Vice-President Johnson as saying that President Kennedy might "visit Dallas and other major Texas cities [that] . . . summer." Our telephone project did reveal an interesting pattern: Ruby's long-distance calls increased significantly in number in the months leading up to the assassination — from twenty-five to thirty-five calls a month in May, June, July, August, and September to some seventy-five calls in October and ninety-six calls during the first three-and-a-half weeks of November. It was perhaps more significant that we discovered a pattern of telephone calls to individuals with criminal affiliations, calls that could only be described as suspicious.

We assembled Ruby's calls into categories. There were calls to close friends (five or more in a day to Ralph Paul, his financial backer, was not unusual) and relatives, especially his brother Earl. He also made numerous calls for business purposes, such as locating striptease dancers for the act at the Carousel. He was often in touch, for example, with Harold Tannenbaum, who ran several New Orleans clubs that were owned at least in part by Carlos Marcello, the Mafia leader. (It was through Tannenbaum that Ruby, when he visited New Orleans in June 1963, hired Janet Conforto, or "Jada," who got him into considerable trouble with her "x-rated" act.) At times Ruby called the strippers directly, as in the case of Juanita Dale Phillips, who was known as "Candy Barr," a girl friend of Mickey Cohen, the West Coast mobster. Then there were the so-called AGVA calls, a lot that were made by Ruby in connection with a dispute he was having with the American Guild of Variety Artists, which was coming to a head in the fall of 1963.

A troublesome question for us was whether the AGVA dispute, or perhaps another purpose not related to the assassination, was an adequate explanation for the increased number of calls, particularly those to organized-crime figures. Ruby told the Warren Commission all the calls in question were related to the AGVA dispute, not to the "underworld," an assurance we did not feel bound to accept.

Ruby placed seven calls to his friend Lewis McWillie: one in June, on the 27th, and six in September — on the 2nd (two calls), the 4th, the 19th, the 20th, and the 22nd. The first two were placed to McWillie's home; the others, to the Thunderbird Casino, where he worked. In his 1978 deposition, McWillie said Ruby was "having some trouble with AGVA" and asked to be put in touch with someone who "knew the president of AGVA." McWillie said he referred Ruby to William Miller, the owner of the Riverside Hotel in Reno. He said the subsequent calls were just to thank him for helping out. On October 26, 1963, Ruby called Irwin S. Weiner in Chicago and talked to him for twelve minutes. Weiner was a bondsman and insurance agent with syndicate connections (he was once described by *The Washington Post* as "the underworld's major financial figure in the Midwest") and ties to the Teamsters Union. In 1962 FBI informant information linked Weiner to the ownership of the Deauville and Capri casinos in Havana, and he was known to have been associated with Allen Dorfman, who managed the Central States Pension Fund for Teamsters' President James R. Hoffa. In 1963 Weiner refused to discuss the call from Ruby with the FBI, and no further effort was made to investigate it. (While Weiner had grown up on the West Side of Chicago and had gone to school with Earl Ruby, he had not had previous contact with Jack Ruby, as far as we knew.) Weiner was subpoenaed by us to testify in executive session. He acknowledged either a personal acquaintance or a business relationship with several syndicate figures, including Felix Alderisio, Santo Trafficante, Sam Giancana, James Allegretti, James Fratianno, Paul Labriola, James Weinberg, Lenny Patrick, Dave Yaras, Robert "Barney" Baker, and Murray "Dusty" Miller. Weiner denied that he had owned an interest in a Cuban gambling establishment, though he acknowledged he had made trips to Cuba. His explanation for the October 26 phone call was that Ruby was contemplating legal action in the AGVA dispute and wanted Weiner to write a bond, which Weiner said he refused to do. (This was the only mention in either the Warren Commission investigation or ours of any form of suit contemplated by Ruby in the AGVA dispute.)

On November 7, 1963, Ruby received a seventeen-minute collect call from Robert "Barney" Baker of Chicago, a liaison man between James Hoffa and underworld leaders. Baker told the FBI in 1963 that he had been called by Ruby earlier that day (a call for which we could find no record), so he called him back. Baker said Ruby, whom he did not know, wanted help in his union dispute, which, Baker said, he declined to give, and that was that. Baker repeated the explanation to us in a deposition in 1978, but the phone records contradicted him. On November 8, 1963, the day after his conversation with Baker, Ruby called Murray "Dusty" Miller at the Eden Roc Hotel in Miami Beach, and they talked for four minutes. Miller, also a Hoffa associate with links to organized-crime figures, told us he had not known Ruby previously and the call was a request for help in the AGVA matter. Ruby said, according to Miller, "Barney Baker gave me your number and told me that maybe you could help out." Miller said he declined to help. Thirty-one minutes after he talked to Miller, Ruby called Baker again, and they talked for fourteen minutes. Baker did not tell the FBI in 1964 about the second call, and he was at a loss to explain it to us.

Finally, although there were no phone records to support it, Eva and Hyman, Ruby's sister and brother, told the Warren Commission in 1964 that Ruby had told them that he called Leonard Patrick in Chicago about his union problems. When the FBI talked to Patrick in 1963, he said he had not seen Ruby in ten to twelve years. In a 1978 deposition Patrick told us he could not remember a phone call from Ruby, and he denied knowing anything about Ruby's dispute with AGVA. Patrick suggested that Ruby may have called his partner, Dave Yaras, who "was closer" to Ruby than he was. (Yaras told the FBI in 1963 that while he had known Ruby as a "young hustler" on the West Side of Chicago, Ruby was "not outfit," and he had had no contact with him in 14 years.) We were no more satisfied with Patrick's explanation than we were with McWillie's, Weiner's, or Baker's.

At Odds with AGVA

Ruby's relations with AGVA, which dated back to when he first arrived in Dallas, had not always been as difficult as they seemed to be in 1963. In fact, from 1958 to 1961 Ruby was closely associated with the AGVA representative in Dallas, James Henry Dolan, who had a criminal record and had been involved with the Mafia organization in Denver run by Clyde and Eugene Smaldone. FBI sources in 1961 termed Dolan's stewardship of the AGVA office in Dallas a "racketeer proposition," and they said Dolan "may have used his position for extra income by requiring payoffs from band leaders and persons seeking entertainers." A 1962 FBI report described Dolan's specialty as the armed robbery of bookmakers, gamblers, and houses of prostitution. Informants also indicated to the FBI that as an enforcer for Santo Trafficante, Dolan was sent to beat up and rob *bolita* operators who were believed to be holding out. In 1963 Dolan was thought to have been involved with Nofio Pecora, a Marcello lieutenant in New Orleans, in at least one robbery, and he was said to be connected to two West Coast organized-crime figures, James Fratianno and Eugene Hale Brading. On November 21, 1963, Dolan was seen by an FBI agent entering a bookmaking establishment in Dallas.

When interviewed by the FBI in 1963, Dolan admitted he had known Ruby since 1957 and that they had seen a lot of each other when Dolan was the AGVA representative, both socially and on business. (Dolan told us in 1978 that from time to time he received complaints from Ruby's employees, such as one from a performer who had refused Ruby's demand that she date a customer.) In 1963 the producer of a nightclub review, Breck Wall, told the FBI that in 1960 he entered into an agreement with Ruby and Dolan to put on his show at Ruby's club, then called the Sovereign. But when Ruby refused to sign a contract, Wall said, he pulled out, which angered Ruby to the point that he punched Wall's assistant, Joseph Peterson. When we asked Dolan about the incident, he referred to it as an "arbitration," and he called Peterson a "little fairy," though he acknowledged that Ruby had been a "bully." The FBI learned of at least two cases of employee complaints against Ruby in which Dolan acted as arbiter. In one, a stripper who had quit over Ruby's advances, said she was told by Dolan to finish out her contract; in another, a stripper said that when she complained that Ruby had slapped her, Dolan told her to forget it, "because Ruby had too much on the Dallas police . . . for such a trivial charge to be taken seriously."

Dolan was succeeded as the Dallas AGVA representative by Thomas Palmer, who held the job in November 1963. It was during Palmer's tenure that Ruby stirred up a dispute over "amateur nights." By hiring nonunion dancers and calling them amateurs, the strip clubs could increase profits by paying less than the wage scale. The practice was apparently introduced in Dallas by two of Ruby's competitors, Barney and Abe Weinstein, who ran the Theater Lounge and the Colony Lounge. At first Ruby tried to beat the Weinsteins at their own game, but when that failed, he asked AGVA to prohibit the amateur night practice. There was evidence that Ruby had a justified complaint, in that it was believed (by Tony Zoppi, the newspaper columnist, for one) that the Weinsteins were paying off the union. In any event, Ruby complained loudly and bitterly. He appealed to Joey Adams, the national president of AGVA, and he went to New York in August 1963 in an attempt to meet with Bobby Faye, the national administrative secretary, who refused to see him. He also placed at least six telephone calls to Faye, four of them on November 13, 1963. Finally, Faye sent a note to Ruby, which read in part: "Tom Palmer [is] handling your situation and [he]

. . . will not do anything to hurt you." Palmer told the FBI in 1964 that he ordered the Weinsteins by letter on November 13, 1963, to discontinue the amateur nights, although Abe Weinstein denied, in a deposition to us in 1978, that he ever received such an order.

Ruby's Financial Plight

Ruby's financial records, as the Warren Commission observed, were "chaotic"; his "pockets and the trunk of his car served as his bank." While he did keep bank accounts and rented a safe-deposit box, they were hardly ever used, at least in 1963, so it was difficult to assess Ruby's pecuniary condition. By his own account, which he would give to anyone who would listen, it was dismal. There was no doubt, moreover, that he had tax problems: he owed the federal government excise taxes going back six years and totaling almost $40,000; and, according to the Warren Commission, he owed "an additional $20,000" in other federal taxes. We therefore considered the possibility that Ruby turned to the lending market to alleviate his financial difficulties. On June 6, 1963, Ruby's lawyer, Graham R. E. Koch, told the Internal Revenue Service that his client hoped to settle his accounts "as soon as arrangements can be made to borrow money. . . ." But according to an FBI check of more than fifty banking institutions, there was no evidence that Ruby borrowed through customary channels. This raised the question: Did Ruby turn to underworld money sources — perhaps a loan shark in Las Vegas — to obtain funds? There was, in fact, evidence that he did.

Paul Roland Jones told the FBI that he saw Ruby on November 10, 1963. Business was poor, Ruby said, and his competitors had become his enemies. Jones said he asked if he could help, and Ruby replied that he had got himself into the situation and he had to get himself out. It was around this time, too, that Ruby met with an old friend from the West Side of Chicago, Alexander Gruber. Gruber told the FBI in 1964 that he had been in Joplin, Missouri, and decided to drop in on Ruby, "since Dallas was about 100 miles from Joplin." (It was 360 miles.) His explanation was no more believable in 1978. He told us he could not remember why he had gone so far out of his way to see someone he had not seen since 1953.

Here were two Ruby contacts in November 1963 that troubled us. Jones, who had documented syndicate connections, having been the mob's man in Dallas in the attempted takeover in 1946, appeared after not having seen Ruby for some time. Gruber, while apparently not syndicate-connected, had come suddenly out of Ruby's Chicago past for a reason he would not be candid about.

While the Warren Commission rejected it, there was credible evidence that Ruby traveled to Las Vegas between November 10 and November 22, 1963. Gilbert Coskey, a cashier at the casino in the Stardust Hotel, told the FBI that Ruby had tried to cash a check, and the casino credit manager, John Tihista, remembered the incident as probably having occurred on a weekend, though he had no records to prove it. In addition, the FBI obtained confidential information that Ruby's visit occurred on the weekend of November 16-17. The FBI was unable to document the trip (which could either mean Ruby did not make it or that he traveled under another name), and Lewis McWillie told the FBI in December 1963 that he had "never known Ruby to visit Las Vegas." The Warren Commission chose to believe McWillie. We, on the other hand, put little faith in McWillie's word, noting the six Ruby-McWillie telephone conversations in September — more, we believed, than could be explained by Ruby's gratitude for having been referred to a hotel manager in Reno for help in the AGVA dispute. (We also noted that McWillie, in his deposition to us in 1978, said that Ruby did not mention in any of the September phone conversations his financial difficulties or his problems with federal tax authorities. Since we knew that Ruby talked of his financial woes and tax troubles with virtually everyone he contacted, we considered this another example of McWillie's lack of candor.) We concluded, therefore, that a Ruby trip to Las Vegas on the weekend before the assassination was a distinct possibility. Further, there was circumstantial evidence that in the days that followed Ruby took some sort of action to resolve his financial problems. On Sunday, November 17, at 9:28 P.M., Ruby called Gruber at his home in Los Angeles, and they talked for eight minutes. Gruber could not remember in 1978 what they had talked about, or so he testified, but we thought it reasonable to suspect it had to do with Ruby's finances. In addition, on November 19 Ruby gave his lawyer, Graham Koch, authorization to deal with the IRS. According to Seth Kantor, Koch said Ruby told him "he had a connection who would supply him money to settle his long-standing government tax problems." When we contacted Koch, he said he did not recall talking to Kantor, and he had no recollection of Ruby coming into a substantial sum of money. He did acknowledge, however, that Ruby may have said something about settling his tax problems.

Again we had the pieces of a jigsaw puzzle — Ruby's phone calls; the AGVA dispute; his trips to New Orleans, New York, and possibly Las Vegas; and his business dealings in Dallas — but, unlike the Cuban episode, they did not form a clear, coherent picture. We did not have all the pieces, and some we had did not fit, that is, they did not necessarily warrant a sinister interpretation. For example, Ruby's dispute with AGVA was real, and it explained some, if not all, of his phone calls, even some of those placed to organized-crime figures. (We were, admittedly, dealing with inferences of circumstantial evidence, but since we were not operating in the context of a criminal trial, the evidence did not have to meet the strict standard of proof beyond a reasonable doubt. We were concerned with history, not personal responsibility in a judicial proceeding.) From a consideration of probability or reasonable likelihood, we had to acknowledge that there was more than one interpretation of the evidence, not all of them sinister. There were, however, three alternative sinister interpretations of certain evidence that could not be precluded. The telephone calls may, as one alternative, have been related to the assassination, although it seemed unlikely that the assassination would have been planned over the phone. As a second alternative, the calls may all have been related to the AGVA dispute, but in the sinister sense that Ruby was seeking illicit mob influence to solve his labor problems. As a third alternative, some of the calls — in conjunction with the visits by Jones and Gruber and the reported trip to Las Vegas — might have been related to Ruby's decision to resolve his financial difficulties by borrowing from a syndicate source. Nothing that we knew established or precluded any of these interpretations, which served to explain why the picture composed of the jigsaw pieces had not come into clearer focus.

We came to realize, however, that the significance of Ruby's conduct in the summer and fall of 1963, with respect to the assassination, lay elsewhere and rested on surer footing. There was in medieval philosophy a dictum called Occam's Razor: "*pluralites non est ponende sine necessitate*" (multiplicity ought not to be posited without necessity), which suggested that a simple explanation should always be preferred to a complicated one. We knew that while a number of inferences could be made from Ruby's activities, none was individually compelling. Consequently, we decided it was sufficient to point out what Ruby's conduct over the summer and fall of 1963 did establish beyond serious question and how his conduct might have fit into a conspiratorial scheme. Ruby's business was in deep financial difficulty, complicated by the dispute with AGVA over "amateur" strippers and serious tax problems. Ruby was not one to keep his troubles to himself. He complained of them to a variety of individuals, including organized-crime figures who were aware of two other qualities of Ruby's character: he was prone to violence and, as his mission to Cuba had demonstrated, he was open to being used in an underworld operation. Organized-crime figures had a motive to kill the President; in Oswald, they had the means to kill him. When Oswald neither escaped nor was killed in flight, they were presented with a motive to silence him. Ruby was also known to be familiar with many Dallas police officers, so he stood a good chance of being admitted to where Oswald was being held. Whatever else may be inferred from Ruby's conduct in the summer and fall of 1963, it at least established that he was an available means to effect Oswald's elimination. Paul Roland Jones, who was in a position to know, alluded to Ruby's availability in 1964, as the FBI indicated in a report: "[Jones] said from his acquaintance with Ruby he doubted he would have become emotionally upset and killed Oswald on the spur of the moment. He felt Ruby would have done it for money. . . ." Jones added that if Ruby had been given orders by anyone to kill Oswald, Joe Civello, the "head of the syndicate" in Dallas, would know about it.

The Stalking of Oswald

The Warren Commission concluded that an examination "of Ruby's activities immediately preceding and following the death of President Kennedy revealed no sign of any conduct which suggest[ed] that he was involved in the assassination." While the Commission did not directly address the issue, its general conclusion extended to the question of whether Ruby stalked Oswald before he killed him, implying he did not. The Commission noted that Ruby had given "several detailed accounts of his activities," and that the accounts were "consistent with the evidence available to the Commission from other sources." The Commission found, it said, "no evidence" that Ruby "conspired with anyone in planning or executing the killing of Lee Harvey Oswald." In arriving at these conclusions, the Commission was making, as Burt Griffin told us, "a professional evaluation" of the evidence available to it, which was then, as Griffin put it, expressed in "code words" such as "no evidence."

   We did not quarrel with the right of the Commission to make "professional evaluations" of any issue, including the difficult question of stalking. Professional evaluations were, we knew, a necessary part of any investigation, but we believed that they should not have been "professional" in the narrow sense that they manifested a high degree of the advocate's craftsmanship. Fact evaluations should be, we believed, characterized by open-mindedness and balanced judgment and should be made from the perspective of an evaluator, not that of an advocate of a particular view. It was in this sense that our appraisal of the Commission's report was most harsh. When we closely examined the Commission's analysis of the stalking issue, we found that substantial evidence that Ruby had in fact stalked Oswald before he killed him had been rejected. In addition, we could find no principle by which the evidence was rejected or accepted, except consistency with a lone-assassin theory (Stalking, in itself, was not consistent with a lone-assassin theory.) For example, some identifications of Ruby at the Dallas police station in the period following the assassination were rejected because the witness had not known Ruby, while the identifications of other witnesses, who had known Ruby previously, were rejected for some other reason. Identifications were rejected, it seemed, if they were inconsistent with a finding that Ruby did not stalk Oswald.

There were well-recognized approaches that should have been applied to the evidence the Commission possessed. First, it is usually appropriate to try to construct from the physical evidence a coherent account of what happened. Witness testimony can then be examined, though it is less reliable and often in conflict with the physical evidence, especially as the number of witnesses increases. (There is a truism among defense counsel that you are better off if your client is not observed at the scene of the crime, but if he must be seen at all, you are better off if it is by a number of witnesses.) Contradictions between physical evidence and witness testimony are usually resolved by relying on the physical evidence. Where contradictions develop between witnesses, and they cannot be resolved by the physical evidence, an effort should be made to construct a view of the facts that assumes no one is mistaken or lying and that the contradictions are only apparent. But where the contradictions are irreconcilable, choices must be made. It is best, first, to examine the process of perception. Was the witness in a position to hear or see what he says he did? Did the witness take advantage of that position? And so on. Only after it has been determined that an honest mistake is not possible is the question of false testimony appropriate. Then, a careful effort should be made to assess the motives to lie, which would include bias, corruption, fear, etc. It is a good practice in assessing evidence — both physical and from witnesses — to posit various hypotheses of what might have happened and then test them against the evidence until a good fit is found, realizing, of course, that perfect fits are seldom possible, since the process of perception is imperfect.

The open-minded, balanced evaluation that seeks the plain truth stands in sharp contrast to the approach of the advocate, who has an obligation — given or assumed, affirmative or negative, prosecution or defense — to take one side or another. The advocate then marshals the evidence around his position, following as best he can the canons of open-minded and balanced analysis, but departing from them whenever he must support the position of his advocacy. The adversary proceeding that pits two advocates against one another in a struggle to convince a judge or jury can be an effective fact-finding mechanism — in fact, there are few devices more effective in exposing mistaken or false testimony than skillful cross-examination conducted by an advocate. But the adversary system presupposes an open-minded judge, or fact-finder;

the role of the advocate in the adversary system is then to assist the judge in making a determination by sharpening his understanding of opposing views. In addition, however objective the process of evaluation might have been, it is possible to write an advocate's brief to support it. While the Warren Commission may have been open-minded in its fact-finding process, its report was not necessarily written from the standpoint of balance and impartiality. Just as critics of the Warren Commission were justifiably censured for arguing solely from the hypothesis of conspiracy, the Commission, we came to believe, was arguing from a single-assassin perspective. It was a point of view that was quite evident in the Commission's treatment of the Ruby-as-stalker issue in its report. The evidence available to us, which indicated that the Commission's central conclusion about conspiracy was wrong, made it all the more necessary that we take another look at the evidence bearing on Ruby's conduct between the assassination and the murder of Oswald. We needed to see for ourselves if it was still appropriate to conclude that there was "no sign" or "no evidence" that Ruby was, as the Commission put it, "delegated to perform the shooting of Oswald on behalf of others who were involved in the slaying of the President."

As our analysis of the physical evidence showed, Ruby's account of his Cuban activities was not consistent with the facts. We found little reason, therefore, to accept his story of the forty-eight hours in question, unless it survived the most exacting analysis. When we had completed that analysis, we determined there was substantial evidence that Ruby had not, as he stated, acted on the spur of the moment when he killed Oswald; that his stated motive — to obviate the necessity for Mrs. Kennedy to return to Dallas for Oswald's trial — was false; and that he was neither acting during an epileptic seizure of a psychomotor variant type, as his lawyer claimed, nor suffering from a temporary form of insanity, as one of his doctors testified at his trial. We concluded, in short, that Ruby consciously set out to kill Oswald — that he stalked him and shot him with no apparent motive other than to silence him. We also concluded that Ruby had been in contact with organized-crime figures before and after the assassination, and we discovered evidence that organized-crime figures were present during at least part of his trial for the murder.

We traced Ruby's activities to the week of the assassination: the call to Gruber at 9:28 P.M. on Sunday, November 17; the granting of the authorization for his lawyer to deal with the IRS and a reported money connection on Tuesday, November 19. Apparently nothing of significance occurred on Wednesday, the 20th, and the Warren Commission considered Thursday, the 21st, to be equally uneventful. During the day, the Commission noted, Ruby attended to his "usual duties" as proprietor of his two clubs, the Carousel and the Vegas, and his activities that evening were a "combination of business and pleasure." He met twice with Lawrence V. Meyers, "a Chicago businessman," once at the Carousel and once at the Cabana Motel, where Meyers was staying. Before meeting Meyers, Ruby had dinner with "his close friend and financial backer" Ralph Paul, the Commission also noted, and it thought it worth mentioning that Ruby saw Don Campbell, an employee of *The Dallas Morning News*, at the restaurant. By merely "noting" these meetings, the Commission indicated it saw little significance in them.

We looked into Meyers, who appeared to be a respectable businessman. In 1963 he was a sales manager in the sporting goods division of Bro Manufacturing Company of Chicago. We were, however, struck by one aspect of his trip to Dallas in November 1963. He was accompanied by Jean West, also known as Jean Aase, who was described by Meyers in a deposition to us as a "dumb but accommodating broad," a "party girl," a "semiprofessional hooker." He said he had picked her up at the 20 East Delaware Lounge in Chicago, which was in a hotel with a "reputation for party girls." In our inspection of telephone records, we had discovered that on September 24, 1963, a fifteen-minute call was made to the number listed for the hotel by David W. Ferrie of New Orleans, who in 1963 was employed by Carlos Marcello and associated, according to several witnesses, with Lee Harvey Oswald. Meyers had no explanation for the call; we were unable to locate West; and Ferrie was dead. We were left with an unanswered question.

There were other circumstances surrounding Ruby's dinner with Ralph Paul that the Warren Commission neglected to take into account. They ate at a restaurant called the Egyptian Lounge at 5610 East Mockingbird Lane in Dallas, which was owned by the Campisi brothers, Joseph and Sam. The Campisis told the FBI in 1963 they had seen Ruby there that night. Joseph said Ruby ate a steak; Sam said that Ruby and Paul were there for about forty-five minutes sometime after 9:45 or 10 P.M. We checked the files on the Campisis and found the one on Joseph particularly interesting. He was classified as a member of organized crime by the Drug Enforcement Administration, and an FBI informant report in 1967 indicated he was slated to replace Joseph Civello as the Mafia leader in Dallas. While other reports listed Campisi's organized-crime status as "definite," "suspected," and even "negative," we interviewed a former senior official of the Dallas Police Department who had no doubts. Captain W. P. Gannaway, who in 1963 was the commander of the Special Service Bureau, stated emphatically that the national syndicate's Dallas representative at that time was Civello, and Joseph Campisi belonged to his organization. Gannaway said further that Campisi had bought the Egyptian Lounge from John Brazil Grissaffi, a "hit man" for the the old Hollis de Lois Green gang, which, according to the FBI, specialized in the late 1940s in burglarizing large drug stores for narcotics and cash. Among the members of the Green gang were James Robert Todd and Russell D. Matthews, both of whom were acquainted with Ruby. (In 1959 Matthews worked in the casino of the Hotel Deauville in Havana, which was owned by Santo Trafficante. When we deposed Matthews in 1978, he admitted having known Ruby but denied knowing Trafficante. Joseph Campisi told us, however, that Matthews had told him that Trafficante "treated him good" when he worked for him in Cuba.) We also learned that Campisi ran gambling tours from Dallas to the Flamingo Hotel in Las Vegas, a substantial part of which was owned by three prominent underworld figures: Meyer Lansky, Anthony Accardo, and Gerardo Catena.

Ruby was also acquainted with Joseph Civello, who took over the Mafia family in Dallas in 1956, succeeding Joseph Piranio. In an FBI interview on January 14, 1964, Civello acknowledged having known Ruby for "about ten years," but he said he had not seen him since 1957. Ovid Demaris, the author of *Jack Ruby,* told us he talked with Civello while doing research for the book. "Yeah, I knew Jack," Civello said, according to Demaris. "We were friends, and I used to go to his club." There was also the testimony of Robert G. Moore, who was interviewed by the FBI on November 26, 1963. Moore, who had worked both in a store owned by Civello and as a piano player for Ruby, said, "Ruby was a frequent visitor [at Civello's store] and [an] associate of Civello. . . ." We were unable to question Civello, who died in 1970.

When we deposed Joseph Campisi in 1978, he said he first met Ruby in 1947, but he did not know the circumstances of Ruby's coming to Dallas, nor did Ruby ever, "that I recall," drop names of people he had known in Chicago. He admitted he knew Ruby was a brawler "who would jump on anybody," and he had warned him: "Jack, you are going to get a knife stuck in your stomach." Campisi acknowledged that Ruby had a lot of friends in the police department. "They all knew Jack," he said. Campisi claimed, however, that he knew little about Ruby's business or about his dispute with AGVA. Despite his statement to the FBI in 1963, he denied having seen Ruby at his restaurant on the night before the assassination. On related matters, Campisi said he was acquainted with Lewis McWillie, and he knew that Ruby had visited McWillie in Cuba. As for Civello, he was a "real close" friend — "like being cousins, you know." Did he know Carlos Marcello in New Orleans? He replied: "[E]very year I send sausage, 260 pounds of Italian sausage . . . for Christmas to give the [Marcello] brothers and what friends I have there." Finally, Campisi's phone records showed as many as twenty calls a day from him to New Orleans.

Ruby had an ironclad alibi for the assassination itself. He told the Warren Commission that he was in the second-floor advertising offices of *The Dallas Morning News* from 11 or 11:30 A.M. to 1:30 P.M., and his story was confirmed by several witnesses, including Don Campbell, the newspaper employee he had seen the night before at the Egyptian Lounge. We understood that, as a nightclub operator who advertised in the papers, Ruby had a legitimate reason for being at the *Morning News*, but we observed that his going there, rather than watching the presidential motorcade, was inconsistent with his professed admiration for President Kennedy.

Ruby told the Warren Commission that upon hearing about the assassination, he went from *The Dallas Morning News* directly to the Carousel, where he started making a series of phone calls. But Seth Kantor, a Scripps-Howard reporter, told a different story. Kantor, who was part of the Washington press corps covering the motorcade and who had rushed to Parkland Memorial Hospital, said that while there he saw Ruby, whom he had known for a number of years (Kantor had been based in Dallas). In his deposition to the Warren Commission, Kantor was somewhat uncertain about the time and place of his encounter with Ruby, though he was certain it was at the hospital shortly after the assassination. In the book he wrote in 1977, *Who Was Jack Ruby?*, Kantor reconstructed it with impressive precision. At 1:27 P.M. he concluded a phone call to his office in Washington and turned in response to a tug on his suit jacket. It was Jack Ruby. Kantor remembered Ruby asking, "Should I close my places ...?" Moments later, Kantor recalled, he went to a press conference at which Malcolm Kilduff of the White House press office announced the President's death. It was 1:33 P.M. Kantor argued in his book that Ruby had ample time to get from the *Morning News*, where he was last seen at 1:10 P.M., to Parkland and back downtown to the Carousel, where his arrival was put by witnesses at 1:40 P.M. On May 14, 1964, Hubert and Griffin wrote a memo to Rankin in which they argued that "we must decide who is telling the truth, for there would be considerable significance if it were concluded that Ruby [was] lying." Ultimately, the Commission decided that Kantor was "probably" mistaken. When Griffin read Kantor's book in 1977, however, he wrote to Kantor that he was "persuaded that the greater weight of evidence supports your claim. . . ." If Kantor was right about the Ruby encounter (and we agreed with Griffin), it meant that Ruby had not told the truth to the Warren Commission. It was difficult to understand why Ruby had gone to the hospital and then was unwilling to admit it, after he had made no effort to conceal his presence there to Kantor, but just the fact that Ruby had lied to the Warren Commission about his post-assassination activities was significant.

Ruby did, as he testified to the Warren Commission, make a number of phone calls after he got back to the Carousel. He called Ralph Paul, his friend and backer; Alice Nichols, a former girl friend; and Eileen Kaminsky, his sister. The subject of the calls, according to Ruby, was his reaction to the assassination and the decision to close his clubs. At 2:37 P.M. he called Alexander Gruber, the friend in Los Angeles who had him visited recently. Gruber told the Warren Commission that Ruby talked about a car-wash business, a dog that was being sent to him, and the assassination. Then he lost his self-control. (Ruby must have recovered quickly, for two minutes after hanging up on Gruber he called Ralph Paul.) The Warren Commission accepted Ruby's explanation for his post-assassination calls at face value; they were a manifestation of genuine disturbance over the President's death. We did not rule out this explanation, although we tended to believe that Ruby was feigning his emotional outbursts. We also realized they might have been genuine manifestations of emotional distress, not over the assassination, but over his as-yet-unplayed role in its aftermath.

Shortly after 1:45 P.M., at the Texas Theatre in the Oak Cliff section of Dallas, where Ruby lived, Oswald was arrested and was taken to the Police and Courts Building, arriving at about 2 P.M. The center of activity was the third floor, where public elevators opened into a lobby that was the midpoint of a seven-foot-wide corridor that extended along the 140-foot length of the building. At one end, there were the offices of Police Chief Jesse E. Curry; at the other, a press room large enough for only a handful of newsmen. Between the press room and the lobby there was a complex of offices occupied by the Homicide Bureau, headed by Captain J. Will Fritz. It was about 2:30 P.M. when Fritz returned to his office from the Texas School Book Depository, and Oswald was brought in for the first of several interrogations. Before sometime after 1:30 Saturday morning, when he was finally bedded down for the night, Oswald was taken to an assembly room in the basement for three lineups (at 4:05 P.M., 6:20 P.M., and 7:40 P.M.); he was questioned on and off in Fritz's office; and he was arraigned twice — at 7:10 P.M., for the murder of Officer J. D. Tippit, and at 1:30 A.M., Saturday, for the assassination of the President. Shortly after midnight, Oswald was taken to the basement assembly room for an appearance before an estimated one hundred reporters and photographers.

During all this time there was virtually no security in the Police and Courts Building. By late Friday afternoon Assistant Police Chief Charles Batchelor had guards stationed at elevator and stairway entrances, but another assistant chief, N. T. Fisher, told the Warren Commission, "Anybody could come up with a plausible reason for going to one of the third-floor bureaus. . . ."

According to the Warren Commission's reconstruction, Ruby left the Carousel and went to the home of his sister Eva Grant, where he stayed for a short time before returning to the club and arranging to close it up. He then bought cold cuts and other snacks at the Ritz Delicatessen and took them back to Eva Grant's, where he made more phone calls while she watched television broadcasts of Oswald's arrest and listened to reports of his defection to the Soviet Union. According to Eva Grant, she said to Ruby, "I could never conceive of anybody in his right mind who would want this President hurt." Saying nothing, Ruby went into the bathroom and "threw up." Ruby left about 7 P.M., telling Eva he was going home to change clothes before going to the synagogue for services.

John Rutledge, a veteran police reporter for *The Dallas Morning News*, put the time at 6 P.M. when he saw Ruby on the third floor of the Police and Courts Building. Rutledge also recalled seeing Ruby get off the elevator between two newsmen, pushed up against them and holding a piece of paper, as they passed by uniformed guards who were checking people entering the third floor. Rutledge was not the only one to tell the Warren Commission of seeing Ruby on the third floor between 6 and 9 Friday night. Detective A. M. Eberhardt, who as a member of the vice squad had come to know Ruby, testified that right after he returned from dinner, around 7 P.M., Ruby spoke with him and shook his hand. Ruby had, Eberhardt said, "a notebook in his hand." Victor F. Robinson, a reporter for WFAA, a Dallas radio and television station, who knew Ruby from having frequented the Carousel, said that between 7 and 8 P.M. he saw Ruby walk up to Captain Fritz's office and start to open the door. "I have no doubts [it was Ruby]," Robinson said. Two officers stopped him and told him, "You can't go in there, Jack." (Only one of the officers at the door remembered the incident, and he said the man was not Ruby. When he was shown photographs of Ruby taken later that night, which Robinson identified "without any qualification," the officer told the FBI that "he [did] not feel that he knew Ruby well enough to make an unqualified identification. . . .") Robinson said Ruby then went back down the hall toward the elevator. The Warren Commission chose to believe that the witnesses who put Ruby on the third floor of police headquarters early Friday evening were mistaken, either in their identification, even though they each knew him, or in the time they gave for having seen him, noting that Ruby himself denied that he was there before 11:15 P.M. On the other hand, the Commission did not find evidence that corroborated Ruby's testimony that he was at his apartment during the time in question.

That Ruby did get to his apartment by 9 P.M. was documented by a long-distance call he placed to his brother Hyman, and to two of his sisters in Chicago. (Hyman recalled that his brother sounded disturbed and talked of returning to Chicago.) From home, Ruby drove to Temple Shearith Israel, arriving toward the end of a two-hour service that had begun at 8 P.M. During refreshments after the service, Ruby was greeted by Rabbi Hillel Silverman, who was surprised, he said later, that while Ruby seemed depressed, he did not mention the assassination.

After he left the synagogue, Ruby told the Warren Commission, it occurred to him that the police who were working late might be hungry, so he stopped to buy sandwiches for them. He then called Richard M. Sims, a homicide detective, to offer to bring the sandwiches up, but he was told they were not needed. "Jack," said Sims, "we wound up our work already." Ruby went to the third floor anyway. He told the Commission he had decided to give the sandwiches to newsmen at radio station KLIF, and he went to police headquarters to find a reporter who knew the KLIF telephone number, which he needed to get into the station. (He had learned by this time from a relative of an employee of the station that the sandwiches were not needed there either.) Ruby was admitted to the third floor of the Police and Courts Building, as he explained to the Commission, because he was a "little domineering." Videotapes confirmed that sometime after midnight Ruby attended a third-floor briefing at which Chief Curry and District Attorney Henry M. Wade announced that Oswald would be shown to newsmen at a press conference in the basement. Ruby told the Commission that he went to the basement, "carried away by the excitement of history," but there was also evidence he went armed with a revolver. In an interview with the FBI on December 25, 1963, Ruby said he had the revolver in his right front pocket all evening, but when he appeared before the Warren Commission on June 7, 1964, he said he had lied about the revolver, "to make [his] . . . defense to save [his] . . . life." At the press conference, Ruby stood on a table in the rear of the room. Seth Kantor, who was there, described the scene in *Who Was Jack Ruby?*

> Reporters stood on tables in front of [Ruby] and a barrier of photographers stood before Oswald. The photographers began to push, shove and close in on Oswald. Questions began to rage at him.

Kantor observed that if Ruby did have his revolver at the press conference and considered using it, "he could not have gotten off a clean shot."

Following the press conference, Ruby did get the night number of KLIF, called the station, and took the sandwiches and some soft drinks, arriving at the station at about 1:45 A.M. He did not return to his apartment until about 6 A.M. He said he went to *The Dallas Times Herald* to check on an ad for his nightclub. Then he spent time with Larry Craford, an employee at the Carousel, and after getting back to his apartment he talked with George Senator, his roommate.

Oswald was questioned three times on Saturday, beginning at 10:25 A.M. in Captain Fritz's office. He was also put in a lineup once and visited by his wife, mother, brother, and the president of the Dallas Bar Association. Oswald placed, or attempted to place, two telephone calls — one to John Apt, a New York lawyer known for defending Communists, and one to his wife. His last interrogation of the day ended at 7:15 P.M.

It was standard procedure in Dallas to transfer a prisoner charged with a felony from city police jurisdiction to the county jail and the jurisdiction of the sheriff. About noon on Saturday, Chief Curry called Captain Fritz to see if Oswald could be transferred at about 4 P.M. Fritz told Curry he thought not, as he had more questions to ask. Nevertheless, arrangements were made for the transfer that afternoon, and Jack Ruby showed unusual interest in those arrangements.

Thomas Brown, an attendant at a parking garage adjacent to the Carousel, told the Warren Commission that at about 1:30 P.M. Saturday he overheard Ruby mention Chief Curry's name in a conversation on a public telephone in the garage. Sometime after 3 P.M., Sergeant D. V. Harkness of the Police Traffic Division, who was expecting Oswald might be moved at 4 P.M., started clearing a crowd that was blocking a driveway entrance to the county jail. Harkness saw Ruby in the crowd. A short time later Ruby drove back to the parking garage, where the manager, Garnett C. Hallmark, heard him place a call to someone he thought Ruby called "Ken," and their discussion seemed to be about the transfer of Oswald. Hallmark testified he did not hear Oswald's name mentioned, but someone was referred to as "he," and he heard Ruby say, "You know I'll be there." Ken Dove, a KLIF announcer, told the Warren Commission that Ruby called him twice that afternoon, and in one of the calls he asked when Oswald was going to be transferred. Five newsmen, none of whom had known Ruby previously, testified that Ruby was at the Police and Courts Building — some said on the third floor — on Saturday afternoon. One of them, Frederick Rheinstein, an NBC producer-director, said Ruby (he was "reasonably certain" it was Ruby, for he "was an irritant, so his face became fixed") tried to watch the activities on the third floor on the closed circuit monitor in his television van. The Warren Commission, noting that Ruby had "not mentioned such a visit," was able to reach "no firm conclusion" about Ruby's alleged presence at police headquarters on Saturday.

The decision was eventually made to transfer Oswald at 10 A.M. Sunday, and it was announced — apparently inadvertently — by Chief Curry at about 7:30 P.M. Saturday. A couple of reporters wanted to go out for dinner on Saturday evening, but they did not want to miss the transfer. Curry told them that if they got back by 10 o'clock the next morning, they "wouldn't miss anything." At a 10:20 P.M. press conference Curry formally announced that Oswald would be moved in an armored truck, and he generally outlined other security precautions.

Ruby's activities on the morning of Sunday, November 24, were, as the Warren Commission put it, the subject of "conflicting testimony." Ruby, as well as George Senator, said he did not leave the apartment until after 11 A.M., although three technicians for WBAP-TV all said they believed they saw Ruby in the vicinity of the Police and Courts Building before 11 o'clock. Ira Walker, the most positive of the technicians, put the time at 10:30, recalling that Ruby had come to the window of his truck and asked, "Has he been brought down yet?" The Commission decided to discount the testimony of the television technicians, because none of them had known Ruby before. It also could be established with some certainty that Ruby was at his apartment at 10:19, for it was then that he received a phone call from Karen Carlin, a striptease dancer who worked at the Carousel, requesting $25 to help pay her rent and grocery bill. Carlin later testified that Ruby was "short" with her, but he said he had "to go downtown anyway," and he agreed to send her the money by Western Union. She remembered that he said he had to dress first. The driving time from Ruby's apartment in Oak Cliff to downtown Dallas was about fifteen minutes. Ruby parked in a lot directly across the street from the Western Union office, where he purchased a $25 money order to be telegraphed to Carlin. The money order was stamped at 11:17 A.M., Central Standard Time. The telegraph clerk recalled that Ruby promptly turned and walked out the door to Main Street and proceeded in the direction of the Police and Courts Building one block away.

Oswald was checked out of his jail cell at 9:30 A.M. and taken to Captain Fritz's office for a final round of questioning. Captain C. E. Talbert, who was in charge of the Patrol Division, had assigned security in the basement to Sergeant Patrick T. Dean. The transfer party left Fritz's office with Oswald in handcuffs at about 11:15 A.M., and when it arrived in the basement, seventy to seventy-five police officers and forty to fifty newsmen were assembled. Fritz came to the jail office door and asked if everything was ready. Someone shouted, "Here he comes!" Oswald, his right wrist handcuffed to Detective J. R. Leavelle's left, and with Detective L. C. Groves walking to his left, came through the door. They had moved about ten feet from the jail office door when Ruby emerged from between a newsman and a detective at the edge of the straining crowd, extended his right hand, which was holding a .38 caliber revolver, and fired a single bullet into Oswald's abdomen. Oswald was declared dead at Parkland Hospital at 1:07 P.M.

The killing of Oswald raised a number of questions: How did Ruby get into the basement of the Police and Courts Building? Did he have help? Was the killing of Oswald part of a plot that had resulted in the President's death? The Warren Commission found nothing in the way that Ruby reached Oswald to indicate a conspiracy, concluding that he "entered the basement unaided, probably via the Main Street ramp," no more than three minutes before the shooting. The Commission recognized that no one observed Ruby's entry. It had to rely on Ruby's own word and the statements of the police officers, who said Ruby "admitted" to them shortly after the shooting that he entered via the ramp.

The testimony of police officers who had been charged with securing the Main Street ramp did not corroborate Ruby's story. Roy E. Vaughn, the patrolman on guard, told the Warren Commission that Ruby did not come down the ramp, and Vaughn passed a polygraph test on the question during a Dallas police investigation in 1964. (Vaughn repeated his statement to us in 1978.) While the Warren Commission intimated that Vaughn had made an honest mistake, his testimony was supported by three officers parked in a squad car on the ramp, who said they did not see Ruby enter. In addition, Sergeant Don Flusche, who did not testify before the Warren Commission, told us that although he was off duty at the time, he was standing across the street, and he was certain that Ruby, whom he knew, did not use the ramp. In all, there were eight witnesses who said Ruby did not use the Main Street ramp to get into the basement.

After Ruby was subdued, he was taken upstairs and questioned by Dallas police together with Forrest V. Sorrels of the Secret Service and Special Agent C. Ray Hall of the FBI, although neither Sorrels nor Hall were present throughout the session. Four police officers who did the questioning, including Sergeant Dean, the basement security officer, said Ruby told them he had entered by the ramp, but the reports the officers filed immediately after the interrogation did not reflect Ruby's explanation. Neither Sorrels nor Hall recalled Ruby's statement; in fact, Hall said he refused to answer the question. Critics of the Warren Commission later seized on these discrepancies, claiming the ramp-entry story was contrived to cover up the assistance that Dallas police wittingly or unwittingly gave Ruby. Much of the attention was directed at the role of Sergeant Dean. While the Warren Commission was not told,

Dean was given a polygraph examination in the 1964 Dallas police investigation, and it was our understanding that he failed on questions related to Ruby's access to the basement. We could not, however, locate a record of the test. Dean acknowledged in an interview in 1978 that he failed the test, but we were unable to arrange for his testimony under oath. Before the issue could be forced, the Committee's term expired. (Dean told *The Dallas Morning News* he had lined up Melvin Belli, who defended Ruby at his murder trial, to represent him if he was subpoenaed by us.)

We learned some interesting facts about Dean anyway. He was a good friend of Ruby, even though he was a principal witness in his prosecution. (That their friendship endured was indicated by a copy of the Warren Commission's report that Ruby sent to Dean. It was inscribed, "Your buddy, Jack Ruby.") We also found from a background check on Dean that he had been on good terms with prominent organized-crime figures; good enough in the case of Joseph Civello, the Dallas Mafia leader in 1963, to have joined him for dinner shortly after Civello returned from the mob meeting in Apalachin in November 1957. As for Dean's testimony in the Ruby trial, the Texas Court of Criminal Appeals found it to be an "item of reasonable error" when it ultimately overturned the guilty verdict. On March 25, 1964, there was a confrontation between Dean and Burt Griffin, the Warren Commission counsel, who suggested in an off-the-record conference that Dean's testimony was false. As a result, Griffin was ordered back to Washington and confined there, with the exception of a one-day trip to Dallas in April, until mid-July, and he was not permitted to question a Dallas police officer again.

(Dean was not Civello's only Dallas law-enforcement connection. After serving six years of a fifteen-year narcotics conviction in 1937, Civello was paroled. He then applied for a pardon, and one of his character witnesses was J. E. (Bill) Decker, the Dallas County sheriff in 1963, into whose custody Oswald was being transferred when he was murdered. And in October 1963 a Dallas police vice-squad detective was disciplined for having a business association with two nightspots that were owned by Civello associates.)

The results of our investigation led to the conclusion that Ruby probably entered the basement, not down the ramp, but from an alley that separated the Western Union office from the Police and Courts Building and ran from Main Street to Commerce Street. At the mid-point of the alley was a door to the first floor of the Police and Courts Building, and it was possible to go from there to the basement by either an elevator or a fire stairway. John O. Servance, who was the head porter in the building in 1963, told the Warren Commission that the door could be opened from within the stairwell, though it was locked on the outside. Dean told the Commission that he secured the door, but his testimony conflicted with that of Servance and two other maintenance employees.

When all of the evidence was assembled, much of it circumstantial, the only firm conclusion we could come to was that Ruby, as well as Dean and the other officers who questioned him, probably did not tell the truth about how Ruby got into the basement. But how the entry was in fact achieved remained theory at best. In addition, we believed it had not been shown that Ruby had witting help from anyone in getting into the basement, and we could find little substance to suggestions of a phone call or other sort of signal, any more than we could put credence in reports of a signal to officials in charge of Oswald's transfer that Ruby was in place. False statements by Dean and the other officers, after all, were just as easily explained as an effort to cover up the inadequacy of the security measures (possibly the failure to lock the fire door). In fact, theories that Ruby had inside assistance were countered by his presence at the Western Union office within minutes of the transfer.

Our conclusions about Ruby's entry into the basement were inconsistent with a conspiracy that called for Ruby to kill Oswald at the specific time he did, but they did not reduce the likelihood of a plot that called for Ruby to kill Oswald whenever he could get to him. The evidence of Ruby's repeated efforts to reach Oswald on Friday and Saturday made it appear probable to us that Ruby was stalking him, ready to shoot him when the opportunity arose. Ironically, when the opportunity did arise, it was so sudden and so dependent on coincidence, that Ruby's act did not appear to be conspiratorial. It would take an evaluation of Ruby's sanity and possible motives — questions that came up at his trial in early 1964 — to tip the scales toward conspiracy.

The State of Texas Versus Jack Ruby

In full view of a nation stunned by the assassination of its President some forty-eight hours earlier, Jack Ruby mortally wounded Lee Harvey Oswald. For those who were not watching the murder live on television, the networks replayed it periodically, until it became the most widely viewed homicide in history. Chief Justice Earl Warren was in his study preparing the eulogy he was to deliver that afternoon at the Capitol Rotunda, where the President's body was lying in state until the funeral the following morning. His daughter, Dorothy, ran in and said, "Daddy, they just killed Oswald." He cautioned her not to "pay attention to . . . wild rumors," to which she reponded, "I just *saw* them do it." For those around the world who missed it on television, there was the Pulitzer Prize-winning photograph by Bob Jackson of *The Dallas*

Times Herald, which showed Ruby, hunched over, firing into Oswald, who is grimacing in pain, as Detective Leavelle looks on in horror. Ultimately, not more than a handful of Americans failed to witness the actual act of Oswald's murder, yet Ruby was entitled to a fair trial. While what people saw on television or on page one of their newspaper comprised the central elements of the crime, they were not all that was involved in assessing Ruby's guilt. As Melvin M. Belli, Ruby's principal trial lawyer, summed it up in *Dallas Justice*: "[T]he whole world knew Ruby had shot Oswald. . . . The question was, why?"

On November 27, 1963, a Dallas County grand jury indicted "Jack Rubenstein, alias Jack Ruby," for "unlawfully, voluntarily and with malice aforethought kill[ing] Lee Harvey Oswald by shooting him with a gun, contrary to the form of the Statute in such cases made and provided, and against the peace and dignity of the State." On February 10, 1964, a hearing was held as part of an effort to secure for Ruby a trial in a county other than Dallas; it was not granted. The selection of the jury began on February 17; it was completed on March 3. The trial opened on March 4. A verdict of guilty — with a punishment of death — was returned on March 14, 1964. An appeal was taken; the verdict was reversed; and a new trial was ordered by the Texas Court of Criminal Appeals on October 5, 1966. On January 3, 1967, while awaiting retrial, Jack Ruby died of cancer in Parkland Memorial Hospital. We carefully examined each of these events for any light they might cast on the President's death.

Independently, five different attorneys were called that Sunday morning, all of whom appeared at the jail prepared to arrange Ruby's release on bail. When Oswald's death was announced, however, the charge, assault with intent to kill, was changed to murder. Obtaining bail was out of the question, and four of the five lawyers departed. Tom Howard, a veteran Dallas criminal lawyer who had been called by Ralph Paul, remained at the jail to act for Ruby. Howard saw Ruby between 1:56 P.M. and 2:02 P.M., immediately after Sorrells of the Secret Service, Hall of the FBI, Sergeant Dean, and the other Dallas police officers had completed their questioning. Ruby had at times been unsure, they said, about how to respond. But when he was taken before Captain Fritz at 3:15 P.M., he had a confident answer to the sort of questions that had given him trouble earlier: "No comment." Within a few hours of Oswald's death a complaint charging Ruby with murder was filed, a warrant for his formal arrest was issued, and he made his initial appearance before a magistrate. Ruby was transferred to the sheriff's custody on Monday, November 25. The unannounced transfer was effected without difficulty.

After he had been replaced as defense counsel, Howard told a number of newspaper reporters how he would have defended Ruby. He would not have tried to secure an acquittal, Howard said, for he did not believe Ruby was insane, at least in the legal sense. Instead, he would have conducted a "deathhouse defense." He told Allan E. Blanchard of *The Detroit News*: "I would have put Jack at the jury's mercy, spending a lot of time in detailed description of an electrocution. No jury can be unaffected by that." Under Texas law, had Howard pleaded him guilty to murder without malice, Ruby could not have received more than five years in prison. John Kaplan and Jon R. Waltz, both law professors, wrote in their study, *The Trial of Jack Ruby,* that a friend of Howard, who was a member of the grand jury, took an informal poll of two hundred Dallas citizens concerning the punishment Ruby ought to receive: it was seven to one for a light sentence. (Miffed by their book, Belli called Kaplan and Waltz "small claims court professors" who "never tried a case." In fact, Kaplan was an assistant U.S. attorney before joining the faculty of Stanford, and Waltz was a trial lawyer for ten years before taking a teaching post at Northwestern.) Howard had tried twenty-five capital cases, and none of his clients had gone to the electric chair. The key to the defense would be to present it, in Howard's own crude words, like it was "just another nigger murder case." (In Dallas, as in most of the South at the time, the punishment of a black for a crime against another black was disproportionately light.) Howard said that he did not want to treat the case like it was a *cause célèbre.* Unfortunately for Ruby, Howard was not to be the principal defense attorney.

How Melvin Belli, a nationally known trial lawyer, was brought in to handle the Ruby defense was a matter of some dispute. We heard a report that Seymour Ellison, a lawyer associated with Belli, got a phone call from "a Las Vegas attorney" who said, "Sy, one of our guys just bumped off the son of a bitch that gunned down the President. We can't move in to handle it, but there's a million bucks net for Mel if he'll take it." Ellison confirmed to us that he received the phone call, but he said he did not remember the name of the Las Vegas attorney, and nothing developed from the call. Belli told us a different story. He said Earl Ruby came to California three days after his brother was arrested; he watched Belli sum up a murder defense in a Los Angeles courtroom; and he asked him to take the case. Belli said he declined at first. He had learned that his fee would be paid by the sale of Ruby's story to newspapers, and he did not care to be involved in that sort of exploitation. Nevertheless, Earl Ruby talked him into it, Belli told us, and he took the case with five goals in mind: to save Jack Ruby; to strengthen the law; to show that current legal tests for insanity were inadequate; to wed modern law to modern science; and to help Dallas "solve its problem."

Belli set out to do, we noted, just what Tom Howard said he would have tried to avoid: to create a *cause célèbre*. Earl Ruby told still another story, which was the version reported by Kaplan and Waltz. He considered and rejected all Texas attorneys, including Percy Foreman of Houston, who was as famous and flamboyant as Belli. He also rejected the famous criminal lawyer, Jake Erlich of San Francisco, because he was Jewish, which might not sit well in Dallas. Earl Ruby next turned to Charles Bellows, a top trial lawyer in Chicago, with whom he was acquainted. (Bellows represented James R. Hoffa, who was scheduled to go on trial in federal court in Chicago for fraud.) Bellows figured Ruby's trial might last several months, so he said he wanted living expenses and a $20,000 fee. Jack Ruby was virtually penniless, and there was no defense fund, so Earl Ruby went to Mike Shore, a friend in Los Angeles. Shore came up with William Woodfield as a writer of Ruby's story, and Woodfield suggested Belli as a defense counsel. Woodfield tried to call Belli and left a message. Belli, in turn, left a message with Woodfield's wife: "Get me that case — I want it so badly I can taste it." Eventually, a meeting was arranged at Belli's Los Angeles home. When the matter of a fee came up, Earl Ruby told Belli he thought his brother's story might raise $25,000. Belli said, "O.K., don't worry about the rest. I'll probably make it by writing a book."

Belli told us he was Jack Ruby's only choice, and he said Ruby told him that he had "checked him out." We were led to believe that Belli, who had probably come to his attention by representing a mobster and a stripper, was, in fact, Jack Ruby's first choice.

Ruby liked to tell friends that he knew Mickey Cohen, the West Coast hoodlum. He also knew Juanita Dale Phillips, a stripper whose stage name was Candy Barr. In the late 1950s Phillips was working for Ruby's competitors, Barney and Abe Weinstein, and starring in a pornographic film, but in 1957 she was arrested by Dallas Detective G. M. Tippit (the Tippit Ruby knew, not the one Oswald killed) for the possession of marijuana. She was prosecuted by William Alexander, the assistant district attorney who handled the case against Ruby in 1964, in a proceeding presided over by Joe B. Brown, the judge in Ruby's 1964 trial. Upon conviction, Phillips was sentenced to fifteen years. While she was out on bail pending appeal, her engagement to Cohen was announced. Belli, who had represented Cohen, was persuaded to handle Phillips's appeal, and even though he put on quite a show in her behalf, she was sent to prison, where she remained until she was paroled by Governor John B. Connally three and a half years later. Ruby was back in touch with Phillips in 1963, calling her a number of times during the summer and visiting her in Edna, Texas, in an effort to get her to go to work in his club as soon as the conditions of her parole permitted. We could not be certain just how well Ruby knew Cohen, who also grew up in Chicago, but he admired him and tried to emulate him. Dean Jennings, who was the AGVA branch manager in Dallas in 1956 and 1957, said Ruby "was somewhat of a tough guy," who often appeared to be acting out a "junior version of Mickey Cohen." Belli also noticed the similarity. Ruby's concern for his personal appearance reminded him of Cohen. They were, he said, "the same type."

We made an effort to examine the financing of Ruby's defense, though Earl Ruby, who handled the money, apparently did not keep adequate records. A defense fund was established, but as Earl Ruby told the Warren Commission (and repeated to us in 1978), it barely brought in enough to cover the cost of soliciting contributions — $1,500 to $2,000. The sale of Ruby's story raised another $45,000, of which Ruby received approximately $30,000, and, according to Earl Ruby, Belli got $11,000. (Belli told us he ended up with $17,000 in unpaid expert-witness bills and other expenses.) Howard received $4,000; Bellows got $2,500; and $11,000 was paid to other lawyers, expert witnesses, and an investigator. Joseph Tonahill, a Texas lawyer Belli brought into the case, declined to accept a fee. That, according to Earl Ruby and Belli, summed up the financing of the defense. We found it difficult to believe that Belli did not receive a substantial fee for his defense of Ruby. (A CIA report stated that Belli flew to Mexico City a few days after the Ruby trial ended, and he met there with Victor Velasquez, a noted trial lawyer but one with a "shabby" reputation in Mexico, according to CIA sources. Velasquez, it had been charged, was involved in "drug smuggling." Belli stayed just one night, then flew to San Francisco. He and Velasquez, when they were asked, denied the meeting had anything to do with the Ruby trial. We considered the possibility that Belli went to Mexico to pick up a fee for the Ruby defense, but we found no proof that he did.)

We also looked into the post-trial financial standing of Ruby's relatives, to see if there was any sign that one or more of them had received payment for the killing of Oswald. The only one to become wealthy in the years following the assassination was Earl Ruby, who explained that his money had come from a company in Detroit, Cobo Cleaners, which he bought for about $120,000 in October 1961. The purchase seemed legitimate, but then we learned that Earl Ruby's income from Cobo Cleaners increased dramatically in the years immediately after 1963. Earl Ruby explained to us that Cobo's principal customer, Hudson's Department Store, signed a contract in December 1962, which accounted for his increased wealth. With limited time and resources, we were not able to verify or refute Earl Ruby's explanation.

Belli was but one of a cast of striking characters in the Ruby trial. The judge, Joe Brantley Brown, was not a man of superior intellect, though he was experienced (thirty years on the bench), and he had a reputation for fairness and courtesy. His record in the Texas Court of Criminal Appeals was not bad (ten reversals out of thirty-four appeals), and he was considered to be a "defense" judge, who called the close questions against the prosecution. If he had one glaring fault, it was his thirst for publicity. (During the trial of Juanita Dale Phillips for marijuana possession, he delighted in posing with her for photographers.)

The prosecution team was led by Henry Wade, who had graduated with highest honors from the University of Texas Law School in 1938 and had served in the FBI and U.S. Navy before his election as Dallas County district attorney. Wade had a reputation for integrity, though his judgment was questioned for his offhand statements, such as those he made during Oswald's detention. (A habit he had not broken by 1980. "Frankly, I don't think there's much organized crime in Dallas," Wade told *The Dallas Morning News*. "I think the whole idea of the Mafia is overrated. I think it's just sort of a romantic thing for reporters to write about.") The number-two man was William Alexander, who was respected, if not liked, by the Dallas bar and known to be an able trial lawyer. The team was rounded out by James Bowie, the prosecution's "book man," whose knowledge of the law, including the recent decisions of the Supreme Court, would, in Kaplan's and Waltz's words, "bring joy to the heart of a law professor." Belli, in short, did not face a team of country bumpkins.

For his part, Belli was well advised in his selection of Joseph Tonahill to assist him. A past-president of the Texas Association of Plaintiff Attorneys, Tonahill was the one lawyer in the case who received from the Texas Senate a resolution commending the "courage, loyalty, and stability" of his actions on behalf of his client, "sustaining respect for the legal profession and what it fights for." Such resolutions may generally be discounted by noting the political nature of their source, but in Tonahill's case it was well deserved. The defense team also had its "book man," Philip Burleson, who previously had headed the appellate section of the Dallas district attorney's office and had written a manual on procedure for the appeal of criminal cases.

In his blunt way, Alexander summed up Belli's problems. "Jack Ruby," he said, "was about as handicapped as you can get in Dallas. First, he was a Yankee. Second, he was a Jew. Third, he was in the nightclub business." As it could be gathered from what he did, rather than what he said, Belli's defense strategy was, therefore, to move the trial from Dallas if possible, but in any event to go for an acquittal — all or nothing at all. Alexander had, of course, overstated Ruby's problems, for he would be tried not by Dallas as a whole, but by twelve Dallas citizens. Besides, Dallas was a city with a tradition of fair play, and Alexander's implications of prejudice were unwarranted.

As soon as Belli entered the case, the defense made a motion for bail. Generally, under Texas law, bail is a matter of right in capital cases, except "where proof is evident." The motion was heard but denied by Judge Brown, "for the present." The prosecution's presentation had not been very impressive on the question of premeditation, in light of the evidence (the testimony of the Western Union clerk, the time of the telegraphed money order to Karen Carlin, and the time of the shooting), so it was not clear that Ruby would fail to get bail the next time around. The second bail hearing at the end of January, however, did not go as expected. Usually, the defense attempts to use preliminary proceedings to learn about the prosecution's case, but Belli, to the surprise of observers, entered most of his evidence of Ruby's insanity. It seemed that Belli was trying as much to educate the Dallas community, from which the jury would be selected, about the special character of Ruby's insanity plea, as he was to get the judge to grant Ruby bail. In fact, after the hearing and before Brown could rule, Belli withdrew the bail motion, and Judge Brown turned to consideration of Belli's motion for a change of venue.

Ruby's story, as written by Woodfield, was published as a three-part copyrighted series in papers across the country between the second bail hearing and the change of venue hearing. There was little in it that was not already known (the Dallas papers did not even carry it), so it seemed to have little effect on the trial. The hearing on the change of venue motion, as the bail hearing had been, was a major production. Belli presented forty-one witnesses, including Stanley Marcus of Nei-man-Marcus, the department store. Marcus said he had "grave reservations" that either the defense or the prosecution could get an impartial jury anywhere in the state, but he thought it more likely elsewhere than Dallas. Dallas had, he said, taken the assassination "personally." Wade countered with thirty-eight affidavits from Dallas citizens, all of whom swore that they thought it possible for a fair trial to be held, and he then made the telling argument: "They say we can't get an impartial jury here. Let's try. The proof is in the pudding." Much of the publicity had been generated by the defense (by Ruby's personal story, for example), and the reaction had not been unfavorable. Belli had a poll taken in mid-December, which showed that 66 percent of the people of Dallas thought Ruby was sane, but when the poll was repeated two months later, after the bail hearing, the figure had dropped to 40 percent. In any event, Judge Brown agreed to try to find an impartial jury in Dallas.

Belli needed, in Kaplan's and Waltz's words, "an educated jury conversant with and receptive to psychiatric testimony." After fourteen days of questioning and challenging, a jury was seated in the box: one hundred sixty-two prospective jurors had been questioned; sixty-two had been excused because they expressed opposition to capital punishment, fifty-eight because they manifested possible prejudice toward Ruby. The average age of the twelve selected was a little over thirty-nine; there were eight men and four women. All were Protestants. All but two were native Texans. Five were from Dallas; the rest were from the suburbs. They were generally of above-average intelligence: two engineers, an accountant, a bookkeeper, a research analyst, a corporation vice-president, a secretary, a postman, two salesmen, an airline mechanic, and a telephone company employee.

The trial began on March 4, 1964. The prosecution presented not just the bare facts of the shooting, but the conduct of Ruby that indicated he was stalking his prey. The purpose was not to show conspiracy; it was to imply premeditation. The prosecution also introduced a series of statements that Ruby allegedly made in the presence of police officers at the time of the shooting or immediately after it. The remarks, quoted more or less verbatim, were at odds with the defense plea of insanity. "You rotten son of a bitch, you shot the President." "I hope the son of a bitch dies." "I hope I killed the son of a bitch." "I did it because you couldn't do it." "I intended to get off three shots." "I did it to show the world that Jews have guts." "I did it so Jackie Kennedy wouldn't have to come to Dallas." "I first thought of killing him at the Friday night press conference." While a number of officers testified against Ruby, the most damaging testimony was given by Sergeant Patrick T. Dean. Dean said that Ruby's statements about showing the world that Jews have guts, doing it out of sympathy for Jackie Kennedy, and thinking about it at the Friday night press conference were made while Ruby was being questioned shortly after the shooting. Texas law prohibits without qualification any statement taken by the police from a person in custody from being used against him in a trial, even if it is obtained without coercion. On the other hand, Texas law admits statements made during the *res gestae* (Latin for "things done") of the offense, an exception that, while somewhat fluid, usually means at the time of the offense and as a natural part of it. Belli was well within the normal expectation of the law, therefore, when he objected to the police officers' testimony, particularly statements attributed to Ruby after he was taken upstairs. Since they carried a high risk of reversal, we wondered why Wade pressed to have the statements admitted, when they were not essential to his case. They did, of course, tend to negate insanity, but Wade's expert testimony ultimately would have to confront the insanity plea.

Belli's two-pronged defense strategy could be simply put, even if facts to support it were not simple to summarize. (Curiously, Belli never attacked the statements that inferred premeditation, as such.) First, the police witnesses to Ruby's alleged statements had lied. Second, Ruby was legally insane at the time of the shooting, since he had sustained (at some undetermined time) organic brain damage, and he was subject to seizures of an epileptic character, having what was medically known as "psychomotor variant epilepsy." When he shot Oswald, he was suffering a seizure and was in a fugue state, so he was not legally responsible for his conduct.

Belli's defense was at its most persuasive on the question of the truthfulness of at least some of the police testimony. A New York City radio newsman, Ike Pappas, had a tape recorder running near the entrance to the jail office when Oswald was brought out, and it did not pick up any remarks by Ruby at the moment he shot Oswald. But other statements were more firmly established. Detective D. R. Archer was not alone in hearing Ruby say he did it because the police could not, and he intended to get off three shots; Forrest Sorrels of the Secret Service testified to the Warren Commission that he heard Ruby make remarks similar to "I hope the son of a bitch dies" and "I did it so Jackie Kennedy wouldn't have to come to Dallas." But the most damaging statement, the one about having thought about it at the Friday night press conference, implying clear premeditation (and stalking), had not been heard by Sorrels. It was in Dean's testimony alone.

The insanity plea rested on medical testimony, which is often difficult for laymen to evaluate. One of the prospective jurors, Harry L. Elledge, summed it up well when he was questioned by one of the prosecutors on his ability to give Ruby a fair trial: "They'll put on their doctors, and you'll put on yours and who am I to believe?" In science, as in philosophy, there is often more than one school of thought on a particular issue. Even where the theory is agreed upon, its application may be more art than science. And where the facts are not clear, reasonable persons can arrive at different points without having to feel that truth is unattainable, or that others are not acting in good faith. Belli's strategy was beset by many such problems. Ruby was examined and electroencephalograms (tests that measure brain-wave patterns) were taken, but the defense and prosecution witnesses disagreed on the interpretation of the graphs. In any event, the graphs could only establish the possibility of brain damage. That the brain damage gave rise to epilepsy and that Ruby was in a fugue state when he shot Oswald remained to be shown. Belli hoped to supply those conclusions with the testimony of Dr. Manfred S. Guttmacher, one of the nation's leading experts in forensic psychiatry. Unfortunately for Belli (and for Ruby), it was at this point that the defense fell apart. Belli himself said of Dr. Guttmacher's testimony, in his book, *Dallas Justice*: "It was not *precisely* what I would have wished for." Instead of supporting Belli's theory that relied on the electroencephalograms to show a psychomotor epileptic seizure, Guttmacher testified that Ruby had shot Oswald in a state of "episodic dyscontrol." That is to say, Ruby was an emotional man with a weak personality structure whose defenses had crumbled under stress, so an impulse to kill had become irresistible. As Kaplan and Waltz put it: "The defense's chief attorney and his principal expert had passed like ships in the night." Privately, Dr. Guttmacher expressed the view that Ruby had exhibited too many indications of uninterrupted consciousness, and the shooting of Oswald had been carried off too efficiently with too little fumbling for an epileptic seizure to be a real possibility. For all practical purposes, the defense's presentation had collapsed. It was now a traditional plea of temporary insanity, and the jury had more than sufficient testimony to discount that diagnosis, if it chose, from both Ruby's pattern of conduct in stalking Oswald, and from expert testimony on the issue of insanity given by the prosecution's psychiatrists.

After eight days of testimony both sides rested. Extensive legal arguments took up the next day; the judge then charged the jury, and final arguments were made. It was at 12:40 A.M., Saturday, March 14, 1964, when a tired Melvin Belli, the last defense counsel to argue, sat down. The closing remarks were reserved for Wade, since the prosecution carried the burden of proof, and got the last word. He, too, was tired. When he finished, the clock read 1:06 A.M.

Most of the press representatives hazarded the guess that Ruby would be found guilty, but only one reporter said he thought Ruby would be sentenced to die. At 9:15 Saturday morning the jury returned to begin deliberations. It did not take long. With only a little discussion, a ballot was taken and the jury was unanimous in finding Ruby sane. Since there was no serious doubt on the question of murder, no ballot was taken. After about fifteen minutes the jury took a ballot on the question of "malice," that is premeditation. There were no dissents, so sentencing was next. The jurors agreed that the choice was life or death. On the first ballot, it was eight to four for death. Several more ballots brought it to eleven to one; fifteen more minutes and the holdout wavered. They had a verdict. In all, the deliberations had taken only two hours and nineteen minutes. When the verdict was announced, Belli railed "May I thank the jury for a victory for bigotry and injustice!" But the jury had spoken, and a fair analysis of the evidence supported the verdict.

The trial also brought out enlightening evidence of Ruby's motive, though it did not become public at the time. It was contained in a note that Ruby passed to Tonahill during the trial. It read:

> Joe, you should know this. Tom Howard told me to say that I shot Oswald so that Caroline and Mrs. Kennedy wouldn't have to come to Dallas to testify. O.K.?

Tonahill later said, "What Ruby wrote down disturbed me very much. I thought about it, walking all the way back to my hotel room. It was very upsetting." Belli himself wrote in *Dallas Justice*:

> Clearly [Ruby's] . . . story of trying to protect Mrs. Kennedy from a harrowing court appearance at a trial for Oswald did not add up. . . . I am sure the story was false because it didn't square with everything else we knew. . . .

Ruby's conviction eventually found its way to the Texas Court of Criminal Appeals, which reversed the verdict. The court's opinion, which was not well reasoned, rested on two points. First, it found that the statements by Ruby testified to by Sergeant Dean, that he decided to kill Oswald two nights before he did so, were not within the *res gestae* of the shooting of Oswald. "The admission of this testimony was clearly injurious," the court held, "and calls for a reversal of [the] . . . conviction." Unfortunately, the court did not consider the possible application of the "harmless error" rule to the Ruby verdict. In light of the other overwhelming evidence of Ruby's guilt, it was hardly likely that the Dean testimony tipped the scale, as damaging as it was. Consequently, the verdict should have been allowed to stand, as the admission of Dean's testimony was "harmless." Second, the court held that a change of venue should have been granted. Unfortunately, here the court's opinion was abbreviated and hardly persuasive. It was difficult to support its judgment that the jury was not impartial. The court had no good answer — and made none — to Wade's telling point: "You test a pudding by eating it." The process of jury selection showed that an impartial jury could be and was chosen.

The Testimony of Jack Ruby

Ruby did not take the stand in his trial; Belli would not let him. But he did appear before the Warren Commission shortly after the trial. His testimony was taken in Dallas by Chief Justice Warren and Congressman Ford of the Commission and J. Lee Rankin, Joseph A. Ball, and Arlen Specter of the Commission staff. (Leon D. Hubert, Jr., and Burt

W. Griffin, who had been assigned to the Ruby aspect of the case, were conspicuously absent.) Sheriff Decker; Leon Jaworski, special counsel to the Texas attorney general; and Tonahill, representing Ruby, were also present. Ruby's testimony could not be accepted at face value, and we found it difficult to frame a coherent theory of it, since a number of interpretations presented themselves. One fair interpretation would propose that there was no coherence to it at all, suggesting that it should be read as the ramblings of a mentally unbalanced man. Ruby was not insane when he killed Oswald, so the theory would go, but the pressure of the trial and the verdict had made him so. As such, the testimony should be dismissed on most points as not reliable; it was only sad and pitiful. Another view would see it, however, as a valiant effort by Ruby to tell the truth, at least as he knew it; yet it would also see it as colored by the stress to which the assassination, the shooting of Oswald, and his trial and sentence of death had subjected him. His testimony, therefore, might be useful both in the details he revealed about the assassination and himself, but it would have to be read with the utmost caution. Much of it would have to be rejected, not as an intentional fabrication, but as the product of stress. This view, we believed, had much to recommend it, if only because it was humane. Yet it was not the view that we ultimately tended toward as we studied Ruby's testimony, for there was another view that, while we did not subscribe to it entirely, seemed to us to offer the best approximation of the truth.

Our view of Ruby's Warren Commission testimony moved in two directions, one basically consistent with the single-assassin theory, the other radically at odds with it. First, it conceded that Ruby was under considerable stress after his trial, especially in light of the verdict, but it interpreted Ruby's testimony as basically calculated, not irrational. Ruby expected there would be another trial. Next time out, he would probably have to adopt the "deathhouse" defense that Tom Howard had proposed. As Ruby himself told the Commission, Belli should not "have tried to vindicate me on an insanity plea, to relieve me of all responsibility, because circumstantially everything look[ed] so bad for me." Ruby must have known that if he could maintain an image of a man under stress, he might be able to establish at least the absence of "malice" in his next trial (or in a clemency hearing before the governor), so he would then face only five years, not death. In fact, Ruby explicitly noted for the Commission the "very bad mental strain" he was under. (We noted that Ruby's jailers believed he was "putting on an act" when he hit his head against the wall of his cell, broke his glasses, threw a spittoon at a light bulb, tried to stick his finger in a light socket, and tore up his coveralls. "O.K., Jack, cut the crap or we won't play cards with you anymore," the jailers would say, according to Ovid

Demaris and Garry Wills in *Jack Ruby*. Ruby would respond, "Oh, you sonsabitches," and then he would calm down.) Ruby's Warren Commission testimony may be read as basically calculated for the simple purpose of furthering his own cause and with no other inferences, an interpretation that would not be at odds with a single-assassin hypothesis. It, too, was an interpretation with much to be said for it, but, again, it was not the one we found the most compelling. An interpretation of Ruby's testimony as basically calculated had an intriguing variation, to wit: Ruby was trying to tell the truth about the conspiracy he knew existed, but he feared for his life and consequently spoke indirectly, as seasoned criminals often do when they are being interrogated.

An argument that Ruby did not reveal the conspiracy because of genuine fear for his life would be strengthened if there was evidence that contacts between Ruby and organized crime continued after the assassination and the murder of Oswald. There was, in fact, such evidence, although the Warren Commission never took account of it. Joseph Campisi, reportedly the number-two man in Dallas to Mafia leader Joseph Civello at the time, told the FBI in 1963 that he visited Ruby in jail after getting a call from Sheriff Decker. (Campisi acknowledged to us in 1978 that he was close to Decker, who, he said, had "no problems with the Italian families" in Dallas.) In a disjointed interview, Campisi told the FBI that Ruby talked about Mrs. Kennedy and the kids; he said he knew nothing about Ruby's background or associates; and he said "the only person present at the time he talked to Ruby was a deputy sheriff." When we deposed Campisi in 1978, he added that his wife, Marie, accompanied him when he went to see Ruby. (One reading of this seemingly incidental information would be that organized-crime figures do not take their wives along when they are conducting business; another would be that Campisi wanted the visit to appear purely social when it was not.) Campisi also told us that he attended at least part of Ruby's trial.

A careful reading of Ruby's Warren Commission testimony revealed the hints of a conspiracy and Ruby's fear to tell of it, and we tried to fit them together, as a craftsman would weave the threads of an intricate tapestry. We wondered: Was Ruby trying to tell the Commission something indirectly in hopes of getting out of Dallas, so he could tell the whole truth? "I want to tell you the truth, and I can't tell it here," he said rather explicitly to Chief Justice Warren. He specifically asked to be taken to Washington: "If you understand my way of talking, you have got to bring me to Washington. . . ." He said his "life was in danger" in Dallas, adding, "[M]y whole family is in jeopardy." He then asked Decker and Tonahill to leave the room, and the sheriff complied, though his lawyer did not. Ruby asked Warren if he could talk to him in private, but Warren told him unequivocally he would not be brought to Washington, for "it could not be done." Only then did Ruby proceed to tell his story, and it was consistent with what he had told the FBI.

Ruby was not questioned extensively, so most of what he said was a narrative constructed by him. We felt it was appropriate, therefore, to read more into his testimony than we would if he had been directed by a skilled interrogator. We suspected that Ruby was trying to bring out certain facts that were intended to point investigators in the right direction, although the basic story was his standard account. He told the Commission, for example, that there was "a certain organization" involved, though the one he named was the John Birch Society. (At one point Ruby apparently tried to underline his effort to speak on two levels by saying, "I must be a great actor. I tell you that.") Ruby said that "no one else requested me to do anything," and he was specific. "No underworld person," he said without being asked, "made any effort to contact me." Then, as if to undermine his own denial, he mentioned his Chicago background. He noted the long-distance calls, giving the AGVA explanation, but he immediately brought up his trip to Cuba and Lewis McWillie, a "key man" at the Tropicana, he said. He said, again without being asked, that he "only made one trip to Havana," when he could easily have realized that the Warren Commission had access to the airline records that would demonstrate he was lying.

Rankin stepped in to question Ruby about his fear for his family, and the answer was clear for what it implied: his family would be in danger, he replied, if he were a "party to a plot to silence Oswald." He turned to Warren and remarked that he was "in a tough spot," and he appeared to be groping for a "solution . . . to save . . . himself." Finally, he said to Ford, "[M]aybe certain people don't want to know the truth that may come out of me." We asked former President Ford, who testified at a Committee public hearing on September 21, 1978, why the Warren Commission declined Ruby's request to be taken from his Dallas jail cell and brought to Washington. Ford replied:

> We believe[d] that we had fully probed from him all of the information that he had available, and the Chief Justice . . . and I reported back to the other members of the Commission the interrogation we had of . . . Ruby. [T]he other members of the Commission agreed with the Chief Justice and myself that it was not necessary to bring . . . Ruby from Dallas to Washington and to go through another interrogation of him in the nation's capital.

When the Commission did not bring him to Washington, Ruby's last hope of extricating himself from his difficult position was gone.

Ruby was not quite finished with the Commission, however. During his testimony in Dallas he asked to be given a polygraph examination, and Warren promised he would "be able to take such a test." In fact, the suggestion that Ruby be given a polygraph had originated with the Warren Commission staff. Assistant Counsel David W. Belin had proposed the idea, but a majority of the staff recommended against it, and Warren sided with the majority, believing also that such tests were of limited use. (The error rate of polygraphs is so high that most courts refuse to admit their results as evidence.) Belin "took matters into his own hands," as he put it. He contacted Rabbi Hillel Silverman, whose synagogue Ruby had occasionally attended, and suggested that Silverman use his influence with Ruby. Belin later took credit for the request by Ruby for the polygraph, and he used the results to argue for the Warren Commission's single-assassin hypothesis.

Ruby was given the polygraph by the FBI on July 18, 1964. Among others, William Robert Beavers, a psychiatrist who had examined Ruby previously and had diagnosed him as a "psychotic depressive," was an observer. Dr. Beavers said that he thought Ruby's "depressive element" had diminished on the day of the examination, but he cautioned that he was not an expert in the area of "interrelationships between mental illness and the polygraph." Nevertheless, J. Edgar Hoover told the Warren Commission that, in light of Beavers's diagnosis, which raised a "serious question" as to Ruby's mental condition, "no significance should be placed on the polygraph." The Commission wrote in its report that it "did not rely on the results of . . . [the] examination" in reaching its conclusions.

We too were concerned with the validity of the polygraph. Ruby had been asked a number of key questions: Was the trip to Cuba solely for pleasure? (Yes) Did he shoot Oswald to silence him? (No) Did he shoot Oswald because of any influence of the underworld? (No) Did he shoot Oswald to save Mrs. Kennedy the ordeal of a trial? (Yes) If Ruby's answers could be relied on, then the questions we had raised about his participation in a conspiracy to silence Oswald could be resolved in the negative. Our own evidence clearly indicated he had lied on some of the questions (the Cuba trip, the "Mrs. Kennedy" motive). But what about the others? It was important to determine if the test was valid.

While our Committee prohibited the use of polygraph examinations for fact-finding, in view of their unreliability, it did ask a panel of distinguished experts to evaluate the validity of tests administered by others. It was the unanimous conclusion of the panel that four key factors, independent of Ruby's mental state, had a negative effect on the reliability of the test: (1) the time lapse since the shooting; (2) Ruby's extensive prior interrogation; (3) the many people present during the examination; and (4) the great number of questions asked. The panel considered that the manner in which the test was administered, citing four major factors and ten others, represented "a gross abuse of basic polygraph principles." No opinion could be rendered on Ruby's credibility, the panel advised, because of the conditions under which the test was conducted.

Ruby died just three months after the Texas Court of Criminal Appeals ordered a new trial. In his last days, his brother Earl smuggled a tape recorder in a briefcase into his hospital room. The fourteen-minute tape was sold to Capitol Records, and the proceeds of a four-minute record were used to bury Ruby. The story Ruby recorded differed little from the one he had told all along. (It included, for example, the demonstrably false explanation of his Cuban travels.) On January 3, 1967, the end came. The Dallas County medical examiner, Earl Rose, performed the autopsy. He found the heaviest cluster of cancer cells in Ruby's right lung. The brain was sectioned, and microscopic tests revealed no organic brain damage, although there were traces of the white cancer tumors coursing through the body. We asked Dr. Rose if Ruby could have had cancer and known it in November 1963. The answer was no.

Ruby was the seventh person to die at Parkland Hospital in 1967. The code number of his corpse was M-67-007 (Oswald had been M-63-356). The code was shortened on jars into which cells and tissues were placed for later examination. Jack Ruby's last identification was "007."

Elements of Conspiracy

As we brought our investigation of Ruby to a close, we came to a number of important conclusions. We could not accept the Warren Commission's benign view of Ruby's background, character, associations, and conduct. Nor could we accept its belief that Ruby killed Oswald out of genuine shock and grief over the President's assassination. For us, the truth was far from benign. Ruby's violent character had been molded in a matrix of crime and corruption in Chicago, one of the nation's centers of organized crime. His business activities were an integral part of a system of criminal operations, even if they were not illegal as such. At least on his trip to Cuba, Ruby played an important, if minor, role in a sophisticated syndicate operation that involved one of the most powerful underworld leaders. Ruby's associates in Dallas for the years and months prior to the assassination included a number of prominent organized-crime figures. He was in serious financial difficulty in the period leading up to the assassination, and a number of organized-crime figures were aware of it. Those same figures, under heavy pressure from the Kennedy organized-crime program, had a strong motive to assassinate the President.

Ruby's professed motive for killing Oswald — that he wanted to spare Mrs. Kennedy the ordeal of a trial — was admittedly false. Ruby told a number of other lies to conceal the truth, the most significant being that he killed Oswald on the spur of the moment, when the evidence was overwhelming that he stalked his prey for nearly two days before gunning him down. The murder of Oswald by Jack Ruby had all the earmarks of an organized-crime hit, an action to silence the assassin, so he could not reveal the conspiracy. It was time to turn to Oswald, to see if his background, character, associations, and conduct might provide new evidence as to the identity of his coconspirators.

12

Lee Harvey Oswald:
His Role Reconsidered

All the Marine Corps did was to teach you to kill, and after you got out . . . you might be [a] good gangster.

Lee Harvey Oswald
Warren Commission *Hearings,*
Volume VIII

Lee Harvey Oswald: 1939–1963

As we undertook to reexamine Lee Harvey Oswald — his background, his character, and his associations with organizations and individuals — we did not expect there would be much to add to what was already known about his role in the assassination. We were wrong. After a careful reconstruction of Oswald's early life in New Orleans, which included an appraisal of his family roots, together with a close look at him in the fateful summer of 1963, we were able to see the President's assassin in an entirely new light.

In August 1939, six years and a month after he married Marguerite Claverie, Robert Lee Oswald collapsed and died of a heart attack while mowing the lawn of his home on Alvar Street in New Orleans. Two months later, on October 18, the Oswalds' second son was born and named Lee (for his late father) Harvey (for his uncle and godfather) Oswald. (Lee was actually Marguerite's third son; the father of her eldest was her first husband, Edward John Pic.) Robert Oswald had not been well-to-do. At the time of his death he was struggling to meet the payments on the house on Alvar Street, and there were few resources on the Claverie side of the family to help Marguerite. She had started to work at age seventeen, after just one year of high school, as a receptionist for a law firm, and she had had to return to the role of breadwinner soon after Lee was born.

As a child, Lee Oswald lived with his aunt and uncle, Lillian (Marguerite's older sister) and Charles F. Murret, remaining with them until, at age three, he was placed in the Evangelical Lutheran Bethlehem Orphan Asylum in New Orleans. He was taken out of the orphanage by his mother in January 1944, as were his brother Robert and half-brother John Pic the following June. With Marguerite's third marriage, to Edwin Ekdahl, it appeared the family would be reunited. The boys did spend the summer of 1946 with their mother in a rented home in Covington, Louisiana, and they lived with the Ekdahls for a time in Benbrook, Texas, a town not far from Fort Worth. But the marriage was a stormy one, and it ended in divorce in 1948.

Since his father was dead and Marguerite never was able to adapt to her maternal role, the closest approximation of normal parents that Oswald had was the Murrets. Catholics of French and German descent (Marguerite and Lillian Claverie had been baptized in the Lutheran church of their mother, but their father was Catholic), the Murrets had five children of their own. Their home at 757 French Street was, however, adequate to accommodate periodic visits by Lee and Marguerite when they were living in Texas and when they moved back to New Orleans in early 1954, having spent a year and a half in New York City. Even though they rented their own apartment, Lee regularly came to the Murrets for Friday-night seafood dinner. He would be back again on Saturday, and Aunt Lillian would give him money to rent a bike and go riding in City Park. While he was attending a Marine Corps radar school in Biloxi, Mississippi, Oswald kept up his visits to the Murrets; he wrote to them from the Soviet Union; and when he returned to New Orleans in April 1963, seeking a job and a home for his new family, he phoned his aunt to ask for a room, and she welcomed him back.

When he testified to the Warren Commission in 1964, Charles Murret said he had kept his distance from his nephew in the summer of 1963: "To tell the truth, after he defected to Russia . . . I just let it go out the window." In fact, Murret said, he had never taken much interest in Oswald: ". . . I just couldn't warm up to him." Murret, who died of cancer in October 1964, had been, we learned, less than candid with the Commission. When Oswald returned to New Orleans from Dallas in the summer of 1963, Murret drove him back to the bus station to pick up his luggage. (Oswald wrote his wife Marina, who had remained at the home of a friend in Irving, Texas: "All is well. Uncle

'Dyuz' [sic] offered me a loan of $200 if needed.'') Once an apartment had been found and Marina and their daughter June arrived, Murret drove the Oswalds to 4907 Magazine Street, a good 99 blocks from his house, and helped them move in. He loaned Oswald $30 or $40 for the first rent payment on the apartment, and he encouraged Lee and Marina, with their daughter, to visit, which they did regularly. Murret told the Warren Commission that if the Oswalds did spend time at his home that summer, it must have been while he was out: "They must have come in the daytime." On the contrary, Lee and Marina were often at the Murrets on weekends and holidays, such as Labor Day (when Murret lectured his nephew on helping his wife learn English). On one weekend Murret drove his wife, a daughter Joyce, and the Oswalds to Mobile, Alabama, where his son, Eugene, was attending a Jesuit seminary. (Oswald gave a talk on Russia to the seminarians.) In addition, the Murrets visited the Oswalds at their Magazine Street apartment, and they took an interest in their well-being. For example, after Oswald was arrested for fighting with anti-Castro Cubans on August 9, 1963 (he had been passing out pro-Castro leaflets), a prominent friend of Murret, a liquor-store owner and state boxing commissioner, Emile Bruneau, bailed him out of jail. Murret himself went to the Oswalds the next night and closely questioned Lee about the incident, telling him to show up in court, get a job, and support his family.

We did not find it unusual that Murret would want to disassociate himself from a nephew who was the accused assassin of the President; nor did we fault Warren Commission Counsel Albert E. Jenner, Jr., for concentrating, in the questioning of Murret, on issues that were pertinent to the case against Oswald: Had there been among Oswald's belongings an object shaped like a tent pole wrapped in tan paper? Had Oswald been left- or right-handed? (In her testimony, Marguerite Oswald suggested her son had been a left-handed rifleman, which might have hampered his ability to fire the bolt-action Mannlicher-Carcano.) Had Oswald ever learned to drive? (Certain conspiracy allegations before the Commission depended on Oswald being at the wheel of an automobile.) But we did consider Murret's effort to direct Jenner away from his relationship with Oswald significant, in light of what we had come to suspect about the participation by organized crime in an assassination conspiracy. While Jenner did not ask Murret about his line of work, he did try to learn it from his wife: "He's a clerk for, well, he works for different companies. . . . He works at different wharves, in other words," Lillian Murret testified. Her answer was incomplete.

To his wife and just about everyone else, Charles Murret was known as "Dutz," a nickname from boyhood. "[I]t just caught on, with me

being in the fight game and all," he told Jenner. As a professional box-
er, Murret had only a couple of bouts, but he went on to be the manager
of other fighters, in particular one named Anthony Sciambra, and he
was successful enough that his obituary was headlined: "Death Claims
Sports Figure." But Murret was, we found, a sports figure in another
sense: he was a professional gambler, a handbook operator, and he was
connected with the organized-crime operations of Carlos Marcello.

In the Warren Commission's investigation, there was a hint about
Murret's career. In an interview with the FBI on November 30, 1963,
John Pic, Oswald's half-brother, stated that something said to him
when he was quite young had left the impression that his uncle "was a
gambler and bookmaker." But that was the only reference to Murret's
illegal activities that we could find in the entire record of the 1964 investigation. (Had the FBI consulted its own files, it would have found a
report dated May 6, 1944, on illegal gambling operations in New Orleans that listed two clubs, ". . . handbooks . . . operated by Dutz Murret at 128 Chartres Street and 837 Iberville Street.") Marguerite Oswald
revealed in 1965 that she had been aware of her brother-in-law's line of
work. Miffed because Lillian Murret had told the Warren Commission
that her son, Gene, was more thrifty as a youth than Lee Oswald, she
told a biographer: "Her boy had a father who was in the bookmaking
business and had a very large income. . . ." In 1978 Marguerite Oswald
told us that Murret had been a bookmaker "for many, many years."

From interviewing members of his immediate family, we learned that
Murret had long been associated with a man named Sam Saia. Lillian
Murret said her husband had been "in the gambling business" with
Saia for a number of years, working at the Lomalinda Club, among
others. "Gambling at that time," she said, "was wide open here."
Gene Murret, who had by 1978 become an official of the state of Loui-
siana, said his father, ". . . certainly has had associations with Sam
Saia," recalling that the Lomalinda had been located at the corner of
Royal and Iberville in the French Quarter. Mrs. Murret added that Murret had started working with Saia in the 1930s, and the association
perhaps had continued through the 1950s and into the 1960s, though it
had been terminated by the time of her husband's death. Sam Saia, we
learned, had been an important organized-crime figure in New Orleans.
The New Orleans Metropolitan Crime Commission, in 1955, called him
"a principal member of a large gambling organization," who had been
arrested "on at least 22 separate charges." Saia had, the report continued, maintained a position of influence in the New Orleans underworld by means of his close ties to various political figures, including a
mayor and a chief of police. When the FBI began to look closely at
organized crime in New Orleans and elsewhere in the 1960s, its atten-

tion was drawn to Saia. In a report on May 28, 1962, Special Agent Regis Kennedy noted that the Internal Revenue Service had identified Saia as a powerful gambling figure. In November 1965, a month after Saia died, an FBI report summed up his career: he had "made his money by dope peddling in the early years" and gone on to become "one of the largest bookmakers" in New Orleans and "the financial backer of numerous [underworld] clubs. . . ." (One of Saia's deputies was Anthony Sciambra, the ex-boxer who had been managed by Murret and who was arrested numerous times and convicted of running an illegal handbook.) Aaron M. Kohn, for years the managing director of the Metropolitan Crime Commission, told us in 1978 that Saia had been "the biggest and most powerful operator of illegal handbooks and other forms of illegal gambling in the city," and he was "very close to Carlos Marcello." Among other dealings with Marcello, Saia was, as was Murret, a subscriber to a Marcello-controlled wire service, an illegal means for bookmakers to obtain race results. As such, they had to make regular payments to Marcello.

What about Murret, we asked ourselves — was he also close to Marcello? Marguerite Oswald suggested to us that Murret ". . . may have come across Marcello in his business — he probably did . . . at some point." She was apparently in a good position to know, for Marguerite Oswald may have had Marcello ties of her own. For example, before and after her marriage to Edward Pic she worked as a secretary for Raoul Sere, a lawyer, who went on to become an assistant district attorney at a time, according to Aaron Kohn, when the New Orleans D.A.'s office was corrupted and subject to Marcello's influence. "Sere," Kohn said, "was an important part of the political establishment during its worst period," a time when "enforcement of the law decidedly took a back seat to racketeer payoffs througout the city government." Marguerite Oswald was also associated with another New Orleans attorney, Clem Sehrt, an old family friend, she explained, from whom she sought advice in 1955 when Lee was urging her to falsify his birth certificate so he could join the Marines. Sehrt, too, we learned, had a shady past: he had been a lawyer and financial adviser to a business associate of Marcello, and his law partner had represented Marcello himself. A former state banking official and a New Orleans banking executive, Sehrt had engaged "in a number of highly questionable deals," according to Kohn.

Corroboration of Marguerite Oswald's underworld associations in New Orleans was supplied to us by a businessman and his wife, who asked for anonymity. They told us that on a Saturday night in 1969 they went with Marguerite Oswald and other friends to a social club in Waco,

Texas, which was managed by Sam Turmani, a former New Orleans underworld figure who, while serving as an officer of the Louisiana state police, had been Marcello's bodyguard and chauffeur. Marguerite Oswald was using an assumed name to avoid attention, but as they were seated in the cocktail lounge, Turmani came over to her and said, "I know you," to which she replied, "I know you, too."

After Turmani sat down at the table, reminiscing with Marguerite about mutual friends and events of the old days, it became apparent that they had been more than just casual friends. They discussed members of Marguerite's family, including Dutz Murret, who Turmani remembered as a gambling associate of Sam Saia, and the Murret children, though they delicately avoided any mention of Lee. And they talked about Marcello. "Carlos is legit now," Turmani said. "He's not involved in much any more. He's been out of narcotics for years."

When we asked Marguerite Oswald about Turmani, who died in 1976, she refused to elaborate. But we learned from Aaron Kohn that he had been mixed up in several syndicate operations that profited from gambling and prostitution, and he had maintained his ties to the Marcello Mafia family after moving to Waco.

Marguerite Oswald argued with us. "[J]ust because Mr. Murret worked for those people and may have known Mr. Marcello," she said, ". . . doesn't mean anything about Lee." Before we would accept her logic (we ultimately did not), we considered the question of Oswald's knowledge of Murret's illegal activities. In a biography of Marina Oswald in 1977, Priscilla Johnson McMillan noted that Oswald "had confided that he suspected the Murrets lived beyond what his uncle's earnings would support," and he "might be engaged in some activity on the side, like bookmaking." (McMillan, not aware of all of the facts, suggested that there was "no evidence that this was so.") Marina Oswald confirmed to us that Oswald had known about Murret's gambling sideline and had discussed it with her. "I know he was suspicious about his uncle and his work and what not, . . ." she said, "but I don't know much about it. I didn't know what gambling really was then in this country, or what those mob people were."

Oswald and David Ferrie

We looked beyond Oswald's immediate family in our examination of his formative years. In particular, we studied his New Orleans environment from January 1954, when he and his mother returned there from New York City, to July 1956, when they moved to Fort Worth. The Oswald home in New Orleans, at 126 Exchange Place in the French Quarter, was an apartment over a pool hall, where Oswald would go to shoot a few games and throw darts. "Of course, I didn't have a fabulous apartment," Marguerite Oswald admitted to the Warren Commission. "But very wealthy people and very fine citizens live in that part of town . . . ." There were fine sections of the French Quarter, but Exchange Place was not one of them. Aaron Kohn called it "the hub of the most notorious underworld joints in the city." It was where Marcello operated openly: "You couldn't walk down the street without literally being exposed to two or three separate forms of illicit activity, . . ." Kohn said. He was elaborating on what he had said in a release put out by the Metropolitan Crime Commission on November 26, 1963, in which he described Exchange Place as a street with "sordidly operated bars, including some in which aggressive homosexuals and prostitutes were frequenters and others the scene of operations for illegal bookies."

While living on Exchange Place, Oswald went to Beauregard Junior High School, which, according to Lillian Murret, "had a very low standard" and "did have a very bad bunch of boys . . . [who] were always having fights and ganging up on other boys, and I guess Lee wouldn't take it, so he got in several scrapes. . . ." Aaron Kohn confirmed the bad reputation of Beauregard, adding that it frequently bred criminal careers. As to Oswald's academic record in New Orleans, there was little to go by. His mother told the Warren Commission he missed only nine days of his one term at Beauregard — he got C grades, and he was promoted to Warren Easton High School. There was reason to believe, however, that Beauregard was Oswald's last school. In October 1955 he tried to join the Marine Corps but was rejected because he was only sixteen, and for the next ten months he worked as a messenger for Tujague and Son, a shipping company. He reentered high school in Fort Worth in 1956 but dropped out when he turned seventeen in October, and then he joined the Marines.

Oswald did not have a police record as a youth, but his closest friend at Beauregard, Edward Voebel, told the Warren Commission that he did consider committing at least one crime, the burglary of a pistol from a store window. Voebel talked him out of it, he said, by pointing out that the gun store was equipped with an alarm system. It was also Voebel who induced Oswald to join a Civil Air Patrol squadron in New Orleans, and who testified in 1964 that he believed the squadron was commanded at the time by David W. Ferrie. Ferrie, a former Eastern Airlines pilot, was an operative for Carlos Marcello in 1963, as well as one or two men seen with Oswald in Clinton, Louisiana, in the late summer of 1963. "I think [Ferrie] was there when Lee attended one of these meetings," Voebel told the Warren Commission, "but I am not sure. . . ." Voebel had, however, been quite certain of it when first interviewed by the FBI on November 25, 1963: "Voebel stated that he and Oswald were members of the Civil Air Patrol in New Orleans with Captain Dave Ferrie during the time they were in school," the report read. (We were unable to reinterview Voebel, who died in 1971.) Evidence that Oswald had served in a CAP unit commanded by Ferrie in 1955 made the sighting of Oswald and Ferrie together in Clinton in late August or early September 1963 far more comprehensible. If Oswald and Ferrie had known each other in the past, there would have been a basis for renewing the friendship that summer. Further, Ferrie would have been, like Murret, an intermediary through whom organized-crime figures could have learned about Oswald, his political beliefs, and his inclination to act rashly, among other character traits.

The testimony of other witnesses tended to confirm the Oswald-Ferrie association in 1955. Frederick S. O'Sullivan, a vice squad detective with the New Orleans Police Department when he was questioned in 1963, told the FBI it was he who had recruited both Voebel and Oswald as CAP cadets in the squadron at Lakefront Airport when Ferrie was the squadron commander. They came to one or two meetings, O'Sullivan said, but did not join. Oswald, he explained, decided it would be more convenient to attend meetings at Moisant Airport. Oswald's decision was apparently made at the same time that Ferrie moved from Lakefront to Moisant. "Ferrie . . . transferred and assumed command of the CAP at Moisant Airport at about the same time . . . Oswald might have joined," an FBI report of an interview with O'Sullivan read. O'Sullivan, who by 1978 had become a security officer for the Hilton hotel chain, told us he could not say for certain he had seen Ferrie and Oswald together, though he thought an encounter was likely. "Ferrie ran the unit then," he said, "and Oswald came a couple or a few times." Another former CAP member, Collin Hamer, told us that in the summer of 1955 he saw Oswald at ten or twelve meetings at the Eastern Airlines hangar at Moisant Airport, and Ferrie was there as well. Hamer, who had not previously been contacted by authorities, declared: "Ferrie was at all the meetings during the time Oswald and I were involved in CAP. He did not always do the teaching, but he was always there." George Boesch, who said he left the Lakefront squadron with Ferrie to help him set up the CAP program at Moisant, recalled that Oswald attended meetings for two or three months while Ferrie was the instructor; and Anthony Atzenhoffer, who served as platoon sergeant of the squadron at Moisant, was certain that Oswald, as a cadet, had been trained by Ferrie. "I can't recall seeing the two of them together," said Atzenhoffer. "I don't have that detailed of a memory. But I am sure they were together at the same time." Finally, another former CAP commander, John Irion, a friend of Ferrie for ten years (he testified in Ferrie's behalf at an Eastern Airlines hearing in August 1963), said he recalled Oswald as a CAP trainee at the time Ferrie was in charge. Irion, who said he had not been questioned in the assassination investigation in 1964, thought that a Ferrie-Oswald contact was highly probable.

Return to Dallas: 1962

In June 1962 Lee Harvey Oswald returned from the Soviet Union with a wife and four-month-old daughter. He had met Marina Prusakova at a dance in Minsk in mid-March 1961 and married the nineteen-year-old Russian woman six weeks later, on April 30, 1961, by which time he had decided to end his self-imposed exile. On May 16, in a letter to the U.S. Embassy in Moscow, he asked for the right to return to the States and demanded presumptuously that he not be "persecuted for any act pertaining to this case. . . ."

It was an abrupt turnaround for a young man who had announced shortly after his arrival in the Soviet Union in October 1959 that he wished to renounce his U.S. citizenship, though he never did; and who had slashed his wrists upon learning that his visa would not be extended, whereupon it was. We sought an explanation from several sources. Priscilla Johnson McMillan, who interviewed Oswald in Moscow in 1959 and whose biography of Marina Oswald, *Marina and Lee*, was published in 1977, suggested he was reacting to the rejection of his application to Patrice Lumumba University and to restrictions on his freedom by the Soviet government. Marina Oswald herself told us: "[H]e might have stayed longer, or maybe forever, if he was granted permission to become a student," though she also implied he was merely homesick. Oswald offered his own reason in an essay he wrote on the betrayal of his Marxist ideals: "The Soviets have committed crimes unsurpassed even by their early day capitalist counterparts, the extermination of their own peoples, with the mass extermination so typical of Stalin, and the individual suppresstion [sic] and regimentation under Krushchev [sic]." But the answer was more likely to be found, we came to conclude, in the paradoxical character of Lee Harvey Oswald: a devoted husband and father, a family man, who would beat his wife regularly and disappear from home for days, even weeks; an avowed Marxist, a follower of Fidel Castro of Cuba, whose fictional hero was Ian Fleming's James Bond, an anti-Communist British spy. Oswald was sullen and antisocial, often physically repulsive by choice, yet he craved approval and public recognition. Finally, he was a loner who was almost never alone.

There was, we realized from the outset, a frustrating scarcity of witnesses who would admit to an intimate familiarity with Oswald in the last year and a half of his life, in particular the summer and fall of 1963, the period in which the plot to kill President Kennedy had to have been planned. His mother could be of no help, for she did not see Oswald from August 1962 until the day after the assassination. As for Robert Oswald, his only contact with his brother after July 1962 was at a Thanksgiving reunion at his home in Fort Worth. And Oswald's only other close relatives, the Murrets in New Orleans, would acknowledge little contact with him at all. As far as we could tell, only Marina Oswald was in regular, if not constant, contact with Oswald throughout the period. Yet there were questions about the candor of her testimony. She had admitted that she lied to the FBI; she did so, she said, in reaction to the abrupt manner of the agents who interrogated her in the aftermath of the assassination. (She lied, for example, when she denied knowing that her husband had traveled to Mexico in September 1963.) Marina swore that her statements to the Warren Commission were truthful, but there was little reason to believe all that she said, or to suppose that she necessarily knew very much about her husband's actions in a strange land, whose language was largely unfamiliar to her. In fact, when she appeared before us on September 13 and 14, 1978, she was not particularly helpful. And yet, Marina Oswald's testimony was the best direct evidence we had for an evaluation of Oswald's basic nature.

The fullest account of the Oswalds' life together was, we found, the biography written by Priscilla McMillan, a scholar in Soviet studies, who was fluent in Russian and who had been able to sit with Marina at a quiet retreat in the summer of 1964, recording her reminiscences in a chronological and orderly fashion. (We considered the possibility, as it bore on her book, that Mrs. McMillan had been a CIA agent in the Soviet Union. A careful review of agency files substantiated her assurance to us that she had never worked for any federal agency, except for a brief stint as a translator.)

The search for enlightenment from nonfamily associates of Oswald was even less fruitful, since few were known to exist. Those we knew about, consisting of a colony of Russian emigres in Dallas-Fort Worth and Ruth and Michael Paine, a couple in close touch with the Oswalds in October and November 1963, were of little help, because they insisted they had had little use for Oswald and had resisted learning very much about him. The one individual who admitted to the Warren Commission that he had been at all close to the accused assassin (and even he took the opportunity of a Commission deposition to renounce his friendship with Oswald), was a man named George de Mohrenschildt, who committed suicide on the very day in 1977 that he was contacted by one of our investigators. (De Mohrenschildt did, however, leave behind written testimony, though its value could be questioned: an unfinished manuscript of a highly personal and opinionated book, in which he contended that Oswald had been an unwitting participant in the plot — a patsy.

On arrival at Love Field, Dallas, on June 14, 1962, Oswald was disappointed at the absence of reporters and photographers, "because he told me there is going to be a whole bunch of them," Marina Oswald told us. Oswald loved the limelight, and he was delighted when Robert Oswald, who met them at the airport and at whose home in Fort Worth they would stay for several weeks, said there had been a front-page story in the newspaper, with a photograph, about his imminent return from Russia. (Oswald's desire for fame and notoriety was one of a half-dozen character traits we examined in a motive analysis of Oswald. Others were alienation and antisociability and an inability to hold a job; a penchant for deception and intrigue; an adherence to a Marxist political philosophy; a willingness to resort to violence to achieve ends or to express feelings; and a tendency to be dependent on strong figures.) Oswald's incivility was a noticeable trait, and he was quick to demonstrate it soon after he and his wife arrived in Texas. One of the Russian refugees, the wife of a prominent Fort Worth attorney, called to invite them for a visit, but Oswald let the woman know he had better things to do. Marina Oswald, angered by her husband's rudeness, told him so and got a beating. It was meted out quietly, in the bedroom, so Robert and his wife Vada would not hear, but the cuffs across her face were painful, and the threat that he would kill her if she said anything to Robert Oswald was terrifying.

It was difficult staying with Oswald's relatives, especially his mother, at whose home they spent a stormy three weeks. So, on August 10, 1962, Marina and Lee moved into their own place, an apartment in a shabby duplex bungalow on Mercedes, a dingy street in a commercial section of Fort Worth, not far from where Oswald had found a job. Three days later Marguerite Oswald paid a visit while her son was out, and he was so incensed with Marina for letting her in that he beat her up a second time, and from then on the assaults occurred with regularity, once or twice a week. The main source of friction was the generous attention Marina was receiving from the emigre Russians, who were supplying groceries and giving her clothes. Oswald was offended by this largesse in light of his inability to provide more than the barest necessities of life.

On October 8 Oswald quit his job with the Leslie Welding Company, having decided to look for work in Dallas, so for the first of many times during their marriage the Oswalds were separated. Marina, along with baby June, stayed for three days in Dallas with De Mohrenschildt's daughter and son-in-law, Alexandra and Gary Taylor, and then returned to Fort Worth, where she spent nearly a month with Elena

Hall, a Russian-American who had befriended her. She saw her husband only on the weekends. Oswald did not resent the attention of the Russians so much that he would not seek their help. On October 9 he called Anna Meller, whose husband, Teofil, got in touch with an official of the Texas Employment Commission, who helped Oswald land a job as a photographic technician with the graphic arts firm of Jaggars-Chiles-Stovall. But according to Priscilla McMillan, his ingratitude offended the Russians. "He so outraged their notions of what decent conduct ought to be that he stunned them into giving him what he wanted," McMillan wrote.

In addition to being boorish, Oswald was behaving in a characteristically deceptive way. He had been laid off by Leslie Welding, he lied (apparently just to gain sympathy), and he made a mystery of his whereabouts. He did not, as Marina Oswald, De Mohrenschildt, and others were led to believe, stay at the Dallas YMCA for all of a certain period in the fall of 1962. He was registered there only for the week of October 15 to 19, which left October 8 to 13 and October 21 to November 2 unaccounted for.

Oswald found an apartment at 604 Elsbeth Street in the Oak Cliff section of Dallas, but when Marina saw it on Sunday, November 4, she was appalled by the filth and had to be coaxed to move in. At about 10 o'clock that evening Oswald left, saying he had paid for his room at the "Y," so he might as well use it, though there was no record that he did, in fact, stay at the YMCA. Marina, who stayed up until 5 A.M. scrubbing the apartment, never did find out where he went that night. Within a day or two they were squabbling again, with Oswald calling his wife a whore for her association with the Russians. (The Oswalds' personal relations had been deteriorating to the point that they had sexual intercourse no more than once a week.) Angrier than she had ever been, Marina sought refuge at the home of the Mellers, vowing never again to "go back to that hell." A week later there was a peace meeting at the De Mohrenschildts, but Marina, despite Oswald's pleadings, was adamant in her refusal to agree to a reconciliation. Although it was decided that they should remain apart for a few months, Oswald was persistent. He had inveigled information about Marina's whereabouts from De Mohrenschildt, and he called her incessantly, begging to see her. She finally agreed to a meeting, at which Oswald literally got down on his knees, crying and imploring her forgiveness. He was, admittedly, a "terrible character," but he would change, not overnight, but bit by bit. Marina yielded.

The Russian emigrés, with the single exception of George de Mohrenschildt and his wife, Jeanne, were furious. "You mean you took advantage of all your friends just to teach Lee a lesson," one of them, Kayata Ford, complained. In fact, Marina had not taught Oswald a thing. Shortly after the reconciliation, angered by her smoking, Oswald snatched a cigarette from Marina's mouth and snuffed it out on her bare shoulder, leaving a second-degree burn. In the view of Priscilla McMillan, the Oswalds had a mutual need to inflict and accept pain. There was, too, the sexual aspect of their difficulties: Marina relished an active sex life, but Oswald, De Mohrenschildt observed, was asexual. De Mohrenschildt claimed to have lost patience with Marina's constant complaints about her husband's inattention, though she indicated that, on at least one occasion, he tried to take advantage of it. He asked her one day, when Oswald was at work, how she found her husband sexually. "Oh, nothing special," she said. "How about I show you some time?" De Mohrenschildt suggested.

On New Year's Eve, 1962, with Oswald in bed and not interested in celebrating, Marina wrote to a former lover, Anatoly Shpanko: "My husband does not love me, and our relationship here in America is not what it was in Russia. I am sad that there is an ocean between us and that there is no way back. . . ." She mailed the letter with insufficient postage, however, and Oswald opened it when it was returned. Enraged, he ordered her to read it aloud. She refused, so he read it, but he stumbled over her handwriting and told her to continue. Again she declined, so he hit her across the face, an open-handed slap, not as brutal a blow as those she had learned to fear. By late January 1963 their relations had taken a momentary turn for the better, however, and one Saturday night, having gone to bed early, they conceived their second child in an act of love that Marina found the most satisfying of their marriage. The next day, using an alias, Oswald mailed an order to Seaport Traders, Inc., in Los Angeles, enclosing a $10 downpayment on a .38 special Smith & Wesson revolver. The balance of the cost, $19.95 plus shipping charges, was paid on delivery.

February was a dreadful month for Marina, as the ferocity of the beatings intensified, and their frequency multiplied. Oswald would attack at the slightest provocation, pummeling her time after time with closed fists. If she balked at sex on demand, he would pin her down and take her by force, and when Marina once called him "crazy" for getting satisfaction from the violence of the struggle, he grabbed her by the throat and vowed to kill her if she ever again questioned his sanity. Oswald was still simmering over her running to the Russians and, as if to compensate for having had to get down on his knees and beg her to come back, he declared the only reason he had groveled was to prove his power over her. "You're my property," he snarled, "and I'll do with you as I please. So long as I want you, you'll stay. If not — then off with you."

"Hunter of Fascists"

On February 13, 1963, a Wednesday, the Oswalds went to dinner at the De Mohrenschildts, and on the way home in George's big gray convertible, the conversation turned to politics. It was in English, and Marina was unable to understand. She sensed, however, that something said that night inspired Oswald to plan a horrendous act, a murder. The victim was to be Edwin A. Walker, a retired Army general, who lived in Dallas and had become a prominent exponent of extreme conservatism and anticommunism. Marina Oswald did not feel that De Mohrenschildt was putting her husband up to it, but he might have "influenced Lee's sick fantasy," as she put it to Priscilla McMillan.

According to Marina, the week of February 17 was the most brutal of the marriage. On Sunday, Oswald forced her to write to the Soviet Embassy in Washington to request officially that she and June be permitted to return to Russia, and despite what she had written to Anatoly Shpanko out of New Year nostalgia, she did not want to go. A day or so later, Oswald hit her so hard her nose bled. He then stormed out, and when he returned to a locked apartment, having forgotten his key, he smashed a glass door pane to get in. Marina fought back with her acid tongue: "You weak, cowardly American. What a fool I was. I was afraid to marry a Russian because Russian men beat their wives. You. You're not worth the soles of their feet." On the evening of Friday, February 22, at the home of Everett Glover, a friend of De Mohrenschildt, Marina met Ruth Hyde Paine, who was ten years her senior and who lived in the Dallas suburb of Irving. Ruth Paine was separated from her husband, Michael, an engineer for Bell Helicopter. A student of the Russian language, she was able to converse haltingly with Marina and soon became her closest confidante.

Oswald did not go to work on Saturday, February 23. He was out all day, but Marina never found out where he went. That night there was a terrible row over how to cook rice and beans, which ended with Marina making an awkward attempt at suicide. Oswald caught her standing on a toilet seat with a clothesline around her neck, and he gave her a hard fist to the face. "Don't ever do that again," he warned. "Only fools try that." Complaints about the constant fighting from the building management convinced Oswald he was being watched, so, not bothering to tell Marina, he found a new apartment at 214 West Neely Street, only a block or so from 604 Elsbeth.

Oswald's hunch about surveillance was not without basis, for on March 11 the wife of the manager of the building on Elsbeth Street reported the move to the FBI. As a matter of fact, the FBI had kept a close watch on Oswald from the moment he had returned to the United States, though the surveillance did not go beyond routine questioning. Oswald was interviewed for the first time in Fort Worth on June 26, 1962, by agents who considered him cold, arrogant, and uncooperative; and on August 16 he was intercepted on his way home from work by two agents, who interviewed him in their parked automobile.

On Saturday or Sunday, March 9 or 10, Oswald went to the vicinity of 4011 Turtle Creek Boulevard, General Walker's address, and took several photographs of the home and its surroundings (the approximate date of the photography was determined for the Warren Commission from the progress of construction of a building in the background). If nothing else, Oswald learned from the photos that there would be a chance for escape if he used a rifle. On March 12, using a coupon clipped from *American Rifleman*, he ordered a Mannlicher-Carcano Italian carbine from Klein's Sporting Goods in Chicago, enclosing a money order for $21.45 and asking that delivery be made to A. Hidell (his alias) at P.O. Box 2915, Dallas. Marina was upset by what she regarded as a frivolous purchase when there was hardly enough money for food, and she was shocked by her husband's new image of himself. On Sunday, March 31, Oswald, dressed all in black, marched into the backyard, where Marina was hanging diapers on a clothesline, and demanded that she take his picture. His holstered .38 revolver was strapped to his waist; and he was holding his rifle in one hand and two newspapers in the other (both were Communist newspapers, a March 11 issue of *The Militant* and a copy of *The Worker* dated March 24). With a bit of coaching, Marina was able to focus and snap the shutter of Oswald's Imperial Reflex at least three times. When she gave him back the camera, he said he would send a print to *The Militant* to show he was "ready for anything." (The authenticity of the pictures had been challenged, but our photographic panel found no evidence of fakery.)

When Ruth Paine came to visit a couple of times in early March, Marina Oswald poured out her troubles. She was pregnant and ashamed of it. Her husband beat her regularly and was threatening to send her back to the Soviet Union against her will. And she was lonely. Mrs. Paine was compassionate, and she too, with a marriage on the rocks, craved companionship. Toward the end of the month she took Marina and June to her home in Irving, and on April 2 she had all the Oswalds, along with her estranged husband Michael, over for dinner. It struck Priscilla McMillan that the Paines turned up at an opportune time for Oswald, since Ruth would be able to offer refuge to Marina and June if he were arrested or killed in his assault on Walker. McMillan also noted that from the day Oswald returned to the United States he was in the protective custody of someone — his family, the Russian emigres, and the Paines. "The one time he was completely on his own," McMillan wrote, "was, interestingly, the one time he did not need help, while he was working at Jaggars-Chiles-Stovall, October 12 to April 6." We did wonder, though, about George de Mohrenschildt, for there was evidence that Oswald's feelings about him bordered on hero worship. Marina Oswald told Priscilla McMillan that except for two friends in Minsk, De Mohrenschildt knew her husband's politics better than anyone — "and that he read Lee like an open book."

In the first week of April 1963, probably on Monday, April 1, Oswald was fired by Jaggars-Chiles-Stovall for poor job performance, a sloppy appearance, and his political attitudes (he had taken to reading *Krokodil*, a Russian humor magazine, during breaks, which marked him as a radical). His last day at work was Saturday, April 6, and when he came home that evening he still had not told Marina he was unemployed. The next day he left the apartment with the rifle and returned about 6 o'clock without it, explaining to Marina later that he had buried it in a wooded area near Walker's house (a story that was difficult for us to accept). After dinner he went out again and came home late, neglecting to give Marina an account of his activities, though he was probably keeping watch on the house on Turtle Creek Boulevard. On Wednesday, April 10, the day he finally told Marina he had lost his job, Oswald went out in his best suit — to look for a job, she supposed. He did not come home for dinner, and after she put the baby to bed she began to worry, even though she had learned not to fret about her husband's absences at all hours. She realized there were dark corners where she had better not probe, parts of her husband's life that were not her business, and generally she complied. At about 10 P.M., she went into Oswald's small study and found a note on the desk: "Send information about what has happened to me to the Embassy, . . ." it read. "I paid the rent . . . . I have also paid for the water and gas. There may be some money from work . . . . Certain of my papers are in the small blue suitcase. My address book is on the table in my study . . . . We have friends here, and the Red Cross will also help you. If I am alive and taken prisoner, the city jail is at the end of the bridge we always used to walk across when we went to town. . . ."

At 11:30, Oswald walked in. He was the color of talc, drenched with sweat, his eyes flashing:

"I shot Walker."

"Dead?"

"I don't know."

"What did you do with the rifle?"

"Buried it."

Marina thought of going to the police, but in the Soviet Union, where the system says you must inform, even on loved ones, it is a point of honor to remain silent. (Even after the Kennedy assassination, Marina would not admit to the FBI that she was aware of the attack on Walker until she was confronted with the incriminating note, which had been discovered among Oswald's belongings.) She was desperate with fear, not knowing what had happened or what would happen to her. Oswald would only tell her that Walker was a "Fascist." "If someone had killed Hitler," he said, "many lives would have been saved." Marina learned from the papers on Thursday, April 11, the immediate details: Walker had survived, narrowly; an aide to the general, Robert Surrey, reported having seen two men in a late-model car in an alley behind the Walker home two nights before the shooting; and a young boy said he had seen two cars that may have been leaving the scene of the shooting. "Americans are so spoiled," Oswald scoffed to Marina. "It never occurs to them that you might use your own two legs. They always think you have a car."

The De Mohrenschildts paid a visit to the Oswalds on Easter eve, April 13. As Marina remembered the occasion, De Mohrenschildt's opening remark to her husband was: "How come you missed?" (De Mohrenschildt's version of the incident was that only after seeing Oswald's rifle stored in a closet did he ask: "Did you take a shot at General Walker, Lee?") It was the last time the De Mohrenschildts saw the Oswalds. There was a card from New Orleans, Jeanne De Mohrenschildt told the Warren Commission, and she had intended to send a Christmas card from Haiti but had not, for the obvious reason. Then, in 1967, after the De Mohrenschildts had returned to Dallas, there was what George de Mohrenschildt dramatically described as a "message from the grave." It was one of the photographs that Marina had taken of her husband with his weapons and copies of *The Militant* and *The Worker*, similar to the one, De Mohrenschildt said, that appeared on the cover of *Life*. There was an inscription on the back: "To my friend George from Lee Oswald, 5/IV/63." And in Russian, in another handwriting (our handwriting experts were unable to determine whose), there was this: "Hunter of Fascists, ha-ha-ha!"

Marina decided it was time to leave Dallas; it was a dangerous place for her husband, who had refused to get rid of his rifle. "I would like to see the city you grew up in," she said, adding that she would enjoy meeting his New Orleans relatives, the Murrets. Oswald apparently was just as eager to get to New Orleans, possibly because he wanted to be closer to the Cuban revolution, and New Orleans had a large Cuban population. He had fashioned a placard that read, "Hands off Cuba,

Viva Fidel,'' and he sometimes carried it with him when he handed out leaflets on the streets of Dallas. As he had told De Mohrenschildt, U.S. policy toward Cuba, the Bay of Pigs invasion, for example, was "an utter disaster." De Mohrenschildt wrote in his unpublished book that he did not know quite how to fathom Oswald's position on Cuba: "The . . . attractive side of Lee's personality was that he liked to play with his own life, he was an actor in real life. A very curious individual."

Return to New Orleans

On April 24, 1963, President Kennedy's forthcoming trip to Texas was banner-headlined on page one of *The Dallas Times Herald*, although the Warren Commission assumed that the trip to Dallas was first reported on September 13 and confirmed on September 26. On the afternoon of Tuesday, April 23, Vice-President Johnson met with executives of the *Times Herald* and KRCD-AM FM and TV, and he was quoted the next day as saying that he hoped that "President Kennedy's schedule [would] . . . permit him to attend a breakfast in Fort Worth, a luncheon in Dallas, and an afternoon tea in San Antonio. . . ." Johnson also commented on widespread criticism of President Kennedy in Texas: "He's the only pilot you have, and if the plane goes down, you go with it. At least wait until November before you shoot him down."

It was also on April 24 that Ruth Paine arrived at the Neely Street apartment and found, to her surprise, the Oswalds sitting on a pile of luggage. She drove them to the bus terminal, where Oswald bought a pair of tickets, one for himself for use that day and one for Marina and June when he was situated in New Orleans. When he returned to the car, Mrs. Paine made a suggestion: Why not leave Marina and June with her in Irving? She also offered to drive them to New Orleans when the time came. Oswald accepted her invitation on the spot, and he went back into the terminal to redeem Marina's ticket, giving her part of the fare for spending money.

Oswald was gratified by the reception he got from the Murrets, Aunt Lillian and Uncle Charles, or "Dutz." He had been afraid that they had not approved of his trip to the Soviet Union, but that was not indicated. Oswald spent the days job hunting, Lillian Murret told the Warren Commission, returning home for supper, after which he would watch television and go to bed. After two weeks he found a job as a maintenance man at the William B. Reily Co., a coffee processor and distributor. (The false information given, for no apparent reason, on his application was a further manifestation of his naturally deceptive nature: he had lived for the past three years at 757 French Street, the Murrets' address; he had graduated from Warren Easton High School, which he had actually attended for only a few weeks; his references were, in two out of three cases, fictitious.) The job was low-paying ($1.50 an hour) and dirty, calling for oiling and cleaning coffee machines, but when interviews with photographic firms were set up by the Louisiana Employment Commission, Oswald did not show up. Lillian Murret was not too impressed with her nephew's job as a "greaser" and suggested that he go back to school and learn a trade. "No, I don't have to go back to school," he replied. "I don't have to learn anything. I know everything."

Marina and June arrived May 9, having been driven to New Orleans by Ruth Paine after Oswald had called to say he had found a job and a place to live. Almost immediately, the Oswalds were at odds. "Bickering," Priscilla McMillan wrote, was the "currency of their relationship." Marina hated the apartment at 4907 Magazine Street, the cockroaches especially, and she was appalled at Oswald's personal appearance. His daily attire was work pants, a dirty T-shirt, and sandals; he stopped shaving and bathing regularly; and he brushed his teeth only at night. "You're my wife," he stormed, when Marina objected to his foul breath. "You're supposed to love me any way I am." Marina recounted her woes in a letter to Ruth Paine: "As soon as you left, all love stopped." The second baby was due in October, and Marina had already decided to accept Ruth's invitation to come then and stay with her in Irving.

Oswald was miserable in his job, and his careless performance showed it. On July 19, just two days after Marina's twenty-second birthday, he was fired. (He never had told his wife the true nature of his work, claiming it had something to do with photography, which she found inconsistent with the grease and coffee dust on his clothing.) On July 22 Oswald went to the state employment office to file a claim for compensation and, presumably, to apply for another job, though he never did look for one in earnest. For the next two months, he did little but sit at home and read, or so it appeared to Marina.

Oswald's chief interest while in New Orleans was Cuba. On May 26 he wrote to Vincent T. Lee, national director of the Fair Play for Cuba Committee, to say he wanted to form a New Orleans chapter. Following his arrest on Friday, August 9, for fighting with anti-Castro Cubans led by Carlos Bringuier, Oswald telephoned the Murrets and arrogantly demanded that they use their influence to get him out of jail. Dutz Murret was on a religious retreat (underworld gambling figures, ironically, are often practicing Catholics); Lillian Murret was in a hospital recovering from ear surgery; so Oswald talked with their daughter, Joyce O'Brien, who had come to visit from Beaumont, Texas. Joyce went down to the police station on Saturday, but when she was told that Oswald had been waving a "Viva Castro" sign, she balked: "Oh, my God," she said, "I'm not going to get him out of here if he's like that." She went to the hospital to confer with her mother, and they decided to call Emile Bruneau, an old friend of the Murrets who had political influence, and Bruneau arranged Oswald's bail that afternoon. When Dutz got back on Sunday, he went over to the apartment on Magazine Street and asked Oswald if he was tied up with any "Commie" group. Oswald said he was not. Murret gave him a fatherly lecture: "You ought to get out and find yourself a job," he said. "You have a wife and child and one coming."

By late August Oswald had become something of a local celebrity, and he was asked to appear in a radio debate with Bringuier. The moderator had been briefed on Oswald by the FBI (his defection to the Soviet Union, his attempt to renounce his citizenship, his marriage), and the exposure of his past turned Oswald's sought-after media appearance into an embarrassment. "I wasn't prepared, and I didn't know what to say," he admitted to Marina.

Discouraged, Oswald decided to go to Cuba to fight for Castro. He would hijack a commercial aircraft with Marina's help, but she disabused him of that notion, since, in her seventh month of pregnancy, she had little interest in holding a pistol on a planeload of passengers while her husband commandeered the cockpit. Oswald decided he could get to Cuba legally — by going via Mexico City, where there was a Cuban embassy. "I'll show them my clippings, show them how much I have done for Cuba, . . ." he said to Marina. In early September he started studying a secretarial notebook in which Marina had listed Spanish words and their Russian equivalents. He also began to dry-fire his Mannlicher-Carcano from the porch of the apartment in the evening. "Fidel Castro needs defenders," he explained to Marina. "I am going to be a revolutionary."

In mid-July Marina received a renewed invitation from Ruth Paine to come and stay with her, "for two months or two years," and Oswald encouraged her to accept. On August 11 Marina mailed her acceptance, being careful to abide by Oswald's instruction not to mention his plan to go to Cuba. (To Marina, it was a sign that she was gaining her husband's confidence that he would let her in on his deceptions, his "black deeds," as she called them.) Mrs. Paine wrote back on August 25, promising to be in New Orleans before dark on September 20. Oswald was grateful to Ruth Paine for again taking his family off his hands when it was time to move, and he showed it by treating her deferentially. He gave her a copy of his W-2 wage statement from Jaggars-Chiles-Stovall to prove that Marina was a Texas resident and therefore entitled to medical care at a cost based on her ability to pay. And he told Mrs. Paine he was going to Houston or Philadelphia to look for work and would come to get Marina and June when he had found a job.

Return to Dallas: 1963

As the Paine station wagon was about to leave New Orleans for Dallas on the morning of September 23, 1963, Oswald's last words to Marina were whispered urgently: under no circumstances was she to tell Ruth about his trip to Mexico or his plan to go to Cuba. Mrs. Paine took Marina and June back to Irving, Texas, and Oswald went to Mexico City. He used his own name in making bus reservations, in speaking with other passengers, and in dealing with Cuban and Russian consular officials in his effort to obtain travel documents. His efforts were frustrated, however, so Oswald returned to the United States — to Texas, not to Louisiana. On his first day back in Dallas, October 3, he did not call Marina at Ruth Paine's. Instead, he took a room, again using his own name, at the YMCA, having already checked in with the Texas Employment Commission. On Friday, October 4, he applied for a job at a printing company, but he was rejected on the strength of a negative recommendation from his former employer, Jaggars-Chiles-Stovall. "Bob Stovall does not recommend this man," the notation on his application read. "He was released because of his record as a troublemaker. Has communistic tendencies." Oswald called Marina after this, his latest disappointment, then hitchhiked to the Paine home in Irving. There he spent the first of several weekends as a visiting husband, having been replaced by Ruth Paine as the principal source of support and guidance, as Marina prepared for the birth of her second baby.

On Monday, October 7, Oswald took a room under his own name at Mary Bledsoe's rooming house, but he was asked to leave after a week. Mrs. Bledsoe would not stand for a boarder who spoke in a foreign language on the public telephone. (It had been supposed that the language was Russian, but Marina Oswald told the Warren Commission that the landlady had also heard Spanish, at least "Adios," suggesting Oswald may have been speaking to someone else.) He was back at Ruth Paine's for the weekend of October 12-13, and on Monday he took a room at 1026 North Beckley, in his old neighborhood, the Oak Cliff section of Dallas. He registered as "O. H. Lee."

During this time Oswald received *The Worker* and *The Militant* at Michael Paine's address in Irving (Michael and Ruth were still separated). An examination of the contents of the two papers for the three-month period prior to the assassination revealed an extremely critical attitude toward President Kennedy and his policy on Cuba. In the middle of October, Oswald told Michael Paine, apparently in all seriousness: "[Y]ou [can] . . . tell what they wanted you to do . . . by reading between the lines, reading the thing and doing a little reading between the lines." Paine thought to himself that Oswald "wanted to be a party to something or a part of a group that had objectives." He "wanted to be an activist of some sort."

On October 14 Oswald applied for a position at the Wiener Lumber Company at Inwood Road and Maple Avenue (which was on the route a motorcade would take from Love Field to downtown Dallas). But Oswald was unable to satisfy Sam Wiener that he had been honorably dischared from the Marine Corps, and he was not hired. On October 15, however, thanks to an inquiry by Ruth Paine, Oswald was hired as an order filler by the Texas School Book Depository, and he started work on October 16. While it could be foreseen that a motorcade through downtown Dallas might well pass through Dealey Plaza, we found no evidence that Oswald got the job as part of a plan by him alone or with others to assassinate the President. On Oswald's birthday, October 18, there was a surprise celebration at Ruth Paine's, and on Saturday night Oswald and Marina watched movies on television, one of which, *Suddenly* (1959), cast Frank Sinatra in the role of a mentally unbalanced exserviceman hired to assassinate the President, and the other, *We Were Strangers* (1949), with John Garfield, was about a revolution in Cuba in which an assassination would mark the beginning of the overthrow of the Machado dictatorship in 1933. Marina went into labor on Sunday night, and Ruth took her to Parkland Hospital, leaving Oswald with June and the two Paine children. Ruth called the hospital shortly after she got back and learned that Marina had given birth to a second daughter. But she did not wake Oswald, deciding to tell him the next morning. After work he went to the hospital, where he and Marina discussed a name for the baby. She had picked Audrey (for Audrey Hepburn, who had played the part of Natasha in a film version of *War and Peace*) and Rachel (for Ruth Paine's niece). Oswald took exception to Rachel, saying it sounded too Jewish (thus betraying a touch of anti-Semitism). He wanted the baby named after her mother, so she became Audrey Marina Rachel Oswald, though she would be called Rachel.

On Friday, November 1, upon arriving at Ruth Paine's, Oswald was told that an FBI agent, James P. Hosty, had been to the house to inquire about him. Marina was surprised at how disturbed Oswald was, though he tried to conceal it. Hosty reappeared on Tuesday, November 5, to ask for Oswald's current address. Oswald was in fact so angered by Hosty's visits that he appeared at the FBI office in Dallas and asked to see him. Hosty was not there, so Oswald left him a note. According to the receptionist, it may have included a threat to "blow up" the FBI office if Hosty did not stop "bothering" Marina. Hosty told us the note had advised him to see Oswald directly if he wanted information, and that if he did not stop "bothering" Marina, Oswald would report it to "proper authorities." (Following the assassination, on instructions from a Dallas superior, Hosty destroyed the note, and its existence did not become public until 1975. Our investigation determined that while the incident demonstrated a breach of conduct, neither the note nor its destruction was related to the assassination.)

Friday, November 8, was the beginning of a long weekend to celebrate Veterans Day, and it was on that Sunday morning that Ruth Paine discovered and copied a draft of a letter from Oswald to the Soviet Embassy in Washington, " . . . to inform you of events since my interview with Comrade Kostine in the Embassy of the Soviet Union, Mexico City, Mexico." He told of the visits by FBI Agent Hosty and attempted to explain the purpose of the trip to Mexico. But it was the incoherence of the letter, not the content, that disturbed Ruth Paine. On Monday Oswald again discussed the FBI contacts with Marina. They had intended to find an apartment together after Christmas, but Oswald's fear of the authorities, according to Marina, made him insist that they keep their address a secret. Marina balked at the idea of hiding her whereabouts from Ruth Paine, and Oswald promised to think of a solution. He did not go to Irving the following weekend and had not telephoned by Sunday night, so Marina put in a call to the rooming house, only to be told there was no Lee Oswald living there. When Oswald called on Monday, Marina asked why she could not reach him, and he explained he was not registered under his real name. When Marina objected angrily to more of his mysterious ways, Oswald got furious. He said he did not want his landlady to know his real name because she might "read in the paper" that he had defected. (The Warren Commission termed this reason "unlikely," since unless Oswald was engaged in some political or other public activity, there would be no reason for reports of his background to appear in the newspapers.) "You don't understand a thing," he said. "I don't want the FBI to know where I live, . . ." and he ordered Marina not to tell Ruth Paine. "You and your long tongue — they just get us into trouble."

Oswald showed up in Irving unexpectedly after work the following Thursday, November 21. He told Marina that he was lonely, and he "wanted to make his peace" with her. Marina refused to speak with him. The next morning he left for work before anyone else arose, taking his rifle with him. He left his wedding ring in a cup on the dresser and $170 in a wallet in a dresser drawer.

Charles Givens, an employee of the Texas School Book Depository, was riding down in an elevator around 11:45 A.M. when he saw Oswald on the sixth floor, clipboard in hand, which held three book invoices.

"Boy, are you going downstairs? It's near lunchtime."

"No, sir."

The three invoices, each dated November 22, were never filled.

Elements of Conspiracy

As we brought our investigation of Oswald to a close, we came to a number of important conclusions. We could no longer accept the Warren Commission's view of Oswald's background, associations, and conduct, although we had no quarrel with the Commission's recognition that Oswald was fully capable of violence. (Apart from the assassination, his physical abuse of Marina, his attempt to assassinate General Walker, and his killing of Officer Tippit showed a willingness to use violence for his own ends.) Nor could we accept the Warren Commission's belief that Oswald killed the President out of a mix of many, essentially personal, motives. For us, the truth was far more complex. Oswald had not, we knew from our reexamination of the evidence in Dealey Plaza, acted alone. Our analysis of his character led us to believe that Oswald was preoccupied with his political ideology, and it was likely that he acted in the assassination in light of that ideology. He defected to the Soviet Union at age twenty, expressing a desire to renounce his citizenship. He offered the Soviets the knowledge he had gained as a Marine, and he told his brother Robert he would fight and kill on behalf of his new country. He even attempted suicide when told he would not be allowed to remain in the Soviet Union. Following his disillusionment with the Soviet system, he returned to the United States, but he did not renounce his commitment to leftist ideology. He subscribed to and read radical journals and was apparently influenced by them to take violent action. He was outspoken in his support of Castro, in whose behalf he demonstrated publicly. He even considered hijacking a plane to flee to Cuba, and then, according to Marina, he contemplated leaving her and their child to go there via Mexico. His attempted assassination of Walker, a "Fascist" to Oswald, showed his willingness to commit murder for a political purpose. Walker and Kennedy hardly shared a common ideology, but from the perspective of an extreme left winger, they could have been seen as related. Kennedy was, after all, the man who invaded Cuba and came within a hairsbreadth of nuclear war over the Soviet missiles in Cuba. We had to believe, therefore, that the plot to assassinate the President, for Oswald at least, was rooted in his fundamentally leftest political beliefs. This judgment inevitably led us to return to the perceptive memorandum of Warren Commission Counsel

William T. Coleman, Jr., and W. David Slawson and the theory that
Oswald had been enlisted in what appeared to be a pro-Castro plot by
anti-Castro agents. The Commission portrayed Oswald as essentially a
loner, but the evidence of his activities in New Orleans in the summer
of 1963, evidence the Commission had access to, contradicted that
portrayal. As the Commission knew from the testimony of Carlos
Bringuier, Oswald made an effort to lend active support to the anti-
Castro Cuban Student Directorate, arguably to infiltrate the organization. And he was photographed handing out pro-Castro leaflets with a
Latin-looking associate who was never identified. There was, moreover, the story offered by Silvia Odio, which we were persuaded was authentic, contrary to the view of the Warren Commission; and we were
struck by the consistency with the Slawson-Coleman thesis of an
Oswald visit to Odio's home in Dallas with two Latin companions, again
possibly for the purpose of infiltrating an anti-Castro group, in this case
the Junta Revolucionaria Cubana, or JURE. Other sightings of Oswald
with "Latins" were not so firmly fixed, but collectively they wove a
convincing pattern: he was seen by a bartender and bar owner in New
Orleans with a man who "spoke Spanish"; he sought legal advice with
respect to his less-than-honorable discharge from the Marines in the
company of a "Mexican"; he went to Western Union in Dallas to
obtain funds with a man "of Spanish descent"; and he spoke Spanish
words over a public telephone at his Dallas rooming house. While these
associations could, from observation, be determined to be Latin, their
political hue — whether pro- or anti-Castro — was not clear.

While Oswald was in New Orleans, the likelihood of a presidential
trip to Texas had been made public. In addition, Oswald arrived in New
Orleans after his assault on General Walker indicated he was capable of
political murder. We considered it unlikely that he would have bragged
openly, least of all to his own relatives, of having tried to assassinate
Walker, but Marina knew, and she might not have been so loath to tell
about it. She had, after all, confided to Ruth Paine about the beatings
she got from Oswald. We, therefore, believed it was quite possible that
the Murrets learned of the Walker incident, and Dutz Murret was in an
ideal position to connect his nephew with organized crime, since he
himself was an underworld figure. We did not have reason to believe
that Murret was a coconspirator in the assassination, but we did regard
him a likely conduit of information about Oswald — his character, his
political beliefs, his violent bent (specifically, the assault on Walker) —
to people who had the motive and the capability to plot the assassination. We recognized that there might not have been a need for a family
link to organized crime, since Oswald's pro-Castro political stance was
public knowledge in New Orleans. In this respect, we deemed signifi-

cant Oswald's adolescent association with David Ferrie; the sightings of Oswald and Ferrie together in Clinton, Louisiana, in late August or early September 1963; and the mysterious 544 Camp Street connection (the address of an office where Ferrie worked was stamped on some of Oswald's "Fair Play for Cuba" leaflets). Here we had a direct link between Oswald and a man who (1) was violently and outspokenly opposed to Castro; who (2) had voiced publicly his hatred for Kennedy; and who (3) was directly connected to — in fact, worked for — Carlos Marcello, the organized-crime leader in New Orleans. There were, therefore, the elements of the conspiracy in New Orleans: knowledge of an expected presidential trip to Texas; a violence-prone, pro-Castro Oswald; and an alliance of anti-Castro and underworld figures whose common bond was a hatred of the U.S. President. We came to believe that these were the elements that matured into the conspiracy that succeeded in November.

There were, however, other items of evidence that led us to believe that the actual contact with Oswald for the ultimate purpose of killing Kennedy may have occurred much closer to the date of the assassination. We found it significant, for example, that on the trip to Mexico City in late September Oswald used his real name. Since he characteristically used an alias when engaged in purchasing weapons or other conspiracy-related activities, this would argue forcefully against the notion that he was an active plotter when he went to Mexico. Upon his return to Dallas Oswald continued to use his own name — at least until he moved into the rooming house at 1026 North Beckley and registered as O. H. Lee. That was on October 15, the same day, incidentally, that he was hired at the Texas School Book Depository. It appeared to us logical, therefore, that it was after he returned to Dallas on October 3 that he was contacted by agents of the conspiracy, who had concluded that his participation in the plot was desirable, since he would, if publicly identified, draw attention away from their own complicity. Oswald must not have expected to escape, since he left his wedding ring and most of his money with his wife. His coconspirators also assumed, it seemed clear, that he would be killed, since there were not many avenues of flight from the Book Depository. When he did escape, it was necessary to silence him, lest the true nature of the plot be learned.

The options of his fellow conspirators were circumscribed once Oswald was in custody. Who was available to silence him? Who could gain access to the police station and smoothly accomplish the objective? Given Jack Ruby's background, he was a logical choice. Unlike Oswald, Ruby knew how to hold his tongue (for fear of retribution to his family, if for no other reason). Ruby was, we noted, not very different from the sort of individual that, as a rule, carries out an organized-crime murder.

He was, in short, a typical hit man. The evidence was together, the inferences drawn, the conclusions reached. We had not named the gunman who was behind the picket fence, but from what we knew about Ruby and Oswald, we could safely infer an identification: he was an agent of organized crime. It remained only to evaluate the plot as a whole.

13

The Plot to Kill the President

The gods must have their due.

Sophocles
Antigone

The Meaning of the Assassination

In our investigation we had an abundance of information to evaluate. There was the evidence gathered by our Committee and by government bodies that had gone before us — the FBI, the CIA, the Secret Service, and the Warren Commission principally, but also the Kefauver Committee, the McClellan Committee, and the Church Committee, to name only some of them. We also assessed the assassination literature (our bibliography consisted of 1,021 titles). When the time came to integrate this wealth of information into a comprehensive set of conclusions, we realized that inevitably those conclusions would depend on the meaning we attached to the assassination itself. Everyone we contacted in our fact-finding process — a former President, a former Attorney General, current and former officials of the FBI and the CIA, members and counsel of the Warren Commission, critics of the Warren Commission — professed to want to know the truth about the assassination of the President. But because it is not possible to know everything about anything, the known facts needed the mucilage of a theory; they had to be held together by a coherent view of what happened in Dallas, which could only be an approximation of the truth. As facts are integrated into theory, we realized further, conclusions are shaped and colored by attitudes and assumptions. No one would quarrel with the favorite remark of Mr. Justice Holmes that the first requirement of a good theory is that it fit the facts, but we also knew that there was more to seeking the truth than a fidelity to facts. Holmes's Supreme Court colleague, Mr. Justice Cardozo, said that no matter how hard we try, we can never see "with any eyes except our own." We believed, therefore, that the broader meaning of the assassination had to be examined before we proceeded to an assessment of the soundness of our judgment that organized crime had a hand in the President's death.

As the symbolic leader of the nation, the President meant many things to many people, so his loss was keenly felt. Because his death was sudden and violent, it was all the more traumatic, and expressions of shock, sorrow, and fear were immediate. Presidents are father figures; they personalize political order. Their sudden death exposes, as it did on November 22, 1963, the fragility of that political order. President Kennedy's assassination, however, evoked intense and universally felt emotions for a special reason. The modern media had made him and his family unusually well known, and his death and burial commanded the full attention of the public for four days. The immediate reaction was one of profound sympathy for the widow and children. Few were not deeply touched when John, age three, took a step forward in front of St. Matthew's Cathedral in Washington, and saluted his father's bier. The President's state funeral — with its riderless horse and military honor guard leading a slow procession across Memorial Bridge to Arlington National Cemetery, the final 21-gun salvo, and interment — offered more than an opportunity to share the loss. It was an opportunity to overcome the dread of death by participating in a public ceremony that demonstrated the cohesiveness and strength of the living. Robert F. Kennedy, an erect figure, his eyes etched in pain, stood beside a stoic Mrs. Kennedy, dressed and veiled in black, as both of them faced the stark reality of death. Through the catharsis of that public expression of human grief, return to the daily tasks of life was facilitated for the survivors.

There remained, however, the eternal questions the assassination seemed to raise. Robert Kennedy, on that terrible night when the President's body was brought back to the White House, broke down and sobbed, "Why, God?" Subsequently, he was to scrawl on a yellow legal pad in his office at the Department of Justice: "The innocent suffer — how can that be possible and God be just?" What came to be called into question for Robert Kennedy and for many others was the very meaning of life: Since President Kennedy's life was so full of purpose, what was the meaning of his death? Was there a purpose for it, or was it, after all, just a chance event for which there was no meaning?

The quest for the meaning of life and death, of course, transcends the search for the meaning of the assassination of the President. Nonetheless, the basic dichotomy that applies to the approach to life itself — purpose versus chance — was reflected, we found, in the way people reacted to the assassination of the President. The word most often used to describe Dallas on November 22, 1963, was tragedy, and it was how people tended to view the tragic in life that most often shaped their view of the assassination. It happens that the two fundamental and diametrically opposite perspectives of tragedy are presented in literature. They, in fact, represent the basic difference between classic Greek drama and the realism of modern theater. It is instructive, therefore, to see how the different interpretations of the nature of life and death have been articulated in literature.

The origin of the term "tragedy" is not known with certainty. The Greek word *tragoedia* literally means "goat song." At Athens, where Greek tragedy was born, there was a spring festival of Dionysius, a Greek god favored by the poor and oppressed, who received relief from the harshness of life in wine and dance. It was part of the festival to award a goat as the prize for a winning play. Greek drama had its genesis, in turn, in folk music, so the origin of tragedy can probably be traced to the gradual metamorphosis of epic poetry and ritual into drama. As a work of art, Greek tragedy was presented by song and dance as well as speech. There were few actors, and emphasis was on unity of action in theme and plot. Tragic drama, serious in purpose, reflected the Greek view of life: a universe was ordered by law, any flouting of which — even by misjudgment — led to disaster. The best tragic drama described a man, not preeminently virtuous, but often a person of nobility, a king or national leader, whose misfortune was caused by a fatal flaw, *hamortia*. For the greatest of the Greek tragedians, Aeschylus, Sophocles, and Euripides, tragic drama was a means of introducing poetic insight into the fundamental human condition of pain and suffering. Aristotle, the Greek philosopher, argued that since all knowledge was beautiful, as well as useful, the effect of witnessing tragic drama was necessarily pleasing, even though it aroused profound emotions of pity and fear: pity from sympathy with the suffering of the protagonist; fear from a recognition of the fate endured by all who violated the eternal laws of the universe. For Aristotle, Greek drama also produced *katharsis*, as the resolution of the inevitable and fitting was portrayed.

For the Greeks, each man's fate included both the good and the bad, but man was free to heighten the pleasure of the good life through virtue or to aggravate his pain and suffering through vice. The Greeks did not insist that all tragic drama have an unhappy ending. (In Euripides' *Alcestis*, the hero's wife is restored to him because, after her death, he recognizes his own folly.) Nevertheless, Aristotle argued that unhappy endings were preferable, and he believed that the most powerful emotional interest in tragedy was stimulated by the reversal of fortune, *peripteia*, and by recognition of the reason why, *anagnorisis*. The greatest of the Greek playwrights, Sophocles, summed up the dominant Greek view in his masterpiece, *Oedipus Rex*, which demonstrated the inexorable working out of the laws of the universe. One of the more poignant moments of the play is when Jocasta, the queen, jubilant before she learns the truth, proclaims that since life is random, it is best to abandon principle and live from hand to mouth. A messenger then attempts to cheer Oedipus, the king, and instead does the opposite by confirming his fears that he has committed both incest and patricide. In horror, Oedipus departs, self-blinded and self-banished.

The development of realism in modern theater began in the nineteenth century as a reaction to the exaggerated sentimentalism of romantic drama, which treated contemporary middle-class life as seriously as great tragedians like Shakespeare had treated the age of aristocracy. Honoré de Balzac started as a romanticist, but eventually showed himself to be a realist in *Pamela Girard*, *La Maratre*, and *Mercadet*. Henrik Ibsen, in *The Doll's House* and other plays, concentrated on psychological truth and the interplay of social forces, showing the condition of modern man in the modern world. For these playwrights, man was not free, able to affect his lot in life for good or for ill; instead, he was a minute particle in a mechanical process. Thus, the prose problem play came to be substituted for the poetic heroic tragedy. In the twentieth century, the philosophy of realism was continued by such masters as Maxim Gorki, the Russian playwright best known for *The Lower Depths*. Tragic guilt was denied by insistence that man was the victim of impersonal forces. Pity and fear were evoked in the portrayal of suffering by the fact that the protagonist was not responsible for, but endured, his fate. New ideas of man, society, and the universe were expressed by showing conflict within man himself, the concerns of disrupted psyche, and man's solitude in an unfriendly world.

As Aristotle had spoken for the Greeks, such German philosophers as Arthur Schopenhauer and Friedrich Nietzsche spoke for the realists. The age of reason had come to an end, and the forces of feudalism seemed to be returning, as the Napoleonic wars had left Europe prostrate. For Schopenhauer, the tragic fact — without which there could be no dramatic tragedy — was "the unspeakable pain, the wail of humanity, the scornful mastery of chance, and the irretrievable fall of the just and innocent." For Nietzsche, too, human suffering was basic to tragedy, but it ought to yield neither to despair nor the manly acceptance of universal laws; it could only be transcended, not understood, by the belief that "despite every phenomenal change, life is at bottom joyful and powerful." Life must be acted out with joy, though it is at bottom absurd.

These two basic philosophies of life lead to fundamentally different interpretations of the assassination. An acceptance of modern realism would facilitate a determination that the President's death was a chance event, while an adherent to the classic Greek view would insist on the need for purpose, a meaning behind the event — a conspiracy. While we recognized that philosophical presumptions might shape and color the evidence, we realized it was the evidence itself that ought to determine the final conclusion. The assassination of the President may well have posed ultimate questions about the meaning of life, but we believed that the answer to why the President was assassinated was a question of fact, not of meaning. Life itself might be meaningful, yet the President's death could have been essentially a chance event; life could be at bottom absurd, yet the President's death might well have been the result of a conspiracy. We believed that predispositions ought to be set to one side. However ultimate questions about the meaning of life were answered, we believed that any interpretation of the assassination had to be rooted in the facts. History, Aristotle noted in his treatise *On Poetics*, deals with what "has been," even though "some historical occurrences may well be in the probable and possible order of things." History, in short, is a question of fact, not meaning.

Assassination as a Method of Organized Crime

As a first step in evaluating our conclusion that organized crime was responsible for the assassination of the President, we examined political assassinations in the United States. Their pattern had been studied by the National Commission on the Causes and Prevention of Violence, which was created in 1968 following the assassinations of Dr. Martin Luther King, Jr., and Senator Robert F. Kennedy. Nine U.S. Presidents, one in four, the commission found, had been targets of assassins, and four had died as a result. In addition, between 1835 and 1968 eighty-one other public officials or political candidates had been assaulted, some fatally. Assassinations by organized groups were, however, the exception. The typical political assassin in the United States was a deranged, self-appointed savior, essentially a loner. Only in the years immediately following the Civil War were terrorist tactics, including assassination, undertaken by organized groups to alter the government. The commission also made a careful study of violence by organized-crime figures, for whom murder was not random brutality, but a consciously selected means to an end. The enforcement of loan shark debts by violence served a business purpose. The killing of informants had an internal security purpose, for it inhibited informing in the future. When rival gangs tried to muscle in on territories, the gangland wars that broke out served an anticompetitive purpose. And when young leaders within an organization rebelled against the old order, the violence that often developed was the result of a thoughtfully conceived tactic in a struggle for power. These findings were to be expected, but what the commission had to say about organized-crime involvement in political assassination was surprising.

The commission identified eleven political assassinations where the motive was related to some objective of organized crime. There was, for example, the Mafia murder of David C. Hennessey, the New Orleans Superintendent of Police, in 1890. In 1926 Mayor Jeff Stone of Culp, Illinois, was shot and killed, probably because he had been corrupted by a bootlegging syndicate. William H. McSwiggin, an assistant state attorney in Chicago, who was believed to have been looking into the activities of Al Capone, was, along with two companions, cut down by a hail of bullets on the night of April 27, 1926. And in 1936 an Illinois state legislator, J. M. Bolton, and State Attorney Thomas J. Courtney were both killed, in all likelihood by the Capone gang. The other killings were of less prominent officials, since office holders who were victims of organized-crime violence generally served at a low level of government. They each had been in close contact with the underworld — either as conscientious opponents or as corrupt collaborators.

Our next step was to examine the President's assassination in light of the *modus operandi* of organized-crime murders, to see if any "fingerprints" left in Dallas had been overlooked. A great deal was known about the typical pattern of organized-crime murders, since records had been kept. The Chicago Crime Commission had, for example, established that between 1919 and 1963 there were 982 gangland slayings in the Chicago area. (The figure was obviously incomplete, since an unknown number of victims whose bodies were not recovered would have been listed as missing persons.) The record of arrests and convictions in gangland slayings was not impressive, however. In the same forty-four year period in Chicago only fifteen convictions were obtained for thirteen murders (law enforcement solves between 85 and 95 percent of homicides generally). A well-designed gangland slaying, in short, defied prosecution. Generally, too, no effort was made to conceal the nature of the killing, which as often as not occurred in a public place. The purpose of the gangland slaying was not just to do away with the victim; it also served notice to others of the authority of the leaders who ordered it.

While the murder of Lee Harvey Oswald by Jack Ruby had all of the earmarks of a gangland slaying (a key witness shot down by a shadowy figure at close range in public), that was not the case in the assassination of the President. Nevertheless, the classic pattern has not been without exceptions. A number of instances have been recorded in which the usual pattern was altered when it was necessary to hide the true nature of the murder, as might be expected in the assassination of a high-level government official. Someone with no traceable ties to the mob would be identified and selected to make the hit. He probably would not be a professional killer, and he would not be told enough so that he could tie the mob to the murder in the event he was caught. Every precaution would be taken to conceal the mob's participation in the hit. The motive, for example, might be made to appear to be run-of-the-mill robbery. And usually the assassin himself would be murdered shortly after the hit, making it extremely difficult to trace it back to those who ordered it. Because it ultimately turned out to have been a gangland murder, a good example of the exception was the attempted assassination, on June 28, 1971, of Joseph Colombo, Jr., the leader of one of the five New York Mafia families, before a crowd of 65,000 at the second annual rally of the Italian-American Civil Rights League at Columbus Circle in Manhattan.

Colombo had established the league to protest, as anti-Italian discrimination, the arrest of his son by the FBI in April 1970 for melting coins into silver ingots. (In his antidiscrimination campaign, Colombo negotiated with Albert S. Ruddy, the producer of *The Godfather,* to remove the name "Mafia" from the script of the film, and he prevailed on the Nixon Administration to get the Justice Department to stop referring to the Mafia and La Cosa Nostra in public releases.) The first rally had been a notable success, with four members of Congress on hand and Anthony Scotto, president of Local 1814, International Longshoremen's Association, as honored guest. (The son-in-law of Albert Anastasia's brother, Anthony, Scotto was reportedly, though he denied it, a *caporegime* in the Mafia family of Carlo Gambino. When he was tried for racketeering in federal court in New York City in October and November 1979, and found guilty on the strength of wiretap evidence, Scotto was able to command character testimony from Governor Hugh L. Carey of New York; two former mayors of New York City, Robert F.

Wagner and John V. Lindsay; and Lane Kirkland, the successor to George Meany as president of the AFL-CIO.) The second annual rally, however, was marred by tragedy. A black man, Jerome Johnson, twenty-four, carrying cameras and press identification, approached the speaker's stand and shot Colombo three times in the head. Johnson was immediately thrown to the ground, three shots rang out, and he was discovered shot and killed after the mass of bodies was untangled. Even as police clustered around, Johnson's killer escaped as professionally as he had carried out the execution. As for Colombo, he survived five hours of brain surgery but remained comatose until his death seven years later.

The police investigation of the Colombo shooting led eventually to Joseph "Crazy Joe" Gallo, a dissident member of the Colombo La Cosa Nostra family, who had rebelled against Joseph Profaci, Colombo's predecessor as family boss, in a bloody gang war in the 1960s. On April 6, 1972, Gallo was shot and killed by five Colombo men, one of whom, Joseph Luparelli, was arrested. Fearing for his life if not given adequate protection, Luparelli acknowledged that revenge was the motive for Gallo's murder. Johnson, who had lived in New Brunswick, New Jersey, was described by police sources as a "nondescript loner" who had been involved in narcotics, pornography, and prostitution. He was also characterized as a "real nut," which suggested he was simply a psychotic misfit acting on an inner compulsion. The better theory, however, was that Gallo, while in prison for extortion, had come to know a group of rising young black hoodlums and had maintained his association with them after his release in March 1971. That association apparently enabled Gallo to have Johnson recruited for the Colombo assault.

While the Kennedy assassination was not a typical gangland slaying, it was similar in many ways to the specialized (Colombo) type of hit. On the other hand, the victims of previous political assassinations were low-level officials of government, and there was always a motive — either the official was in hot pursuit of the underworld figures who ordered his killing, or he had somehow been compromised by them. Obviously, President Kennedy was not a low-level public official. His administration was, on the other hand, in dogged pursuit of underworld figures, as the anticrime program of Attorney General Kennedy, with the full backing of the President, marked a sharp departure from the past. What was at stake was power and wealth, possessions for which the mob had murdered repeatedly in the past. That the mob had the motive seemed beyond serious question. For the first time ever, there was a sustained and comprehensive attack on organized crime by the federal government. A corresponding departure on the part of organized crime from the pattern of past assassinations should not, therefore, have been unexpected.

The question of compromise was more difficult to assess. Prosecutors and other law officers have been generally agreed that organized crime does not pose a personal threat to them. Gangsters, they feel assured, will not retaliate for what is done in the line of duty. In fact, there have been occasions when the subject of a prosecution has let it be known that he believed the case was well conducted, that no unfair advantage was taken, and he recognized it was a business matter — that is, nothing personal. (A sense of this attitude was captured by Mario Puzo in *The Godfather* when Tessio, after Michael Corleone has caught him in a plot and ordered his death, says to Hagen, the *consiglieri*, "Tell Mike it was business. I always liked him.")

The best illustration of this so-called code concerned Thomas E. Dewey, the New York prosecutor who gained fame in the 1930s by bringing top members of the underworld to justice. As an assistant U.S. attorney in 1933, Dewey had obtained an indictment, for tax evasion, of Arthur "Dutch Schultz" Flegenheimer, a former bootlegger who had used his political connections to take over the numbers racket in Harlem. But Schultz was found not guilty, a verdict that Federal Judge Frederick H. Bryant termed "a blow against law enforcement and . . . aid and encouragement to the people who would flout the law." Dewey was subsequently appointed a special state prosecutor by Governor Herbert H. Lehman, and he went after Schultz again. This time Schultz responded by letting a contract on Dewey's life to Albert Anastasia, who promptly told Charles Luciano. Luciano called a meeting of the New York mob leaders, and it was decided that Schultz himself would be killed. On October 23, 1935, Schultz went to the Palace Chop House and Tavern in Newark, New Jersey, with two bodyguards, Abe Landau and Bernard Rosencranz, and a friend and financial adviser, Otto Berman. All four were gunned down (all died, though Schultz lingered briefly in a hospital) by a hit team headed by Charles "The Bug" Workman, a reliable Luciano bodyguard and chauffeur. (In an unusual outcome for a gangland slaying, Workman was tried and convicted for the murders.)

The code cuts both ways. It is well understood by prosecutors and police that there is a line that must not be crossed. You are all right, it is said, just as long as you do not "sleep with them," that is, you do not take favors, either money or sex. For the prosecutor or cop or other government official who does cross the line and then takes action against them, retaliation awaits. The public official's world is one of laws; the gangster's world is one of violence; so once the public official crosses the line, he invites violent retribution.

The Vulnerability of John F. Kennedy

Rumors had circulated for years of a connection between Joseph P. Kennedy, the President's father, and organized crime. Not long before he died in 1973, Frank Costello told an author, Peter Maas, that he had been in the liquor business with Kennedy in the 1930s (before the repeal of Prohibition, which would have made it illegal). Costello had, he said, "helped Kennedy become wealthy." There had been a falling-out since then, and Costello was deeply angered over the way Kennedy had snubbed him. Similarly, Joseph "Doc" Stacher, a longtime associate of Costello, as well as of Charles Luciano and Meyer Lansky, told of Joseph Kennedy's alleged rumrunning activities when he was interviewed by newspapermen in Israel not long before he died in 1976. Stacher also told of conflicts between Kennedy and underworld bootleggers.

Since all the principals had died, little of certainty could be established. As expected, the Kennedy family maintained that there was nothing in the elder Kennedy's business records to show a relationship with Costello or that he was involved in illegally importing liquor.

A resolution to repeal the 18th (Prohibition) Amendment was introduced in Congress on February 20, 1933, but it was not until December 5, 1933, that the 21st Amendment was ratified, making the sale of liquor legal again. In September 1933 Joseph Kennedy and his wife, along with President Roosevelt's son James and his wife, sailed for England. The British distillers, conscious of rank and station, treated Kennedy royally, and since he seemed to have the right connections, he secured an appointment as American agent for certain English and Scottish liquor interests, including Haig & Haig and Gordon's Dry Gin. Using "medicinal" licenses Kennedy had secured in Washington, his company, Somerset Importers, warehoused considerable stocks, and Kennedy made a killing. As for Costello, he had established Alliance Distributors as exclusive agents for Scotland's Whiteley Company, maker of King's Ransom and House of Lords Scotch. Lansky, Luciano, and other underworld figures also had a hand in the imported liquor business, as the British apparently were not too choosy about "connections."

While there was no evidence that Joseph Kennedy was connected with Costello or with any other crime figure, we noted that he was widely regarded in the underworld in less-than-flattering terms. John Roselli, for example, told Sam Giancana on December 21, 1961, that Frank Sinatra had been in touch with the elder Kennedy. "He's got it in his head," Roselli said, "that they're going to be faithful to him." Giancana replied, "In other words, then, the donation that was made,

. . ." Roselli interrupted, "That's what I was talking about." Giancana made an observation: "In other words, if I ever get a speeding ticket, none of these f____s would know me." "You told that right, buddy," Roselli replied. Later on, Giancana told a girl friend, Judith Campbell, that Joseph Kennedy was "one of the biggest crooks who ever lived," and in Doc Stacher's view, the Kennedy brothers' drive against organized crime was inspired by their father's hostility. "The Kennedy family," said Stacher, "was thirsting for . . . [my] blood. . . ." That is why Stacher left for Israel. The Kennedys "were out to get us," he said. "They had a personal grudge."

It is doubtful that a relationship between Joseph Kennedy and the underworld, even if it had existed, would have done more than color attitudes toward the President. Standing alone, it would hardly be enough to make assassination thinkable.

During the long night of November 8, 1960, when victory was far from certain, John Kennedy placed a call to Mayor Richard J. Daley of Chicago. "Mr. President," Daley said, according to Benjamin C. Bradlee, author of *Conversations with Kennedy,* "with a little bit of luck and the help of a few close friends, you're going to carry Illinois." It was, in fact, thanks to massive vote stealing in Illinois (where Daley-controlled wards in Cook County supplied the necessary 10,000-vote plurality) and Texas (where 100,000 big-city votes were simply disqualified), that the Kennedy-Johnson ticket eked out its razor-thin margin of victory. Even Theodore H. White, an author who basically respected Kennedy, found troubling overtones in the 1960 election, which he explained in his book, *Breach of Faith.* The nature of those overtones in Chicago went beyond the force of the personality of Irish-Catholic Democrat Richard Daley. The stark fact was that the West Side Bloc, a handful of legislators and ward politicians who controlled the working-class Italian, Hispanic, Polish, and black wards that skirted the Chicago River, had contributed mightily to the late-night victory. The West Side Bloc was controlled by the Chicago syndicate, which was, therefore, justified in taking some credit for Kennedy's election. "[T]he presidency was really stolen in Chicago," said Mickey Cohen, the Los Angeles gangster. And Sam Giancana boasted to Judith Campbell, "Listen, honey, if it wasn't for me, [Kennedy] wouldn't . . . be in the White House."

The mob's support for Kennedy's election was apparently neither sought nor rejected, and any political coalition embraces a variety of groups, not all of them upstanding. Traditionally, Republican prosecutors have been more willing to pursue organized-crime and political-corruption cases than their Democratic counterparts. Mickey Cohen put it this way:

> I know that certain people in the Chicago organization knew that they had to get John Kennedy in. There was no thought that they were going to get the best of it with John Kennedy. See, there may be different guys running for an office, and none of them may be . . . what's best for a combination. The choice becomes the best of what you've got going. John Kennedy was the best of the selection. But nobody in my line of work had an idea that he was going to name Bobby Kennedy attorney general. That was the last thing anyone thought.

The mob surely had its own reasons for wanting to see a Democratic victory in Illinois. The failure to reject mob support that he never specifically sought did not mean that Kennedy had crossed the line. It may have fixed perceptions of him, but it would not have been enough to bring his murder within the realm of contemplation.

There was much about John F. Kennedy that women admired and men envied. He was young, handsome, intelligent, rich, powerful, and well married. He also had, according to his good friend George Smathers, the Florida senator, "the most active libido of any man I've ever known." If the reports could be credited (and probably not all of them could), he had affairs or casual liaisons with a number of women, not only as a senator, but as a candidate for the presidency and as President. The French Ambassador, Herve Alphand, and his wife Nicole were good friends of the Kennedys, and Alphand worried about the President's indiscretions. "He loves pleasure and women," said the ambassador. "His desires are difficult to satisfy without causing fear of a scandal and its use by his political adversaries." Max Lerner, the journalist, aptly summed up the contrast between Kennedy's public image and his private conduct:

> He was beset from without by Nikita Khrushchev, who crowded and tried to cow him, and by Fidel Castro, who competed with him for the commitment of the young in the West. His image, in his mid-forties, was publicly that of the radiant and maturing world leader. But his . . . private life — aside from his marriage and his children — was that of the erotically focused male enjoying the risks of sexual adventure along with the power game of world politics.

In November 1959 Judith Campbell, a twenty-six-year-old, dark-haired divorcee who, though pretty enough to be a starlet and under contract to Warner Brothers, MGM, and Universal, had never quite made it in the movies, met Frank Sinatra and began an affair with him.

Sinatra was at the time the leader of the "Rat Pack," a fast-living bunch of actors and entertainers, which included such notables as Dean Martin, Sammy Davis, Jr., and Peter Lawford, who at the time was married to Kennedy's sister Patricia. The Rat Pack's escapades attracted a number of hangers-on, including John Roselli, a Las Vegas figure who represented the interests of the Chicago mob in the Desert Inn and the Stardust. They were a fun-loving crowd — lots of high times and antics like "girl-passing," which was the practice of sharing sexually satisfying young women. Judith Campbell insisted that she only had "affairs," yet her own version of events in those days revealed that she was passed around — at least on two important occasions.

In February 1960 the Rat Pack was in Las Vegas filming *Oceans Eleven,* a movie about some ex-servicemen who rob a casino, and Sinatra was appearing at the Sands, a hotel-casino whose secret owners numbered Anthony Accardo of Chicago, Meyer Lansky of Miami, and Gerardo Catena, the acting boss of the Genovese Mafia family in New Jersey. Senator Kennedy, whose presidential campaign was just getting into high gear, was in Las Vegas, visiting his sister Patricia Lawford. On Sunday evening, February 7, as he was sitting at Sinatra's table in the Sands lounge with his brother Edward, Kennedy was introduced by Sinatra to Judith Campbell, and a relationship began. They met again on March 7, 1960, at the Plaza Hotel in New York City, which was the first contact involving intimacy, according to Campbell. During the affair, which continued until March 22, 1962, there were repeated liaisons — in Las Vegas, Los Angeles, Chicago, Palm Beach, and Washington. Not known for being a lavish gift-giver, Kennedy made at least one contribution to Campbell's livelihood in the form of a check for $2,000. They were also in regular contact by telephone. Campbell's phone records indicated calls to Evelyn Lincoln (Kennedy's secretary) at the White House, while White House logs showed some seventy calls either to or from Campbell during the period. At the same time, Campbell was in contact with a number of shady individuals, including Paul "Skinny" D'Amato, a New Jersey underworld figure who reportedly had represented Sam Giancana's interests at the Cal-Neva Lodge in Lake Tahoe, Nevada; with John Roselli; and with Giancana himself. It was Roselli who brought Campbell to the attention of the FBI.

John Roselli, who was listed among the "top 40 hoodlums" targeted in the Justice Department's organized-crime drive, was staying at the Crest Hotel in Beverly Hills, California, in the fall of 1961. When the FBI checked his telephone records, it found he had made six calls to Judith Campbell, and a check of her phone records turned up two calls to the White House — on November 7 and 15, 1961. Campbell was first interviewed by the FBI on November 27, 1961, in Palm Springs, California. Little of significance was developed from the interview, even though Campbell was in close touch with both Roselli and Giancana. (In her book, *My Story*, Campbell said that during this time she had been a publicist for Jerry Lewis Productions, and she had gone to Giancana and Roselli in an effort to kill a story in *Confidential* that would have embarrassed Lewis.) The FBI investigation of Campbell continued into 1962, and on February 27, J. Edgar Hoover advised Attorney General Kennedy by memorandum of her two calls to the White House in November. The FBI director also noted her contacts with Giancana, "a prominent Chicago underworld figure," and with Roselli, "one of the second group of forty hoodlums receiving concentrated attention." The memorandum added: "The relationship between Campbell and Mrs. Lincoln or the purpose of these calls is not known." On March 22 Hoover lunched with the President at the White House. Since both men were dead in 1978, we could only infer what they talked about, but the White House records showed that the last telephone contact with Judith Campbell occurred a few hours after the luncheon.

On March 28, 1960, seven weeks after he introduced Campbell to Senator Kennedy, Sinatra was performing at the Fontainebleau Hotel in Miami Beach. It was cocktail hour in the French Room, and Sinatra had just introduced Campbell to "Joe Fish," or Joseph Fischetti, a cousin of Al Capone who was paid for services as a "talent scout" whenever Sinatra appeared at the Fontainebleau. "Hey, Frank," said Fischetti, "look who's here." Sinatra turned and said, "Come here, Judy. I want you to meet a good friend of mine, Sam Flood." The middle-aged, medium-built man with a ruddy complexion was Sam Giancana.

Campbell insisted she was not intimate with Giancana for more than a year and a half after they met, but she acknowledged meeting with him several times while she was "dating" the President. On April 6, 1960, she went to see Giancana in Chicago, stopping off to visit then-candidate Kennedy at his home in Washington, where they were intimate. Campbell and Giancana were often together at the Armory Lounge in Forest Park, Illinois, Giancana's hangout, where he would conduct "meets" in a back room, always in Sicilian. He told her, "You don't want to hear what I've got to say to these people." During her relationship with Giancana, which remained close at least until October 1962, Campbell received a number of gifts from him, including a Ford Thunderbird. On more than one occasion she saw Giancana immediately before or after being with Kennedy. On April 28, 1961, for example, the day after she and Giancana went to the wedding of Anthony Accardo's daughter, Linda Lee, Campbell was visited by the President, who was in Chicago for a fund-raising dinner, at her suite (room 839-40) in the Ambassador East Hotel. Though he stayed for only twenty minutes, they were intimate. On August 8, 1961, she lunched with the President at the White House. They argued and were not intimate as Kennedy had hoped, according to her account. That evening, Giancana and Anthony Tisci, his son-in-law and the administrative assistant to Congressman Roland V. Libonati, visted Campbell in room 353 of the Mayflower Hotel in Washington. According to Campbell, Giancana would only say he was in town on "some business."

During the period of his relationship with Campbell Giancana had access to electronic surveillance equipment through his CIA contacts, and on at least one occasion, he put it to use for his own purposes. The incident was widely reported. In October 1960 Giancana got Robert Maheu, the former FBI agent who was the CIA-Mafia go-between, to arrange the bugging of the Las Vegas apartment of Dan Rowan, the comedian, to find out if his girl friend, Phyllis McGuire, was, as Giancana suspected, being unfaithful. (Both Giancana and Roselli, as well as Maheu, became the subjects of an FBI investigation after Arthur Zalletti, a private detective who was monitoring the equipment, was caught, and Roselli had to bail him out of jail.) Giancana may have inadvertently indicated what he was up to during a confrontation with FBI agents at O'Hare International Airport in Chicago on July 12, 1961. Angered by the agents' insistent questioning of Phyllis McGuire, Giancana stormed, "I know all about the Kennedys . . . and one of these days . . . [I am] going to tell all." Campbell also betrayed an interest in eavesdropping equipment while she was seeing the President, asking a private detective in West Hollywood, California, if he could supply her with something "to put in her handbag to record telephone conversations."

Kennedy's break with Campbell in March 1962 was followed that summer by the termination of his friendship with Sinatra. The singer had built a helicopter pad and added a wing to his home in Palm Springs, California, in anticipation of a presidential visit but, the President told Peter Lawford, "I can't stay there . . . while Bobby's handling [the Giancana] investigation." Kennedy stayed at the Palm Desert home of Bing Crosby instead. Justice Department attorneys, too, were concerned, and they complained to Robert Kennedy that the effort against organized crime was being undermined by the President's public relationship with Sinatra. At the Attorney General's request, a nineteen-page report on Sinatra was prepared and delivered on August 3, 1962. While indicating no illegal activity by the entertainer, it documented his long-standing association with major mob figures. The report was forwarded to the President. (On June 30, 1962, an incident occurred that lent force to the Sinatra report. Charles English, a Giancana henchman, came out of the Armory Lounge and challenged an FBI agent who was keeping Giancana under surveillance. English told the agent that if the Attorney General was interested in Giancana, he should set up a meeting through Sinatra.)

In contrast to his father's alleged association with Costello and the mob's help in winning the 1960 election, Kennedy's relationship with Campbell was quite possibly of significance with respect to the assassination. Campbell may not have been aware of the full implications of her affair with the President, although she conceded in her book that perhaps she had been "used [by Giancana] almost from the beginning." She was not "some kind of Phi Beta Kappa," her former husband observed, as he explained that she would not have understood the CIA-Mafia plots. Campbell claimed that she thought the President was "in love" with her, though she had no grounds for believing that anything other than sex was involved, since all she did was "service" him. As Mickey Cohen put it to his biographer: "Frank [Sinatra] got . . . [Kennedy] all the broads he could ever have used. And these girls were not unknowns. They were all starlets. . . ." From the mob's point of view, Kennedy had been compromised. He had crossed the line. In the Greek sense, the liaison with Judith Campbell was, we came to believe, Kennedy's fatal flaw, the error in judgment for which the gods would demand their due.

"Since when is f_____g a federal offense?" an unidentified mob figure asked in an FBI-monitored conversation, referring to a bureau investigation of Gil Beckley, a bookmaker, on a vice matter. And he elaborated:

> . . . and if it is, . . . I want the President indicted, because I know he was whacking all those broads. Sinatra brought him out. . . . I'd like to . . . [hit] Kennedy. . . . I would gladly go to the penitentiary for the rest of my life, believe me. . . .

Giancana had considered Sinatra his hot line to the White House, but it did not go as he had hoped. On December 12, 1961, Roselli commiserated with Giancana:

> He's got big ideas, Frank does, about being ambassador or something. You f__k them, you pay them, and then they're through. You got the right idea, Moe, so . . . f__k everybody. . . . We'll use them every f_____g way we can. They only know one way. Now let them see the other side of you.

Roselli then told Giancana:

I had a chance to quiz [Sinatra in Las Vegas]. . . . I said, Frankie, can I ask one question? He says, Johnny, I took Sam's name, and wrote it down, and told Bobby Kennedy, this is my buddy. This is my buddy, this is what I want you to know, Bob. And he says Johnny, he. . . .

Giancana laughed and commented: "You could have answered it yourself."

On January 31, 1962, Giancana had a conversation with John D'Arco, a politician from Chicago's First Ward, about the upcoming election for Cook County sheriff and the possible candidacy of Roswell Spencer, a former FBI man:

Giancana:	*[Spencer is] like Kennedy. He'll get what he wants out of you, but you won't get anything out of him.*
D'Arco:	*That f____r Kennedy! Is Sinatra gonna work on . . .?*
Giancana:	*No.*
D'Arco:	*I heard that the President, when he is in California, is with Sinatra all the time.*
Giancana:	*He can't get change of a quarter.*
D'Arco:	*Sinatra can't?*
Giancana:	*That's right. Well, they got the whip and they're in office and that's it. . . . So they're going to knock us guys out of the box and make us defenseless.*

After Kennedy broke off with Sinatra, a Giancana underling, Johnny Formosa, suggested that Sinatra ought to be hit. "I could," said Formosa, "knock out a couple of those guys — Lawford and that Martin prick — and I could take the nigger and put his other eye out." "No," Giancana replied. "I got other plans. . . ."

The Assassination, According to John Roselli

Our conclusion that elements of organized crime participated in the plot to assassinate President Kennedy was based on more than an analysis of character, motive, and association. It was independently confirmed in information that John Roselli, the mob figure, secretly provided to Jack Anderson, the syndicated columnist, between early 1967 and August 7, 1976, when Roselli's body was found in an oil drum floating in Dumfoundling Bay near North Miami Beach, Florida.

Born Filippo Sacco in Esperia, Italy, on July 4, 1905, Roselli arrived with his mother and brother in Boston in 1911 to join his father, Vincenzo. By the 1940s he was the Chicago mob's representative in Los Angeles, until he was tried and sent to prison for his part in the $2 million movie industry extortion. Upon his release in 1947, Roselli returned to Hollywood, where he was hired as an "assistant producer" by Byron Foy, who headed Eagle Lion Studios and who had sponsored Roselli's parole. Roselli actually worked on three movies: *He Walked by Night, T-Men,* and *Canyon City.* He offered, one producer who knew him said, "direct knowledge about prisons and cops." The studio position was, however, a cover, for Roselli was again the Chicago emissary to the Los Angeles Mafia family of Jack Dragna. He was also spending a great deal of time in Las Vegas, which was fast becoming a mob-dominated gambling town, as a result of a project that was undertaken in the late 1940s by Benjamin "Bugsy" Siegel, an old friend and early criminal associate of Meyer Lansky. Siegel was killed on June 20, 1947, by five 30-30 slugs fired through a living-room window of the Beverly Hills mansion of his paramour, Virginia Hill. (The execution had been ordered by Charles Luciano and other Mafia leaders, and approved by Lansky, at a meeting in Havana during Christmas week, 1946, which was ostensibly called to honor Frank Sinatra, who was appearing at the Hotel Nacional. The charge against Siegel: embezzling mob money, which was deposited in a Swiss bank account by Virginia Hill. The contract was carried out by Dragna's men.)

After Siegel's death Roselli became a familiar, even prominent, figure in Las Vegas, and, when Jack Dragna died in 1957, his career reached its zenith. His considerable influence was due, among other reasons, to his close association over the years with Dragna's successor, Frank DeSimone (Roselli's lawyer in the movie-industry extortion trial had been Otto Christensen, DeSimone's law partner). One of Roselli's chief accomplishments during the decade or so that he held sway in Las Vegas was arranging for Anthony Giordano, the Mafia leader in St. Louis, and Anthony Zerilli, a *caporegime* in Detroit, to buy a hidden interest in the Frontier Hotel in Las Vegas in 1966 and 1967. He was also instrumental in the sale of the Sands and the Desert Inn to Howard Hughes in March 1967, for which he received a $95,000 finder's fee. With the death of DeSimone on January 10, 1968, Roselli considered trying to take over the West Coast organization, since Nicholas Licata, who had succeeded DeSimone, was not highly regarded. Roselli had the backing of Santo Trafficante, but he was opposed by the powerful Zerilli family in Detroit. The issue became academic, however, when Roselli and four associates were convicted on December 2, 1968, of organizing and participating in a scheme to cheat in card games at the exclusive Friars Club in Beverly Hills. Roselli had been sponsored as a member of the Friars by Frank Sinatra, Dean Martin, and George Jessel, the club's founder, but he gave them reason to regret it. For four years, from 1962 to 1966, Roselli was a regular at the high-stakes gin rummy table along with such luminaries as Tony Martin, the singer, comedians Phil Silvers and Zeppo Marx, and Harry Karl, the millionaire husband of actress Debbie Reynolds. What his unwitting victims did not know, as they dropped an estimated $400,000, was that Roselli, or confederates sitting in for him, were taking signals, transmitted electronically by observers stationed at peepholes. The scam was exposed, however, by one of the peepmen, George Sears, who told about it to the FBI. Roselli asked Frank Bompensiero, a Mafia strong-arm man from San Diego, to kill Sears, but the FBI kept him hidden until the trial. Roselli was convicted and sentenced to five years in the federal penitentiary at McNeil Island, Washington. His career had crested, and he did not stand up well to the rigors of prison life.

During the period Roselli was facing prosecution for his rigged card games, he was feeling the pressure of what remained of the federal organized-crime drive. In May 1966 the FBI threatened to have him deported unless he cooperated in its investigation of Mafia activities. Roselli contacted Sheffield Edwards, who as director of the CIA's Office of Security had been one of the planners of the Castro assassination plots. Edwards notified the FBI that Roselli wanted to "keep square with the Bureau," but he was afraid he would be killed for "talking." Nevertheless, the government proceeded. On October 20, 1967, Roselli was indicted under the Alien Registration Act; he was convicted on May 23, 1968; and he received a six-month sentence, to be served concurrently with the term for cheating at cards. Deportation proceedings were subsequently begun, but they were still pending at the time of Roselli's death. It was during this period (March 1967) that Drew Pearson and Jack Anderson published a report that Fidel Castro had ordered the assassination of President Kennedy in retaliation for the CIA-Mafia plots. The information had apparently come from Edward P. Morgan, a lawyer for Robert Maheu, the CIA-Mafia go-between. Roselli, through Maheu, had also contacted Morgan.

Following his release from McNeil Island in 1973, Roselli was in direct touch with Anderson. (Anderson did not know it, but Roselli had been called before a federal grand jury in 1970 to testify about several matters, including hidden Mafia ownership of Las Vegas casinos. At first he refused to answer on grounds of self-incrimination, but when he was given immunity and faced the prospect of having time added to his sentence, he agreed to talk, although he carefully avoided giving any information of value. Nevertheless, it would have appeared to his organized-crime associates that he had cooperated, for shortly after his grand jury appearance the government successfully prosecuted Anthony Giordano and Anthony Zerilli for hidden ownership of the Frontier Hotel. The word in the underworld was, in fact, that Roselli had been turned. While Roselli undoubtedly denied to his associates that he had cooperated with the government, he had to know that he was a marked man.) Bit by bit over the next two years Roselli, according to Anderson, confided in him what he knew about the Kennedy assassination, on the condition that Anderson not reveal his identity. In 1971 Anderson had reported in some detail on the CIA-Mafia plots, naming Roselli as one of the principal participants. The FBI had tried to "pump Roselli for information," Anderson wrote on February 23, 1971, but he had been "sworn to silence by the CIA, and up to this moment, he hasn't broken it." The details that Roselli supplied in their face-to-face meetings, according to Anderson, linked the Mafia directly to the assassination. It was the work of Cubans connected to Santo Trafficante, according to Roselli, and Oswald had been recruited as a decoy. Oswald may have fired at the President, but the fatal shot was fired from close range. Once Oswald was captured, the mob arranged to have him killed by Ruby, who, Roselli told Anderson, had not been in on the assassination itself. (Anderson told us that Roselli had characterized Ruby as just a "punk.") Roselli said it was also his theory that Castro was behind the assassination, along with Trafficante. He said he knew that a team that had been sent to kill Castro had been captured and tortured, and he believed that Castro might have formed an alliance with Trafficante to kill Kennedy.

We found Roselli's statements difficult to evaluate, and there even were reasons to dismiss it. We knew, for example, that Roselli had told James Fratianno, a West Coast mob figure, that there was no truth to it. It would not have surprised us to learn that Roselli had contrived the whole story as leverage in his effort to avoid prosecution for the Friars Club fraud and deportation as an alien. We realized he could have fashioned the account out of sheer speculation, based on his participation in the CIA-Mafia plots. On the other hand, Roselli's story may have been essentially true, with only the speculation about Castro's role added to "shake up" the government and strengthen his bargaining position. Roselli could have reasoned logically that out of fear that its role in the Castro plots would be exposed, with an inference that the plots resulted in the assassination of the President, the government would halt prosecutive action against him.

In making a credibility assessment, we were impressed by the fact that certain aspects of Roselli's account came tellingly close to what we knew to be the truth. To be sure, Roselli could have based his account to Anderson on the speculation of published Warren Commission critics (Anderson told us that from talking to Roselli, he did not believe he had read the assassination literature), but it would have been asking too much of coincidence for that to explain how Roselli's statements contained *all* of the essential elements. In addition, an important aspect of Roselli's account — the fact that the fatal shot had been fired from close range — was not shown to be true (at least to the extent that a shot *was* fired from the grassy knoll, although it actually missed) until our investigation in 1978. Roselli could not, in short, have been aware of the fact of a shot from the knoll unless he had inside information, for up until the time of his death, in July 1976, the official view was that all of the shots had come from behind. We knew from the acoustics evidence that there was, in fact, a close-range ambush in Dealey Plaza, as Roselli said there had been. And while Roselli was wrong about the fatal shot having been fired from that ambush, which was positioned behind the picket fence on the grassy knoll, he and others privy to the conspiracy would have been justified in thinking that it had. We learned from the analysis of the acoustics evidence that the shot from the grassy knoll, fired some 111 feet from the limousine, preceded the fatal head shot, which was fired by Oswald from the Texas School Book Depository, by less than seven-tenths of a second. The gunman behind the picket fence on the knoll could not have heard the report of Oswald's rifle due to the near-simultaneous sound of his own weapon. He had watched as Oswald fired the first two shots — missing completely on the first and just wounding the President on the second. Then, as he squeezed the trigger, the President's head exploded, so he must have believed — and have told the men who sent him to Dealey Plaza — that it was his shot that killed the President. (Both the grassy-knoll gunman and his underworld coconspirators must have been perplexed but pleased when the Warren Commission announced its conclusion that there was no evidence that a second gunman even existed, much less had actually assassinated the President.) Roselli's report that Kennedy was killed by a close-range ambush, therefore had the ring of inside information to it, information that could only have originated with the gunman himself.

The same sort of analysis could be applied to Roselli's report that Cubans were Oswald's coconspirators, since Oswald did, in fact, have a number of associations with Cubans. With some justification, many of the sightings of Oswald with Latins, quite probably Cubans, could be questioned or explained as innocent, and none of them alone could be deemed conclusive evidence of conspiracy. Woven together, however, they formed a pattern that was significant and potentially sinister. The efforts of the Warren Commission to dismiss Oswald's Cuban associations — particularly the photograph of Oswald and an accomplice handing out "Fair Play for Cuba" leaflets in New Orleans, and the account by Silvia Odio of a visit by Oswald and two Cuban confederates to her home in Dallas — seemed to us to be strained and artificial. Taken together with the fact of the second gunman and the Roselli account of how Oswald was recruited by Cuban agents of Santo Trafficante, the pattern of Oswald's Latin associations could be stitched, we believed, into a tapestry that depicted the true nature of the plot.

Roselli made two appearances before the Church Committee. On June 24, 1975, he told in detail of his part in the CIA-Mafia plots, and ten months later, on April 23, 1976, he was grilled about his Castro retaliation theory. He told the Church Committee that he had no evidence to support it. It was following Roselli's appearance in June 1975 that a contract for his murder was approved by the national organized-crime commission, according to Nicholas Gage of *The New York Times*, who said his information came from a Mafia figure who was in a position to know. Gage said his informant told him that killing Roselli proved to be a difficult feat, since he was behaving cautiously. He had moved into the home of his sister and brother-in-law, Edith and Joseph Daigle, in Plantation, Florida, where he spent his days reading by the pool and his evenings watching television, and whenever he went out, to eat in a restaurant or to play golf, he did so in the company of relatives or close friends. Only twice, as far as we could tell, did he stray from this pattern: on July 16, 1976, he had dinner with Santo Trafficante at The Landing in Fort Lauderdale; twelve days later he disappeared.

On July 28, 1976, Roselli and his sister ate a late brunch, and at 12:50 P.M., he left in her car, a 1975 silver Chevrolet Impala, and drove to a nearby marina, where, Gage was told, he was met by two men, one an old friend, the other a visitor from Chicago. They boarded a private yacht and set out for a cruise, while someone drove the Impala to the Miami International Airport and checked it into a parking lot, evidently to make it appear that Roselli had fled the country. As Roselli sat on deck, sipping a glass of vodka, the man from Chicago slipped up from behind, asphyxiated him, and taped a washcloth over his mouth to make sure he was dead. Roselli's legs were sawed off, so the body could be stuffed into a 55-gallon oil drum, which was weighted down with chains and dumped in Dumfoundling Bay. It was, however, found by fishermen ten days later, after the gases created by decomposition had supplied enough buoyancy to float the drum to the surface. The investigation that followed did not result in an identification of Roselli's killers.

Sound reasons for Roselli's murder were offered by FBI sources. The word was out that he had breached the underworld code when he appeared before the grand jury probing the ownership of the Frontier Hotel and, again, when he appeared before the Church Committee.

Either infraction would have been sufficient to mark him for execution, and Gage reported that his Mafia informant had confirmed that Roselli's utterances had been his undoing. Still, a mystery remained, for Roselli's death was not typical. Had he been publicly slain or had his body been routinely found, either of the explanations would have been adequate — he was simply the victim of mob justice. But the carefully devised effort to make it appear that Roselli had left the country cast his killing in a different light. It suggested that someone knew what else Roselli might divulge publicly or already had divulged privately, and this was reason enough to have him silenced; yet the someone did not want it to appear that Roselli had been murdered. Roselli's murderer, or murderers, may have believed that if it was indicated that Roselli's death was related to his testimony to the Church Committee, a vigorous murder investigation would follow, an investigation that would get to the substance of Roselli's Senate testimony — the CIA-Mafia plots and their connection with the death of the President. (If Roselli's murderers did hold that view, however justified they may have been, nothing that happened after the body was discovered confirmed the infallibility of their foresight.)

The Death of Sam Giancana

If Roselli was killed for what he knew about the assassination, and if the killing was related to the CIA-Mafia plots, what about the murder of Sam Giancana, who had come to Miami on September 24, 1960, to plot the assassination of Castro with Roselli and Trafficante? Like Roselli, Giancana was being pursued by the authorities in the period following the CIA-Mafia plots, and he too had had an unpleasant taste of prison. Giancana was called before a federal grand jury in Chicago on May 14, 1965, and questioned extensively for three days. David Shippers, the head of the Organized Crime Section of the U.S. attorney's office in Chicago, called it an effort "to break the mob's inner circle." Shippers elaborated: "We wanted to get information on the national commission [of organized crime], and Giancana was the Chicago representative to the commission." (Giancana's subpoena was in keeping with a sophisticated strategy of the Department of Justice. All Chicago mob figures and politicians associated with them were called before the grand jury and questioned at length, even if they refused to answer, so no one would know who was and who was not talking. Americo DiPietto, for example, was called from Leavenworth, where he was serving a twenty-year sentence on a narcotics conviction, and while he was too terrified to give even his name, he was kept in town for two days. In addition to Giancana, Charles English, Fiore Buccieri, and Gus Alex of the Chicago syndicate were called; as were John D'Arco, Pat Marcy, and Benjamin Jacobson of the First Ward; and Anthony Tisci, Giancana's son-in-law, the former aide to Congressman Libonati, along with Tisci's new boss, U.S. Representative Frank Annunzio.)

On June 1, 1965, Giancana was brought before Chief Judge William S. Campbell. After hearing from Shippers, Judge Campbell asked him, "Do you continue to refuse?" "Yes, sir," Giancana replied, and Judge Campbell ordered him jailed until he testified, telling him he had the key to his own cell. Giancana spent twelve difficult months in jail, obtaining his release only upon the termination of the grand jury's eighteen-month term. Justice Department attorneys in the field wanted to call him before a successor grand jury, but they were overruled by Washington. One factor in the decision not to recall Giancana was the intervention of the CIA, which was fearful that his assistance in the plots against Castro would become public.

Upon his release, Giancana fled to Mexico, where he lived initially in Cuernavaca, at Las Nubes 2, and in a plush condominium on Amsterdam Avenue in Mexico City. Eventually he settled in an expensive walled estate in the Las Quintas section of Cuernavaca. For all that luxury, Giancana was a broken man. As an alien, his residency status was precarious, and it cost him $2,000-a-week in bribes to remain in Mexico. And as an exile, he was reduced to the rank of soldier in the Chicago syndicate, as day-to-day command had been assumed by Sam Battaglia, under the guidance of Felice DeLucia and Anthony Accardo, both retired Chicago bosses. Giancana did not return to his home in Oak Park, Illinois, for eight years, and when he did return, he did so involuntarily. On July 18, 1974, Mexican authorities unexpectedly ordered his deportation — so unexpectedly, in fact, that most of his assets remained in the hands of Mexican citizens who had held them for him.

When Giancana stepped off the plane in Chicago, he showed the effects of age as well as a stomach ailment. He saw an FBI agent with whom he had fought over the years and told him, almost meekly, that he wanted to forget the past — he was "retired." He was, however, greeted with a grand jury subpoena, which meant the ordeal was beginning anew. He appeared before the grand jury on four occasions and met with federal investigators three other times, but according to Peter Vaira, the chief of the Department of Justice Strike Force in Chicago in 1974, he was "evasive and uncooperative." He had again been immunized, but instead of remaining defiantly mute, he adopted a tactic of saying as little as possible and at times resorting to lies, preferring to risk a perjury charge rather than an open-ended jail term for contempt. Privately, Giancana told friends he would do anything to keep from "rotting in jail," but he assured Accardo and other mob leaders that he was not cooperating.

On Thursday, July 19, 1975, staff representatives of the Church Committee arrived in Chicago to arrange for Giancana's appearance in Washington five days later to testify about the CIA-Mafia assassination plots. That evening, Giancana had a few friends over to his Oak Park home. Charles English was there, and they were joined around 7 P.M. by Giancana's daughter Francine and her husband, Jerome DePalma, as well as Dominic "Butch" Blasi. Shortly after a quiet dinner of chicken, baked potatoes, and mixed vegetables, English and Blasi left, and near 10 P.M., the DePalmas also left, to take their little daughter home to bed. Later that evening Giancana was in his finished basement with someone he apparently knew and trusted. This was where he relaxed. He kept his golf bags there, as well as his movie equipment and his favorite full-length features, *The Manchurian Candidate* and *The Man with the Golden Arm,* both starring his old friend, Frank Sinatra. He was cooking sausage, escarole, and beans when he felt the silencer on a 10-shot High Standard Duromatic .22 target pistol tickle the back of his head. As with the President, it was a bullet in the back of the head that ended his life. But Giancana was shot also in the mouth and neck — seven times in all. No arrest was made in his murder.

As with Roselli, there were several theories offered for Giancana's death. It may have been feared that he was trying to regain his old position in the Chicago hierarchy, but that was unlikely. David Shippers, the government lawyer who had pursued Giancana, thought he had been silenced. "When there's a hit like this one — shots in the face and throat," Shippers observed, "it is typical of a Mafioso killing, indicating they believe he has been talking — in the throat to show you've been talking, and in the mouth to show you won't talk any more." Yet it was unclear what Giancana might have been talking about — mob activities in Chicago, the CIA-Mafia plots, the assassination of President Kennedy? Members of Giancana's family thought they knew. One of his daughters, Antoinette, insisted that her father had been killed "by the same people responsible for killing the Kennedys."

The Anguish of Robert F. Kennedy

As in Greek tragedy, there was in the President's character a fatal flaw, a *hamortia*, one that could have made him vulnerable to assassination by organized crime. There was also in the President's assassination a dramatic reversal of fortune, a *perripteia*. President Kennedy had sought in the trip to Dallas to bolster his prospects in the coming election; instead he was killed. Life would imitate art almost too perfectly, if it were also possible to say that through this reversal of fortune, the President suffered, and through his suffering he came to recognize the nature of his error of judgment. But life is not Greek drama, and the President did not suffer — he was either unconscious or dead by the time the bell heard on the police dispatch tape tolled his passing. In addition, it was not possible to say that President Kennedy ever suspected, much less understood, the reasons for his death. For him, there was no moment of *anagnorisis.* Life for him was not a Greek tragedy.

There was, nevertheless, another way to view the assassination. It is commonly supposed that each element of Greek tragedy had to find its fulfillment in a single protagonist, while, in fact, Greek drama was about life, not necessarily people. So long as each element was present, the tragic in life was appropriately portrayed. As Greek tragedy, the meaning of the President's death may appropriately be found in someone other than the President.

November 20, 1963 was Robert Kennedy's thirty-eighth birthday, and there was a party at the Justice Department. The Kennedys were given to irony, and the Attorney General climbed on the desk of his cavernous office and made a few tongue-in-cheek remarks. It was, he said, great to have done so much in so little time, to have worked so hard and elected a President and now to have assured his reelection by the popularity of his policies on civil rights, Hoffa, wiretapping. . . .

Two days later the Attorney General presided over an organized-crime meeting — it was the second day of a two-day conference, attended by Kennedy's senior staff and U.S. attorneys from around the country. At about noon the subject of Sam Giancana and corruption in Chicago was taken up, but then there was a lunch break. The meeting was never reconvened. Kennedy went with Robert M. Morgenthau, the U.S. attorney for the Southern District of New York, to Hickory Hill, his Virginia estate, for lunch, and it was there that he heard the news from Dallas. Late that afternoon he was with Edwin Guthman, his press assistant. "I thought they might get one of us," he said, "but Jack, after all he'd been through, never worried about it. . . . I thought it would be me."

Robert Kennedy was, as Arthur Schlesinger noted, "a desperately wounded man." John Seigenthaler, a friend and an aide at Justice, said it was "as if he were on the rocks. . . ." To Pierre Salinger, the White House press secretary, "He was the most shattered man I had ever seen." His first public appearance after the assassination was at a Christmas party at an orphanage that had been arranged by Mary McGrory of *The Washington Star.* Guthman, who wrote a reminiscence of his days at Justice, *We Band of Brothers*, remembered how one of the children, a black boy, no more than six or seven, ran up to Kennedy and chanted, "Your brother's dead! Your brother's dead!" "The little boy knew he had done something wrong," Guthman wrote, "but he didn't know *what*, so he started to cry. Bobby stepped forward and picked him up, in kind of one motion, and held him very close for a moment, and he said, 'That's all right. I have another brother.' "

In *Robert Kennedy and His Times*, Schlesinger traced Kennedy's effort to come to grips with his grief. Over Easter 1964 he went with Jacqueline Kennedy to Paul Mellon's house in Antigua. While there, she showed him a copy of Edith Hamilton's little classic, *The Greek Way*. It introduced him to Greek literature, and he soon came to appreciate it, often quoting passages from *Oedipus Rex*. "He knew the Greeks cold," recalled Jeff Greenfield, one of his Senate staffers. "He'd cite some play and say, 'You know that?' " Greek insights into grief obviously touched a deep chord within him.

Those who knew Robert Kennedy best talked of the depths of his suffering during this period. Many also speculated that there was more to it than merely the loss of his brother. Schlesinger, for example, reported a conversation with Kennedy on December 9, 1963, when he said that there could be no serious doubt that Oswald was involved, but there was still argument as to whether he had done it by himself or as part of a larger plot, "whether organized by Castro or by gangsters." There is an element of doubt in life, even for those who deeply believe that it ultimately has meaning. What many of those who knew Robert Kennedy well speculated about was to what degree one element of his suffering was related to his own uncertain knowledge. Kennedy knew about the early CIA-Mafia plots. Could they have resulted in retaliation? Kennedy knew about his brother's relationship with Judith Campbell and the mob's attitude toward him. Could that have resulted in the assassination? The uncertainty about these points must surely have added immeasurably to the burden of grief that he carried. Even though he had his *anagnorisis*, he could never have been sure what really happened. That might have been the most agonizing part.

Robert Kennedy carried a recognition of the true nature of these factors, which went beyond that possible for the President, who was not particularly religious. Robert Kennedy knew that neither he nor his brother had played a role in the assassination plots against Castro. Had they brought about the President's death, the pain of undeserved suffering would have been felt. As for the President's relationship with Judith Campbell, Robert Kennedy was a man whose private life reflected traditional Catholic values. It had been suggested that he had had an affair with at least one woman, Marilyn Monroe. William

Sullivan, who was assistant director of the FBI and the man in charge of its intelligence organization, wrote:

> Although Hoover was desperately trying to catch Bobby . . . red-handed at anything, he never did. Kennedy was almost a Puritan. We used to watch him at parties, where he would order one glass of Scotch and still be sipping from the same glass two hours later. The stories about Bobby . . . and Marilyn Monroe were just stories. The original story was invented by a so-called journalist, a right-wing zealot who had a history of spinning wild yarns. It spread like wildfire, of course, and J. Edgar Hoover was right there, gleefully fanning the flames.

Kitty Kelly, who collected every known story of the President's indiscretions for her book, *Jackie Oh!*, called the Attorney General "a monk," noting that he "objected strongly to what was going on in his brother's White House." Those who knew Robert Kennedy were well aware that, on this count, he was not one with his brother. In the Greek sense, therefore, Robert Kennedy was a tragic hero, not preeminently virtuous, but whose great misfortune was caused by a fatal flaw in his brother's character, a flaw that caused Robert Kennedy a full measure of mental anguish.

It seemed evident, too, that Robert Kennedy carried his burden well and brought other sufferers both insight and relief. "For the next two and a half years," wrote Rita Dallas, his father's nurse, "Robert Kennedy became the central focus of strength and hope for the family. . . ." "Despite his own grief and loneliness," she wrote, "he radiated an inner strength. . . . Bobby was the one who welded the pieces back together."

Los Angeles: June 4, 1968

In June 1968 Robert Kennedy was in California seeking the Democratic nomination for President. On June 3, the day before the primary, as his motorcade moved slowly through cheering crowds in San Francisco's Chinatown, there were sounds that appeared to be shots. Kennedy stood still but kept waving, and he motioned toward Ethel, his wife, who, pale and stricken, had slumped in her seat. The scare had been caused by Chinese firecrackers.

On June 4, at about 6:30 P.M., Kennedy went to the Hotel Ambassador in Los Angeles to hear the returns from California and South Dakota. George McGovern called. Kennedy had, he said, beaten him, as well as Hubert Humphrey, in McGovern's home state, carrying both the farmers and the Indians. Then Kennedy learned he had won California, beating Eugene McCarthy. John Glenn, the astronaut, later a senator from Ohio, remembered how Kennedy went around the living room of his hotel suite, personally thanking each member of his inner circle. He was confident, Glenn recalled, that he was headed for the nomination and victory in November. He then went downstairs to express his appreciation to a throng of jubilant supporters. He said:

> [California], the most urban state, . . . South Dakota, . . . the most rural. . . . We were able to win them both. I think we can end the divisions within the United States. [W]e can work together . . . . We are a great country, an unselfish country, and a compassionate country. I intend to make that the basis for running.

The crowd in the ballroom cheered as Kennedy departed with Rafer Johnson, the Olympic decathalon champion, and Roosevelt Grier, the Los Angeles Rams tackle, clearing the way. He took a short cut through the kitchen.

As with his brother, the shot that killed Robert Kennedy was fired into the back of his head. In all, eight shots were fired from the Iver Johnson .22 revolver. The Los Angeles Police Department and the FBI concluded that a young Palestinian, Sirhan Sirhan, acting alone, had assassinated him. A jury found Sirhan guilty, and he was ultimately sentenced to a life term (he will be eligible for parole on September 1, 1984). Robert F. Kennedy had reached the end of his corridor of grief.

A Witness to Two Tragedies

What about a conspiracy in the Robert Kennedy assassination? Did evidence point to organized crime complicity there as well? It had not been a subject of our investigation, since the Committee's mandate specifically prescribed the murders of President Kennedy and Dr. King. We knew, however, that William Sullivan, the assistant director of the FBI, was not satisfied with the 1968 investigation. "There were," he wrote, "so many holes in the case. We never could account for Sirhan's presence in the kitchen of the Ambassador Hotel." The problem for Sullivan was not *if* Sirhan had killed Robert Kennedy, but *why*. "You can work on a case for years," he added, "and still not know the real answers." We also knew that Sirhan had got a job as a "hot-walker" at the Santa Anita racetrack through Henry Ramistella, also known as Frank Donnarauma, who, it had been suggested, was connected to organized crime in New Jersey. (We could not confirm the New Jersey crime ties, but we did learn that Ramistella had a record of narcotics violations in New York and Florida.) We had, in short, little to add to the investigation of Robert Kennedy's murder. There was, however, one troubling Dallas-Los Angeles parallel.

In our investigation we were interested in one Jim Braden, who was held for questioning in Dallas on November 22, 1963. Braden reportedly was picked up after the assassination as he was leaving the Dal-Tex Building, directly across the Houston-Elm intersection from the Texas School Book Depository. A deputy sheriff, C. L. Lewis, thought he was "acting suspiciously." After three hours he was released. If the Dallas authorities had done a general background check on Jim Braden, they would have found nothing to stir their suspicions. What they did not know then, however, was that a few weeks prior to the assassination, Braden had legally changed his name. As Eugene Hale Brading, he had a criminal record that dated back to 1934, and he was, on November 22, 1963, on parole, having been convicted of mail fraud and the interstate transportation of stolen property.

Braden, or Brading, told a parole officer that he was scheduled to visit an office in the Mercantile Bank Building at 1704 Main Street in Dallas at about the same time, it turned out, that Jack Ruby was to be there to show a young woman where she might find employment. (Both Braden and Ruby subsequently denied that they went to that office.) In addition, Braden stayed at the Cabana Motel in Dallas on the night of November 21, the same night that Ruby went to the Cabana to visit a friend who also was staying at the motel. (We also learned that in the summer and fall of 1963 Braden was in and out of an office in New Orleans — room 1701 of the Pere Marquette building, the office of Vernon Main, Jr., an oil geologist — at least twelve times. Room 1707 of the Pere Marquette building was the office at the time of Carlos Marcello's lawyer, G. Wray Gill, who employed David W. Ferrie as an investigator, also in the summer and fall of 1963.) Peter Noyes, a former CBS producer and author of a meticulously documented book, *Legacy of Doubt*, had connected Braden to a number of underworld figures, including Meyer Lansky, for whom, according to Noyes, Braden had worked as a "personal courier." We sought to hear from Braden an elaboration of his allegation that Noyes's book had wronged him. He gave us a deposition and testified in executive session. In the end, we reached no firm judgment on Braden's mob connections or on whether his activities in Dallas were in any way related to the assassination.

Braden said he had flown to Dallas by private plane on business, oil business. He had told his parole officer in California, he acknowledged, that he would be in Dallas from Wednesday, November 20, to Monday, November 25, when he would leave for Houston. At the moment of the assassination, he said, he was visiting the probation office in Dallas.

After his interview with the parole officer (who could not recall the meeting), Braden walked the six blocks to Dealey Plaza in search of a taxicab. He said he went into the Dal-Tex Building to find a telephone, so he could call his mother and tell her about the assassination, but a freight elevator operator became suspicious, and, he admitted, he was held for questioning. He said that while he was in custody, he told the sheriff's department that he was walking and "police cars were passing [him] coming down toward the triple underpass. . . ." (Braden's statement had been read as an acknowledgment that he was in Dealey Plaza at the moment of the assassination, and sheriff's deputies identified him in a photograph taken in Dealey Plaza. Nevertheless, Braden told us he was not in Dealey Plaza.) Braden testified that his companions on the trip from California, who were expecting to meet him at the Cabana Motel at 2 P.M., had checked out and flown to Houston; he said he did not have a chance to call them. (The motel records put their departure time from the Cabana at 2:01 P.M., November 22, 1963.) Braden testified that he had caught a commercial flight to Houston that night. He denied knowing Jack Ruby, David Ferrie, or Carlos Marcello. He denied any association with organized-crime elements, and he denied having had anything to do with the assassination of the President. He did acknowledge, however, that on the night of June 4, 1968, the night Robert Kennedy was killed, he was staying at the Century Plaza Hotel in Los Angeles, located less than fifteen minutes away from the Hotel Ambassador.

Murder Will Out

On September 28, 1978, as our public hearings were drawing to a close, the final witness before the Committee was Burt W. Griffin, who in 1964 was one of two Warren Commission attorneys responsible for the Ruby aspect of the assassination investigation. The Committee asked Judge Griffin to reflect on the successes and failures of the Commission and the FBI in light of his experience as a staff counsel, as well as a former prosecutor and current member of the judiciary with criminal jurisdiction. He showed extraordinary insight and candor in his comments, especially when he put his finger on a crucial fact, one often overlooked in analyses of the President's death: the great problem of obtaining "proof of conspiracy" in a free society. He directed the Committee's attention to the "reality that under the American system of civil liberties and the requirement [for a criminal conviction] of proof beyond a reasonable doubt, . . . it is virtually impossible to prosecute or uncover a well-conceived and well-executed conspiracy." Almost prophetically, Judge Griffin said: "The few successful . . . [prosecutions of a sophisticated conspiracy] . . . almost always result from accidental discover[ies]." That explained, he suggested, why our society had "almost totally failed in its efforts . . . to prosecute the organized commission of crime."

It was difficult to disagree with Judge Griffin's perceptive comments. That freedom carries with it a certain price — and one that is well worth paying — ought to be obvious to experienced observers of American history. Proof of conspiracy in a free society only comes when there has been the right mixture of diligence and luck. Successful prosecution of conspiracy is in fact rare. Yet there is another point that must be made. History, if not prosecution, is well served, for truth has a way of taking care of itself. Chaucer said it well, as our investigation showed. Murder will out.

Principal Sources

Official Reports and Court Cases

Chicago Crime Commission, *A Report on Chicago Crime for 1963,* Chicago, Ill., 1964.

New Orleans Metropolitan Crime Commission, *The Assassination of President Kennedy,* 11-26-63, New Orleans, La.

New Orleans Metropolitan Crime Commission, *Report,* 8-24-66, New Orleans, La.

Attorney General of the United States, *Conference on Organized Crime,* 1950.

Attorney General of the United States, *Annual Report,* 1963.

The President's Commission on the Assassination of President Kennedy, *Hearings,* Volumes I-XXXVI, Government Printing Office, Washington, D.C. 1964.

Commission on Law Enforcement and Administration of Justice, *Task Force Report: Organized Crime,* Government Printing Office, Washington, D.C., 1967.

The National Commission on Causes and Prevention of Violence, *Assassination and Political Violence,* Government Printing Office, Washington, D.C., 1969.

The National Commission on Causes and Prevention of Violence, *Final Report,* Government Printing Office, Washington, D.C., 1969.

Commission on CIA Activities within the United States, *Report to the President,* Government Printing Office, Washington, D.C., 1975.

U.S. Congress, *The Congressional Record,* 1-6-76, 9-17-76, 9-30-76, 2-1-77, 2-2-77, 2-16-77, 3-8-77, 3-30-77, 4-28-77, Government Printing Office, Washington, D.C.

U.S. Congress, Senate, Special Committee to Investigate Organized Crime in Interstate Commerce, *First Interim Report,* Government Printing Office, Washington, D.C., 1950.

U.S. Congress, Senate, Special Committee to Investigate Organized Crime in Interstate Commerce, *Second Interim Report,* Government Printing Office, Washington, D.C., 1951.

U.S. Congress, Senate, Special Committee to Investigate Organized Crime in Interstate Commerce, *Third Interim Report,* Government Printing Office, Washington, D.C., 1951.

U.S. Congress, Senate, Special Committee on Improper Activities in the Labor or Management Field, *First Interim Report,* Government Printing Office, Washington, D.C., 1958.

U.S. Congress, Senate, Special Committee on Improper Activities in the Labor or Management Field, *Second Interim Report,* Government Printing Office, Washington, D.C., 1959.

U.S. Congress, Senate, Special Committee on Improper Activities in the Labor or Management Field, *Final Report,* Government Printing Office, Washington, D.C., 1960.

U.S. Congress, Senate, Permanent Subcommittee on Investigations, Committee on Government Operations, *James R. Hoffa and Continued Underworld Control of New York Teamsters Local 239,* Government Printing Office, Washington, D.C., 1962.

U.S. Congress, Senate, Permanent Subcommittee on Investigations, Committee on Government Operations, *Gambling and Organized Crime,* Government Printing Office, Washington, D.C., 1962.

U.S. Congress, Senate, Permanent Subcommittee on Investigations, Committee on Government Operations, *American Guild of Variety Artists,* Government Printing Office, Washington, D.C., 1963.

U.S. Congress, Senate, Permanent Subcommittee on Investigations, Committee on Government Operations, *Organized Crime and Illicit Traffic in Narcotics, Parts One-Five,* Government Printing Office, Washington, D.C., 1963.

U.S. Congress, Senate, Permanent Subcommittee on Investigations, Committee on Government Operations, *Organized Crime and Illicit Traffic in Narcotics,* Final Report, Government Printing Office, Washington, D.C., 1965.

U.S. Congress, Senate, Subcommittee on Criminal Laws and Procedures, Committee on Judiciary, *Controlling Crime through More Effective Law Enforcement,* Government Printing Office, Washington, D.C., 1967.

U.S. Congress, Senate, Subcommittee on Criminal Laws and Procedures, Committee on Judiciary, *Measures Relating to Organized Crime,* Government Printing Office, Washington, D.C., 1969.

U.S. Congress, Senate, Select Committee to Study Governmental Operations with respect to Intelligence Activities, *Alleged Assassination Plots Involving Foreign Leaders,* Government Printing Office, Washington, D.C., 1975.

U.S. Congress, Senate, Select Committee to Study Governmental Operations with respect to Intelligence Activities, *The Investigation of the Assassination of President Kennedy: Performance of the Intelligence Agencies,* Government Printing Office, Washington, D.C., 1976.

U.S. Congress, Senate, *Organized Crime Control Act of 1970,* Ninety-first Congress, First Session, 1969.

Capone v. *United States,* 56 F.2d 927 (7th Cir. 1932).

Costello v. *United States,* 350 U.S. 359 (1956).

Giancana v. *Hoover,* 322 F.2d 789 (7th Cir. 1963).

Giancana v. *Johnson,* 335 F.2d 372 (7th Cir. 1964).

Giancana v. *United States,* 352 F.2d 921 (7th Cir. 1965).

Hoffa v. *United States,* 385 U.S. 293 (1966).

Osborn v. *United States,* 385 U.S. 323 (1966).

People v. *Hines,* 284 N.Y. 93, 29 N.E.2d 483 (1940).

People v. *Luciano,* 277 N.Y. 348, 14 N.E.2d 433 (1938).

People v. *Sirhan,* 102 Cal. 305, 497 P.2d 1121 (1972).

Rubenstein v. *State,* 407 S.W. 2d 793 (Ct. of Crim. App. of Tex. 1966).

United States v. *Agueci,* 310 F.2d 812 (2d Cir. 1962).

United States v. *Aviles,* 274 F.2d 179 (2d Cir. 1960).

United States v. *Bufalino,* 285 F.2d 408 (2d Cir. 1960).

United States v. *Compagna,* 146 F.2d 524 (2d Cir. 1944).

United States v. *Isaacs,* 493 F.2d 1124 (7th Cir. 1973).

United States v. *Kahaner,* 317 F.2d 459 (2d Cir. 1963).

United States v. *Polizzi,* 500 F.2d 856 (9th Cir. 1974).

United States v. *Roselli,* 432 F.2d 879 (9th Cir. 1970).

Pursuant to agreement with the Select Committee on Assassinations, the Central Intelligence Agency and the Federal Bureau of Investigation reviewed this book in manuscript form to determine that the classified information it contained had been properly released for publication and that no informant was identified. Neither the CIA nor the FBI warrants the factual material or endorses the views expressed.

Bibliography

Books and Articles

Addams, Jane, *Twenty Years at Hull House,* The Macmillan Company, New York, N.Y., 1910.

Aristotle, *On Poetics,* Britannica Great Books, Encyclopedia Britannica, Inc., Chicago, Ill., 1952.

Aronson, Harvey, *The Killing of Joey Gallo,* G.P. Putnam's Sons, New York, N.Y., 1973.

Ashman, Charles, *The CIA-Mafia Link,* Manor Books, Inc., New York, N.Y., 1975.

Attwood, William, *The Reds and the Blacks,* Hutchinson, London, 1967.

Barron, John, *KGB: The Secret Work of Soviet Secret Agents,* Reader's Digest Press, New York, N.Y., 1974.

Belli, Melvin M. (with Maurice C. Carroll), *Dallas Justice: The Real Story of Jack Ruby and his Trial,* David McKay Company, Inc., New York, N.Y., 1964.

Bickel, Alexander M., "The Failure of the Warren Report," *Commentary,* October 1966.

Bradlee, Benjamin C., *Conversations with Kennedy,* W.W. Norton & Company, Inc., New York, N.Y., 1975.

Brashler, William, *The Don: The Life and Death of Sam Giancana,* Harper & Row, New York, N.Y., 1977.

Brill, Steven, *The Teamsters,* Simon and Schuster, New York, N.Y., 1978.

Busch, Francis X. *Enemies of the State,* Bobbs-Merrill Company, Inc., New York, N.Y., 1954.

Campbell, Rodney, *The Luciano Project,* McGraw-Hill Book Company, New York, N.Y., 1977.

Chandler, David L., *Brothers in Blood: The Rise of the Criminal Brotherhoods,* E.P. Dutton & Co., Inc., New York, N.Y., 1975.

Chavez, Judy (with Jack Vitek), *Defector's Mistress,* Dell Publishing Co., Inc., New York, N.Y., 1979.

Cohen, Mickey (with John Peer Nugent), *In My Own Words,* Prentice-Hall, Inc., Englewood Cliffs, N.J., 1975.

Cook, Fred J., *Mafia,* Fawcett Publications, Inc., Greenwich, Conn., 1973.

Cressey, Donald R., *Theft of the Nation,* Harper & Row, New York, N.Y., 1969.

Crile, George, and Taylor Branch, "The Kennedy Vendetta," *Harper's,* August 1975.

Demaris, Ovid, and Garry Wills, *Jack Ruby,* New American Library, New York, N.Y., 1968.

Demaris, Ovid, *Captive City,* Lyle Stuart, Inc., New York, N.Y., 1969.

Lord Devlin, "Death of a President: The Established Facts," *The Atlantic,* March 1965.

Diapoulos, Peter, and Steven Linakis, *The Sixth Family,* E.P. Dutton & Co., Inc., New York, N.Y., 1976.

Dodgson, Charles Lutwidge (Lewis Carroll), *Through the Looking Glass and What Alice Found There,* Random House, New York, N.Y., 1946.

Eisenberg, Dennis, Uri Dan, and Eli Landau, *Meyer Lansky: Mogul of the Mob,* Paddington Press, Ltd., New York, N.Y., 1979.

Epstein, Edward Jay, *Inquest: The Warren Commision and the Establishment of Truth,* Viking Press, New York, N.Y., 1966.

Epstein, Edward Jay, *Counterplot,* Viking Press, New York, N.Y., 1969.

Epstein, Edward Jay, *Legend: The Secret World of Lee Harvey Oswald,* Reader's Digest Press, New York, N.Y., 1978.

Exner, Judith Campbell (with Ovid Demaris), *My Story,* Grove Press, Inc., New York, N.Y., 1977.

Feder, Sid, and Joachim Joesten, *The Luciano Story,* David McKay Company, Inc., New York, N.Y., 1954.

Fensterwald, Bernard, Jr., and Michael Ewing, *Coincidence or Conspiracy,* Kensington Publishing Corp., New York, N.Y., 1977.

Ford, Gerald R., *Portrait of the Assassin,* Simon and Schuster, New York, N.Y., 1965.

Fraley, Oscar, *4 Against the Mob,* Award, New York, N.Y., 1948.

Frasca, Dom, *King of Crime,* Crown Publishers, Inc., New York, N.Y., 1959.

Gage, Nicholas, *The Mafia Is Not an Equal Opportunity Employer,* McGraw-Hill Book Company, New York, N.Y., 1971.

Gage, Nicholas, *Mafia, USA,* Playboy Press, Chicago, Ill., 1972.

Garrison, Jim, *A Heritage of Stone,* G.P. Putnam's Sons, New York, N.Y., 1970.

Gentile, Nicola, *Vita di Campmafia,* Rome, 1963.

Goldberg, Alfred, *Conspiracy Interpretations,* University of California, 1968.

Goodhart, A.L., "The Mysteries of the Kennedy Assassination and the English Press," *The Law Quarterly Review,* January 1967.

Guthman, Edwin, *We Band of Brothers,* Harper & Row, New York, N.Y., 1971.

Hamilton, Edith, *The Greek Way,* W.W. Norton & Company, Inc., New York, N.Y., 1980.

Hirsch, Phil, *The Mafia,* Pyramid Books, New York, N.Y., 1971.

Houghton, Robert A. (with Theodore Taylor), *Special Unit Senator,* Random House, New York, N.Y., 1970.

Jennings, Dean, *We Only Kill Each Other,* Prentice-Hall, Inc., Englewood Cliffs, N.J., 1967.

Johnson, Haynes, *The Bay of Pigs,* W.W. Norton & Company, Inc., New York, N.Y., 1964.

Johnson, Lyndon B., *The Vantage Point: Perceptions of the Presidency, 1963–69,* Holt, Rinehart & Winston, New York, N.Y., 1971.

Kantor, Seth, *Who Was Jack Ruby?,* Everest House, New York, N.Y., 1978.

Kaplan, John, and Jon R. Waltz, *The Trial of Jack Ruby,* The Macmillan Company, New York, N.Y., 1965.

Kaplan, John, "The Assassins," *Stanford Law Review,* May 1967.

Katz, Leonard, *Uncle Frank,* Drake Publications, Inc., New York, N.Y., 1973.

Kefauver, Estes, *Crime in America,* Doubleday & Company, Inc., Garden City, N.Y., 1951.

Kelley, Kitty, *Jackie Oh!,* Lyle Stuart, Inc., Secaucus, N.J., 1978.

Kennedy, Robert F., *The Enemy Within,* Harper and Brothers, New York, N.Y., 1960.

Kobler, John, *Capone: the Life and World of Al Capone,* G.P. Putnam's Sons, New York, N.Y., 1971.

Koskoff, David E., *Joseph P. Kennedy: A Life and Times,* Prentice-Hall, Inc., Englewood Cliffs, N.J., 1974.

Landesco, John, "Organized Crime in Chicago," from *Illinois Crime Survey of 1929,* University of Chicago Press, 1968.

Lane, Mark, *Rush to Judgment,* Holt, Rinehart & Winston, New York, N.Y., 1966.

Lazo, Mario, *Dagger in the Heart,* Funk & Wagnalls, New York, N.Y., 1968.

Lerner, Max, *Ted and the Kennedy Legend: A Study in Character and Destiny,* St. Martin's Press, New York, N.Y., 1980.

McMillan, Priscilla J., *Marina and Lee,* Harper & Row, New York, N.Y., 1977.

Maas, Peter, *The Valachi Papers,* G.P. Putnam's Sons, New York, N.Y., 1968.

Manchester, William, *The Death of a President,* Harper & Row, New York, N.Y., 1967.

Meagher, Sylvia, *Accessories after the Fact,* Vintage Books, New York, N.Y., 1976.

Meskill, Paul S., *The Luparelli Tapes,* Playboy Press, Chicago, Ill., 1976.

Messick, Hank, *The Silent Syndicate,* The Macmillan Company, New York, N.Y., 1967.

Messick, Hank, *Lansky,* G.P. Putnam's Sons, New York, N.Y., 1971.

Messick, Hank, and Burt Goldblatt, *The Mobs and the Mafia: An Illustrated History of Organized Crime,* Crowell, New York, N.Y., 1972.

Mills, James, *The Prosecutor,* Farrar, Straus, and Giroux, New York, N.Y., 1969.

Moldea, Dan E., *The Hoffa Wars,* Paddington Press Ltd., New York, N.Y., 1978.

Mollenhoff, Clark R., *Strike Force,* Prentice-Hall, Inc., Englewood Cliffs, N.J., 1972.

Moore, William H., *The Kefauver Committee and the Politics of Crime,* University of Missouri Press, 1974.

Navasky, Victor S., *Kennedy Justice,* Atheneum, New York, N.Y., 1971.

Nelli, Humbert S., *The Business of Crime: Italians and Syndicate Crime in the United States,* Oxford University Press, 1976.

Ness, Eliot (with Oscar Fraley), *The Untouchables,* Julian Messner, Inc., New York, N.Y., 1957.

Noyes, Peter, *Legacy of Doubt,* Pinnacle Books, New York, N.Y., 1973.

Oswald, Robert L. (with Myrick and Barbara Land), *Lee: A Portrait of Lee Harvey Oswald,* Coward-McCann, Inc., New York, N.Y., 1967.

Peterson, Virgil W., *Barbarians in Our Midst,* Little, Brown and Company, Boston, Mass., 1952.

Puzo, Mario, *The Godfather,* G.P. Putnam's Sons, New York, N.Y., 1969.

Reid, Ed, *The Grim Reapers,* Henry Regnery & Co., Chicago, Ill., 1969.

Reid, Ed, *Mickey Cohen: Mobster,* Pinnacle Books, New York, N.Y., 1973.

Salerno, Ralph, and John S. Tompkins, *The Crime Confederation,* Doubleday & Company, Inc., Garden City, N.Y., 1969.

Schlesinger, Arthur M., Jr., *A Thousand Days: John F. Kennedy in the White House,* Houghton Mifflin Company, Boston, Mass., 1965.

Schlesinger, Arthur M., Jr., *Robert Kennedy and His Times,* Houghton Mifflin Company, Boston, Mass., 1978.

Schorr, Daniel, *Clearing the Air,* Houghton Mifflin Company, Boston, Mass., 1977.

Seedman, Albert A., and Peter Hellman, *Chief!,* Arthur Fields Books, Inc., New York, N.Y., 1974.

Shakespeare, William, *Hamlet,* Britannica Great Books, Encyclopedia Britannica, Inc., Chicago, Ill., 1952.

Sheridan, Walter, *The Fall and Rise of Jimmy Hoffa,* Saturday Review Press, New York, N.Y., 1972.

Sophocles, *Oedipus Rex,* from *The Complete Greek Tragedies,* edited by David Green and Richmond Lattimore, The University of Chicago Press, 1954.

Sorenson, Theodore C., *Kennedy,* Harper & Row, New York, N.Y., 1965.

St. George, Andrew, "The Cold War Comes Home," *Harper's,* November 1973.

Stafford, Jean, *A Mother in History,* Farrar, Straus, and Giroux, New York, N.Y., 1965.

Sullivan, William C. (with Bill Brown), *The Bureau: My Thirty Years in Hoover's FBI,* W.W. Norton & Company, Inc., New York, N.Y., 1979.

Teresa, Vincent (with Thomas C. Renner), *My Life in the Mafia,* Doubleday & Company, Inc., Garden City, N.Y., 1973.

Thompson, Josiah, *Six Seconds in Dallas,* B. Geis Associates, New York, N.Y., 1968.

Thrasher, Frederic, *The Gang,* University of Chicago Press, 1927.

Turkus, Burton B., and Sid Feder, *Murder, Inc.,* Manor Books, Inc., New York, N.Y., 1974.

Turner, William W., and John C. Christian, *The Assassination of Robert F. Kennedy,* Random House, New York, N.Y., 1978.

United Press International, *Four Days: The Historical Record of the Death of President Kennedy,* American Heritage, New York, N.Y., 1964.

Voltz, Joseph, and Peter J. Bridge, *The Mafia Talks,* Fawcett Publications, Inc., Greenwich, Conn., 1969.

Warren, Earl, *The Memoirs of Earl Warren,* Doubleday & Company, Inc., New York, N.Y., 1977.

Weisberg, Harold, *Whitewash,* Hyattstown, Md., 1966.

Whalen, Richard J., *The Founding Father: The Story of Joseph P. Kennedy,* New American Library, New York, N.Y., 1964.

White, Theodore H., *Breach of Faith: The Fall of Richard Nixon,* Atheneum, New York, N.Y., 1975.

Wilson, Theodore, "The Kefauver Committee 1950," from *Congress Investigates: A Documented History: 1792–1974,* edited by Arthur M. Schlesinger, Jr., and Roger Bruns, Chelsea House, New York, N.Y., 1975.

Wilson, Woodrow, *Congressional Government,* Peter Smith Publishers Inc., Magnolia, Mass., 1958.

Wirth, Louis, *The Ghetto,* University of Chicago Press, 1928.

Wyden, Peter, *Bay of Pigs,* Simon and Schuster, New York, N.Y., 1979.

Zeiger, Henry A., *Sam the Plumber,* Mentor, New York, N.Y., 1971.

Zeiger, Henry A., *Frank Costello,* Berkley Medallion Books, New York, N.Y., 1974.

Zeiger, Henry A., *The Jersey Mob,* Signet, New York, N.Y., 1975.

Zola, Emile, "J'Accuse . . . !," *L'Aurore,* January 13, 1898.

Index

Index

*Numbers in italics signify a photograph
of the referenced subject on the
indicated page*

411